THE TOP 10 OF MUSIC

THE TOP 10 OF MUSIC

RUSSELL ASH AND LUKE CRAMPTON
WITH BARRY LAZELL

HEADLINE

Copyright © 1993 HEADLINE BOOK PUBLISHING PLC/
Russell Ash and Luke Crampton

First published in 1993
by HEADLINE BOOK PUBLISHING PLC

10 9 8 7 6 5 4 3 2 1

British Library Cataloguing in Publication Data

Ash, Russell
Top Ten of Music
I. Title II. Crampton, Luke
781.64

ISBN 0 7472 0798 4

Cover photographs

Left (top to bottom): Retna Pictures/Photofest;
Tom Farrington/Redferns; Michel Linssen/Redferns.
Centre: Mick Hutson/Redferns.
Right (top to bottom): Mick Hutson/Redferns;
Justin Thomas/All Action; Retna Pictures/Photofest.
Background: Image Bank.

Design and computer make up by Penny Mills

Illustration reproduction by Global Colour

Printed and bound in Great Britain by
BPCC Hazells Ltd, member of BPCC Ltd

HEADLINE BOOK PUBLISHING PLC
Headline House
79 Great Titchfield Street
London W1P 7FN

CONTENTS

ABOUT THE AUTHORS

Russell Ash studied anthropology and was diverted into a brief career as an aviation insurance broker before eventually finding his way into book publishing and writing, which has occupied him since 1967. He has written and contributed to more than 50 books on subjects as diverse as art and humour (not to mention pigs, cats, Paddington Bear, epitaphs, the Wright brothers, strange books and vampires). He has a special interest in compiling popular reference books, among them *The Londoner's Almanac* and, since 1989, the annual bestseller, *The Top 10 of Everything*, which has now been published internationally. He is also the co-author (with Ian Morrison) of *The Top 10 of Sport*. He lives with his wife and two sons in Sussex where he is a partner in an illustrated book production company.

Luke Crampton, a former child actor, journalist and one-time Crown FM music phone-in host, was the co-founder of the British media research organization MRIB in 1981. He has written and contributed to a dozen titles, all music- and media-related, including the bestselling and ongoing series of the *Guinness Book of Rock Stars* (with Dafydd Rees), *The Great Rock and Roll Trivia Quiz Book*, *The Steve Wright In The Afternoon Book* and the *Official Wham! Biography*. He has recently married and relocated to Atlanta, USA, where he has established Songfinder, a music research company devoted to finding hit material for artists, record companies and motion picture soundtracks.

Barry Lazell used to have a proper job as a teacher, but since 1977 has made his living from his hobby, writing about and researching popular music and the record industry, becoming founder of the Record Business research department and of MRIB, for which he continues to research video. He was a columnist for *Sounds*, *Music Week* and other publications and is a regular contributor to *Vox* magazine and associate editor of its *Record Hunter* supplement. Among books which he has written or co-authored are *40 Years of NME Charts*, a biography of Bryan Ferry and Roxy Music, music quiz and pop and movie list books and *The Essential Guide to Rock Records*. He lives in Essex with his wife, two daughters and collections of books, CDs, records and videos that have long since passed the unwieldy stage.

INTRODUCTION

From its first year (and it's now in its fifth), Russell Ash's *The Top 10 of Everything* has contained a substantial selection of music Top 10s, and it was felt that the time was right for a book devoted specifically to this subject. More than almost any other topic, music lends itself naturally to ranking in list form, with the record charts the most widely known manifestation. The charts are, however, by their very nature ephemeral and show only this week's bestsellers. At best, year-end charts round up the top-sellers of the preceding year, after which the success of a record is largely forgotten, while the lifetime achievements of individual artists or groups, songwriters, producers and record labels are seldom, if ever, subjected to quantitative scrutiny – an omission that *The Top 10 of Music* attempts to rectify.

To make clear what we mean by a 'Top 10' list, we define it as a 'definitive' list: something that can be measured (bestselling, highest chart positions, most expensive, firsts – even 'favourite', provided this results from a poll of a sufficiently large number of people). Additionally, although they are not strictly 'Top 10s', some non-definitive or non-quantified lists also appear from time to time: these are simply lists of 10 somethings-or-other that we have included for interest with no claim that they are superlative or even ranked in any way (they generally appear alphabetically). Such lists can be instantly identified by their lack of 'Top 10' logos and by the spinning records in their backgrounds.

The majority of quantitative Top 10 lists, which comprise the bulk of the book, are based on sales data and/or chart performance. Definitive record sales figures can be difficult to garner (commercial confidentiality is usually cited), but the authors maintain an accurate database of a substantial number of record sales totals covering the most successful or notable singles and albums in the UK and USA. An aid to accuracy are the sales awards (silver, gold and platinum) certified by the UK and US industry associations, the BPI and RIAA. The weekly compilation of increasingly accurate charts in both these territories also provides a consistent sales research base, from which many of these lists have been collated. For the purposes of this book, therefore, rankings are based, in the first instance, on sales information (where known) and also on the chart statistics dating back to 1952 (the year of the first UK singles survey). Thus, most of the Top 10 lists are a reliable if not definitive assessment of data culled from a number of sources and, in most instances, are relevant up to the end of 1992 unless otherwise indicated.

While the work of compiling charts, which were initially collated in-house by music magazines such as *New Musical Express* and *Billboard* in the 1950s, has spawned its own industry (not least the UK's first dedicated music research company, MRIB, which was formed in 1981) and a wealth of valuable reference books (most notably the *Guinness British Hit Singles* and *Hit Albums* volumes, Joel Whitburn's definitive US tomes, *Top Pop Singles 1955–1990*, *Top Pop Albums 1955–1992*, *Top Country Singles* and *R & B Singles 1942–88* and Adam White's *Gold & Platinum Records*), each decade has seen significant improvements in both the collection of sales and radio airplay data and a number of spin-off specialist music charts (classical, Country, heavy metal, independent, rap, soul, etc), making today's surveys more accurately representative of weekly market moves. While this is certainly the case for the UK and North America, many other territories are only in the formative stages of gathering reliable sales data, often making national lists and global assessments all the more difficult to collate.

It is worth noting that where years are given with singles and albums they generally refer to year of release. However (especially with year-end releases), the record's peak sales may occur later, placing it among the best-sellers of a subsequent year. Thus *Saturday Night Fever*, a 1977 release, became the bestselling album of 1978 in both the UK and USA. A further discrepancy may seem apparent between two different Top 10 lists that share common ground, and it should be borne in mind that some rankings are affected by their own research criteria. For example, while the list of the Top 10 Indie Singles of All Time in the UK maintains that Joy Division's *Love Will Tear Us Apart* is at number two, the Top 10 Singles on the Factory Label alternatively suggests that this disc is only the company's sixth most successful title – even though all Factory-released product was eligible for the UK indie chart. The answer lies in the fact that the label list is based purely on sales information, whereas the indie ranking is primarily an assessment of indie chart performance (on which *Love Will Tear Us Apart* resided for some three years), itself compiled from sales information from specialist 'indie' retailers. The overall objective for each quantitative list is to provide the most accurate order of comparative success using the most dependable and relevant research source available in each instance, but apparent conflicts of this kind can inevitably occur where the parameters of the various data sources differ.

Why should we be interested in analysing the successes and failures of often long-forgotten (as well as some unforgettable) artists? The ranking order enables us to compare and classify, to get a sense of who are the winners and losers, how one artist stacks up against another, while the Top 10 list itself often provides a convenient 'time capsule' of the successes of a particular era, the annual lists evoking in shorthand the musical fashions and the rising stars of each successive year in both the UK and USA. Chronological lists add perspective by showing the progressive arrival of rock on the scene and the introduction of new music genres such as heavy metal, reggae, Punk and rap, the impact of technological innovations such as the CD revolution, social trends, high earners, fashions in bestselling music books and even T-shirts. Minority musical interests are represented in lists on, for example, ska, while major music genres are given treatment that accords approximately with the size of their audiences. Although classical music and opera do not offer the same scope for list-compiling

as pop music, we hope their aficionados will not be disappointed by our coverage of these subjects.

The book is as up-to-date as is practically possible: while we were working on it, Whitney Houston's *I Will Always Love You* and its parent album (*The Bodyguard* soundtrack collection) broke numerous records and altered often long-standing Top 10 lists, while a number of artists, from long-established but recent multi-award-winner Eric Clapton to new Canadian reggae/hip-hop artist Snow clocked up further achievements, thereby rearranging our carefully-constructed lists. As this introduction was being written, it was still proving difficult to confirm the entry of the aforementioned Whitney Houston single in the book's very first list, The Top 10 Singles of All Time Worldwide. With the global jury still out on this one, as it were, Whitney may have to wait for the book's second edition for her definitive placing among the all-time singles elite.

Certain lists throw up some pretty surprising bedfellows – charts in which old timers and newcomers jostle for supremacy (Ken Dodd outselling the Beatles, for example, as he did, astonishingly, in 1965), and the relative strengths of individuals and groups with careers spanning long periods are exposed: how do the Rolling Stones compare with the Who for instance, or a modern superstar like Prince or Michael Jackson with Elvis Presley?

Special thematic features encompass subjects from Rock and the Movies to Phil Spector, while there are challenging quizzes throughout (if it's any consolation, one of the authors set the quiz questions and one of the others got eight right on one and three on the next he tackled).

We hope that *The Top 10 of Music* will return in due course in a new edition. If you have any comments on any of our lists or suggestions for new ones, please write to us c/o the publishers. With your help the next book will be even better.

Russell Ash
Luke Crampton
Barry Lazell

SINGLES

THE TOP 10 SINGLES OF ALL TIME WORLDWIDE

	Title	Artist	Sales exceed
1	White Christmas	Bing Crosby	30,000,000
2	Rock Around The Clock	Bill Haley & His Comets	17,000,000
3	I Want To Hold Your Hand	Beatles	12,000,000
4	It's Now Or Never	Elvis Presley	10,000,000
5=	Hound Dog/Don't Be Cruel	Elvis Presley	9,000,000
5=	Diana	Paul Anka	9,000,000
7=	Hey Jude	Beatles	8,000,000
7=	I'm A Believer	Monkees	8,000,000
9=	Can't Buy Me Love	Beatles	7,000,000
9=	Do They Know It's Christmas?	Band Aid	7,000,000
9=	We Are The World	USA For Africa	7,000,000

Something to smile about: Bing Crosby's 1942 recording of White Christmas *made the US chart every Christmas for 21 years, and is the world's biggest-selling single of all time.*

Global sales are notoriously difficult to calculate, particularly in countries outside the UK and USA and especially in the Far East. 'Worldwide' is thus usually taken to mean the known minimum 'western world' sales. Bing Crosby's 1942 record, *White Christmas,* is indisputably the all-time bestselling single, and the *song,* recorded by others and sold as sheet music, has also achieved such enormous sales that it would additionally appear in the number one position in any list of bestselling songs

THE TOP 10 SINGLES OF ALL TIME IN THE UK

	Title	Artist	Year	Approximate UK sales
1	Do They Know It's Christmas?	Band Aid	1984	3,510,000
2	Bohemian Rhapsody	Queen	1975/1991	2,130,000
3	Mull Of Kintyre	Wings	1977	2,050,000
4	Rivers Of Babylon/Brown Girl In The Ring	Boney M	1978	1,995,000
5	She Loves You	Beatles	1963	1,890,000
6	You're The One That I Want	John Travolta and Olivia Newton-John	1978	1,870,000
7	Relax	Frankie Goes To Hollywood	1984	1,800,000
8	Mary's Boy Child/Oh My Lord	Boney M	1978	1,790,000
9	I Just Called To Say I Love You	Stevie Wonder	1984	1,775,000
10	I Want To Hold Your Hand	Beatles	1963	1,640,000

A total of 46 singles have sold over 1,000,000 copies apiece in the UK during the last 40 years, and these are the cream of that crop. The Band Aid single had a host of special circumstances surrounding it, and it is difficult to imagine, even if a similarly special case arose in the future, such sales ever being approached again by a single in this country. Two years, 1978 and 1984, were the all-time strongest for million-selling singles, and this chart fittingly has three representatives from each. Prior to the huge sales of Queen's *Bohemian Rhapsody* in the wake of Freddie Mercury's death in 1991, it stood at number 23 in this list, its elevation to the Top 10 ousting Ken Dodd's *Tears* (1965).

THE TOP 10 SINGLES OF ALL TIME IN THE USA

	Title	Artist	Year
1	*White Christmas*	Bing Crosby	1942
2	*I Want To Hold Your Hand*	Beatles	1964
3	*Hound Dog/Don't Be Cruel*	Elvis Presley	1956
4	*It's Now Or Never*	Elvis Presley	1960
5	*We Are The World*	USA For Africa	1985
6	*I Will Always Love You*	Whitney Houston	1992
7	*Hey Jude*	Beatles	1968
8	*The Chipmunk Song*	Chipmunks	1958
9	*Love Letters In The Sand*	Pat Boone	1957
10	*You Light Up My Life*	Debby Boone	1977

White Christmas remains the United States' all-time most-charted single, having been a major Yuletide seller every Christmas for 21 years from its original release. Total US sales are thought to be in the region of 15,000,000.

THE TOP 10 EPs OF ALL TIME IN THE UK

	Title	Artist	Year
1	*Twist And Shout*	Beatles	1963
2	*Magical Mystery Tour* (6-track double EP)	Beatles	1968
3	*Crackers International*	Erasure	1988
4	*The Roussos Phenomenon*	Demis Roussos	1976
5	*The Beatles' Hits*	Beatles	1963
6	*The Special AKA Live*	Specials	1980
7	*Got Live If You Want It*	Rolling Stones	1965
8	*The One In The Middle*	Manfred Mann	1965
9	*All My Loving*	Beatles	1964
10	*Long Tall Sally*	Beatles	1964

In the mid-1960s, when seven of the titles listed were released, four- (or occasionally five- or six-) track EPs were half the price again of standard singles, and therefore normally sold in much smaller quantities. This was no barrier to the Beatles, most of whose EPs made the singles chart, with *Twist And Shout* selling almost 700,000 copies. The format was virtually killed by the advent of budget albums, then re-emerged in the mid-1970s (when Demis Roussos topped the chart) essentially as four-track – and identically-priced – singles.

THE WORLD'S BESTSELLING SINGLES

For roughly the first 70 years of the century, from the inception of recording technology, the single record, in one form or another, was the bestselling music format, and remained for decades the basis of the ever-expanding international recording industry. In the 1970s, however, the album format overhauled it, to become totally dominant in the Western world (and particularly the USA, the biggest single domestic market) during the 1980s.

This is the reason why the biggest-selling singles of all time, by and large, come from the middle decades of the century, when (a) the Western consumer society bloomed, and (b) teenagers also became consumers, with Rock 'n' Roll arriving just in time to cater to them. *Rock Around The Clock* was the key single of this latter cultural turning point. It was the first rock single most people around the world bought – and clearly, since its global sales were never matched by anything else in the genre, it was the *only* one some of them ever bought. Rock, though, was also the great global cultural communicator of the 1950s and 1960s, and it is inevitable that the biggest international stars of those

years, particularly Elvis Presley and the Beatles, would have singles that reached the very largest numbers of record buyers. By the 1980s, with the format in decline, the singles which deliberately grabbed the international conscience were those that retained the widest appeal, hence the uncharacteristically large sales of the charity releases by Band Aid and USA For Africa.

However, the single which most fully defines the concept of universal, timeless appeal is *White Christmas*. First released in 1942, the Bing Crosby rendition (there have, of course, been thousands of others subsequently) effortlessly rejuvenates itself every December, and is almost certainly the only single in the all-time Top 10 that is still selling in regular quantities in the 1990s. There is no possibility of any single ever catching it up in terms of total sales – although it has been overtaken by the world's bestselling album, Michael Jackson's *Thriller*, which achieved global sales of 40,000,000, and did this in only a tenth of the time it took *White Christmas* to amass its total. The name of that game is evolution.

THE TOP 10 SINGLES OF 1952 IN THE UK

	Title	Artist
1	Auf Wiedersehen (Sweetheart)	Vera Lynn
2	Wheel Of Fortune	Kay Starr
3	Cry/The Little White Cloud That Cried	Johnnie Ray
4	Unforgettable	Nat 'King' Cole
5	Here In My Heart	Al Martino
6	High Noon	Frankie Laine
7	There's Always Room At Our House	Guy Mitchell
8	Half As Much	Rosemary Clooney
9	The Homing Waltz	Vera Lynn
10	You Belong To Me	Jo Stafford

The first year in which record sales were reliably charted in Britain was – as had been the case throughout the whole post-war period – heavily dominated by American acts, whose hits the UK record industry merely tended to cover. There were notable exceptions, however, and Vera Lynn, harking back to her wartime popularity, took an English translation of a German ballad to international popularity, as well as outselling everything at home.

THE TOP 10 SINGLES OF 1952 IN THE USA

	Title	Artist
1	Cry/The Little White Cloud That Cried	Johnnie Ray
2	Wheel Of Fortune	Kay Starr
3	Auf Wiedersehen (Sweetheart)	Vera Lynn
4	Here In My Heart	Al Martino
5	I Went To Your Wedding	Patti Page
6	You Belong To Me	Jo Stafford
7	Blue Tango	Leroy Anderson
8	Why Don't You Believe Me	Joni James
9	Half As Much	Rosemary Clooney
10	Kiss Of Fire	Georgia Gibbs

Vera Lynn's hit was in many ways the sensation of 1952, being the first single by a British artist ever to top the US chart – which it did for almost two months. Ballads had almost completely taken over from the big bands by this time, though Johnnie Ray's double-sided smash also introduced more than a hint of R & B emotion into the normally starched-white US ballad scene of the early 1950s.

(Top) *'Forces' sweetheart' Vera Lynn's* Auf Wiedersehen (Sweetheart) *was not only the UK's bestselling single of 1952 but also achieved the distinction of being the first single by a British artist to top the US chart.*

(Above) Cry/The Little White Cloud That Cried *took Johnnie Ray, dubbed 'the Nabob of Sob' because of his tear-jerking performances, to the top of the 1952 US bestseller rankings.*

THE TOP 10 SINGLES OF 1953 IN THE UK

	Title	Artist
1	I Believe	Frankie Laine
2	Answer Me	Frankie Laine
3	Limelight	Frank Chacksfield
4	Song From Moulin Rouge	Mantovani
5	She Wears Red Feathers	Guy Mitchell
6	Don't Let The Stars Get In Your Eyes	Perry Como
7	Look At That Girl	Guy Mitchell
8	Outside Of Heaven	Eddie Fisher
9	Answer Me	David Whitfield
10	Pretend	Nat 'King' Cole

With Mantovani and David Whitfield asserting British interests, this was another heavily American-dominated year. Whitfield's big success was overshadowed by Frankie Laine's US version of the same song, and this was in every way Laine's big year in the UK. For two weeks in October, he had three singles in the top four chart positions, and I Believe was No. 1 for a staggering total of 18 weeks.

THE TOP 10 SINGLES OF 1953 IN THE USA

	Title	Artist
1	Song From Moulin Rouge	Percy Faith
2	How Much Is That Doggie In The Window	Patti Page
3	Vaya Con Dios	Les Paul and Mary Ford
4	Don't Let The Stars Get In Your Eyes	Perry Como
5	Rags To Riches	Tony Bennett
6	You, You, You	Ames Brothers
7	Till I Waltz Again With You	Teresa Brewer
8	St George And The Dragonet	Stan Freberg
9	I'm Walking Behind You	Eddie Fisher
10	I Believe	Frankie Laine

Frankie Laine did not dominate the US chart in 1953 quite as he did in Britain, but nevertheless this was a year almost wholly populated by similarly well-established artists. The big oddity, in more senses than one, was the success of musical satirist Stan Freberg, whose hit single retold the St George and the Dragon story as it might be narrated by Sgt Joe Friday of the hit TV police series Dragnet!

THE TOP 10 SINGLES OF 1954 IN THE UK

	Title	Artist
1	Secret Love	Doris Day
2	Oh Mein Papa	Eddie Calvert
3	Cara Mia	David Whitfield
4	Little Things Mean A Lot	Kitty Kallen
5	Three Coins In The Fountain	Frank Sinatra
6	Hold My Hand	Don Cornell
7	Such A Night	Johnnie Ray
8	My Son, My Son	Vera Lynn
9	I See The Moon	Stargazers
10	Let's Have Another Party	Winifred Atwell

Doris Day's two months atop the chart with arguably her most popular film song ever, comfortably clinched her the year's biggest seller. Frank Sinatra's hit, his first UK No. 1 success, was also from a movie (of the same title). Johnnie Ray's Such A Night, suggestive (though only just) more of bed than sleep, was not at all welcome on BBC airwaves, but nevertheless also reached No. 1.

THE TOP 10 SINGLES OF 1954 IN THE USA

	Title	Artist
1	Little Things Mean A Lot	Kitty Kallen
2	Secret Love	Doris Day
3	Hey There	Rosemary Clooney
4	Wanted	Perry Como
5	Oh Mein Papa	Eddie Fisher
6	Mr Sandman	Chordettes
7	Make Love To Me	Jo Stafford
8	Sh-Boom (Life Could Be A Dream)	Crew Cuts
9	I Need You Now	Eddie Fisher
10	Three Coins In The Fountain	Four Aces

A good year for female performers, who occupied the top three placings plus two more entries in the year's Top 10. Eddie Fisher was the most consistent male performer, while the Crew Cuts' Sh-Boom represented the first of a rash of bland white (and in this case, Canadian) hit covers of R & B originals which would shortly characterize the developing Rock 'n' Roll era.

THE TOP 10 SINGLES OF 1955 IN THE UK

	Title	Artist
1	Rose Marie	Slim Whitman
2	Rock Around The Clock	Bill Haley & His Comets
3	Give Me Your Word	Tennessee Ernie Ford
4	Softly, Softly	Ruby Murray
5	Cherry Pink And Apple Blossom White	Perez Prado
6	Cherry Pink And Apple Blossom White	Eddie Calvert
7	Unchained Melody	Jimmy Young
8	Cool Water	Frankie Laine
9	Stranger In Paradise	Tony Bennett
10	Unchained Melody	Al Hibbler

THE TOP 10 SINGLES OF 1955 IN THE USA

	Title	Artist
1	Rock Around The Clock	Bill Haley & His Comets
2	Cherry Pink And Apple Blossom White	Perez Prado
3	Sincerely	McGuire Sisters
4	The Yellow Rose Of Texas	Mitch Miller
5	The Ballad Of Davy Crockett	Bill Hayes
6	Sixteen Tons	Tennessee Ernie Ford
7	Autumn Leaves	Roger Williams
8	Love Is A Many-Splendored Thing	Four Aces
9	Unchained Melody	Les Baxter
10	Dance With Me Henry	Georgia Gibbs

Rock 'n' Roll arrived in Britain this year, via the American movie *The Blackboard Jungle* and the song highlighted in that film, Bill Haley's *Rock Around The Clock*. A chart-topper late in 1955, this would, by the end of January 1957, become the first single ever to sell over 1,000,000 copies in the UK alone. Slim Whitman's *Rose Marie,* meanwhile, set a new record for consecutive weeks (11) at No. 1.

Despite Bill Haley's success with 1955's top single marking the first year of the Rock 'n' Roll era in the US, the phenomenon did not manifest itself noticeably in the bulk of the top 10 sellers, though both the McGuire Sisters and Georgia Gibbs' hits were white major label covers (with a title cleaned up from *Roll With Me Henry* in the latter case) of successful R & B group records.

Slim Whitman by that old photographer's studio campfire. In 1955 he set a new record of 11 consecutive weeks at UK No. 1 with the show ballad Rose Marie. *Its success meant that* Rock Around The Clock *by Bill Haley (top) & His Comets, the top single of the year in the USA, was held to number two position in the UK.*

THE TOP 10 SINGLES OF 1956 IN THE UK

	Title	Artist
1	I'll Be Home	Pat Boone
2	Whatever Will Be Will Be	Doris Day
3	Memories Are Made Of This	Dean Martin
4	Why Do Fools Fall In Love?	Teenagers
5	It's Almost Tomorrow	Dream Weavers
6	Sixteen Tons	Tennessee Ernie Ford
7	The Poor People Of Paris	Winifred Atwell
8	Just Walkin' In The Rain	Johnnie Ray
9	No Other Love	Ronnie Hilton
10	Rock And Roll Waltz	Kay Starr

Pat Boone arrived on the scene as a rock singer, covering songs by the likes of Fats Domino and Little Richard, but it soon became apparent that rather old-fashioned ballads were his real forte, and I'll Be Home, the top seller of 1956, had the greatest longevity of any of his records in the UK, due to its being tailor-made for BBC radio's Two-Way Family Favourites show – on which it was constantly requested for the next decade.

THE TOP 10 SINGLES OF 1956 IN THE USA

	Title	Artist
1	Hound Dog/Don't Be Cruel	Elvis Presley
2	Love Me Tender	Elvis Presley
3	Heartbreak Hotel	Elvis Presley
4	Singing The Blues	Guy Mitchell
5	The Wayward Wind	Gogi Grant
6	Memories Are Made Of This	Dean Martin
7	Rock And Roll Waltz	Kay Starr
8	The Poor People Of Paris	Les Baxter
9	Lisbon Antigua	Nelson Riddle
10	My Prayer	Platters

Elvis Presley arrived like an atom bomb on the US music scene in 1956, laying waste entire swathes of it, as the styles of half the performers of the early 1950s suddenly became redundant overnight in the eyes (or ears) of the teenage audience who, suddenly, comprised the biggest record-buying group. Hound Dog/Don't Be Cruel sold a staggering 6,000,000 copies in the US alone, and Heartbreak Hotel and Love Me Tender between 2,000,000 and 3,000,000 each.

THE TOP 10 SINGLES OF 1957 IN THE UK

	Title	Artist
1	Diana	Paul Anka
2	Mary's Boy Child	Harry Belafonte
3	All Shook Up	Elvis Presley
4	Love Letters In The Sand	Pat Boone
5	Young Love	Tab Hunter
6	Singing The Blues	Guy Mitchell
7	Yes, Tonight Josephine	Johnnie Ray
8	Island In The Sun	Harry Belafonte
9	Teddy Bear	Elvis Presley
10	When I Fall In Love	Nat 'King' Cole

Record sales boomed in the UK in 1957, partly as the advent of Rock 'n' Roll turned a generation of teenagers into record buyers, as it already had in the United States. Both Mary's Boy Child and Diana and sold 1,000,000 copies in the UK, only the second and third in history to do so. This entire Top 10 features American artists, British rock not yet having got off the ground or extricated itself from the home-grown skiffle movement.

THE TOP 10 SINGLES OF 1957 IN THE USA

	Title	Artist
1	Love Letters In The Sand	Pat Boone
2	Jailhouse Rock	Elvis Presley
3	All Shook Up	Elvis Presley
4	Teddy Bear	Elvis Presley
5	Too Much	Elvis Presley
6	Young Love	Tab Hunter
7	Tammy	Debbie Reynolds
8	Diana	Paul Anka
9	Honeycomb	Jimmie Rodgers
10	April Love	Pat Boone

This was Elvis Presley's year again, with four 2,000,000-selling singles in succession, though ironically Pat Boone outsold his rival to the year's chart with his own biggest seller of all time – Love Letters In The Sand moved more than 3,000,000 copies in the United States alone. Tammy and April Love were both movie title songs, while Tab Hunter was a movie actor who could not really sing at all!

THE TOP 10 SINGLES OF 1958 IN THE UK

	Title	Artist
1	Jailhouse Rock	Elvis Presley
2	All I Have To Do Is Dream/Claudette	Everly Brothers
3	Who's Sorry Now	Connie Francis
4	Magic Moments/Catch A Falling Star	Perry Como
5	Stupid Cupid/Carolina Moon	Connie Francis
6	When	Kalin Twins
7	Hoots Mon	Lord Rockingham's XI
8	It's Only Make Believe	Conway Twitty
9	Tulips From Amsterdam/ You Need Hands	Max Bygraves
10	Whole Lotta Woman	Marvin Rainwate

THE TOP 10 SINGLES OF 1958 IN THE USA

	Title	Artist
1	The Chipmunk Song	Chipmunks
2	Catch A Falling Star/Magic Moments	Perry Como
3	Tom Dooley	Kingston Trio
4	It's All In The Game	Tommy Edwards
5	Don't	Elvis Presley
6	At The Hop	Danny & The Juniors
7	The Purple People Eater	Sheb Wooley
8	All I Have To Do Is Dream/Claudette	Everly Brothers
9	Tequila	Champs
10	(Volare) Nel Blu Dipinto Di Blu	Domenico Modugno

Still the Americans dominated Britain's top sellers, with Max Bygraves and Lord Rockingham's XI (the resident band on the *Oh Boy!* TV show) as somewhat incongruous domestic representatives in the Top 10. *Jailhouse Rock* was Elvis Presley's biggest-yet UK seller, entering the singles chart at No. 1 (an unprecedented feat), and selling over 500,000 copies in three days.

Gimmicky novelties were starting to permeate American Rock 'n' Roll by 1958, as witness the success of *The Chipmunk Song* (a staggering 4,000,000-seller at Christmas) and *The Purple People Eater*. The Champs' *Tequila*, meanwhile, instituted another strong movement in the form of the rock instrumental, and was also the first rock disc to win a category of the newly established Grammy Awards (as 'Best R & B Performance', oddly enough).

The Everly Brothers, Don and Phil, had a bestselling single of 1958 in both the UK and USA with their fourth hit, the double A-side All I Have To Do Is Dream/Claudette.

THE TOP 10 SINGLES OF 1959 IN THE UK

	Title	Artist
1	*Living Doll*	Cliff Richard
2	*What Do You Want To Make Those Eyes At Me For*	Emile Ford
3	*What Do You Want?*	Adam Faith
4	*It Doesn't Matter Anymore*	Buddy Holly
5	*Side Saddle*	Russ Conway
6	*Travellin' Light*	Cliff Richard
7	*Smoke Gets In Your Eyes*	Platters
8	*A Fool Such As I/I Need Your Love Tonight*	Elvis Presley
9	*Only Sixteen*	Craig Douglas
10	*Dream Lover*	Bobby Darin

British rock-based acts finally came into their own commercially during 1959, and in fact dominate this Top 10 with six of the listings. By far the most important arrival was Cliff Richard, who showed his versatility early on by spurning a 100 per cent rock repertoire for two Country-style beat ballads in *Living Doll* and *Travellin' Light*. Cliff, Adam Faith, Emile Ford and Russ Conway all stood out from the prevailing UK trend, by recording original material rather than covering American hits.

THE TOP 10 SINGLES OF 1959 IN THE USA

	Title	Artist
1	*Mack The Knife*	Bobby Darin
2	*The Battle Of New Orleans*	Johnny Horton
3	*A Fool Such As I/I Need Your Love Tonight*	Elvis Presley
4	*Venus*	Frankie Avalon
5	*Stagger Lee*	Lloyd Price
6	*A Big Hunk O' Love*	Elvis Presley
7	*The Three Bells*	Browns
8	*Lonely Boy*	Paul Anka
9	*Come Softly To Me*	Fleetwoods
10	*Donna/La Bamba*	Ritchie Valens

Though Elvis Presley was in the US Army (and out of the United States) during 1959, his stock stayed high via a pair of singles he had actually recorded during a weekend's leave early in his service career. Some of the rough edges of Rock 'n' Roll were smoothing away by now, and several artists who had arrived on its wave were widening their sights – none more than Bobby Darin, whose *Mack The Knife*, a two-month chart-topper, was a Sinatra-style jazzy fingerpopper.

THE TOP 10 SINGLES OF 1960 IN THE UK

	Title	Artist
1	*It's Now Or Never*	Elvis Presley
2	*Cathy's Clown*	Everly Brothers
3	*Apache*	Shadows
4	*Please Don't Tease*	Cliff Richard
5	*My Old Man's A Dustman*	Lonnie Donegan
6	*Handy Man*	Jimmy Jones
7	*Why*	Anthony Newley
8	*Poor Me*	Adam Faith
9	*A Mess Of Blues/Girl Of My Best Friend*	Elvis Presley
10	*I Love You*	Cliff Richard

It's Now Or Never, initially prevented from release in the UK because of its apparent copyright infringement of *O Sole Mio*, became, when it did reach the market, the country's fastest-selling single to date, topping 1,000,000 in the UK within six weeks. The Everly Brothers' *Cathy's Clown* was to be their all-time UK bestseller, as was the Shadows' *Apache*, their first success independent of Cliff Richard. (*Apache*, ironically, dethroned Cliff's *Please Don't Tease* from No. 1.)

THE TOP 10 SINGLES OF 1960 IN THE USA

	Title	Artist
1	*It's Now Or Never*	Elvis Presley
2	*Are You Lonesome Tonight?*	Elvis Presley
3	*Theme From 'A Summer Place'*	Percy Faith
4	*Cathy's Clown*	Everly Brothers
5	*Stuck On You*	Elvis Presley
6	*I'm Sorry*	Brenda Lee
7	*The Twist*	Chubby Checker
8	*Save The Last Dance For Me*	Drifters
9	*Running Bear*	Johnny Preston
10	*El Paso*	Marty Robbins

Out of the army in the spring of 1960, Elvis Presley wasted no time in re-establishing his pre-eminence, with his first three post-army singles among the year's top five US sellers. Elvis was now noticeably ballad-oriented, however, and elsewhere uptempo R & B (as exemplified by the Drifters) and dance records (such as *The Twist*) were supplanting Rock 'n' Roll as the major teenage fare, along with commercialized Nashville Country music like that from Brenda Lee and Marty Robbins.

THE TOP 10 SINGLES OF 1961 IN THE UK

	Title	Artist
1	Are You Lonesome Tonight?	Elvis Presley
2	Runaway	Del Shannon
3	Wooden Heart	Elvis Presley
4	Are You Sure	Allisons
5	Walkin' Back To Happiness	Helen Shapiro
6	Surrender	Elvis Presley
7	You Don't Know	Helen Shapiro
8	Well I Ask You	Eden Kane
9	Halfway To Paradise	Billy Fury
10	Stranger On The Shore	Mr Acker Bilk

THE TOP 10 SINGLES OF 1961 IN THE USA

	Title	Artist
1	Runaway	Del Shannon
2	Big Bad John	Jimmy Dean
3	Tossin' And Turnin'	Bobby Lewis
4	Wonderland By Night	Bert Kaempfert
5	Calcutta	Lawrence Welk
6	Travelin' Man/Hello Mary Lou	Ricky Nelson
7	Pony Time	Chubby Checker
8	Will You Love Me Tomorrow?	Shirelles
9	Blue Moon	Marcels
10	Michael	Highwaymen

Del Shannon, whose *Runaway* was, globally, the year's bestselling record, was a significant arrival on the scene in being a self-contained rock-based singer/songwriter not necessarily reliant on others' material – Buddy Holly and Eddie Cochran, both dead, had earlier presaged this trend, but many more would follow Shannon. Acker Bilk's hit straddled 1961 and 1962 almost equally, selling 500,000 by the year's end but doubling its total through amazing chart longevity the following year.

The main trend of 1961 in the United States (as it would be for the next two years) was a lack of clear musical trends. Country, folk, novelties such as the Marcels' outrageous gymnastic vocal revival of *Blue Moon*, and even two very square orchestral instrumental offerings from Bert Kaempfert and Lawrence Welk, tended to reinforce this farrago by aligning in unlikely configuration as the year's top sellers.

Helen Shapiro had two records among the bestselling singles of 1961 and gained the distinction of being the youngest artist to that date with a UK No. 1.

THE TOP 10 SINGLES OF 1962 IN THE UK

	Title	Artist
1	*I Remember You*	Frank Ifield
2	*The Young Ones*	Cliff Richard
3	*Telstar*	Tornados
4	*Lovesick Blues*	Frank Ifield
5	*Stranger On The Shore*	Mr Acker Bilk
6	*Wonderful Land*	Shadows
7	*Return To Sender*	Elvis Presley
8	*Can't Help Falling In Love*	Elvis Presley
9	*I Can't Stop Loving You*	Ray Charles
10	*Good Luck Charm*	Elvis Presley

THE TOP 10 SINGLES OF 1962 IN THE USA

	Title	Artist
1	*I Can't Stop Loving You*	Ray Charles
2	*Big Girls Don't Cry*	Four Seasons
3	*Sherry*	Four Seasons
4	*The Twist*	Chubby Checker
5	*Return To Sender*	Elvis Presley
6	*Roses Are Red*	Bobby Vinton
7	*Peppermint Twist*	Joey Dee & The Starliters
8	*Stranger On The Shore*	Mr Acker Bilk
9	*Monster Mash*	Bobby 'Boris' Pickett & The Crypt-Kickers
10	*Duke Of Earl*	Gene Chandler

The top six UK bestsellers this year were all British records, and three of them – Frank Ifield's *I Remember You* and the entries by Cliff Richard and Mr Acker Bilk – also became the first three singles by UK acts to sell over 1,000,000 copies in the UK. Ifield, the Tornados and Bilk, perhaps even more astonishingly for the time, went on to repeat their success in the US charts, normally rarely frequented by non-American artists.

The Four Seasons arrived with two chart-topping million-sellers on the trot, ushering in a major presence for vocal groups (of many styles and both genders) in the US charts. Dance craze of the year was the Twist, and Chubby Checker became the most consistent hitmaker of 1962 on the back of it, his original *The Twist* single from 1960 reappearing to sell 1,000,000 copies all over again.

I Can't Stop Loving You *by Ray Charles, extracted from his equally successful album* Modern Sounds In Country & Western Music, *was the top single of 1962 in the USA.*

THE TOP 10 SINGLES OF 1963 IN THE UK

	Title	Artist
1	She Loves You	Beatles
2	I Want To Hold Your Hand	Beatles
3	The Next Time/Bachelor Boy	Cliff Richard
4	You'll Never Walk Alone	Gerry & The Pacemakers
5	From Me To You	Beatles
6	Twist And Shout (EP)	Beatles
7	How Do You Do It	Gerry & The Pacemakers
8	Summer Holiday	Cliff Richard
9	Confessin' (That I Love You)	Frank Ifield
10	I Like It	Gerry & The Pacemakers

Pop music changed for ever in 1963 with the arrival of the Beatles: lively chart pretenders in January but by December selling as many records as the rest of the market put together. *She Loves You*, their biggest domestic seller, would remain the UK's all-time biggest-selling single for 14 years. Its follow-up, *I Want To Hold Your Hand*, shattered records by entering the chart at No. 1 and selling over 1,000,000 copies within five days. Other (mainly similarly provincial) UK groups flooded the charts in the Beatles' wake.

THE TOP 10 SINGLES OF 1963 IN THE USA

	Title	Artist
1	Sugar Shack	Jimmy Gilmer & The Fireballs
2	Dominique	The Singing Nun
3	Hey! Paula	Paul and Paula
4	Blue Velvet	Bobby Vinton
5	I Will Follow Him	Little Peggy March
6	Sukiyaki	Kyu Sakamoto
7	He's So Fine	Chiffons
8	Fingertips, Part 2	Little Stevie Wonder
9	Walk Like A Man	Four Seasons
10	My Boyfriend's Back	Angels

Though it didn't know it, American popular music was holding its breath before a British onslaught in 1963, and the generally unfocused nature of the year's biggest sellers does, in retrospect, indicate the fact. Two of the hits in the list, by the Singing Nun and Kyu Sakamoto, were novelties sung in foreign languages – French and Japanese respectively! Twelve-year-old Stevie Wonder, meanwhile, gave upwardly mobile Motown its biggest success to date.

THE TOP 10 SINGLES OF 1964 IN THE UK

	Title	Artist
1	Can't Buy Me Love	Beatles
2	I Feel Fine	Beatles
3	Glad All Over	Dave Clark Five
4	Needles And Pins	Searchers
5	Anyone Who Had A Heart	Cilla Black
6	I Love You Because	Jim Reeves
7	A Hard Day's Night	Beatles
8	I Won't Forget You	Jim Reeves
9	Oh, Pretty Woman	Roy Orbison
10	Do Wah Diddy Diddy	Manfred Mann

The new breed of UK beat groups and associated soloists (like Cilla Black, who shared background and management with the Beatles) totally dominated the UK charts in 1964, with new star names appearing weekly. Roy Orbison, entering his strongest sales period ever (and a frequent UK visitor, which obviously helped), fought back on America's behalf, while Jim Reeves' death in the summer led to huge sales for two of his singles.

THE TOP 10 SINGLES OF 1964 IN THE USA

	Title	Artist
1	I Want To Hold Your Hand	Beatles
2	Can't Buy Me Love	Beatles
3	She Loves You	Beatles
4	I Feel Fine	Beatles
5	Baby Love	Supremes
6	Oh, Pretty Woman	Roy Orbison
7	There! I've Said It Again	Bobby Vinton
8	Hello Dolly	Louis Armstrong
9	I Get Around	Beach Boys
10	A Hard Day's Night	Beatles

The Beatles-led 'British Invasion', a totally unprecedented phenomenon, caused United States record-buying tastes to change for good virtually overnight – yet interestingly, apart from the Beatles themselves, who had the year's four bestselling singles, none of the other invaders managed to oust native acts from the rest of the year's Top 10. Louis Armstrong's show tune, a timeless novelty, was the first US chart-topper to break a months-long Beatles stranglehold at No. 1.

Beating the Beatles: incredibly, fellow Liverpudlian Ken Dodd's Tears *was the UK's bestselling single of 1965 – and, until recently ousted from the list, was one of the Top 10 UK singles of all time.*

THE TOP 10 SINGLES OF 1966 IN THE UK

	Title	Artist
1	Green, Green Grass Of Home	Tom Jones
2	Distant Drums	Jim Reeves
3	Strangers In The Night	Frank Sinatra
4	Yellow Submarine/ Eleanor Rigby	Beatles
5	These Boots Are Made For Walkin'	Nancy Sinatra
6	Paperback Writer	Beatles
7	19th Nervous Breakdown	Rolling Stones
8	Keep On Running	Spencer Davis Group
9	The Sun Ain't Gonna Shine Anymore	Walker Brothers
10	What Would I Be	Val Doonican

THE TOP 10 SINGLES OF 1965 IN THE UK

	Title	Artist
1	Tears	Ken Dodd
2	We Can Work It Out/Day Tripper	Beatles
3	The Carnival Is Over	Seekers
4	Help!	Beatles
5	The Last Time	Rolling Stones
6	I'll Never Find Another You	Seekers
7	I Got You Babe	Sonny and Cher
8	(I Can't Get No) Satisfaction	Rolling Stones
9	Ticket To Ride	Beatles
10	It's Not Unusual	Tom Jones

THE TOP 10 SINGLES OF 1965 IN THE USA

	Title	Artist
1	Help!	Beatles
2	(I Can't Get No) Satisfaction	Rolling Stones
3	Yesterday	Beatles
4	I Can't Help Myself	Four Tops
5	Mrs Brown You've Got A Lovely Daughter	Herman's Hermits
6	King Of The Road	Roger Miller
7	I Got You Babe	Sonny and Cher
8	You've Lost That Lovin' Feelin'	Righteous Brothers
9	Downtown	Petula Clark
10	We Can Work It Out/Day Tripper	Beatles

Tom Jones' excursion into Country music with *Green, Green Grass Of Home*, after experiencing falling sales on his rock/pop releases, paid handsome dividends, topping the Christmas-period UK charts and selling more than 1,000,000 copies in Britain alone. All the top three sellers this year were by male soloists, and 1966 was not one of the Beatles' strongest years in terms of sales, with only two singles on the market.

The top three sellers of 1965 each sold more than 1,000,000 copies in the UK, but it seems ironic that at the height of a sales boom generated by group music and ignited by the Beatles, a hopelessly square record by an unlikely fellow Liverpudlian, comedian Ken Dodd, should have outsold everything else that year – including the Beatles' own releases. Note that Sonny and Cher are the sole American presence in this Top 10.

The Rolling Stones really established themselves internationally as the major rivals to the Beatles in 1965, and it was the American-recorded *(I Can't Get No) Satisfaction* – a US million-seller before even being released in Britain – that did the trick. The Beatles' *Yesterday* was not, in fact, released in the UK as a single at all at the time, despite being the third biggest US hit of the year; British fans had to buy the *Help!* album to hear it.

THE TOP 10 SINGLES OF 1966 IN THE USA

	Title	Artist
1	*The Ballad Of The Green Berets*	Staff Sergeant Barry Sadler
2	*I'm A Believer*	Monkees
3	*Winchester Cathedral*	New Vaudeville Band
4	*Last Train To Clarksville*	Monkees
5	*Monday, Monday*	Mamas and the Papas
6	*Cherish*	Association
7	*(You're My) Soul And Inspiration*	Righteous Brothers
8	*Reach Out I'll Be There*	Four Tops
9	*Summer In The City*	Lovin' Spoonful
10	*96 Tears*	? & The Mysterians*

* So called on the original release; '(Question Mark)' was added on later versions.

Thanks to a smash-hit TV show, the Monkees arrived in no uncertain fashion among the year's bestsellers with their first two releases, though they shared the top four with two novelties: the British, largely instrumental, *Winchester Cathedral*, and the extraordinary right-wing anthem by real-life Green Beret Staff Sergeant Barry Sadler, who roused the silent moral majority in America to the tune of more than 2,000,000 sales – and even had a chart-topping album!

(Above) *How green was his valley: Tom Jones's* Green, Green Grass Of Home, *borrowing an arrangement from a Jerry Lee Lewis LP version, held the UK top spot in 1966.*

(Below) *The original heavy metal group? Newcomers the Monkees, aided just a little by a popular TV show, had two records among the 10 bestselling US singles of 1966.*

THE TOP 10 SINGLES OF 1967 IN THE UK

	Title	Artist
1	Release Me	Engelbert Humperdinck
2	The Last Waltz	Engelbert Humperdinck
3	There Goes My Everything	Engelbert Humperdinck
4	Hello Goodbye	Beatles
5	I'm A Believer	Monkees
6	A Whiter Shade Of Pale	Procol Harum
7	Puppet On A String	Sandie Shaw
8	Magical Mystery Tour (Double EP)	Beatles
9	All You Need Is Love	Beatles
10	This Is My Song	Petula Clark

THE TOP 10 SINGLES OF 1967 IN THE USA

	Title	Artist
1	To Sir With Love	Lulu
2	Ode To Billie Joe	Bobbie Gentry
3	Windy	Association
4	The Letter	Box Tops
5	Light My Fire	Doors
6	Groovin'	Young Rascals
7	Daydream Believer	Monkees
8	Somethin' Stupid	Frank and Nancy Sinatra
9	Happy Together	Turtles
10	Hello Goodbye	Beatles

Ballads reasserted themselves in the UK in a major way in 1967. The 'Summer of Love' and the Underground Rock Revolution notwithstanding, much of this popularity was due to the advent of the romantically voiced (and outrageously named) Engelbert Humperdinck, who had the year's three biggest sellers. Meanwhile, Britain won the Eurovision Song Contest with *Puppet On A String*, and Sandie Shaw had her biggest-ever seller as a result.

Lulu's biggest US hit, which sold more than 2,000,000 copies, was the title song to the British-made Sidney Poitier movie in which the singer herself had a small acting part. Oddly, the song was released in the UK only as a B-side, and its potential was therefore wasted. The Doors and Association titles also, inexplicably, failed to impress Britain, despite major airplay in the final weeks of the pirate radio stations.

Release Me, The Last Waltz *and* There Goes My Everything *gave Engelbert Humperdinck a straight run of the top three singles in the UK in 1967 – which oddly is better remembered as the year of psychedelia and the 'Summer of Love'.*

His hit rendition of Stairway To Heaven *24 years away, Rolf Harris made his mark in 1969 with* Two Little Boys.

THE TOP 10 SINGLES OF 1968 IN THE UK

	Title	Artist
1	Hey Jude	Beatles
2	Those Were The Days	Mary Hopkin
3	Lily The Pink	Scaffold
4	What A Wonderful World	Louis Armstrong
5	Cinderella Rockefella	Esther and Abi Ofarim
6	The Good, The Bad And The Ugly	Hugo Montenegro
7	Young Girl	Union Gap
8	The Ballad Of Bonnie And Clyde	Georgie Fame
9	Honey	Bobby Goldsboro
10	Delilah	Tom Jones

The Beatles returned to annual dominance with their longest single (7 minutes 11 seconds), and the longest ever to top the UK chart. It was the first release on the group's own Apple label, while Mary Hopkin's debut was the second. There were also Beatle connections to the year's third biggest single – Paul McCartney's brother Mike was one-third of Scaffold. 'The Union Gap featuring Gary Puckett' was how the original release of *Young Girl* was billed; its re-release six years later reversed the name to 'Gary Puckett and the Union Gap'.

THE TOP 10 SINGLES OF 1968 IN THE USA

	Title	Artist
1	Hey Jude	Beatles
2	Love Is Blue	Paul Mauriat
3	Harper Valley PTA	Jeannie C. Riley
4	Honey	Bobby Goldsboro
5	People Got To Be Free	Rascals
6	(Sittin' On) The Dock Of The Bay	Otis Redding
7	Mrs Robinson	Simon and Garfunkel
8	I Heard It Through The Grapevine	Marvin Gaye
9	This Guy's In Love With You	Herb Alpert
10	Young Girl	Union Gap

As in the UK, the Beatles outsold all comers with *Hey Jude*. This was one of their biggest US sellers of all, with sales in the region of 4,000,000. Otis Redding's biggest-ever single was, ironically, a hit only after his tragic death on 1 December 1967 (it had been recorded just days before), while Herb Alpert achieved his greatest single success to date by putting aside his customary trumpet and singing.

THE TOP 10 SINGLES OF 1969 IN THE UK

	Title	Artist
1	Sugar Sugar	Archies
2	Two Little Boys	Rolf Harris
3	Get Back	Beatles
4	Honky Tonk Women	Rolling Stones
5	Israelites	Desmond Dekker and The Aces
6	Ruby Don't Take Your Love To Town	Kenny Rogers and The First Edition
7	Albatross	Fleetwood Mac
8	I Heard It Through The Grapevine	Marvin Gaye
9	Where Do You Go To, My Lovely	Peter Sarstedt
10	In The Year 2525 (Exordium And Terminus)	Zager & Evans

In a year characterized by long song titles, one of the most simple (and, it must be said, simple-minded) became 1969's biggest-selling single. The Archies did not, in fact, exist as a real performing group at all, but were based upon comic-book characters and voiced by studio session singers. The lead vocalist on *Sugar Sugar* was revealed to be Ron Dante, who later became Barry Manilow's producer.

THE TOP 10 SINGLES OF 1969 IN THE USA

	Title	Artist
1	Sugar Sugar	Archies
2	Aquarius/Let The Sunshine In	5th Dimension
3	Get Back	Beatles
4	Honky Tonk Women	Rolling Stones
5	In The Year 2525 (Exordium And Terminus)	Zager & Evans
6	Everyday People	Sly & The Family Stone
7	Dizzy	Tommy Roe
8	I Can't Get Next To You	Temptations
9	Crimson And Clover	Tommy James & The Shondells
10	Come Together/Something	Beatles

As in the UK, the non-existent Archies had the biggest seller of the year (more than 3,000,000 copies in the US), though they were run quite close by the 5th Dimension, whose medley of two songs from *Hair* was the biggest of a flurry of hit cover versions from the smash Broadway musical. Zager & Evans never managed to follow up their very odd Sci-Fi prophecy song, and thus became one of the biggest one-hit-wonder acts of all time.

THE TOP 10 SINGLES OF 1970 IN THE UK

	Title	Artist
1	The Wonder Of You	Elvis Presley
2	I Hear You Knocking	Dave Edmunds
3	In The Summertime	Mungo Jerry
4	All Right Now	Free
5	Wand'rin' Star	Lee Marvin
6	Band Of Gold	Freda Payne
7	Bridge Over Troubled Water	Simon and Garfunkel
8	Love Grows	Edison Lighthouse
9	Spirit In The Sky	Norman Greenbaum
10	Yellow River	Christie

THE TOP 10 SINGLES OF 1970 IN THE USA

	Title	Artist
1	I'll Be There	Jackson 5
2	Bridge Over Troubled Water	Simon and Garfunkel
3	Raindrops Keep Fallin' On My Head	B. J. Thomas
4	(They Long To Be) Close To You	Carpenters
5	I Think I Love You	Partridge Family
6	American Woman	Guess Who
7	Let It Be	Beatles
8	ABC	Jackson 5
9	Ain't No Mountain High Enough	Diana Ross
10	Mama Told Me Not To Come	Three Dog Night

This was not a year of markedly huge-selling singles in the UK: the top title (recorded live by Presley in Las Vegas) sold fewer than 600,000 copies. Both this and *I Hear You Knocking* were astute revivals of 1950s songs, while Lee Marvin's hit was purely a one-off from the film *Paint Your Wagon*, in which he co-starred with another unlikely crooner, Clint Eastwood (singing *I Talk To The Trees* on the record's B-side).

The Jackson 5 (featuring 11-year-old lead singer Michael) arrived in sensational fashion in 1970, their first four Motown singles all hitting No. 1 in the United States, and the fourth of these, *I'll Be There*, selling almost 3,000,000 copies. B. J. Thomas' hit was the featured song from the hit movie *Butch Cassidy And The Sundance Kid*, while the Partridge Family's debut (with David Cassidy vocalizing) was a spin-off from their successful weekly TV show.

Simon and Garfunkel's Bridge Over Troubled Water, *though it had but a fraction of the eventual sales of its namesake album, was one of the Top 10 singles of 1970 in the UK and USA.*

BEATLES QUIZ

1 What was the title of the full-length cartoon film featuring Beatles music?

2 Which 1968 Beatles single was some seven minutes in length, and by and about whom was it written?

3 Who played drums with the Beatles before Ringo Starr?

4 Who was the Beatles' manager?

5 What was the only Beatles Top 10 hit *not* written by Lennon and McCartney?

6 Who was credited as the featured musician on *Get Back*?

7 Which reclusive producer produced the *Let It Be* sessions?

8 What was the name of the Liverpool club where the Beatles made their lunchtime debut on 21 February 1961?

9 What was the title of the group's TV film which featured *Fool On The Hill*?

10 Which year marked the advent of Beatlemania in the USA?

THE TOP 10 SINGLES OF 1971 IN THE UK

	Title	Artist
1	My Sweet Lord	George Harrison
2	Ernie (The Fastest Milkman In The West)	Benny Hill
3	Grandad	Clive Dunn
4	Chirpy Chirpy Cheep Cheep	Middle Of The Road
5	Maggie May	Rod Stewart
6	Hot Love	T. Rex
7	Knock Three Times	Dawn
8	Coz I Luv You	Slade
9	Amazing Grace	Judy Collins
10	Get It On	T. Rex

George Harrison had the first really big-selling hit by an ex-Beatle, though *My Sweet Lord* would later be overtaken by solo efforts by both Paul McCartney and John Lennon. The year 1971, meanwhile, marked the arrival of Glam-Rock, heralded by Slade and T. Rex – though novelties by two comedy actors were the year's second and third bestselling singles.

THE TOP 10 SINGLES OF 1971 IN THE USA

	Title	Artist
1	Joy To The World	Three Dog Night
2	It's Too Late	Carole King
3	Maggie May	Rod Stewart
4	One Bad Apple	Osmonds
5	How Can You Mend A Broken Heart	Bee Gees
6	My Sweet Lord	George Harrison
7	Knock Three Times	Dawn
8	Indian Reservation	Raiders
9	Go Away Little Girl	Donny Osmond
10	Just My Imagination	Temptations

The Osmonds arrived on the scene with a bang in the United States in 1971. *One Bad Apple*, their breakthrough hit, was virtually a clone of the successful Jackson 5 sound of the previous year, but they quickly branched out, with young Osmond brother Donny initiating a parallel hit career. Songwriter Carole King, meanwhile, finally scored as an artist after first trying nine years earlier, while her early 1960s contemporary Tony Orlando was lead singer of Dawn.

THE TOP 10 SINGLES OF 1972 IN THE UK

	Title	Artist
1	I'd Like To Teach The World To Sing	New Seekers
2	Long-Haired Lover From Liverpool	Little Jimmy Osmond
3	Without You	Nilsson
4	Amazing Grace	Royal Scots Dragoon Guards Band
5	Puppy Love	Donny Osmond
6	My Ding-A-Ling	Chuck Berry
7	Crazy Horses	Osmonds
8	Mouldy Old Dough	Lieutenant Pigeon
9	Mother Of Mine	Neil Reid
10	Son Of My Father	Chicory Tip

Little Jimmy Osmond would eventually overtake the New Seekers in total sales – his Christmas-time smash continued selling well into 1973. This was the first year of 'Osmondmania', with older brother Donny and the group themselves also represented among the top 10 sellers. *Amazing Grace* scored for the second year running, this time in a bagpipe version, following Judy Collins' vocal hit.

THE TOP 10 SINGLES OF 1972 IN THE USA

	Title	Artist
1	The First Time Ever I Saw Your Face	Roberta Flack
2	Alone Again (Naturally)	Gilbert O'Sullivan
3	American Pie	Don McLean
4	Without You	Nilsson
5	I Can See Clearly Now	Johnny Nash
6	Brand New Key	Melanie
7	I Gotcha	Joe Tex
8	A Horse With No Name	America
9	Let's Stay Together	Al Green
10	Baby, Don't Get Hooked On Me	Mac Davis

America's top seller of 1972 was a British song, written and originally recorded by folk singer Ewen MacColl. Roberta Flack's version was a three-year-old album track, released as a single after being featured in the Clint Eastwood film *Play Misty For Me*. Nilsson's *Without You* was also of UK origin, being penned by two members of the group Badfinger.

THE TOP 10 SINGLES OF 1973 IN THE UK

	Title	Artist
1	I Love You Love Me Love	Gary Glitter
2	Eye Level	Simon Park Orchestra
3	Tie A Yellow Ribbon Round The Ole Oak Tree	Dawn
4	Merry Xmas Everybody	Slade
5	Welcome Home	Peters and Lee
6	Blockbuster	Sweet
7	I'm The Leader Of The Gang (I Am)	Gary Glitter
8	See My Baby Jive	Wizzard
9	My Coo-Ca-Choo	Alvin Stardust
10	Cum On Feel The Noize	Slade

Three of these singles were UK million-sellers, though only Gary Glitter's *I Love You...* achieved the figure during 1973. Simon Park Orchestra's *Eye Level* and Slade's *Merry Xmas Everybody* reached seven figures after steady sales through the subsequent five years – in fact, after re-charting almost annually during December, Slade's single has subsequently overhauled everything else here, Glitter included.

THE TOP 10 SINGLES OF 1973 IN THE USA

	Title	Artist
1	Tie A Yellow Ribbon Round The Ole Oak Tree	Dawn
2	My Love	Wings
3	Killing Me Softly With His Song	Roberta Flack
4	Crocodile Rock	Elton John
5	You're So Vain	Carly Simon
6	Bad, Bad Leroy Brown	Jim Croce
7	Let's Get It On	Marvin Gaye
8	Keep On Truckin'	Eddie Kendricks
9	Midnight Train To Georgia	Gladys Knight & The Pips
10	Touch Me In The Morning	Diana Ross

An almost entirely home-grown Top 10 in the United States in 1973, with the exceptions of Elton John and Paul McCartney's Wings. Roberta Flack made a second strong showing (with a song about Don McLean of *American Pie* fame), while Jim Croce had two chart-topping hits (the other was *Time In A Bottle*, which straddled the year's end) before tragically dying in a plane crash while travelling between concerts.

THE TOP 10 SINGLES OF 1974 IN THE UK

	Title	Artist
1	You Won't Find Another Fool Like Me	New Seekers
2	Tiger Feet	Mud
3	Lonely This Christmas	Mud
4	Billy Don't Be A Hero	Paper Lace
5	Gonna Make You A Star	David Essex
6	When Will I See You Again?	Three Degrees
7	The Show Must Go On	Leo Sayer
8	Seasons In The Sun	Terry Jacks
9	She	Charles Aznavour
10	Kung Fu Fighting	Carl Douglas

Not a year of classic, memorable hits, despite the fact that some of them sold very well indeed – over 850,000 in the New Seekers' case. Mud's Elvis Presley Christmas pastiche has since become something of a Yule perennial, while Charles Aznavour's *She* is now, unfortunately, a karaoke staple.

THE TOP 10 SINGLES OF 1974 IN THE USA

	Title	Artist
1	The Way We Were	Barbra Streisand
2	Seasons In The Sun	Terry Jacks
3	Show And Tell	Al Wilson
4	Billy Don't Be A Hero	Bo Donaldson & The Heywoods
5	The Loco-Motion	Grand Funk
6	The Streak	Ray Stevens
7	TSOP (The Sound Of Philadelphia)	MFSB
8	(You're) Having My Baby	Paul Anka
9	You Make Me Feel Brand New	Stylistics
10	The Joker	Steve Miller Band

The year 1974 marked the return of Paul Anka, a hitmaker from a decade-and-a-half earlier, and also a song from the early 1960s in the form of *The Loco-Motion*, here in an unlikely revival by heavy metal specialists Grand Funk. Steve Miller's *The Joker* was to be a UK chart-topper 16 years later.

THE TOP 10 SINGLES OF 1975 IN THE UK

	Title	Artist
1	Bohemian Rhapsody	Queen
2	Bye Bye Baby	Bay City Rollers
3	Sailing	Rod Stewart
4	I Can't Give You Anything (But My Love)	Stylistics
5	Stand By Your Man	Tammy Wynette
6	Whispering Grass	Windsor Davies and Don Estelle
7	Give A Little Love	Bay City Rollers
8	Space Oddity	David Bowie
9	Hold Me Close	David Essex
10	I Only Have Eyes For You	Art Garfunkel

THE TOP 10 SINGLES OF 1975 IN THE USA

	Title	Artist
1	Love Will Keep Us Together	Captain and Tennille
2	Rhinestone Cowboy	Glen Campbell
3	Philadelphia Freedom	Elton John
4	Island Girl	Elton John
5	Fame	David Bowie
6	He Don't Love You (Like I Love You)	Tony Orlando & Dawn
7	Fly Robin Fly	Silver Convention
8	Pick Up The Pieces	Average White Band
9	Bad Blood	Neil Sedaka
10	Shining Star	Earth, Wind & Fire

Queen's *Bohemian Rhapsody* sold 1,300,000 copies in the UK during a nine-week spell atop the chart, cementing the group's superstar status, as well as alerting the record industry to the potential of an effective promotional video – clearly a major factor in bringing this single to such a wide audience. Also worth noting is David Bowie's *Space Oddity*, a very successful reissue of a single which first charted in 1969.

This was a comeback year for Neil Sedaka, who wrote the year's bestseller, *Love Will Keep Us Together*, and also scored as an artist with *Bad Blood* – on which he duetted with Elton John, himself hugely popular in the United States at this time, as entries at numbers three and four in the year's Top 10 attest.

Those trousers! Those boots! Bye Bye Baby, *a song borrowed from the Four Seasons' back catalogue, was the Bay City Rollers' 1975 UK smash.*

THE TOP 10 SINGLES OF 1976 IN THE UK

	Title	Artist
1	Save Your Kisses For Me	Brotherhood of Man
2	Under The Moon Of Love	Showaddywaddy
3	Mississippi	Pussycat
4	When A Child Is Born	Johnny Mathis
5	Don't Go Breaking My Heart	Elton John and Kiki Dee
6	Dancing Queen	Abba
7	If You Leave Me Now	Chicago
8	A Little Bit More	Dr Hook
9	Fernando	Abba
10	I Love To Love	Tina Charles

Brotherhood of Man sold over 1,000,000 copies in the UK of what was essentially their comeback single (the group had first charted in 1970, albeit with a different line-up), after the song won the 1976 Eurovision Song Contest for Britain. Europe had a major impact on this year's biggest hits, not only via two huge sellers from Abba (also previous Eurovision winners), but also in the form of *Mississippi* by Dutch group Pussycat.

THE TOP 10 SINGLES OF 1976 IN THE USA

	Title	Artist
1	Disco Lady	Johnnie Taylor
2	Play That Funky Music	Wild Cherry
3	Kiss And Say Goodbye	Manhattans
4	Disco Duck	Rick Dees and his Cast Of Idiots
5	Don't Go Breaking My Heart	Elton John and Kiki Dee
6	Tonight's The Night	Rod Stewart
7	Silly Love Songs	Wings
8	December 1963 (Oh What A Night)	Four Seasons
9	Afternoon Delight	Starland Vocal Band
10	A Fifth Of Beethoven	Walter Murphy

The Record Industry Association of America began in 1976 to certify platinum discs for singles that sell more than 2,000,000 copies; the hits by Johnnie Taylor, Wild Cherry, the Manhattans and Rick Dees qualified for the first four. The year's major comeback was by the Four Seasons, while the Walter Murphy hit was a disco version of part of Beethoven's 5th Symphony!

THE TOP 10 SINGLES OF 1977 IN THE UK

	Title	Artist
1	Mull Of Kintyre	Wings
2	Don't Give Up On Us	David Soul
3	Don't Cry For Me Argentina	Julie Covington
4	When I Need You	Leo Sayer
5	Silver Lady	David Soul
6	Knowing Me, Knowing You	Abba
7	I Feel Love	Donna Summer
8	Way Down	Elvis Presley
9	The Floral Dance	Brighouse & Rastrick Brass Band
10	So You Win Again	Hot Chocolate

Wings' *Mull Of Kintyre*, spending two months at the top of the UK chart, became the first single ever to sell over 2,000,000 copies in Britain alone (though it failed completely in America, where it was released as a B-side!). This now replaced the Beatles' *She Loves You* as the bestselling single of all time in the UK, a distinction it would hold for the next seven years.

THE TOP 10 SINGLES OF 1977 IN THE USA

	Title	Artist
1	You Light Up My Life	Debby Boone
2	Star Wars Theme/Cantina Band	Meco
3	Car Wash	Rose Royce
4	I Just Want To Be Your Everything	Andy Gibb
5	Best Of My Love	Emotions
6	Evergreen: Love Theme From 'A Star Is Born'	Barbra Streisand
7	Torn Between Two Lovers	Mary MacGregor
8	Dancing Queen	Abba
9	Boogie Nights	Heatwave
10	Got To Give It Up	Marvin Gaye

Debby Boone was the youngest daughter of former hitmaker Pat Boone, and her *You Light Up My Life*, the theme song from the film of the same title, was America's biggest-selling single since the Beatles' *Hey Jude* in 1968. It spent over two months at the top of the chart – exceptional longevity in a year when two-thirds of the No. 1 singles held the slot for only a week apiece. Curiously, Debby failed significantly to follow up her hit.

THE TOP 10 SINGLES OF 1978 IN THE UK

	Title	Artist
1	Rivers Of Babylon/Brown Girl In The Ring	Boney M
2	You're The One That I Want	John Travolta and Olivia Newton-John
3	Mary's Boy Child/Oh My Lord	Boney M
4	Summer Nights	John Travolta and Olivia Newton-John
5	Three Times A Lady	Commodores
6	The Smurf Song	Father Abraham and the Smurfs
7	Night Fever	Bee Gees
8	Rat Trap	Boomtown Rats
9	Take A Chance On Me	Abba
10	Wuthering Heights	Kate Bush

Record sales boomed in 1978, as evidenced by the fact that the top four of this year's list all sold more than 1,000,000 copies in the UK. The boom had little to do with Punk or New Wave (which were filling the music press), but rather with the explosion of commercial disco, exemplified by the year's biggest act, Boney M, and the massive success of the film *Grease*, from which both Travolta/Newton-John duets came, together with a soundtrack album that sold 1,000,000 copies.

THE TOP 10 SINGLES OF 1978 IN THE USA

	Title	Artist
1	Night Fever	Bee Gees
2	Stayin' Alive	Bee Gees
3	Shadow Dancing	Andy Gibb
4	Boogie Oogie Oogie	A Taste Of Honey
5	Grease	Frankie Valli
6	Hot Child In The City	Nick Gilder
7	Three Times A Lady	Commodores
8	You're The One That I Want	John Travolta and Olivia Newton-John
9	Le Freak	Chic
10	Emotion	Samantha Sang

As in the UK, record sales in the United States boomed in 1978, all 10 singles listed here receiving platinum awards for selling over 2,000,000 copies. The acceleration was fuelled by the growth of disco music and the success of the films *Saturday Night Fever* and *Grease*, with the Bee Gees bridging the gap between all three: they wrote and produced the Andy Gibb, Frankie Valli and Samantha Sang hits, as well as their own top two entries.

THE TOP 10 SINGLES OF 1979 IN THE UK

	Title	Artist
1	Y.M.C.A.	Village People
2	Heart Of Glass	Blondie
3	Bright Eyes	Art Garfunkel
4	Hit Me With Your Rhythm Stick	Ian Dury & The Blockheads
5	Sunday Girl	Blondie
6	We Don't Talk Anymore	Cliff Richard
7	I Don't Like Mondays	Boomtown Rats
8	Another Brick In The Wall, Part 2	Pink Floyd
9	When You're In Love With A Beautiful Woman	Dr Hook
10	I Will Survive	Gloria Gaynor

The top three singles this year provided another trio of UK 1,000,000-sellers, though all were by American acts. Oddly, Art Garfunkel's *Bright Eyes*, the theme from the film *Watership Down* (and a British song penned by Mike Batt), failed utterly in his native United States. The Pink Floyd single's total sales would have put it in 4th place in this list, but its peak selling period straddled the year-end 1979–80, placing some 400,000 of its sales in the next decade!

THE TOP 10 SINGLES OF 1979 IN THE USA

	Title	Artist
1	I Will Survive	Gloria Gaynor
2	Do Ya Think I'm Sexy?	Rod Stewart
3	My Sharona	Knack
4	Y.M.C.A.	Village People
5	Bad Girls	Donna Summer
6	Reunited	Peaches and Herb
7	Too Much Heaven	Bee Gees
8	Le Freak	Chic
9	Hot Stuff	Donna Summer
10	Ring My Bell	Anita Ward

Disco ruled the 1979 US charts; even Rod Stewart was (successfully) on the bandwagon, and the only rock song here is the Knack's *My Sharona*. Singles sales were still at an all-time high – again, all those listed here sold more than 2,000,000 copies. Even among this stellar company, Chic's *Le Freak* appears for the second year running; it sold a staggering 4,000,000 copies between November 1978 and April 1979.

THE TOP 10 SINGLES OF 1980 IN THE UK

	Title	Artist
1	Don't Stand So Close To Me	Police
2	Woman In Love	Barbra Streisand
3	Feels Like I'm In Love	Kelly Marie
4	The Tide Is High	Blondie
5	(Just Like) Starting Over	John Lennon
6	D.I.S.C.O.	Ottawan
7	Super Trouper	Abba
8	Geno	Dexy's Midnight Runners
9	Together We Are Beautiful	Fern Kinney
10	Stop The Cavalry	Jona Lewie

No million-selling singles in the UK this year; sales of the Police single were just under 800,000. John Lennon's ironically-titled entry was the first sales beneficiary of his tragic death, just prior to Christmas, and there would be two further huge Lennon sellers at the beginning of the following year.

THE TOP 10 SINGLES OF 1980 IN THE USA

	Title	Artist
1	Another One Bites The Dust	Queen
2	Funkytown	Lipps, Inc.
3	Take Your Time (Do It Right)	S.O.S. Band
4	Call Me	Blondie
5	Lady	Lionel Richie
6	Upside Down	Diana Ross
7	Another Brick In The Wall, Part 2	Pink Floyd
8	Crazy Little Thing Called Love	Queen
9	Rock With You	Michael Jackson
10	Woman In Love	Barbra Streisand

The year's top three singles in the United States all topped 2,000,000 sales. It was Queen's biggest year for American sales, with both singles in this Top 10 reaching No. 1 even though neither was a chart-topper in the UK. Blondie's disco-style *Call Me* was from the film *American Gigolo*, while the Lipps, Inc. and S.O.S. Band records were also disco/dance-style records – as, in many respects, was *Another One Bites The Dust*.

THE TOP 10 SINGLES OF 1981 IN THE UK

	Title	Artist
1	Don't You Want Me	Human League
2	Tainted Love	Soft Cell
3	Stand And Deliver	Adam & The Ants
4	Vienna	Ultravox
5	Making Your Mind Up	Bucks Fizz
6	Prince Charming	Adam & The Ants
7	Antmusic	Adam & The Ants
8	This Ole House	Shakin' Stevens
9	Woman	John Lennon
10	Imagine	John Lennon

Human League's year-end smash sold over 1,450,000 copies, to become one of the five biggest-selling UK singles of the 1980s. John Lennon's *Imagine* sold nearly 700,000 copies when it topped the chart after he died; added to its 1975 total, this pushed the single's cumulative sales to over 1,000,000, making it Lennon's all-time biggest British seller. *Making Your Mind Up* by Bucks Fizz was a rare UK Eurovision Song Contest winner.

THE TOP 10 SINGLES OF 1981 IN THE USA

	Title	Artist
1	Endless Love	Diana Ross and Lionel Richie
2	Physical	Olivia Newton-John
3	Celebration	Kool & The Gang
4	Elvira	Oak Ridge Boys
5	Bette Davis Eyes	Kim Carnes
6	Jessie's Girl	Rick Springfield
7	Waiting For A Girl Like You	Foreigner
8	Arthur's Theme (Best That You Can Do)	Christopher Cross
9	Kiss On My List	Daryl Hall and John Oates
10	I Love A Rainy Night	Eddie Rabbitt

Endless Love (the theme from the film of the same title) and *Physical* each spent two months atop the US charts; the latter was eventually the bigger seller, but its hit tenure extended over into 1982. All the top four titles sold more than 2,000,000 copies, and the year was notable for two exceptionally strong Country music singles, from the Oak Ridge Boys and Eddie Rabbitt.

(Above) *Police's* Don't Stand So Close To Me *was the UK's bestselling single of 1980 and the group's most successful single of all time.*

(Right) *Top of the league:* Don't You Want Me *put Human League in number one place in 1981, and was also one of the decade's bestselling singles.*

THE TOP 10 SINGLES OF 1982 IN THE UK

	Title	Artist
1	*Come On Eileen*	Dexy's Midnight Runners
2	*Fame*	Irene Cara
3	*Eye Of The Tiger*	Survivor
4	*The Lion Sleeps Tonight*	Tight Fit
5	*Pass The Dutchie*	Musical Youth
6	*Do You Really Want To Hurt Me*	Culture Club
7	*Save Your Love*	Rene and Renato
8	*I Don't Wanna Dance*	Eddy Grant
9	*The Land Of Make-Believe*	Bucks Fizz
10	*Seven Tears*	Goombay Dance Band

THE TOP 10 SINGLES OF 1982 IN THE USA

	Title	Artist
1	*Eye Of The Tiger*	Survivor
2	*I Love Rock 'n' Roll*	Joan Jett & The Blackhearts
3	*Ebony And Ivory*	Paul McCartney and Stevie Wonder
4	*Centerfold*	J. Geils Band
5	*Maneater*	Daryl Hall and John Oates
6	*Jack And Diane*	John Cougar
7	*Don't You Want Me*	Human League
8	*Abracadabra*	Steve Miller Band
9	*Hurts So Good*	John Cougar
10	*Hard To Say I'm Sorry*	Chicago

Come On Eileen was 1982's and Dexy's Midnight Runners' only single to sell 1,000,000 copies, while the runner-up for the year's top seller was a testament to the promotional power of TV: Irene Cara's *Fame* had been the title song from Alan Parker's 1980 movie of the same title, but it found British chart success only when the BBC began screening the spin-off TV series, *The Kids From Fame*. The big screen, meanwhile, aided Survivor, as *Eye Of The Tiger* was the theme from *Rocky III*.

Once again a theme from a film was the top-selling US single; both *Eye Of The Tiger* and Joan Jett's single sold more than 2,000,000 copies. Human League's UK million-seller repeated its success across the Atlantic some seven months later, while John Cougar (later Mellencamp) achieved the rare distinction of placing both his first two US Top 10 hits in the year's overall Top 10.

THE TOP 10 SINGLES OF 1983 IN THE UK

	Title	Artist
1	Karma Chameleon	Culture Club
2	Uptown Girl	Billy Joel
3	Red Red Wine	UB40
4	Total Eclipse Of The Heart	Bonnie Tyler
5	True	Spandau Ballet
6	Only You	Flying Pickets
7	Let's Dance	David Bowie
8	Down Under	Men At Work
9	Billie Jean	Michael Jackson
10	All Night Long (All Night)	Lionel Richie

Culture Club sold over 1,300,000 of their biggest hit, *Karma Chameleon*, which made it the seventh bestselling single of the 1980s. The Flying Pickets' hit, meanwhile, actually outsold those by UB40, Bonnie Tyler and Spandau Ballet in final sales reckonings, but its success straddled the 1983–84 Christmas and New Year period, with some 150,000 of those sales falling in the latter year.

THE TOP 10 SINGLES OF 1983 IN THE USA

	Title	Artist
1	Islands In The Stream	Kenny Rogers and Dolly Parton
2	Every Breath You Take	Police
3	Billie Jean	Michael Jackson
4	Flashdance...What A Feeling	Irene Cara
5	Total Eclipse Of The Heart	Bonnie Tyler
6	All Night Long (All Night)	Lionel Richie
7	Down Under	Men At Work
8	Beat It	Michael Jackson
9	Baby, Come To Me	Patti Austin and James Ingram
10	Let's Dance	David Bowie

The Country superstar duet *Islands In The Stream* was America's only single of 1983 to sell 2,000,000 copies, but it did not have the longest run at No. 1 – that honour belonged to the Police's *Every Breath You Take*, the trio's biggest United States seller, which had an unbroken eight weeks at the top. Michael Jackson's two entries were the highest-charting singles (both No. 1s) from his mega-selling album, *Thriller*.

THE TOP 10 SINGLES OF 1984 IN THE UK

	Title	Artist
1	Do They Know It's Christmas?	Band Aid
2	Relax	Frankie Goes To Hollywood
3	I Just Called To Say I Love You	Stevie Wonder
4	Two Tribes	Frankie Goes To Hollywood
5	Last Christmas	Wham!
6	Careless Whisper	George Michael
7	Hello	Lionel Richie
8	Ghostbusters	Ray Parker Jr
9	Agadoo	Black Lace
10	We All Stand Together	Paul McCartney and the Frog Chorus

The year 1984 was unprecedented in UK record history. The top six singles all sold more than 1,000,000 copies (the highest number ever within a 12-month calendar period), and indeed, six of the top eight singles of the 1980s were 1984 hits – Band Aid's release, as noted elsewhere, being the UK's all-time biggest-selling single. George Michael sang on three of these hits, giving him the personal distinction of being on three records to sell 1,000,000 copies in the same year with different billings (Wham!, George Michael and Band Aid).

THE TOP 10 SINGLES OF 1984 IN THE USA

	Title	Artist
1	When Doves Cry	Prince
2	What's Love Got To Do With It	Tina Turner
3	I Just Called To Say I Love You	Stevie Wonder
4	Against All Odds (Take A Look At Me Now)	Phil Collins
5	Footloose	Kenny Loggins
6	Jump	Van Halen
7	Hello	Lionel Richie
8	Ghostbusters	Ray Parker Jr
9	Wake Me Up Before You Go-Go	Wham!
10	Like A Virgin	Madonna

When Doves Cry was taken from Prince's starring movie debut *Purple Rain*, the soundtrack of which also provided the year's bestselling album in the United States. Films were again the flavour of the year, since the hit singles by Stevie Wonder, Phil Collins, Kenny Loggins and Ray Parker Jr were also themes from successful movies. Note that Madonna's *Like A Virgin* would have made the top five if its peak sales had not carried over into 1985.

(Opposite above) *Billy Joel's* Uptown Girl *was held to second place in the UK in 1983 by Culture Club.*

(Below) *The former Annie Mae Bullock paid her dues as a live performer for many years as Mrs Ike Turner, before finally hitting superstar stride in the 1980s as a solo Tina Turner.*

THE TOP 10 SINGLES OF 1985 IN THE UK

	Title	Artist
1	The Power Of Love	Jennifer Rush
2	I Know Him So Well	Elaine Paige and Barbara Dickson
3	19	Paul Hardcastle
4	Take On Me	a-ha
5	Into The Groove	Madonna
6	Frankie	Sister Sledge
7	Dancing In The Street	David Bowie and Mick Jagger
8	Saving All My Love For You	Whitney Houston
9	Move Closer	Phyllis Nelson
10	Easy Lover	Philip Bailey and Phil Collins

While 1985 could not match the previous year in the UK for huge-selling singles, Jennifer Rush's hit passed seven figures. It was an outstanding year for female talent, however, with six of the Top 10 singles being by women soloists or groups. For the first time in many years, an instrumental (Paul Hardcastle's keyboards-dominated *19*, whose only vocal parts were spoken-word samples) was also among the biggest sellers.

THE TOP 10 SINGLES OF 1985 IN THE USA

	Title	Artist
1	We Are The World	USA For Africa
2	Careless Whisper	Wham! featuring George Michael
3	I Want To Know What Love Is	Foreigner
4	Crazy For You	Madonna
5	Party All The Time	Eddie Murphy
6	Do They Know It's Christmas?	Band Aid
7	Money For Nothing	Dire Straits
8	Everybody Wants To Rule The World	Tears For Fears
9	We Built This City	Starship
10	The Power Of Love	Huey Lewis & The News

We Are The World, America's top recording artists' response to the British Band Aid initiative, with the identical aim of raising money for African famine relief, became one of the biggest-selling singles of all time in the United States, its estimated 4,500,000 sales being comparable to the UK performance of *Do They Know It's Christmas?* The latter also sold 1,000,000 copies in the USA, as did *Careless Whisper*, which in crossing the Atlantic lost George Michael's solo billing and gained a group credit!

THE TOP 10 SINGLES OF 1986 IN THE UK

	Title	Artist
1	Every Loser Wins	Nick Berry
2	Don't Leave Me This Way	Communards
3	So Macho	Sinitta
4	Living Doll	Cliff Richard with The Young Ones
5	Chain Reaction	Diana Ross
6	When The Going Gets Tough, The Tough Get Going	Billy Ocean
7	Caravan Of Love	Housemartins
8	Take My Breath Away	Berlin
9	I Want To Wake Up With You	Boris Gardiner
10	The Lady In Red	Chris De Burgh

Rather unexpectedly, the year's biggest seller was a ballad sung by actor Nick Berry, from TV's *EastEnders*, which narrowly outpaced the Communards' Hi-NRG (ie fast) revival of a 1977 hit. Cliff Richard, uniquely, placed *Living Doll* at both the chart top and in an annual Top 10 for the second time (*see* The Top 10 Singles of 1959 in the UK), after recording a comedy version with the TV cast of *The Young Ones* for the charity Comic Relief.

THE TOP 10 SINGLES OF 1986 IN THE USA

	Title	Artist
1	That's What Friends Are For	Dionne Warwick and Friends
2	On My Own	Patti LaBelle and Michael McDonald
3	Kiss	Prince
4	Say You, Say Me	Lionel Richie
5	The Greatest Love Of All	Whitney Houston
6	Kyrie	Mr Mister
7	Stuck With You	Huey Lewis & The News
8	Rock Me Amadeus	Falco
9	Papa Don't Preach	Madonna
10	How Will I Know	Whitney Houston

Uncharacteristically, the only non-American credit in the 1986 US Top 10 went to the Austrian artist Falco rather than to a UK act – although Elton John was one of the 'Friends' on Dionne Warwick's record (the others being Stevie Wonder and Gladys Knight), which was a charity project to benefit AIDS research. Lionel Richie's single outsold both *On My Own* and *Kiss* in the final reckoning, but 30 per cent of its sales had occurred at the tail end of 1985.

THE TOP 10 SINGLES OF 1987 IN THE UK

	Title	Artist
1	Never Gonna Give You Up	Rick Astley
2	Nothing's Gonna Stop Us Now	Starship
3	China In Your Hand	T'Pau
4	Respectable	Mel and Kim
5	You Win Again	Bee Gees
6	Let It Be	Ferry Aid
7	Reet Petite	Jackie Wilson
8	Stand By Me	Ben E. King
9	I Wanna Dance With Somebody (Who Loves Me)	Whitney Houston
10	Pump Up The Volume	M/A/R/R/S

The two oddest entries on 1987's UK Top 10 are the songs by Jackie Wilson and Ben E. King, which originally charted in 1957 and 1961 respectively. Their revivals (both spectacularly bigger than the original entries) were due to their use on British TV commercials. Wilson's *Reet Petite* would actually have been placed at the top of this list, had not some 250,000 of its sales occurred in the second half of December 1986.

THE TOP 10 SINGLES OF 1987 IN THE USA

	Title	Artist
1	I Wanna Dance With Somebody (Who Loves Me)	Whitney Houston
2	Lean On Me	Club Nouveau
3	I Just Can't Stop Loving You	Michael Jackson
4	Nothing's Gonna Stop Us Now	Starship
5	La Bamba	Los Lobos
6	Alone	Heart
7	Livin' On A Prayer	Bon Jovi
8	At This Moment	Billy Vera & The Beaters
9	With Or Without You	U2
10	I Think We're Alone Now	Tiffany

Only the first three singles on this list were officially certified as having sold 1,000,000 copies in the USA, an indication of the decline in singles sales since the end of the 1970s, when the entire annual Top 10 would be comprised of records that had topped 2,000,000 or more. The hits by Starship and Los Lobos were both from films, while Billy Vera's *At This Moment* was a 1981 obscurity elevated to success after being strongly featured on the TV series *Family Ties*.

THE TOP 10 SINGLES OF 1988 IN THE UK

	Title	Artist
1	Mistletoe And Wine	Cliff Richard
2	The Only Way Is Up	Yazz and The Plastic Population
3	I Should Be So Lucky	Kylie Minogue
4	Especially For You	Kylie Minogue and Jason Donovan
5	I Think We're Alone Now	Tiffany
6	First Time	Robin Beck
7	Nothing's Gonna Change My Love For You	Glenn Medieros
8	A Groovy Kind Of Love	Phil Collins
9	He Ain't Heavy, He's My Brother	Hollies
10	With A Little Help From My Friends	Wet Wet Wet

Cliff Richard's Christmas song gave him his first chart-topper for nine years, and his second biggest-selling UK single of all time, after *The Young Ones*. Kylie and Jason's duet would have made number two had its sales not almost equally straddled the 1988–89 New Year divide. TV ads, meanwhile, were responsible for both the Robin Beck (Coca-Cola) hit, and the successful Hollies (Miller Lite) revival, while Phil Collins' new version of the old Mindbenders hit was taken from his film *Buster*.

THE TOP 10 SINGLES OF 1988 IN THE USA

	Title	Artist
1	Kokomo	Beach Boys
2	Never Gonna Give You Up	Rick Astley
3	Don't Worry, Be Happy	Bobby McFerrin
4	A Groovy Kind Of Love	Phil Collins
5	I'll Always Love You	Taylor Dayne
6	What's On Your Mind (Pure Energy)	Information Society
7	Roll With It	Steve Winwood
8	Sweet Child O' Mine	Guns N' Roses
9	One More Try	George Michael
10	Anything For You	Gloria Estefan & Miami Sound Machine

More than two decades after their heyday, the Beach Boys' *Kokomo* ironically proved to be their all-time bestselling single (well over 1,000,000 copies) in the United States. It gained valuable exposure from its use in the Tom Cruise film *Cocktail*, as did Phil Collins' *A Groovy Kind Of Love* by featuring in Collins' own movie, *Buster*.

THE TOP 10 SINGLES OF 1989 IN THE UK

	Title	Artist
1	Ride On Time	Black Box
2	Swing The Mood	Jive Bunny & The Mastermixers
3	Do They Know It's Christmas?	Band Aid II
4	Too Many Broken Hearts	Jason Donovan
5	Eternal Flame	Bangles
6	Let's Party	Jive Bunny & The Mastermixers
7	Hand On Your Heart	Kylie Minogue
8	Something's Gotten Hold Of My Heart	Marc Almond and Gene Pitney
9	All Around The World	Lisa Stansfield
10	Back To Life	Soul II Soul featuring Caron Wheeler

In a year when dance beats ruled, Italian club act Black Box sold almost 850,000 copies of *Ride On Time*, and medley sampling specialists Jive Bunny had two of the top six singles. Meanwhile, the new version of *Do They Know It's Christmas?*, produced by Stock Aitken Waterman, fell nearly 3,000,000 short of the British sales total of the original single, though it topped the Christmas week chart with ease.

THE TOP 10 SINGLES OF 1989 IN THE USA

	Title	Artist
1	Wild Thing	Tone Loc
2	Straight Up	Paula Abdul
3	Miss You Much	Janet Jackson
4	Right Here Waiting	Richard Marx
5	Like A Prayer	Madonna
6	Girl You Know It's True	Milli Vanilli
7	On Our Own	Bobby Brown
8	Batdance	Prince
9	Funky Cold Medina	Tone Loc
10	Blame It On The Rain	Milli Vanilli

By the final year of the 1980s, the bestselling singles in America were virtually all dance, rap, or dance-oriented pop tracks, bought almost exclusively by teenagers, while the market as a whole was almost completely album-oriented. The only genre-buster from this list (these were the only 10 singles whose sales topped 1,000,000 in the US this year) was Richard Marx's radio-friendly ballad *Right Here Waiting*.

THE TOP 10 SINGLES OF 1990 IN THE UK

	Title	Artist
1	Unchained Melody	Righteous Brothers
2	Nothing Compares 2 U	Sinead O'Connor
3	Sacrifice	Elton John
4	Killer	Adamski
5	Dub Be Good To Me	Beats International
6	Ice Ice Baby	Vanilla Ice
7	Vogue	Madonna
8	World In Motion	England New Order
9	The Power	Snap!
10	Show Me Heaven	Maria McKee

THE TOP 10 SINGLES OF 1990 IN THE USA

	Title	Artist
1	Vogue	Madonna
2	Nothing Compares 2 U	Sinead O'Connor
3	Pump Up The Jam	Technotronic
4	Ice Ice Baby	Vanilla Ice
5	Blaze Of Glory	Jon Bon Jovi
6	Step By Step	New Kids On The Block
7	Hold On	En Vogue
8	The Power	Snap!
9	Poison	Bell Biv Devoe
10	All Around The World	Lisa Stansfield

The Phil Spector-produced *Unchained Melody* by the Righteous Brothers, a track originally released (and charted) in 1965, found over 900,000 new sales in the UK when used as the love theme in *Ghost*, the year's biggest movie box-office success. Elton John's *Sacrifice* finally gave him his first solo UK chart-topper after more than two decades of hitmaking. Sinead O'Connor's hit was a previously obscure composition by Prince.

As in the previous year, 1990's biggest US singles were largely dance-oriented, the exceptions this time being Jon Bon Jovi's heavy rock ballad *Blaze Of Glory* (the theme from the film *Young Guns 2*), and Sinead O'Connor's cover of an obscure Prince song, which reprised its UK success. Many of the 10 bestsellers were by new acts, in several cases with their first singles.

Madonna's Vogue *was the bestselling single of 1990 in the USA, spending so long in the Top 100 that her follow-up single* Hanky Panky *came, sold and went within its duration.*

THE TOP 10 SINGLES OF 1991 IN THE UK

	Title	Artist
1	(Everything I Do) I Do It For You	Bryan Adams
2	Bohemian Rhapsody	Queen
3	The Shoop Shoop Song (It's In His Kiss)	Cher
4	I'm Too Sexy	Right Said Fred
5	The One And Only	Chesney Hawkes
6	Do The Bartman	Simpsons
7	Any Dream Will Do	Jason Donovan
8	I Wanna Sex You Up	Color Me Badd
9	3 a.m. Eternal	KLF
10	Don't Let The Sun Go Down On Me	George Michael and Elton John

This was a year when other entertainment media threw up many of the hits. In addition to Bryan Adams' song from *Robin Hood – Prince Of Thieves* (which sold over 1,600,000 and set a new record of 16 consecutive weeks at No. 1), the Cher and Chesney Hawkes hits were from movies, *Do The Bartman* was a spin-off from the animated TV show *The Simpsons*, and *Any Dream Will Do* came from Andrew Lloyd Webber's London stage hit *Joseph And The Amazing Technicolor Dreamcoat*.

THE TOP 10 SINGLES OF 1991 IN THE USA

	Title	Artist
1	(Everything I Do) I Do It For You	Bryan Adams
2	Gonna Make You Sweat	C & C Music Factory
3	Justify My Love	Madonna
4	One More Try	Timmy T
5	I Wanna Sex You Up	Color Me Badd
6	Motownphilly	Boyz II Men
7	Summertime	DJ Jazzy Jeff & The Fresh Prince
8	Black Or White	Michael Jackson
9	The First Time	Surface
10	More Than Words	Extreme

As in the UK, Bryan Adams' love song from *Robin Hood* was by far the most successful single of 1991 in the United States, selling more than 3,000,000 copies by the year's end. Several new dance and rap acts arrived with major debut hits (plus Extreme, a heavy rock band who found their first major single success with an acoustic ballad), and Madonna kept up her consistent annual appearances.

THE TOP 10 SINGLES OF 1992 IN THE UK

	Title	Artist
1	I Will Always Love You	Whitney Houston
2	Rhythm Is A Dancer	Snap!
3	Stay	Shakespears Sister
4	Please Don't Go	K.W.S.
5	Abba-esque (EP)	Erasure
6	End Of The Road	Boyz II Men
7	Ain't No Doubt	Jimmy Nail
8	Would I Lie To You?	Charles & Eddie
9	Ebeneezer Goode	Shamen
10	Deeply Dippy	Right Said Fred

Following a quite familiar pattern, the single topping the UK chart as 1992 ended proved to be the year's biggest seller. However, Whitney Houston's *I Will Always Love You*, from the film *The Bodyguard*, in which the singer co-starred with Kevin Costner, proved to have still wider appeal than even the usual Christmas chart-topper: by the end of December it had already sold 1,200,000 copies, to overtake Jennifer Rush's 1985 hit *The Power Of Love* and become the biggest-selling single ever in the UK by a female artist

THE TOP 10 SINGLES OF 1992 IN THE USA

	Title	Artist
1	I Will Always Love You	Whitney Houston
2	Baby Got Back	Sir Mix-A-Lot
3	End Of The Road	Boyz II Men
4	Jump	Kris Kross
5	Achy Breaky Heart	Billy Ray Cyrus
6	Rump Shaker	Wreckx-N-Effect
7	Tears In Heaven	Eric Clapton
8	I'm Too Sexy	Right Said Fred
9	Smells Like Teen Spirit	Nirvana
10	Under The Bridge	Red Hot Chili Peppers

Well on its way to becoming one of the bestselling singles in American chart history, the Dolly Parton-penned *I Will Always Love You* sold an incredible 4,000,000 copies in only nine weeks in the United States and continued amassing similar numbers well into 1993. Rap accounted for three entries in the top six: numbers two, four and six.

MUSICAL TRENDS AND FADS

From the advent of Rock 'n' Roll, founded around the swivelling hips of Elvis Presley in the mid-1950s, 'rock' music has taken many twists and turns. Some have been genuine and lasting musical trends, others little more than a concerted marketing campaign by the record industry, always desperate to establish a new brand. Rock 'n' Roll easily transformed into the Teen Beat era of the late 1950s and early 1960s, giving rise to the careers of virtually any American teen act whose first name was Bobby (Vinton, Darin, Vee, Rydell, *et al*) while Cliff Richard quickly established himself as the British Elvis in 1958, making way for UK teen-beaters like Adam Faith and Billy Fury.

While the UK market was temporarily sidelined into traditional jazz success (Acker Bilk, Kenny Ball) in 1961 and 1962, the US record-buying public embraced the Twist, the first of a series of dance craze fads (including the Pony, the Fly and even the Limbo), which saw some knock-on success in the UK. Next up was the California-based surfing phenomenon initiated by Jan & Dean and the Beach Boys in 1962, which lasted just long enough to witness the dawn of the Beatles, who changed everything in 1963 in Britain with the beginning of the Mersey Sound. Becoming known as the British Invasion in the US, the Beatles' arrival on the American scene opened the floodgates for a host of similar bands including the Searchers, Herman's Hermits, Gerry & The Pacemakers and the Hollies. Fused into the British Invasion was a different pack of R & B-based groups, the vanguard of which were the Rolling Stones, the Animals and Manfred Mann.

America's response lay in the mid-1960s 'protest' folk rock of Bob Dylan who began a singer-songwriter movement which included Joni Mitchell, Joan Baez and the Byrds, a genre which has never really died, Tracy Chapman and Suzanne Vega being two recent protagonists. As hair length increased and drugs came to the forefront of the late 1960s popular culture, music moved into the psychedelic era, spawning Hendrix and the Doors and peaking with the Woodstock Festival in August 1969.

Passing through the shortlived American-launched 'bubblegum' fad epitomized by the Archies' *Sugar Sugar*, the next major genre became heavy metal, inaugurated by Cream, Black Sabbath, Deep Purple and, most notably, Led Zeppelin, at the beginning of the 1970s. Relying on what may be rock music's most dedicated fan base, heavy metal has survived ever since, constantly churning out a succession of stadium-filling acts including most recently Def Leppard and Guns N' Roses.

Pop's offshoot of the heavy guitar base of heavy metal proved to be the successful glam rock movement, principally a British phenomenon, led by T. Rex, the Sweet, Gary Glitter and even the early recordings by Queen, acts which dominated the UK chart between 1972 and 1975. While heavy metal also spawned a number of 'intellectual' grandiose rock acts (Emerson Lake & Palmer, Yes), their overblown theatrical excesses gave rise to an allergic reaction: Punk arrived with all its angry do-it-yourself anti-music posturing in 1976–77, heralded by the spit and venom of the Sex Pistols, the Clash and the Damned. This strictly British genre was quickly over-marketed and transformed into a broader New Wave movement encompassing the likes of Elvis Costello and the Jam, although its lasting effect was to introduce the indie scene which has flourished to this day via bands like Joy Division (Factory Records) and the Smiths (Rough Trade).

While the United States embraced a handful of its own New Wave acts (Blondie, Patti Smith, the Ramones, Talking Heads), it was mostly busy in the mid- and late-1970s burning up the dance floor as disco music took its grip on American culture and *Saturday Night Fever* became a global success. Dance music has always been an important part of the music scene, but never was its popularity greater than during this period of Donna Summer and flared white suits.

As the UK evolved its own disco/dance industry, the British record fraternity frantically searched for the next big trend, moving through a succession of hyped-up fads including power pop and the New Romantic movement. The latter craze actually opened the door for the likes of Spandau Ballet, Duran Duran and Ultravox and made the synthesizer the instrument of choice, leading to the success of acts including Depeche Mode and Orchestral Manoeuvres In The Dark. Although the last five years have seen the emergence of a number of specialist dance-based styles (including house, acid, techno and even the rave scene), the most enduring has been rap (once written off as a shortlived craze under the title hip-hop) which continues its multi-platinum growth on both sides of the Atlantic.

Perhaps the most consistently successful musical trend in the USA has been Country, which has racked up huge sales since Hank Williams in the 1940s right up to America's most popular artist (of any genre) in the 1990s, Garth Brooks. Its only rival may be R & B/soul music whose eras have encompassed Motown and Philly and whose popularity defies trend (from Sam Cooke to Whitney Houston).

Interest in reggae has always been simmering though never explosive, and many other fads have come, gone and even been revived (ska, mod, oi and even the current grunge rock movement led by Nirvana and Pearl Jam). Many of the most popular acts of the past 10 years can only be loosely defined as adult contemporary (a recognized radio format in the United States), embracing the likes of Phil Collins, George Michael, Michael Bolton and Barbra Streisand. And where on earth does David Bowie belong in all this?

THE TOP 10 SINGLES OF THE 1950s IN THE UK

	Title	Artist	Release year
1	Rock Around The Clock	Bill Haley & His Comets	1955
2	Diana	Paul Anka	1957
3	Mary's Boy Child	Harry Belafonte	1957
4	The Harry Lime (Third Man) Theme	Anton Karas	1950
5	Living Doll	Cliff Richard	1959
6	Jailhouse Rock	Elvis Presley	1958
7	What Do You Want To Make Those Eyes At Me For	Emile Ford	1959
8	All I Have To Do Is Dream/ Claudette	Everly Brothers	1958
9	What Do You Want?	Adam Faith	1959
10	All Shook Up	Elvis Presley	1957

Record sales boomed in the 1950s with the advent of Rock 'n' Roll in 1955–56, and thus most of this Top 10 are from the latter half of the decade, with the top three representing the first three singles (and the only ones of the 1950s) to sell over 1,000,000 copies apiece in the UK. Anton Karas's zither instrumental theme from the film *The Third Man* predates any of the annual charts in this book, but sold 900,000 between 1950 and 1954 – virtually all on 78-rpm singles.

THE TOP 10 SINGLES OF THE 1950s IN THE USA

	Title	Artist	Release year
1	Hound Dog/Don't Be Cruel	Elvis Presley	1956
2	The Chipmunk Song	Chipmunks	1958
3	Love Letters In The Sand	Pat Boone	1957
4	Rock Around The Clock	Bill Haley & His Comets	1955
5	Tom Dooley	Kingston Trio	1958
6	Love Me Tender	Elvis Presley	1956
7	Tennessee Waltz	Patti Page	1950
8	Volare (Nel Blu Dipintu Di Blu)	Domenico Modugno	1958
9	Jailhouse Rock	Elvis Presley	1957
10	All Shook Up	Elvis Presley	1957

Rock 'n' Roll and Elvis Presley were the twin catalysts which ignited record sales in the United States in the middle of the 1950s, and both are represented strongly in the decade's biggest sellers, the former mostly in the person of the latter! Whilst Presley's double-sider, topping 6,000,000, was the decade's top single by a wide margin, the fastest seller was *The Chipmunk Song*, which moved a remarkable 3,500,000 copies in five weeks.

THE TOP 10 SINGLES OF THE 1960s IN THE UK

	Title	Artist	Release year
1	She Loves You	Beatles	1963
2	I Want To Hold Your Hand	Beatles	1963
3	Tears	Ken Dodd	1965
4	Can't Buy Me Love	Beatles	1964
5	I Feel Fine	Beatles	1964
6	We Can Work It Out/ Day Tripper	Beatles	1965
7	The Carnival Is Over	Seekers	1965
8	Release Me	Engelbert Humperdinck	1967
9	It's Now Or Never	Elvis Presley	1960
10	Green, Green Grass Of Home	Tom Jones	1966

The Beatles' domination of the 1960s is clear, with five of the decade's top six singles being by the group. Intriguingly, all the other five in this Top 10 are ballads of varying degrees of what, in those days, would have been termed squareness. This was an era when the great silent majority of occasional record buyers purchased singles, not albums, and Messrs Dodd, Humperdinck, *et al*, were the lucky recipients of their custom.

THE TOP 10 SINGLES OF THE 1960s IN THE USA

	Title	Artist	Release year
1	I Want To Hold Your Hand	Beatles	1964
2	It's Now Or Never	Elvis Presley	1960
3	Hey Jude	Beatles	1968
4	The Ballad Of The Green Berets	Staff Sergeant Barry Sadler	1966
5	Love Is Blue	Paul Mauriat	1968
6	I'm A Believer	Monkees	1966
7	Can't Buy Me Love	Beatles	1964
8	She Loves You	Beatles	1964
9	Sugar Sugar	Archies	1969
10	The Twist	Chubby Checker	1960

Though the 1960s are recalled as the decade in which British music invaded America, the only UK representatives among the decade's 10 biggest sellers in the United States are by the leaders of that invasion, the Beatles – although they do completely dominate the list, holding numbers one, three, seven and eight. Elvis Presley's *It's Now Or Never*, with sales of around 5,000,000, almost equalled his total on *Hound Dog/Don't Be Cruel* which had made it the previous decade's biggest single.

THE TOP 10 SINGLES OF THE 1970s IN THE UK

	Title	Artist	Release year
1	Mull Of Kintyre	Wings	1977
2	Rivers Of Babylon/ Brown Girl In The Ring	Boney M	1978
3	You're The One That I Want	John Travolta and Olivia Newton-John	1978
4	Mary's Boy Child/Oh My Lord	Boney M	1978
5	Summer Nights	John Travolta and Olivia Newton-John	1978
6	Y.M.C.A.	Village People	1979
7	Bohemian Rhapsody	Queen	1975
8	Heart Of Glass	Blondie	1979
9	Merry Xmas Everybody	Slade	1973
10	Don't Give Up On Us	David Soul	1977

Most of the biggest sellers of the 1970s in the UK occurred in an 18-month period between December 1977 and May 1979. The single which started this golden (or, rather, platinum) era, *Mull Of Kintyre*, was the first-ever in Britain to top 2,000,000 copies, and it inherited the 'All-time Biggest Seller' title from the Beatles' *She Loves You*, which had held it for 14 years. Queen's *Bohemian Rhapsody* was destined almost to double its sales in 1991, following Freddie Mercury's death, allowing it to just overtake *Mull* on an all-time basis.

THE TOP 10 SINGLES OF THE 1970s IN THE USA

	Title	Artist	Release year
1	You Light Up My Life	Debby Boone	1977
2	Le Freak	Chic	1978
3	Night Fever	Bee Gees	1978
4	Stayin' Alive	Bee Gees	1978
5	Shadow Dancing	Andy Gibb	1978
6	Disco Lady	Johnnie Taylor	1976
7	I'll Be There	Jackson 5	1970
8	Star Wars Theme/ Cantina Band	Meco	1977
9	Car Wash	Rose Royce	1976
10	Joy To The World	Three Dog Night	1971

During the last four years of the 1970s, singles sales in the United States rose to their highest-ever level, and chart-topping records were almost routinely selling over 2,000,000 copies. Also at their commercial peak in the States during this period were the Bee Gees, who appropriately have the biggest presence on this chart, both with two of their own songs and as writer/producers of younger brother Andy Gibb's *Shadow Dancing*.

THE TOP 10 SINGLES OF THE 1980s IN THE UK

	Title	Artist	Release year
1	Do They Know It's Christmas?	Band Aid	1984
2	Relax	Frankie Goes To Hollywood	1984
3	I Just Called To Say I Love You	Stevie Wonder	1984
4	Two Tribes	Frankie Goes To Hollywood	1984
5	Don't You Want Me	Human League	1981
6	Last Christmas	Wham!	1984
7	Karma Chameleon	Culture Club	1983
8	Careless Whisper	George Michael	1984
9	The Power Of Love	Jennifer Rush	1985
10	Come On Eileen	Dexy's Midnight Runners	1982

Singles from the boom year of 1984 dominate the UK 1980s Top 10, two of them by newcomers Frankie Goes To Hollywood, and two by Wham!/George Michael (who also sang one of the Band Aid leads – as did Boy George from Culture Club). Stevie Wonder and Jennifer Rush are the sole US entrants; in fact, they were the only two Americans to have UK million-sellers during this decade.

THE TOP 10 SINGLES OF THE 1980s IN THE USA

	Title	Artist	Release year
1	We Are The World	USA For Africa	1985
2	Physical	Olivia Newton-John	1981
3	Endless Love	Diana Ross and Lionel Richie	1981
4	Eye Of The Tiger	Survivor	1982
5	I Love Rock 'n' Roll	Joan Jett & The Blackhearts	1982
6	When Doves Cry	Prince	1984
7	Celebration	Kool & The Gang	1981
8	Another One Bites The Dust	Queen	1980
9	Wild Thing	Tone Loc	1989
10	Islands In The Stream	Kenny Rogers and Dolly Parton	1983

America's top-selling single of the 1980s was, rather fittingly, a record which included contributions from many of those artists who had become the recording elite during the decade – the charity single for Africa's famine victims, *We Are The World*. Meanwhile, three of the close runners-up, *Endless Love* (same film), *Eye Of The Tiger* (from *Rocky III*) and *When Doves Cry* (from Prince's *Purple Rain*) were all taken from movies.

THE TOP 10 SINGLES OF ALL TIME IN AUSTRALIA

	Title	Artist	Year
1	Fernando	Abba	1976
2	Never Gonna Give You Up	Rick Astley	1987
3	Unchained Melody	Righteous Brothers	1965/1990
4	Dancing In The Dark/ Pink Cadillac	Bruce Springsteen	1984
5	Hey Jude/Revolution	Beatles	1968
6	Mamma Mia	Abba	1965
7	Moon River	Henry Mancini, Jerry Butler	1961
8	She Loves You	Beatles	1963
9	Australiana	Austen Tayshus	1983
10	Simply Irresistible	Robert Palmer	1988

THE TOP 10 SINGLES OF 1991 IN BELGIUM

	Title	Artist
1	Everything I Do (I Do It For You)	Bryan Adams
2	Wind Of Change	Scorpions
3	James Brown Is Dead	L.A. Style
4	Anitouni	Wamblee
5	Désenchantée	Mylene Farmer
6	Le Dormeur	Pleasure Game
7	Senza Una Donna	Zucchero featuring Paul Young
8	Gipsy Woman	Crystal Waters
9	Geet Het Op	Clouseau
10	Breek De Stilte	Stef & Bob

Source: *IFPI Belgium.*

A typically European mix of international hits and domestic success: numbers three, four, six, nine and 10 were all by Belgian artists.

THE TOP 10 SINGLES OF ALL TIME IN CANADA

	Title	Artist
1	Tears Are Not Enough	Northern Lights
2	I Just Called To Say I Love You	Stevie Wonder
3	We Are The World	USA For Africa
4	(Everything I Do) I Do It For You	Bryan Adams
5	Billie Jean	Michael Jackson
6	Eye Of The Tiger	Survivor
7	Physical	Olivia Newton-John
8	Karma Chameleon	Culture Club
9	Y.M.C.A.	Village People
10	Black Velvet	Alannah Myles

The top three have all sold more than 300,000 copies each. The Northern Lights single was Canada's response to both the Band Aid (UK) and USA For Africa (US) charity singles of 1984–85 and featured a number of the country's top performers, including Bryan Adams, Joni Mitchell and Neil Young.

THE TOP 10 INTERNATIONAL SINGLES OF ALL TIME IN FINLAND

	Title	Artist
1	It's Now Or Never	Elvis Presley
2	The Young Ones	Cliff Richard
3	We Are The World	USA For Africa
4	It's A Sin	Pet Shop Boys
5	Garage Days (EP)	Metallica
6	Lambada	Kaoma
7	What's Another Year	Johnny Logan
8	Always On My Mind	Pet Shop Boys
9	Woman In Love	Barbra Streisand
10	We Don't Need Another Hero (Thunderdome)	Tina Turner

Source: *Finnish Group of IFPI*

This list, up to the end of 1991, excludes domestic releases. *It's Now Or Never* sold over 31,000 copies when released, a substantial margin over Cliff Richard's number two hit which sold only 10,000 copies.

THE TOP 10 SINGLES OF 1991 IN GERMANY

	Title	Artist
1	Wind Of Change	Scorpions
2	(Everything I Do) I Do It For You	Bryan Adams
3	Sadness – Part One	Enigma
4	Joyride	Roxette
5	Bacardi Feeling	Kate Yanai
6	Beinhart	Torfrock
7	Ice Ice Baby	Vanilla Ice
8	The Shoop Shoop Song	Cher
9	Senza Una Donna	Zucchero featuring Paul Young
10	Ich Bin Der Martin, Ne	Diether Krebs and Gundula

Source: Der Musikmarkt.

Veteran German heavy metal outfit the Scorpions hit global pay-dirt with their 'fall of communism' rock anthem *Wind Of Change*, which was so popular that the band was even invited to meet then President Gorbachev in the Kremlin.

THE TOP 10 SINGLES OF ALL TIME IN THE NETHERLANDS

	Title	Artist
1	La Danse De Zorba	Trio Hellenique
2	This Strange Effect	Dave Berry
3	Je T'aime...Moi Non Plus	Jane Birkin and Serge Gainsbourg
4	Hello Josephine	Scorpions
5	Il Silenzio	Nino Rosso
6	My Special Prayer	Percy Sledge
7	Huilen Is Voor Jou Te Laat	Corry en de Rekels
8	Non, Rien N'a Changé	Les Poppys
9	You've Got Your Troubles	Fortunes
10	Paint It Black	Rolling Stones

Source: NVPI.

THE TOP 10 SINGLES OF EACH YEAR IN ITALY, 1982–91

	Title	Artist	Year
1	Paradise	Phoebe Cates	1982
2	Juliet	Robin Gibb	1983
3	Fotoromanza	Gianna Nannini	1984
4	We Are The World	USA For Africa	1985
5	Live To Tell	Madonna	1986
6	Who's That Girl?	Madonna	1987
7	Adamento Lento	Tullio De Piscopo	1988
8	Viva La Mamma	Edoardo Bennato	1989
9	Un' Estate Italiana	Gianna Nannini and Edoardo Bennato	1990
10	Perché Lo Fai	Marco Masini	1991

Source: Musica Edischi.

THE TOP 10 SINGLES OF 1991 IN PORTUGAL

	Title	Artist
1	Taras E Manias	Marco Paulo
2	(Everything I Do) I Do It For You	Bryan Adams
3	Blue Velvet	Bobby Vinton
4	Nao Ha Estrelas No Ceu	Rui Veloso
5	I Can See Clearly Now	Johnny Nash
6	A Paixao	Rui Veloso
7	Innuendo	Queen
8	Don't Cry	Guns N' Roses
9	Hotel California	Gypsy Kings
10	Joyride	Roxette

Source: Associacao Fonografica Portuguesa.

THE TOP 10 SINGLES IN THE UK ON THE APPLE LABEL

	Title	Artist	Year
1	Imagine	John Lennon	1975
2	Hey Jude	Beatles	1968
3	My Sweet Lord	George Harrison	1971
4	Those Were The Days	Mary Hopkin	1968
5	Happy Xmas (War Is Over)	John Lennon & Yoko Ono	1972
6	Get Back	Beatles	1969
7	The Ballad Of John And Yoko	Beatles	1969
8	Goodbye	Mary Hopkin	1969
9	Give Peace A Chance	Plastic Ono Band	1969
10	Knock Knock, Who's There?	Mary Hopkin	1970

Although they appeared with Apple labels, the records (from *Hey Jude* on) by the Beatles and most later ex-Beatle solos did so only by special dispensation of EMI, since the Beatles were always contracted to EMI's Parlophone label. If these releases, carrying Parlophone numbers, are omitted, list numbers one to three and five to seven disappear, in which case the Top 10 would be completed by: *Come And Get It* (Badfinger), *Instant Karma* (John Lennon/Plastic Ono Band), *No Matter What* (Badfinger), *Temma Harbour* (Mary Hopkin), *That's The Way God Planned It* (Billy Preston), and *Hare Krishna Mantra* (Radha Krishna Temple).

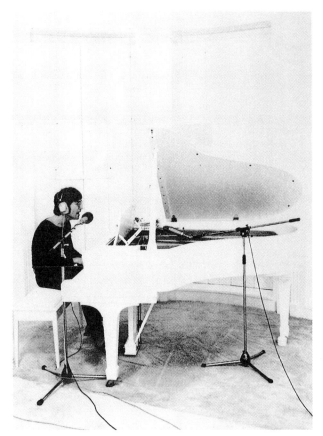

John Lennon's Imagine *is the all-time top seller on the Apple label, finally passing the million mark in the UK after Lennon died.*

THE TOP 10 SINGLES IN THE UK ON THE ATLANTIC LABEL

	Title	Artist	Year
1	Rivers Of Babylon/Brown Girl In The Ring	Boney M	1978
2	Mary's Boy Child/Oh My Lord	Boney M	1978
3	I Got You, Babe	Sonny and Cher	1965
4	Frankie	Sister Sledge	1985
5	Rasputin	Boney M	1978
6	I Want To Know What Love Is	Foreigner	1984
7	Stand By Me	Ben E. King	1987
8	Chanson D'Amour	Manhattan Transfer	1977
9	When A Man Loves A Woman	Percy Sledge	1966
10	Working My Way Back To You	Detroit Spinners	1980

Atlantic first emerged over 40 years ago as one of America's brightest independent labels, initially specializing in R & B. By 1964, when it first gained its own UK identity, it was an established hit source, and in later years became a respected United States major. Boney M, who dominate the biggest sellers, were actually released on a split Atlantic-Hansa label, acknowledging the German source of their records.

THE TOP 10 SINGLES IN THE UK ON THE CBS LABEL

	Title	Artist	Year
1	The Power Of Love	Jennifer Rush	1985
2	Bright Eyes	Art Garfunkel	1979
3	Uptown Girl	Billy Joel	1983
4	Stand And Deliver	Adam & The Ants	1981
5	When A Child Is Born	Johnny Mathis	1976
6	Take My Breath Away	Berlin	1986
7	Prince Charming	Adam & The Ants	1981
8	Woman In Love	Barbra Streisand	1980
9	If You Leave Me Now	Chicago	1976
10	Antmusic	Adam & The Ants	1981

After many years of licensed releases in Britain, CBS Records UK was launched in 1965, scoring its first chart-topper (*Mr Tambourine Man* by the Byrds) in the same year. The label's biggest sellers, however, are all from the mid-1970s to the mid-1980s, and dominated by US acts – with the notable exception of thrice-represented Adam & The Ants. Ironically, though, each of the top two singles, both of which sold more than 1,000,000 copies in the UK, failed to become big sellers in the artists' native USA.

THE TOP 10 SINGLES IN THE UK ON THE CHRYSALIS LABEL

	Title	Artist	Year
1	Heart Of Glass	Blondie	1979
2	Vienna	Ultravox	1981
3	Sunday Girl	Blondie	1979
4	19	Paul Hardcastle	1985
5	The Tide Is High	Blondie	1980
6	Denis (Denee)	Blondie	1978
7	When I Need You	Leo Sayer	1977
8	Atomic	Blondie	1980
9	Dreaming	Blondie	1979
10	Darlin'	Frankie Miller	1978

The Deborah Harry-fronted Blondie, consistent hitmakers in the late 1970s and early 1980s, were clearly Chrysalis' most successful act. *Heart Of Glass* was the label's one domestic million-selling single, with Ultravox's *Vienna* just 100,000 or so sales short of the magic million.

THE TOP 10 SINGLES IN THE UK ON THE DECCA LABEL

	Title	Artist	Year
1	Release Me	Engelbert Humperdinck	1967
2	Green, Green Grass Of Home	Tom Jones	1966
3	The Last Waltz	Engelbert Humperdinck	1967
4	Telstar	Tornados	1962
5	The Harry Lime (Third Man) Theme	Anton Karas	1950
6	There Goes My Everything	Engelbert Humperdinck	1967
7	Auf Wiedersehen (Sweetheart)	Vera Lynn	1952
8	The Last Time	Rolling Stones	1965
9	(I Can't Get No) Satisfaction	Rolling Stones	1965
10	The Smurf Song	Father Abraham	1978

Launched in 1929, Decca was one of the UK's major labels for over four decades, until during the 1970s it went into steep decline through failing to recognize and adapt to changing pop music trends. The glory years were the 1950s and 1960s, when some 30 per cent of the biggest-selling acts of the day recorded for Decca. The top three singles in this list sold more than 1,000,000 copies in the UK.

THE TOP 10 SINGLES IN THE UK ON THE COLUMBIA (EMI) LABEL

	Title	Artist	Year
1	Tears	Ken Dodd	1965
2	The Carnival Is Over	Seekers	1965
3	Diana	Paul Anka	1957
4	Stranger On The Shore	Mr Acker Bilk	1961
5	I Remember You	Frank Ifield	1962
6	The Young Ones	Cliff Richard	1962
7	Eye Level	Simon Park Orchestra	1973
8	The Next Time/Bachelor Boy	Cliff Richard	1962
9	Two Little Boys	Rolf Harris	1969
10	Glad All Over	Dave Clark Five	1963

Columbia was a British trademark of EMI Records for several decades until it reverted to US owner CBS (and then the latter's new owner Sony) at the beginning of the 1990s. All these singles are, therefore, EMI recordings, and almost all are from the 1960s. The top seven all sold more than 1,000,000 copies in the UK.

THE TOP 10 SINGLES IN THE UK ON THE EMI LABEL

	Title	Artist	Year
1	Bohemian Rhapsody	Queen	1975
2	Mistletoe And Wine	Cliff Richard	1988
3	We Don't Talk Anymore	Cliff Richard	1979
4	Whispering Grass	Windsor Davies and Don Estelle	1975
5	Wuthering Heights	Kate Bush	1978
6	Daddy's Home	Cliff Richard	1981
7	The Model	Kraftwerk	1981
8	Is There Something I Should Know	Duran Duran	1983
9	9 To 5	Sheena Easton	1980
10	We Are The Champions	Queen	1977

After several decades of dominance as the UK's leading record conglomerate, EMI finally launched a label bearing its own logo in 1973, in order to boost corporate identity. At the same time, EMI labels such as Columbia and Parlophone were semi-retired, and certain acts – among them Cliff Richard – shifted across to the newcomer. EMI's bestseller, Queen's two-time chart-topper *Bohemian Rhapsody*, had achieved UK sales in excess of 2,000,000 by early 1992, while *Mistletoe And Wine* just reached 1,000,000.

THE TOP 10 SINGLES IN THE UK ON THE FACTORY LABEL

	Title	Artist	Year
1	Blue Monday	New Order	1983
2	World In Motion	Englandneworder	1990
3	True Faith	New Order	1987
4	Step On	Happy Mondays	1990
5	Kinky Afro	Happy Mondays	1990
6	Love Will Tear Us Apart	Joy Division	1980
7	Fine Time	New Order	1988
8	Getting Away With It	Electronic	1989
9	Confusion	New Order	1983
10	Thieves Like Us	New Order	1984

Forced to close down in 1992 despite a string of hits through the previous decade by New Order, Factory was Manchester-based and always idiosyncratic, supporting much worthwhile but wholly uncommercial talent. *Blue Monday*, a UK Top 20 hit three times, is the UK's all-time biggest-selling 12″ single, having sold virtually 1,000,000 copies in that format alone. New Order teamed up with the 1990 England World Cup squad for the label's number two bestseller.

LABELS QUIZ

1 Berry Gordy Jr was the founder of which famous record label in Detroit?
2 Where is Sun Records based?
3 Name the label formed in the late 1960s by members of the Beatles.
4 Which one of the following artists did not record for the ground-breaking Stiff Records label: Ian Dury, Specials, Elvis Costello, Jona Lewie?
5 Who founded Atlantic Records in the 1950s?
6 Who founded Radar F-Beat principally to release Elvis Costello's records?
7 Which innovative rap label formed by Sylvia Robinson boasted hits by the Sugarhill Gang and Grandmaster Flash, Melle Mel & The Furious Five?
8 The Reprise label was established by which famous crooner in the 1950s?
9 What was the name of the RCA spin-off label started in the late 1980s by Eurythmic Dave Stewart?
10 With which of the following record companies has George Michael not had a legal dispute: Innervision, Warner Brothers, Epic?

THE TOP 10 SINGLES IN THE UK ON THE MOTOWN LABEL

	Title	Artist	Year
1	I Just Called To Say I Love You	Stevie Wonder	1984
2	Hello	Lionel Richie	1984
3	Three Times A Lady	Commodores	1978
4	I Heard It Through The Grapevine	Marvin Gaye	1969
5	One Day In Your Life	Michael Jackson	1981
6	Being With You	Smokey Robinson	1981
7	All Night Long (All Night)	Lionel Richie	1983
8	Reach Out, I'll Be There	Four Tops	1966
9	I'm Still Waiting	Diana Ross	1971
10	Tears Of A Clown	Smokey Robinson & The Miracles	1970

Perhaps surprisingly, only two of these bestsellers are from the Tamla-Motown 'Golden Era' of the 1960s. The Stevie Wonder track, by far the label's biggest seller, hails from the 1980s, as do the Lionel Richie, Michael Jackson (released years after he left the label) and (solo) Smokey Robinson songs. Lionel Richie is the most represented artist, being lead singer and writer of the Commodores track as well as his two solo entries.

THE TOP 10 SINGLES IN THE UK ON THE PARLOPHONE LABEL

	Title	Artist	Year
1	Mull Of Kintyre	Wings	1977
2	She Loves You	Beatles	1963
3	I Want To Hold Your Hand	Beatles	1963
4	Can't Buy Me Love	Beatles	1964
5	I Feel Fine	Beatles	1964
6	We Can Work It Out/ Day Tripper	Beatles	1965
7	Help!	Beatles	1965
8	Anyone Who Had A Heart	Cilla Black	1964
9	A Hard Day's Night	Beatles	1964
10	We All Stand Together	Paul McCartney and the Frog Chorus	1984

EMI's Parlophone label, largely reserved for comedy talent before the Beatles put it on the rock map, is predictably dominated by that group, though this list ignores their singles and solo efforts (*Imagine, Hey Jude, My Sweet Lord*) which were on Apple, even though they retained Parlophone catalogue numbers. *Mull Of Kintyre* is one of only three singles ever to have achieved more than 2,000,000 UK sales.

INDEPENDENT LABELS

Perhaps the most enduring impact of the shortlived Punk and New Wave era, a British movement whose initial ideals were a specific anti-establishment backlash against the corporate excesses of major record conglomerates, was the notion that anyone could start their own band, record their own songs and even set up their own home-made label and find a distribution outlet for their music which was 'independent' from the main six corporate distributors. By the mid-1970s WEA, CBS, Polygram, RCA, EMI and PRT had come to dominate the crucial link between the artist and the retailer, but with the explosion of Punk in 1976 and 1977, the record industry establishment was threatened for the first time by the very principles of the wave's leading protagonists. Although the companies responded simply by buying every angry, pimple-faced, foul-mouthed band they could find (it should be remembered that, for all their anti-establishment howlings, the Sex Pistols signed to EMI, A&M and finally Virgin while Punk's second biggest act, the overtly political anti-greed Clash, immediately inked a lucrative deal with the multi-national corporation, CBS), many of the less commercial artists, who couldn't get signed to any label once the noise of Punk died down in 1979, decided to go it alone.

During the late 1970s, therefore, a large number of small labels (including Small Wonder, Cherry Red, Mode, No Future, Fresh, Crass, Safari, Graduate, Truth and Fast) sprang up, often established to issue just one record or to release product by one act, which often owned and operated the label itself. The most successful of these proved to be Rough Trade, based in London, and Factory Records, launched by Tony Wilson in Manchester and the home of Joy Division. Either unable or unwilling to secure distribution of their alternative releases via one of the big six, some labels began distributing records themselves (for example, Rough Trade), while others took advantage of the ad hoc and more casual distribution agreements which could be negotiated with either Stage One, Spartan or Pinnacle, often for a very small number of records (anything from 500 copies upwards). Together with Rough Trade, these three 'independent' distributors became the cornerstone of the burgeoning indie industry between 1977 and 1985 and provided an accessible, reasonably efficient, low-cost national distribution opportunity for thousands of small bands and labels that would otherwise never have seen the light of day. The alternative spirit that this engendered was termed 'indie', and the movement proved successful enough to warrant its own singles and albums charts which began publication in the trade journal *Record Business* in February 1980. The criterion for inclusion on these weekly surveys, still compiled today by MRIB, remains the same: any record released which is not distributed by the main record company conglomerates (the original six, minus PRT who went bust, and, of course, any TV advertising company such as Telstar, Stylus, etc).

With its raw creativity and open-minded position on A & R (Artists & Repertoire – the management of contracted artists), the indie sector blossomed in the 1980s, opening the door for a great number of seminally influential and successful acts, whose sales would often outperform those of their major label rivals. These included the Smiths, Everything But The Girl, the Cocteau Twins, New Order (formerly Joy Division), Crass, Depeche Mode, Pigbag, Yazoo and, more recently, Erasure, the Farm, Happy Mondays, Shamen, KLF and Primal Scream. Many other popular bands, such as UB40, Scritti Politti, House Of Love and the Stone Roses, began life as indie acts but eventually signed major label and distribution deals as the bigger record companies began to see the benefits of signing the top performing acts on the indie charts, and lured them away with large advances.

With small but popular artist rosters, a number of highly successful indie labels emerged that commanded extreme loyalty, both from their acts (New Order never signed a contract with Factory Records) and from alternative music fans, who would often buy a record unheard, simply because it was released on, for example, Crass, Factory or Creation. Although Factory Records were a notable indie victim of the recession in 1992 (despite successfully launching and holding on to New Order and the Happy Mondays), many of these labels have survived and grown over the past 10 years, including 4AD, One Little Indian, Creation, Rough Trade (who fell as a distributor at the beginning of the 1990s, but who, together with Revolver, remains one of the oldest indie labels) and, most successfully, Daniel Miller's Mute which has flourished with the always independent Depeche Mode, Yazoo, Assembly and Erasure.

While the indie sector seems constantly plagued by financial woes (Stage One and Spartan fell by the wayside in the mid-1980s, Pinnacle nearly went bust around the same time but has since been turned around and is now an efficient and profitable distributor) new labels and distributors always seem to quickly replace any casualties. The sector's greatest loss, however, was the demise in 1990 of the Cartel, a national distribution coalition of innovative regional labels, led by Rough Trade in London (and whose members included Fast Forward, Revolver, Backs and Red Rhino) and who, when they were operative, had been responsible for servicing over 50 per cent of all indie product.

THE TOP 10 SINGLES IN THE UK ON THE PWL LABEL

	Title	Artist	Year
1	Especially For You	Kylie Minogue and Jason Donovan	1989
2	I Should Be So Lucky	Kylie Minogue	1988
3	Do They Know It's Christmas?	Band Aid II	1989
4	Too Many Broken Hearts	Jason Donovan	1989
5	When You Come Back To Me	Jason Donovan	1989
6	Hand On Your Heart	Kylie Minogue	1989
7	The Loco-Motion	Kylie Minogue	1988
8	Ferry Cross The Mersey	Various	1989
9	Got To Be Certain	Kylie Minogue	1988
10	Wouldn't Change A Thing	Kylie Minogue	1989

Stock Aitken Waterman, Britain's most successful record production team of recent years, scored a fair proportion of that success on their own PWL label. Where would they have been, though, without Australian ex-*Neighbours* stars Kylie and Jason? Without eight of the label's 10 bestsellers, if nothing else. The remaining two were charity singles, *Ferry Cross The Mersey* being in aid of the Hillsborough disaster fund, and featuring Gerry Marsden, Paul McCartney and others.

THE TOP 10 SINGLES IN THE UK ON THE STIFF LABEL

	Title	Artist	Year
1	Hit Me With Your Rhythm Stick	Ian Dury	1978
2	Stop The Cavalry	Jona Lewie	1980
3	It's My Party	Dave Stewart and Barbara Gaskin	1981
4	Baggy Trousers	Madness	1980
5	Embarrassment	Madness	1980
6	It Must Be Love	Madness	1981
7	Our House	Madness	1982
8	They Don't Know	Tracey Ullman	1983
9	House Of Fun	Madness	1982
10	My Girl	Madness	1980

One of the first of the UK's successful independent record labels of the late 1970s, Stiff launched itself with artists like Nick Lowe, Elvis Costello and Ian Dury (the latter providing its all-time bestseller), but had its best hitmaking period during the first half of the 1980s, courtesy of the extraordinarily consistent Madness, who made the Top 10 with 14 of their first 15 Stiff singles, and occupy 60 per cent of this chart.

THE TOP 10 SINGLES IN THE UK ON THE RCA LABEL

	Title	Artist	Year
1	It's Now Or Never	Elvis Presley	1960
2	Mary's Boy Child	Harry Belafonte	1957
3	Sugar Sugar	Archies	1969
4	I Know Him So Well	Elaine Paige and Barbara Dickson	1985
5	Are You Lonesome Tonight	Elvis Presley	1961
6	Never Gonna Give You Up	Rick Astley	1987
7	Without You	Nilsson	1972
8	Making Your Mind Up	Bucks Fizz	1981
9	Jailhouse Rock	Elvis Presley	1958
10	Amazing Grace	Royal Scots Dragoon Guards	1972

RCA was launched in the UK in 1957, and one of its earliest releases, by Harry Belafonte, still remains its second all-time biggest single. Both *Mary's Boy Child* and Presley's 1960 hit *It's Now Or Never* sold more than 1,000,000 copies in the UK, while the Archies' single sold some 950,000. The label's continued major presence during the 1980s, however, is represented by the Elaine Paige/Barbara Dickson, Rick Astley and Bucks Fizz hits.

In spite of stiff competition, Ian Dury's 1978 record Hit Me With Your Rhythm Stick *is Stiff's bestselling single.*

THE FIRST 10 SINGLES RELEASED IN THE USA ON THE TAMLA LABEL

	A/B Side	Artist	Matrix	Date
1	Come To Me/Whisper	Marv Johnson	101	Jan 1959
2	Merry Go Round/It Moves Me	Eddie Holland	102	Jan 1959
3	Ich-I-Bon-I/Cool & Crazy	Nick & The Jaguars	5501	May 1959
4	Solid Sender/I'll Never Love Again	Chico Leverette	54024	Jun 1959
5	Snake Walk (Part I)/ Snake Walk (Part II)	Swinging Tigers	54024*	Jun 1959
6	It/Don't Say Bye Bye	Ron & Bill	54025	Aug 1959
7	Money (That's What I Want)/ Oh I Apologise	Barrett Strong	54027**	Aug 1959
8	Going To The Hop/Motor City	Satintones	54026	Oct 1959
9	The Feeling Is So Fine/ You Can Depend On Me	Miracles	54028	Mar 1960
10	The Feeling Is So Fine (2nd version)/ You Can Depend On Me	Miracles	54028	Apr 1960

* Snake Walk (Part I) was released a few days after Solid Sender in June 1959 and was mistakenly allocated the same matrix (catalogue) number.

** Released chronologically out of sequence with the 54000 series catalogue numbers.

The Tamla label preceded Motown, whose first single was the Satintones' *My Beloved* (matrix no. 1000), released in September 1961.

THE TOP 10 SINGLES IN THE UK ON THE VIRGIN LABEL

	Title	Artist	Year
1	Don't You Want Me	Human League	1981
2	Karma Chameleon	Culture Club	1983
3	Do You Really Want To Hurt Me	Culture Club	1982
4	In The Air Tonight	Phil Collins	1981
5	A Good Heart	Feargal Sharkey	1985
6	Against All Odds (Take A Look At Me Now)	Phil Collins	1984
7	You Can't Hurry Love	Phil Collins	1982
8	Victims	Culture Club	1983
9	A Groovy Kind Of Love	Phil Collins	1988
10	The Chicken Song	Spitting Image	1986

Virgin Records was launched in the early 1970s with Mike Oldfield's mega-selling *Tubular Bells* album, but it was during the 1980s, when the label acquired three consistently successful acts in Culture Club, Human League and, especially, the soloing Genesis singer/drummer Phil Collins, that its major hit singles were all scored. Both numbers one and two on this list sold more than 1,000,000 copies in the UK.

10 LABELS ON WHICH BEATLES RECORDS HAVE APPEARED IN THE USA

1	Apple
2	Atco
3	Capitol
4	Decca
5	MGM
6	Polydor
7	Swan
8	Tollie
9	United Artists
10	Vee Jay

Prior to the 1964 release of *I Want To Hold Your Hand* in the United States, EMI's American licensee Capitol Records often failed to take up its first option on every Beatles release, allowing smaller labels such as Vee Jay and Swan to pick them up. When Beatlemania finally gripped the country in 1964, these labels were quick to cash in, particularly Vee Jay, which held the rights to all of the band's singles prior to *She Loves You*, notably *Please Please Me*, *Do You Want To Know A Secret*, *Twist And Shout* and *Love Me Do*, which they issued via their Tollie label subsidiary. Swan Records held the rights only to *She Loves You*, which hit US No. 1. United Artists gained record rights to the soundtrack of *A Hard Day's Night*, since its parent company produced the film, while Apple was the Beatles' own label for later releases, marketed through Capitol. The remaining labels – Atco, Decca, MGM and Polydor – have at various times all licensed the use of tracks from the early Beatles sessions recorded in Hamburg for Polydor, Germany.

THE FIRST TOP 10 SINGLES CHART IN THE UK

	Title	Artist
1	Here In My Heart	Al Martino
2	You Belong To Me	Jo Stafford
3	Somewhere Along The Way	Nat 'King' Cole
4	Isle Of Innisfree	Bing Crosby
5	Feet Up	Guy Mitchell
6	Half As Much	Rosemary Clooney
7	High Noon	Frankie Laine
8	Sugar Bush	Doris Day and Frankie Laine
9	Homing Waltz	Vera Lynn
10	Auf Wiedersehen (Sweetheart)	Vera Lynn

'An authentic weekly survey of the best-selling "pop" records' is how the *New Musical Express* heralded the first-ever British singles chart, which it published on Friday 14 November 1952. Before it was instituted, charts were based only on sheet music sales. In subsequent weeks, *You Belong To Me* also reached No. 1, *Feet Up* rose to No. 2 and *Half As Much* to No. 3.

THE FIRST TOP 10 SINGLES CHART IN THE USA

	Title	Artist
1	I'll Never Smile Again	Tommy Dorsey
2	The Breeze And I	Jimmy Dorsey
3	Imagination	Glenn Miller
4	Playmates	Kay Kyser
5	Fools Rush In	Glenn Miller
6	Where Was I	Charlie Barnet
7	Pennsylvania 6-5000	Glenn Miller
8	Imagination	Tommy Dorsey
9	Sierra Sue	Bing Crosby
10	Make-Believe Island	Mitchell Ayres

This was the first singles Top 10 compiled by *Billboard* magazine, for its issue dated 20 July 1940. Since the 7″ 45-rpm single was still the best part of a decade in the future, all these would have been 10″ 78-rpm discs. Note the almost total domination of big-name big bands more than a half century ago – and spare a thought for Mitchell Ayres, who crept in at the bottom of this very first chart, and then never had a hit again.

THE FIRST TOP 10 EUROPEAN SINGLES CHART*

	Title	Artist
1	Let's Dance	David Bowie
2	Billie Jean	Michael Jackson
3	99 Luftballons	Nena
4	Too Shy	Kajagoogoo
5	Major Tom	Peter Schilling
6	You Can't Hurry Love	Phil Collins
7	Electric Avenue	Eddy Grant
8	Together We Are Strong	Mireille Mathieu and Patrick Duffy
9	Words	F. R. David
10	Just An Illusion	BZM

* Week ending 21 April 1983.

Long before MTV Europe, BBC's *Top Of The Pops* featured a shortlived weekly European singles chart. This first Top 10, compiled by MRIB, was broadcast on 19 April 1983, and includes singles that were chart hits in from three to (in the case of Michael Jackson) seven European countries.

THE 10 SINGLES WITH MOST WEEKS AT NO. 1 IN THE UK

	Title	Artist	Weeks
1	I Believe	Frankie Laine	18
2	(Everything I Do) I Do It For You	Bryan Adams	16
3	Bohemian Rhapsody	Queen	14
4	Rose Marie	Slim Whitman	11
5=	Cara Mia	David Whitfield	10
5=	I Will Always Love You	Whitney Houston	10
7=	Diana	Paul Anka	9
7=	Here In My Heart	Al Martino	9
7=	Mull Of Kintyre	Wings	9
7=	Oh Mein Papa	Eddie Calvert	9
7=	Secret Love	Doris Day	9
7=	Two Tribes	Frankie Goes To Hollywood	9
7=	You're The One That I Want	John Travolta and Olivia Newton-John	9

The totals for *I Believe* and *Bohemian Rhapsody* are cumulative of more than one run at the top, in the former case because the single dropped to No. 2 for two weeks in what otherwise would have been a 20-week spell at No. 1, and in the latter case through a return to the top for a second lengthy run 16 years after its first. All other totals are for consecutive chart-topping weeks, which means Bryan Adams is the champion in terms of an unbroken No. 1 run.

THE 10 HIGHEST DEBUTING SINGLES IN THE USA (1955–93)

	Title	Artist	Position	Debut date
1	Let It Be	Beatles	6	21 Mar 70
2=	Hey Jude	Beatles	10	14 Sep 68
2=	Get Back	Beatles	10	10 May 69
4	Mrs Brown You've Got A Lovely Daughter	Herman's Hermits	12	7 Apr 65
5=	I'll Be There	Mariah Carey	13	30 May 92
5=	Erotica	Madonna	13	17 Oct 92
7	That's The Way Love Goes	Janet Jackson	14	1 May 93
8	Rescue Me	Madonna	15	2 Mar 91
9=	Something	Beatles	20	18 Oct 69
9=	Imagine	John Lennon	20	23 Oct 71
9=	Thriller	Michael Jackson	20	11 Feb 84

Madonna's *Rescue Me* is unusual: though it became the highest debuting single by a female artist in US pop chart history (replacing Joy Layne's 1957 No. 30 bowing hit, *Your Wild Heart*) it peaked at only No. 9 and quickly left the survey, thereby being the only record in this Top 10 list that did not subsequently hit US No. 1. She beat her own record, and equalled Mariah Carey's earlier 1992 entry, with the mighty No. 13 debut position of *Erotica*. Tied for 11th position would be USA For Africa's *We Are The World* and the Beatles' *A Hard Day's Night*, both of which entered the chart at No. 21.

THE 10 SINGLES THAT STAYED LONGEST IN THE UK CHARTS

	Title	Artist	First chart entry	Weeks in charts
1	My Way	Frank Sinatra	1969	122
2	Amazing Grace	Judy Collins	1970	67
3	Rock Around The Clock	Bill Haley & His Comets	1955	57
4	Release Me	Engelbert Humperdinck	1967	56
5	Stranger On The Shore	Mr Acker Bilk	1961	55
6	Relax	Frankie Goes To Hollywood	1983	52
7	Blue Monday	New Order	1983	49
8	I Love You Because	Jim Reeves	1964	47
9	Let's Twist Again	Chubby Checker	1961	44
10	White Lines (Don't Don't Do It)	Grandmaster Flash and Melle Mel	1983	43

10 BRITISH SINGLES THAT HIT NO. 1 IN THE USA WITHOUT CHARTING IN THE UK

	Title	Artist	Year
1	Eight Days A Week	Beatles	1965
2	Mrs Brown You've Got A Lovely Daughter	Herman's Hermits	1965
3	I'm Henry VIII, I Am	Herman's Hermits	1965
4	To Sir With Love	Lulu	1967
5	The Long And Winding Road	Beatles	1970
6	How Can You Mend A Broken Heart	Bee Gees	1971
7	Uncle Albert/Admiral Halsey	Paul and Linda McCartney	1971
8	Have You Ever Been Mellow	Olivia Newton-John	1975
9	Saturday Night	Bay City Rollers	1976
10	(Love Is) Thicker Than Water	Andy Gibb	1978

For a British artist to top the US chart and fail even to make the British survey is a very rare event – and one that has not occurred since 1978. For the Beatles, Herman's Hermits and Paul McCartney, it was simply the case that these singles were not released in the UK as 45s. Lulu's *To Sir With Love* (from the movie of the same name) was the B-side of her British hit *Let's Pretend*, but never appeared as a single in its own right. The Bay City Rollers' achievement may be the most extraordinary: just as they began to fall out of favour in their home territory in 1976, they were about to enjoy their first American hit (and only US chart-topper) with *Saturday Night*.

THE RISE AND FALL OF THE CHART SINGLE

The year 1992 witnessed a bizarre chart achievement: the Wedding Present, a Leeds based band little known outside the alternative music scene, equalled a 35-year-old record held by Elvis Presley, notching up twelve Top 30 UK chart singles in one calendar year. Rather than being an impressive sales achievement, this statistical feat merely confirms the dire straits that singles sales are in, a trend which began in the late 1980s and continues on a downward slide which threatens the future of the British singles charts themselves.

None of the dozen titles released by the Wedding Present in 1992 sold more than 10,000 copies, a fact simply evident in their strictly limited edition release, yet singles sales are now so weak that when *Come Play With Me*, their fifth 45 of the year, was issued in May, it entered the chart in the Top 10. For Elvis to realize the same achievement in 1957, average sales of each of his 12 hits needed to exceed 250,000 copies.

Since the dawn of the rock era, the level of British singles sales has always fluctuated, but unit totals for the past five years have plunged to dangerously low depths. While Elvis, Cliff Richard and the Rolling Stones regularly sold between 300,000 and 600,000 copies of their Top 10 singles in the late 1950s and early 1960s, the Beatles improved on these impressive tallies, shifting between 500,000 and 1,000,000 units of the majority of their single releases during the 1960s, when 45-rpm sales routinely outsold those of albums. While there was a recessionary decline throughout the industry between 1970 and 1975, 1978 proved to be the biggest singles sales bonanza ever with the average Top 10 hit often accumulating 500,000 sales, boosted, not least, by the million-selling status of two Boney M discs (*Rivers Of Babylon* and *Mary's Boy Child*) and the global popularity of singles released from the *Grease* soundtrack.

Sales held steady for the next 10 years, another notable high coming in 1984 when a plethora of platinum-selling singles (by Wham!, Stevie Wonder, George Michael, Frankie Goes To Hollywood and, of course, the Band Aid charity effort) lifted overall chart sales beyond normal levels. Since the mid-1980s, however, sales have declined sharply, to the point where a million-seller has become the exception rather than the rule and when many Top 10 records need sell less than a five-figure number per week to claim what was once considered a notable chart achievement. All this, despite an ever-increasing consumer market and media coverage of music.

Is this recent downsurge merely recession linked, or are there fundamental problems underlying the collapse of the single? Aside from the simple rise in the cost of buying a single (1974, 55p; 1992, anything up to £4.99 for a CD single), another factor which indicates a fundamental problem is the number of records that made the chart in 1992: for the first time ever, more than 1,000 singles entered the UK survey, made possible simply by the declining number of sales needed to break into the chart. This compares to an average of 300 per annum during the 1960s (which, even though only a Top 50 was collated back then, versus the current Top 75, nevertheless reflects a substantial change in both the desperate release tactics of the record companies and the increasingly fickle and specialist allegiances of the more fragmented record-buying tastes of the public in the 1990s). Each of the Wedding Present efforts in 1992 entered the Top 30 in its first week of release, only to fall immediately out of this territory the following week, a trend currently afflicting a great number of chart singles and one which was unheard of as recently as the mid-1980s.

Perhaps part of the problem is the failure of the industry, from an A & R stance, to find and cultivate acts that consistently raise the sales profile of the market: while a Presley, Sinatra or Beatles is a rare phenomenon, where are the Bay City Rollers, Wham!, Duran Duran, Culture Club or even Gary Glitters of the 1990s? These were artists who, whatever criticism may be levelled at their musical merits in hindsight, could be relied upon to provide a stream of hit singles over a two- or three-year period, and who commanded generic loyalty among hundreds of thousands of teen fans, always the most likely foundation of singles sales. These have been replaced by a collection of 15-minute wonders or by the specialist, and therefore limited, success of a dance rave single or heavy metal outing. While the ageing baby boomers now support the healthier albums market via acts such as Simply Red and Phil Collins, the singles arena is overpopulated with cover versions and monotonous dance cuts.

Exceptions in recent years have yielded successful but isolated results, and are always ballads: the last three discs to sell more than 1,000,000 copies in the UK have been *I Will Always Love You* (Whitney Houston, 1992–93), *Everything I Do (I Do It For You)* (Bryan Adams, 1991) and *The Power Of Love* (Jennifer Rush, 1985), while the platinum sales level has been reduced by the British Phonographic Industry from 1,000,000 to 500,000 copies in a typical admission of self-defeat. Annual UK singles sales totals have declined from 63,000,000 in 1987 to little over 50,000,000 in 1992.

THE 10 SINGLES THAT STAYED LONGEST AT NO. 1 IN THE USA

	Title	Artist	Release year	Weeks at No. 1
1	*I Will Always Love You*	Whitney Houston	1992	14
2	*End Of The Road*	Boyz II Men	1992	13
3	*Hound Dog/Don't Be Cruel*	Elvis Presley	1956	11
4=	*Cherry Pink And Apple Blossom White*	Perez Prado	1955	10
4=	*You Light Up My Life*	Debby Boone	1977	10
4=	*Physical*	Olivia Newton-John	1981	10
7=	*Mack The Knife*	Bobby Darin	1959	9
7=	*Hey Jude*	Beatles	1968	9
7=	*Endless Love*	Diana Ross and Lionel Richie	1981	9
7=	*Bette Davis Eyes*	Kim Carnes	1981	9
7=	*Singing The Blues*	Guy Mitchell	1956	9
7=	*Theme From 'A Summer Place'*	Percy Faith	1960	9

This listing covers the period from 1955 when *Billboard*'s US Top 100 was inaugurated for singles. Long No. 1 runs were actually more commonplace in the pre-Rock 'n' Roll days of the 1940s and early 1950s when the market was generally slower-moving. Oddly enough, 1981 holds the record for the greatest number of singles (three) having runs of two months or more.

THE FIRST 10 SINGLES TO ENTER THE UK CHART AT NO. 1

	Title	Artist	Date
1	*Jailhouse Rock*	Elvis Presley	25 Jan 58
2	*I Got Stung/One Night*	Elvis Presley	24 Jan 59
3	*My Old Man's A Dustman*	Lonnie Donegan	26 Mar 60
4	*It's Now Or Never*	Elvis Presley	5 Nov 60
5	*Surrender*	Elvis Presley	27 May 61
6	*The Young Ones*	Cliff Richard	13 Jan 62
7	*I Want To Hold Your Hand*	Beatles	7 Dec 63
8	*Can't Buy Me Love*	Beatles	28 Mar 64
9	*A Hard Day's Night*	Beatles	18 Jul 64
10	*I Feel Fine*	Beatles	5 Dec 64

Now a regular occurrence – due not least to the relatively small number of sales required today to enter the UK singles chart in pole position – Elvis started this singles sales phenomenon when *Jailhouse Rock* sold nearly 500,000 copies in just three days in January 1958.

My Old Man's A Dustman, Lonnie Donegan's 1960 smash hit, was the first single by a British artist to enter the chart at No. 1.

THE FIRST 10 FEMALE SINGERS TO HAVE A NO. 1 HIT IN THE UK

	Artist	Title	Date at No. 1
1	Jo Stafford	*You Belong To Me*	9 Jan 53
2	Kay Starr	*Comes A-Long A-Love*	23 Jan 53
3	Lita Roza	*(How Much Is That) Doggie In The Window?*	17 Apr 53
4	Doris Day	*Secret Love*	16 Apr 54
5	Kitty Kallen	*Little Things Mean A Lot*	10 Sep 54
6	Vera Lynn	*My Son, My Son*	5 Nov 54
7	Rosemary Clooney	*This Ole House*	26 Nov 54
8	Ruby Murray	*Softly Softly*	19 Feb 55
9	Alma Cogan	*Dreamboat*	16 Jul 55
10	Anne Shelton	*Lay Down Your Arms*	22 Sep 56

THE FIRST 10 FEMALE SINGERS TO HAVE A NO. 1 HIT IN THE USA

	Artist	Title	Date at No. 1
1	Dinah Shore	*I'll Walk Alone*	5 Oct 44
2	Betty Hutton	*Doctor, Lawyer, Indian Chief*	21 Feb 46
3	Peggy Lee	*Manana*	5 Mar 48
4	Margaret Whiting	*A Tree In The Meadow*	1 Oct 48
5	Evelyn Knight	*A Little Bird Told Me*	14 Jan 49
6	Teresa Brewer	*Music! Music! Music!*	10 Mar 50
7	Eileen Barton	*If I Knew You Were Comin', I'd Have Baked A Cake*	7 Apr 50
8	Patti Page	*Tennessee Waltz*	22 Dec 50
9	Rosemary Clooney	*Come On-A My House*	20 Jul 51
10	Kay Starr	*Wheel Of Fortune*	7 Mar 52

In 1944 I'll Walk Alone *made Dinah Shore the first female artist to hit US No. 1.*

THE FIRST 10 BRITISH SOLO ARTISTS TO HAVE A NO. 1 HIT IN THE USA

	Artist	Title	Date at No. 1
1	Vera Lynn	*Auf Wiedersehen (Sweetheart)*	4 Jul 52
2	Mr Acker Bilk	*Stranger On The Shore*	26 May 62
3	Petula Clark	*Downtown*	23 Jan 65
4	Donovan	*Sunshine Superman*	3 Sep 66
5	Lulu	*To Sir With Love*	21 Oct 67
6	George Harrison	*My Sweet Lord*	26 Dec 70
7	Rod Stewart	*Maggie May*	2 Oct 71
8	Gilbert O'Sullivan	*Alone Again Naturally*	29 Jul 72
9	Elton John	*Crocodile Rock*	3 Feb 73
10	Ringo Starr	*Photograph*	24 Oct 73

The majority of British acts which topped the US chart in the 1960s were groups – UK solo artists found the going much harder. There is a curious irony in Vera Lynn's achievement: the date of the first-ever British No. 1 in the US – and one containing German lyrics – was coincidentally American Independence Day.

Clearly, it was much easier for American solo artists to top the UK survey than it was for British artists to compete in the US market.

THE FIRST 10 AMERICAN SOLO ARTISTS TO HAVE A NO. 1 HIT IN THE UK

	Artist	Title	Date at No. 1
1	Al Martino	*Here In My Heart*	14 Nov 52
2	Jo Stafford	*You Belong To Me*	9 Jan 53
3	Kay Starr	*Comes A-Long A-Love*	23 Jan 53
4	Eddie Fisher	*Outside Of Heaven*	30 Jan 53
5	Perry Como	*Don't Let The Stars Get In Your Eyes*	6 Feb 53
6	Guy Mitchell	*She Wears Red Feathers*	23 Mar 53
7	Frankie Laine	*I Believe*	24 Apr 53
8	Doris Day	*Secret Love*	16 Apr 54
9	Johnnie Ray	*Such A Night*	30 Apr 54
10	Kitty Kallen	*Little Things Mean A Lot*	10 Sep 54

It was not until 1977, when Manfred Mann's Earthband hit US No. 1 with *Blinded By The Light,* that the number of British groups to top the American survey reached 20.

THE FIRST 10 BRITISH GROUPS TO HAVE A NO. 1 HIT IN THE USA

	Artist	Title	Date at No. 1
1	Tornados	*Telstar*	22 Dec 62
2	Beatles	*I Want To Hold Your Hand*	1 Feb 64
3	Peter and Gordon	*A World Without Love*	27 Jun 64
4	Animals	*House Of The Rising Sun*	5 Sep 64
5	Manfred Mann	*Do Wah Diddy Diddy*	17 Oct 64
6	Freddie & The Dreamers	*I'm Telling You Now*	10 Apr 65
7	Wayne Fontana & The Mindbenders	*The Game Of Love*	24 Apr 65
8	Herman's Hermits	*Mrs Brown You've Got A Lovely Daughter*	1 May 65
9	Rolling Stones	*(I Can't Get No) Satisfaction*	10 Jul 65
10	Dave Clark Five	*Over And Over*	25 Dec 65

Numbers four, five and seven scored higher on the UK chart than in their native country.

THE FIRST 10 AMERICAN GROUPS TO HAVE A NO. 1 HIT IN THE UK

	Artist	Title	Date at No. 1
1	Bill Haley & His Comets	*Rock Around The Clock*	12 Nov 55
2	Dream Weavers	*It's Almost Tomorrow*	17 Mar 56
3	Teenagers featuring Frankie Lymon	*Why Do Fools Fall In Love?*	21 Jul 56
4	Crickets	*That'll Be The Day*	2 Nov 57
5	Johnny Otis Show	*Ma, He's Making Eyes At Me*	4 Jan 58
6	Everly Brothers	*All I Have To Do Is Dream*	28 Jun 58
7	Kalin Twins	*When*	23 Aug 58
8	Platters	*Smoke Gets In Your Eyes*	14 Mar 59
9	Marcels	*Blue Moon*	6 May 61
10	Highwaymen	*Michael*	7 Oct 61

THE TOP 10 SINGLES THAT DID NOT MAKE NO. 1 IN THE UK*

	Title	Artist	Chart peak
1	Last Christmas	Wham!	2
2	Blue Monday	New Order	3
3	Ghostbusters	Ray Parker Jr	2
4	Vienna	Ultravox	2
5	I Love You Because	Jim Reeves	5
6	Agadoo	Black Lace	2
7	The Birdie Song	Tweets	2
8	There Goes My Everything	Engelbert Humperdinck	2
9	Antmusic	Adam & The Ants	2
10	I Won't Forget You	Jim Reeves	3

* Based on sales.

Interestingly, most of these non-No. 1 big sellers (all achieving sales of more than 750,000 copies in the UK) were from the 1980s, the exceptions being the Engelbert Humperdinck and Jim Reeves singles from the mid-1960s (the two by Reeves registered high sales and extreme chart longevity in the immediate wake of his death.) Wham!'s Last Christmas sold 1,500,000, and was unlucky to fetch up below Band Aid's Do They Know It's Christmas?, the biggest-selling UK single of all time.

THE FIRST 10 MILLION-SELLING ROCK 'N' ROLL SINGLES IN THE USA

	Title	Artist	Year
1	Rock Around The Clock	Bill Haley & His Comets	1954
2	Shake Rattle And Roll	Bill Haley & His Comets	1954
3	Maybelline	Chuck Berry	1955
4	Ain't That A Shame	Fats Domino	1955
5	Ain't That A Shame	Pat Boone	1955
6	Seventeen	Boyd Bennett	1955
7	I Hear You Knocking	Gale Storm	1955
8	See You Later Alligator	Bill Haley & His Comets	1955
9	Tutti Frutti	Little Richard	1955
10	Heartbreak Hotel	Elvis Presley	1956

Widely regarded as the first Rock 'n' Roll hit, Rock Around The Clock saw the dawn of a new musical era, a hybrid of R & B and Country which would explode as its own genre in the mid-1950s.

THE FIRST 10 MILLION-SELLING SINGLES IN THE UK

	Title	Artist	Year
1	Rock Around The Clock	Bill Haley & His Comets	1954
2	Mary's Boy Child	Harry Belafonte	1957
3	Diana	Paul Anka	1957
4	It's Now Or Never	Elvis Presley	1960
5	The Young Ones	Cliff Richard	1962
6	Stranger On The Shore	Mr Acker Bilk	1961
7	I Remember You	Frank Ifield	1962
8	She Loves You	Beatles	1963
9	I Want To Hold Your Hand	Beatles	1963
10	Can't Buy Me Love	Beatles	1964

The Beatles are the all-time platinum singles sales kings: they amassed five million-selling UK singles in the 1960s, while John Lennon added one with Imagine and McCartney another with Wings' Mull Of Kintyre/Girls School in 1978. Bing Crosby's 1942 release White Christmas is also a UK million-seller – but it took until 1977 to achieve that status!

In the UK, Paul Anka's Diana, the bestselling single of 1957, also qualifies him for entry in the Top 10 lists of the first million-selling singles and the longest stays at No. 1, as well as making him one of the youngest artists to achieve a No. 1 hit – not to mention being one of the 10 bestselling singles of all time.

10 SONGS THAT HAVE BEEN UK HITS IN FOUR OR MORE VERSIONS

	Title	Artists
1	Garden Of Eden	Dick James, Gary Miller, Joe Valino, Frankie Vaughan
2	My Way	Elvis Presley, Sex Pistols, Frank Sinatra, Dorothy Squires
3	Stranger In Paradise	Tony Bennett, Eddie Calvert, Don Cornell, Bing Crosby, Four Aces, Tony Martin
4	Sucu Sucu	Ted Heath, Laurie Johnson, Joe Loss, Nina & Frederick, Ping Ping and Al Verlaine
5	Sunny	Boney M, Cher, Georgie Fame, Bobby Hebb
6	The Story Of My Life	Alma Cogan, Michael Holliday, Dave King, Gary Miller
7	Unchained Melody	Les Baxter, Al Hibbler, Liberace, Righteous Brothers, Leo Sayer, Jimmy Young
8	Volare (Nel Blu Dipinto Di Blu)	Charlie Drake, Marino Marini, Dean Martin, Domenico Modugno, Bobby Rydell
9	Walk Hand In Hand	Ronnie Carroll, Gerry & The Pacemakers, Tony Martin, Jimmy Parkinson
10	White Christmas	Michael Bolton, Pat Boone, Bing Crosby, Darts, Keith Harris and Orville, Mantovani, Freddie Starr

White Christmas has charted seven times in the UK via different, and markedly disparate, acts, with Michael Bolton reviving the old chestnut as recently as December 1992.

THE TOP 10 SINGLES BY FEMALE SINGERS IN THE UK

	Title	Artist	Year
1	I Will Always Love You	Whitney Houston	1992
2	The Power Of Love	Jennifer Rush	1985
3	Don't Cry For Me Argentina	Julie Covington	1977
4	Fame	Irene Cara	1982
5	Anyone Who Had A Heart	Cilla Black	1964
6	Feels Like I'm In Love	Kelly Marie	1980
7	Woman In Love	Barbra Streisand	1980
8	Nothing Compares 2 U	Sinead O'Connor	1990
9	Chain Reaction	Diana Ross	1986
10	Like A Virgin	Madonna	1984

Perhaps the most significant aspect of this list is how comparatively recent most of its entries are. Only two singles were released before 1980, and only Cilla Black's 1964 chart-topper is of real vintage. Statistically, therefore, a female artist stands a better chance of chart success today than in any of pop music's past golden ages – indeed, Madonna (who has obviously helped this state of affairs) was the bestselling act of the 1980s.

THE TOP 10 SOLO SINGERS OF THE 1980s IN THE UK

1	Madonna
2	Michael Jackson
3	Phil Collins
4	Cliff Richard
5	Shakin' Stevens
6	Paul McCartney
7	Kylie Minogue
8	Whitney Houston
9	Prince
10	David Bowie

This Top 10 is based on estimated UK record sales from 1980 to 1989. In that period, the top performer, Madonna, scored 21 Top 10 hit singles (including six No. 1s), while all five of her albums were entries in the album Top 10, two of them reaching the No. 1 position, an achievement that far outstrips that of any other artist of the decade.

THE TOP 10 GROUPS OF THE 1980s IN THE UK

1	Police
2	Wham!
3	Dire Straits
4	U2
5	Queen
6	Simple Minds
7	Pet Shop Boys
8	Duran Duran
9	Adam & The Ants
10	Madness

This list is based on estimated UK record sales (both singles and albums), taking account of both highest chart positions and chart longevity. The Police and Simple Minds shared the position of groups with most No. 1 albums during the 1980s (four each), while Pet Shop Boys had the most No. 1 singles (four). Many other groups were consistently successful during the decade, among them UB40, Culture Club and Eurythmics, who are all close contenders for the number 10 slot. The most successful female group was Bananarama, although they never had a single higher than No. 3 and fell just short of qualifying for the list.

THE 10 ARTISTS WITH THE LONGEST US CHART CAREER RUNS, 1955–93

	Artist	Chart span years	months
1	Paul Simon	33	0
2	Roy Orbison	32	11
3	Ray Charles	32	4
4	Smokey Robinson	32	1
5	B.B. King	31	8
6	Dion	31	3
7	Ronald Isley	30	9
8=	Darlene Love	30	4
8=	Little Richard	30	4
10	Tina Turner	29	5

Simon, who first charted during the week ending 23 December 1957 as half of the harmony duo Tom & Jerry (with Art Garfunkel), scored most recently in December 1990 with his solo hit *The Obvious Child*, though he seems assured to extend this run with each release throughout the 1990s. Roy Orbison's achievement is all the more remarkable since his chart career, which began in 1956, stalled in 1967. He did not chart again until 1980 and left it another nine years to make the survey with the memorable Top 10 smash, *You Got It*, just prior to his death.

DUOS QUIZ

1. Who was the duettist with Marvin Gaye on *It Takes Two*?
2. Which brother and sister act scored with *Deep Purple* and *I'm Leaving It All Up To You*?
3. Which vocal duo of the 1960s comprised songwriters Roger Greenaway and Roger Cook?
4. What was John Travolta and Olivia Newton-John's No. 1 follow-up to their *Grease* chart-topper, *You're The One That I Want*?
5. Which comedy duo posthumously hit UK No. 2 in 1975 with *The Trail Of The Lonesome Pine*?
6. Which female artist has secured duet hits with both Kenny Rogers and Prince?
7. Which pair of American brothers, whose chart career began in the 1950s, played a reunion concert in London in 1983?
8. Who comprised the Eurythmics?
9. Who are Bobby Hatfield and Bill Medley?
10. Which brother and sister duo suffered the death of one of the act in 1983?

THE TOP 10 SINGLES BY HUSBANDS AND WIVES IN THE UK CHARTS

	Title	Artists	Year	Highest chart position
1	*I Got You, Babe*	Sonny & Cher	1965	1
2	*Cinderella Rockefella*	Esther & Abi Ofarim	1968	1
3	*River Deep, Mountain High*	Ike & Tina Turner	1966	3
4	*I Want To Stay Here*	Steve & Eydie	1963	3
5	*Little Donkey*	Nina & Frederick	1960	3
6	*Solid*	Ashford & Simpson	1985	3
7	*Teardrops*	Womack & Womack	1988	3
8	*Nutbush City Limits*	Ike & Tina Turner	1973	4
9	*Little Man*	Sonny & Cher	1966	4
10	*Do That To Me One More Time*	Captain & Tennille	1980	7

Sonny & Cher's I Got You, Babe, *released in 1965, is still the UK's bestselling single by a husband and wife duo.*

Marital harmony in the charts does nothing for domestic togetherness, it seems: several of the couples above, including Sonny and Cher, Nina and Frederick, the Ofarims and the Turners, were subsequently divorced. Yoko Ono's credit on a couple of John Lennon singles has been ignored for the purposes of this list, since there is little audible evidence of her presence on the records.

THE 10 OLDEST SINGERS TO HAVE A NO. 1 SINGLE IN THE UK*

	Artist	Title	yrs	Age mths
1	Louis Armstrong	*What A Wonderful World*	67	10
2	Frank Sinatra	*Somethin' Stupid*	51	4
3	Telly Savalas	*If*	51	1
4	Cliff Richard	*Saviour's Day*	50	2
5	Righteous Brothers	*Unchained Melody*	50 50	2/ 1
6	Charles Aznavour	*She*	50	1
7	Clive Dunn	*Grandad*	49	0
8	Ben E. King	*Stand By Me*	48	5
9	Gene Pitney	*Something's Gotten Hold Of My Heart*	48	0
10	Mantovani	*Theme From 'Moulin Rouge'*	47	9

* To 31 December 1992.

The ages listed are those of the artists during the final week of their last (to date) No. 1 hit. Gene Pitney was just a day over 48 as his 1989 duet success with Marc Almond finished its chart-topping run. Eight of the 10 are still alive, so there is room for further improvement.

THE 10 OLDEST SINGERS IN THE UK TOP 10*

	Artist	Title	yrs	Age mths
1	Frank Sinatra	*New York, New York*	70	4
2	Louis Armstrong	*What A Wonderful World*	68	0
3	Honor Blackman	*Kinky Boots*	64	0
4	James Brown	*Living In America*	56	10
5	Ted Heath	*Swingin' Shepherd Blues*	56	2
6	Petula Clark	*Downtown '88 Remix*	56	0
7	Bobby Vinton	*Blue Velvet*	55	6
8	Nina Simone	*My Baby Just Cares For Me*	54	10
9	Bing Crosby	*Around The World*	54	2
10	Cliff Richard	*I Still Believe In You*	52	2

* To 31 December 1992.

The ages listed are those of the artists at the end of the Top 10 run by their most recent (to date) Top 10 hit. Posthumous Top 10 entries – such as two by Bing Crosby – are not counted. With several of the artists here still actively and successfully recording, many may have further Top 10 hits yet to deliver.

THE 10 YOUNGEST SINGERS TO HAVE A NO. 1 SINGLE IN THE UK*

	Artist	Title	yrs	Age mths
1	Little Jimmy Osmond	*Long Haired Lover From Liverpool*	9	8
2	Donny Osmond	*Puppy Love*	14	6
3	Helen Shapiro	*You Don't Know*	14	10
4	Paul Anka	*Diana*	16	0
5	Tiffany	*I Think We're Alone Now*	16	3
6	Nicole	*A Little Peace*	17	0
7	Glenn Medeiros	*Nothing's Gonna Change My Love*	18	0
8	Mary Hopkin	*Those Were The Days*	18	4
9	Cliff Richard	*Living Doll*	18	8
10	Adam Faith	*What Do You Want*	19	5

* To 31 December 1992.

The ages are those of the artists in the week in which they first topped the UK chart. Kylie Minogue just missed this list, having been 19 years 8 months old when she first hit No. 1 in 1988 with *I Should Be So Lucky*.

THE 10 YOUNGEST SINGERS OF ALL TIME IN THE UK SINGLES CHARTS

	Artist	Title	Year	Highest chart position	Age yrs	mths
1	Microbe (Ian Doody)	Groovy Baby	1969	29	3	0
2	Natalie Casey	Chick Chick Chicken	1984	72	3	0
3	Little Jimmy Osmond	Long Haired Lover From Liverpool	1974	1	9	7
4	Lena Zavaroni	Ma He's Making Eyes At Me	1974	10	10	4
5	Neil Reid	Mother Of Mine	1972	2	11	0
6	Michael Jackson	Got To Be There	1972	5	13	5
7	Laurie London	He's Got The Whole World In His Hands	1957	12	13	9
8	Jimmy Boyd	I Saw Mommy Kissing Santa Claus	1953	3	13	10
9	Marie Osmond	Paper Roses	1973	2	14	1
10	Helen Shapiro	Don't Treat Me Like A Child	1961	3	14	5

The ages given are those reached by these artists during their first-ever week in the UK singles chart. Since this is a chart of solo acts, assorted hitmaking children's choirs are not included, nor is Michael Jackson's initial impact with the Jackson 5, made when he was only 10. With a few honourable exceptions, most of these precocious stars never achieved a follow-up chart success.

10 HIT SINGLES BY ACTORS

	Title	Artist	Year	Chart peak
1	Ain't No Doubt	Jimmy Nail	1992	UK No. 1
2	Wand'rin' Star	Lee Marvin	1970	UK No. 1
3	If	Telly Savalas	1975	UK No. 1
4	MacArthur Park	Richard Harris	1968	UK No. 1/US No. 2
5	Theme From Dr Kildare (Three Stars Will Shine Tonight)	Richard Chamberlain	1962	UK No. 12/US No. 10
6	Let's Get Together	Hayley Mills	1961	UK No. 17/US No. 8
7	Ringo	Lorne Greene	1964	UK No. 22/US No. 1
8	The Way You Look Tonight	Edward Woodward	1971	UK No. 42
9	The Ballad Of Thunder Road	Robert Mitchum	1958	US No. 62
10	Married Man	Richard Burton	1965	US No. 64

Both Richard Harris and Richard Chamberlain went on to score a few more hit singles and albums before returning to their day jobs, while Richard Burton also contributed narration to Jeff Wayne's Top 5 hit album War Of The Worlds in 1978.

THE TOP 10 CHRISTMAS SINGLES OF ALL TIME IN THE UK

	Title	Artist	Year
1	Do They Know It's Christmas?	Band Aid	1984
2	Mary's Boy Child/Oh My Lord	Boney M	1978
3	Last Christmas	Wham!	1984
4	Merry Xmas Everybody	Slade	1973
5	Mary's Boy Child	Harry Belafonte	1957
6	White Christmas	Bing Crosby	1977*
7	Mistletoe And Wine	Cliff Richard	1988
8	When A Child Is Born	Johnny Mathis	1976
9	Happy Xmas (War Is Over)	John Lennon	1980*
10	Lonely This Christmas	Mud	1974

* Year of highest chart position.

Band Aid's *Do They Know It's Christmas?* has now sold over 3,500,000 copies in the UK alone. Slade's *Merry Xmas Everybody* has charted on eight seasonal occasions. Bing Crosby's *White Christmas*, despite having sold over 30,000,000 copies worldwide since 1942, charted for the first time in the UK as late as 1977, a few weeks after the singer's death.

THE TOP 10 CHRISTMAS SINGLES OF ALL TIME IN THE USA

	Title	Artist
1	White Christmas	Bing Crosby
2	Silent Night/Adeste Fideles	Bing Crosby
3	Rudolph The Red-Nosed Reindeer	Gene Autry
4	The Chipmunk Song	Chipmunks
5	I Saw Mommy Kissing Santa Claus	Jimmy Boyd
6	The Little Drummer Boy	Harry Simeone Chorale
7	Do They Know It's Christmas?	Band Aid
8	I'll Be Home For Christmas	Bing Crosby
9	Grandma Got Run Over By A Reindeer	Elmo & Patsy
10	Jingle Bell Rock	Bobby Helms

Most of America's bestselling Christmas singles come from the middle years of the century, with five of this Top 10 list pre-dating the rock era, and only two titles – Band Aid's *Do They Know It's Christmas?* and Elmo & Patsy's comedy item (which has sold over 1,000,000 in recent years without, curiously, ever making the US singles chart) – are more recent than the 1950s.

THE TOP 10 COUNTRY SINGLES OF THE 1950s IN THE USA

	Title	Artist
1	The Battle Of New Orleans	Johnny Horton
2	Sixteen Tons	Tennessee Ernie Ford
3	Singin' The Blues	Marty Robbins
4	Crazy Arms	Ray Price
5	I'm Moving On	Hank Snow
6	In The Jailhouse Now	Webb Pierce
7	I Don't Hurt Anymore	Hank Snow
8	Slowly	Webb Pierce
9	Jambalaya (On The Bayou)	Hank Williams
10	Slow Poke	Pee Wee King

Not only did *The Battle Of New Orleans* spend 10 weeks atop the Country chart in 1959, it also claimed a six-week residence in pole position on the pop chart and sold over 1,000,000 copies, a rare achievement in the 1950s.

THE TOP 10 COUNTRY SINGLES OF THE 1960s IN THE UK

	Title	Artist
1	I Love You Because	Jim Reeves
2	I Won't Forget You	Jim Reeves
3	Ruby (Don't Take Your Love To Town)	Kenny Rogers
4	King Of The Road	Roger Miller
5	Distant Drums	Jim Reeves
6	I'll Never Fall In Love Again	Bobbie Gentry
7	A Boy Named Sue	Johnny Cash
8	Devil Woman	Marty Robbins
9	Big Bad John	Jimmy Dean
10	Welcome To My World	Jim Reeves

score=

THE TOP 10 COUNTRY SINGLES OF THE 1960s IN THE USA

	Title	Artist
1	A Boy Named Sue	Johnny Cash
2	King Of The Road	Roger Miller
3	Harper Valley P.T.A.	Jeannie C. Riley
4	Big Bad John	Jimmy Dean
5	Ode To Billy Joe	Bobbie Gentry
6	He'll Have To Go	Jim Reeves
7	She's Got You	Patsy Cline
8	Walk On By	Leroy Van Dyke
9	Love's Gonna Live Here	Buck Owens
10	Please Help Me, I'm Falling	Hank Locklin

The first five hits all sold over 1,000,000 copies while the bottom five each spent more than five weeks atop the Country singles chart.

Johnny Cash, whose A Boy Named Sue *(complete with strategic bleep where he sang 'son of a bitch') was the bestselling Country single of the 1960s in the USA. It was recorded live at San Quentin prison.*

THE TOP 10 COUNTRY SINGLES OF THE 1970s IN THE UK

	Title	Artist
1	Lucille	Kenny Rogers
2	Stand By Your Man	Tammy Wynette
3	It's Four In The Morning	Faron Young
4	Rose Garden	Lynn Anderson
5	The Most Beautiful Girl	Charlie Rich
6	Convoy	C. W. McCall
7	If I Said You Had A Beautiful Body Would You Hold It Against Me	Bellamy Brothers
8	Honey Come Back	Glen Campbell
9	What I've Got In Mind	Billie Jo Spears
10	Don't It Make My Brown Eyes Blue	Crystal Gayle

THE TOP 10 COUNTRY SINGLES OF THE 1970s IN THE USA

	Title	Artist
1	Convoy	C. W. McCall
2	Rose Garden	Lynn Anderson
3	The Devil Went Down To Georgia	Charlie Daniels Band
4	Don't It Make My Brown Eyes Blue	Crystal Gayle
5	The Most Beautiful Girl	Charlie Rich
6	9 To 5	Dolly Parton
7	You Needed Me	Anne Murray
8	Thank God I'm A Country Boy	John Denver
9	Coward Of The County	Kenny Rogers
10	Here You Come Again	Dolly Parton

Of these million-selling discs, *Convoy* is perhaps best remembered by British music buyers. The lengthy Country CB rap about the travels of a convoy of juggernauts was a rare UK Country smash in 1976 when it hit No. 2.

THE TOP 10 COUNTRY SINGLES OF THE 1980s IN THE UK

	Title	Artist
1	Coward Of The County	Kenny Rogers
2	Islands In The Stream	Kenny Rogers and Dolly Parton
3	Teddy Bear	Red Sovine
4	Lady	Kenny Rogers
5	Angel Of The Morning	Juice Newton
6	9 To 5	Dolly Parton
7	Always On My Mind	Willie Nelson
8	The Wind Beneath My Wings	Lee Greenwood
9	I Love A Rainy Night	Eddie Rabbitt
10	Forever And Ever, Amen	Randy Tavis

Country music hits virtually disappeared from the UK chart in the 1980s – *Coward Of The County* was the only genre single to hit UK No. 1 in the entire decade, while none of the the bottom six titles even made the Top 40. Two classics lurk in this section, however: *Always On My Mind* (amazingly, Willie Nelson's only solo UK chart entry) and *Wind Beneath My Wings* which Bette Midler turned into a sizeable pop hit in 1989.

THE TOP 10 COUNTRY SINGLES OF THE 1980s IN THE USA

	Title	Artist
1	Islands In The Stream	Kenny Rogers and Dolly Parton
2	Elvira	Oakridge Boys
3	Drivin' My Life Away	Eddie Rabbitt
4	Lady	Kenny Rogers
5	Queen Of Hearts	Juice Newton
6	I Love A Rainy Night	Eddie Rabbitt
7	Lookin' For Love	Johnny Lee
8	Angel Of The Morning	Juice Newton
9	Theme From 'The Dukes Of Hazzard' (Good Ol' Boys)	Waylon Jennings
10	Swingin'	John Anderson

Number seven proved to be a big crossover hit single from the 1980 million-selling *Urban Cowboy* film soundtrack starring the unlikeliest Country cowboy, John Travolta.

THE TOP 10 COUNTRY SINGLES OF ALL TIME IN THE UK

	Title	Artist
1	I Love You Because	Jim Reeves
2	I Won't Forget You	Jim Reeves
3	Ruby (Don't Take Your Love To Town)	Kenny Rogers
4	King Of The Road	Roger Miller
5	Lucille	Kenny Rogers
6	Stand By Your Man	Tammy Wynette
7	Coward Of The County	Kenny Rogers
8	Distant Drums	Jim Reeves
9	Rose Marie	Slim Whitman
10	Give Me Your Word	Tennessee Ernie Ford

Even though *I Love You Because* only made UK No. 5, it is still the bestselling Country single ever in Britain, shifting over 750,000 copies in 1964 alone. Reeves has been by far the most popular Country artist in the UK, amassing 29 chart entries between 1960 and 1972 – although *Distant Drums* was his only chart-topper.

THE TOP 10 COUNTRY SINGLES OF ALL TIME IN THE USA

	Title	Artist
1	Islands In The Stream	Kenny Rogers and Dolly Parton
2	Elvira	Oakridge Boys
3	Achy Breaky Heart	Billy Ray Cyrus
4	Convoy	C. W. McCall
5	A Boy Named Sue	Johnny Cash
6	Rose Garden	Lynn Anderson
7	King Of The Road	Roger Miller
8	The Devil Went Down To Georgia	Charlie Daniels Band
9	Don't It Make My Brown Eyes Blue	Crystal Gayle
10	The Most Beautiful Girl	Charlie Rich

Numbers one and two are the only Country singles to sell more than 2,000,000 copies in the USA, though Billy Ray Cyrus' huge hit, *Achy Breaky Heart*, approached the same sales achievement in the summer of 1992. All of the other titles listed have sold over 1,000,000 copies.

THE TOP 10 SKA SINGLES OF ALL TIME IN THE UK

	Title	Artist
1	Ghost Town	Specials
2	The Special A.K.A. Live! (EP)	Specials
3	Do Nothing/Maggie's Farm	Specials
4	Mirror In The Bathroom	Beat
5	Gangsters	Specials AKA
6	One Step Beyond	Madness
7	Tears Of A Clown/Ranking Full Stop	Beat
8	Rat Race/Rude Boys Outa Jail	Specials
9	Too Nice To Talk To	Beat
10	On My Radio	Selecter

Although there were a handful of original ska hits in the late 1960s (notably Prince Buster's *Al Capone* and the Ethiopians' *Train To Skaville*), the commercial resurgence of ska around 1980, led by the Specials and the 2-Tone label, has proved to be its most dominant period. All of these Top 10 hits charted between 1979 and 1981.

THE TOP 10 COVER VERSIONS OF ALL TIME IN THE UK*

	Title	Original version	Cover version
1	Rivers Of Babylon	Melodians	Boney M
2	Mary's Boy Child	Harry Belafonte	Boney M
3	Tears	Rudy Vallee	Ken Dodd
4	I Will Always Love You	Dolly Parton	Whitney Houston
5	Release Me	Jimmy Dean	Engelbert Humperdinck
6	Green, Green Grass Of Home	Johnny Darrell	Tom Jones
7	I Remember You	Dorothy Lamour	Frank Ifield
8	Tainted Love	Gloria Jones	Soft Cell
9	I'd Like To Teach The World To Sing	Hillside Singers	New Seekers
10	Unchained Melody	Al Hibbler	Righteous Brothers

* Based on sales.

The top seven of these well-chosen cover versions were all million-sellers in the UK. Elvis Presley's *It's Now Or Never* and the Seekers' *The Carnival Is Over* are excluded from this list since they were radical adaptations of existing songs (the 1901 Neapolitan ballad *O Sole Mio* and the Russian folk song *Stenjka Ruzin* respectively) with newly written English lyrics.

THE TOP 10 DANCE SINGLES OF 1992 IN THE UK

	Title	Artist
1	I Will Always Love You	Whitney Houston
2	Rhythm Is A Dancer	Snap!
3	Please Don't Go	K.W.S.
4	End Of The Road	Boyz II Men
5	The Best Things In Life Are Free	Luther Vandross and Janet Jackson
6	I'm Gonna Get You	Bizarre Inc featuring Angie Brown
7	Ebeneezer Goode	Shamen
8	People Everyday	Arrested Development
9	Would I Lie To You?	Charles & Eddie
10	It's My Life	Dr Alban

Though it was taken from a dance-oriented album (the soundtrack from the film *The Bodyguard*), Whitney Houston's *I Will Always Love You* was actually a slow ballad, and probably only classifiable as dance if the definition includes end-of-the-evening smooches. Nevertheless, it sold just as hugely through dance/black music-oriented outlets as mainstream shops, hence its peak position. The Boyz II Men track was also a slow ballad; the rest of the 10 raised the tempo.

THE FIRST TOP 10 DISCO SINGLES CHART

	Title	Artist
1	Three Times A Lady	Commodores
2	Galaxy Of Love	Crown Heights Affair
3	British Hustle	Hi-Tension
4	Let The Music Play	Charles Earland
5	You Make Me Feel (Mighty Real)	Sylvester
6	Let's Start The Dance	Bohannon
7	Supernature	Cerrone
8	I Thought It Was You	Herbie Hancock
9	Hot Shot	Karen Young
10	Stuff Like That	Quincy Jones

A necessary by-product of the disco boom in the record industry in the mid-1970s, the first-ever UK Disco Chart appeared on 28 August 1978. It is still compiled today by MRIB, though the now dated monicker 'disco' has been replaced with 'dance'. It is somewhat ironic that the only soul ballad in this Top 10 should debut at No. 1.

THE TOP 10 RE-RELEASES OF ALL TIME IN THE UK

	Title	Artist	Original	Reissue
1	*Bohemian Rhapsody*	Queen	1975	1991
2	*Unchained Melody*	Righteous Brothers	1965	1990
3	*Imagine*	John Lennon	1975	1981
4	*Reet Petite*	Jackie Wilson	1957	1986
5	*Sacrifice*	Elton John	1989	1990
6	*Chi Mai*	Ennio Morricone	1978	1981
7	*Stand By Me*	Ben E. King	1961	1987
8	*He Ain't Heavy, He's My Brother*	Hollies	1969	1988
9	*Blue Velvet*	Bobby Vinton	1963	1990
10	*Holiday*	Madonna	1984	1985

Hit reissues are a fairly common phenomenon of the British record scene, while being virtually unknown in the United States. Of the 10 here, all were bigger sellers the second time around, with the exception of *Bohemian Rhapsody* (which nonetheless added 940,000 sales to the original release's 1,200,000). The Ennio Morricone and Bobby Vinton records had failed to chart at all on their original release.

THE TOP 10 SURFING SINGLES OF ALL TIME IN THE USA

	Title	Artist
1	*Wipe Out*	Surfaris
2	*Surf City*	Jan and Dean
3	*Surfin' USA*	Beach Boys
4	*Pipeline*	Chantays
5	*Surfer Girl*	Beach Boys
6	*Surfin' Bird*	Trashmen
7	*Surfin' Safari*	Beach Boys
8	*Ride The Wild Surf*	Jan and Dean
9	*Penetration*	Pyramids
10	*Surfer's Stomp*	Mar-Kets

Selling predominantly in the surf mecca of California in the early 1960s, nearly 30 surf-related singles made the national US chart. Although *Wipe Out* made only US No. 4 in August 1963 (whereas *Surf City* hit US No. 1 one month earlier) it re-charted to reach No. 11 in 1966, making it the most successful single of the genre. All 10 records were released between 1962 and 1964. Numbers one, four, nine and 10 are instrumentals.

THE FIRST TOP 10 UK HEAVY METAL SINGLES CHART*

	Title	Artist
1	*For Those About To Rock*	AC/DC
2	*Freebird*	Lynyrd Skynyrd
3	*Heat Of The Moment*	Asia
4	*You Keep Me Hangin' On*	Rods
5	*Crimson And Clover*	Joan Jett & The Blackhearts
6	*The Number Of The Beast*	Iron Maiden
7	*Rendezvous*	Tygers Of Pan Tang
8	*She Don't Fool Me*	Status Quo
9	*Fantasy*	Aldo Nova
10	*I Believe In You*	Y & T

* *Compiled by MRIB.*

Chart compilation pioneers MRIB produced the world's first heavy metal sales charts on 10 July 1982, which appeared in both *Sounds* and the specialist heavy metal publication, *Kerrang!*

THE TOP 10 HEAVY METAL SINGLES OF THE 1970s IN THE UK

	Title	Artist
1	*All Right Now*	Free
2	*Paranoid*	Black Sabbath
3	*School's Out*	Alice Cooper
4	*Down Down*	Status Quo
5	*Black Night*	Deep Purple
6	*Voodoo Chile*	Jimi Hendrix Experience
7	*Silver Machine*	Hawkwind
8	*Rockin' All Over The World*	Status Quo
9	*You Ain't Seen Nothin' Yet*	Bachman Turner Overdrive
10	*The Devil's Answer*	Atomic Rooster

Hawkwind's enduring metal anthem, *Silver Machine*, featuring the throaty vocals of future Motorhead founder Lemmy, in addition to hitting No. 3 in 1972, charted again in both 1978 and 1983. Status Quo's *Rockin' All Over The World*, in addition to being the opening song of the Live Aid spectacular in July 1985, was re-cut by the band in 1988 as *Running All Over The World*, helping to raise funds for the same charity.

THE TOP 10 HEAVY METAL SINGLES OF THE 1980s IN THE UK

	Title	Artist
1	Eye Of The Tiger	Survivor
2	The Final Countdown	Europe
3	I Want To Know What Love Is	Foreigner
4	Kayleigh	Marillion
5	In The Army Now	Status Quo
6	Alone	Heart
7	Livin' On A Prayer	Bon Jovi
8	Poison	Alice Cooper
9	What You're Proposing	Status Quo
10	Gimme All Your Lovin'	ZZ Top

UK No. 1 hits by heavy metal acts are extremely rare – only the top three on this list hit the top spot during the decade and so far in the 1990s only Iron Maiden has held pole position with *Bring Your Daughter...To The Slaughter*. (Although the band notched up 23 chart hits during the 1980s, few of their singles spent more than four to five weeks on the survey and hence fail to make this list.) Status Quo are Britain's most successful and enduring hard rock act: between 1970 and 1990 the band amassed 35 Top 30 hits.

THE TOP 10 HEAVY METAL SINGLES OF ALL TIME IN THE UK

	Title	Artist
1	Eye Of The Tiger	Survivor
2	The Final Countdown	Europe
3	I Want To Know What Love Is	Foreigner
4	All Right Now	Free
5	Paranoid	Black Sabbath
6	School's Out	Alice Cooper
7	Down Down	Status Quo
8	Black Night	Deep Purple
9	Voodoo Chile	Jimi Hendrix Experience
10	Silver Machine	Hawkwind

Having sold over 750,000 copies in the UK, Survivor's *Eye Of The Tiger* benefited greatly from its exposure in the *Rocky III* movie. *All Right Now* has charted on four further occasions since originally hitting UK No. 2 in 1970, twice on the *Free* EP in 1978 and 1982, re-charting in its own right in 1973 and yet again in 1991 – thanks to its use in a Wrigley chewing gum commercial – reaching UK No. 8. In addition to hitting UK No. 1 in 1970, Jimi Hendrix Experience's *Voodoo Chile* also sold as one of three tracks on the 1990 No. 52 *All Along The Watchtower* EP.

THE TOP 10 HEAVY METAL SINGLES OF 1992 IN THE UK

	Title	Artist
1	Let's Get Rocked	Def Leppard
2	Keep The Faith	Bon Jovi
3	Come As You Are	Nirvana
4	November Rain	Guns N' Roses
5	Be Quick Or Be Dead	Iron Maiden
6	To Be With You	Mr Big
7	Everything About You	Ugly Kid Joe
8	Bohemian Rhapsody/These Are The Days Of Our Lives	Queen
9	Knockin' On Heaven's Door	Guns N' Roses
10	Highway To Hell (Live)	AC/DC

The traditional big names of heavy metal, as in the genre's album category, were those who, by and large, saw their singles find general chart success, with few of the vast array of second-league metallurgists having sufficiently large fan bases to expand their sales out of the specialist bracket – their problem being that there are very few airplay outlets for heavy rock in the UK. Relative newcomers Mr Big, Nirvana and Ugly Kid Joe (all of them American) did, however, break through with particularly commercial offerings.

THE TOP 10 HEAVY METAL SINGLES OF THE 1970s IN THE USA

	Title	Artist
1	Babe	Styx
2	You Ain't Seen Nothin' Yet	Bachman Turner Overdrive
3	Whole Lotta Love	Led Zeppelin
4	Hot Blooded	Foreigner
5	Double Vision	Foreigner
6	Dust In The Wind	Kansas
7	Smoke On The Water	Deep Purple
8	Smokin' In The Boy's Room	Brownsville Station
9	I Want You To Want Me	Cheap Trick
10	Beth/Detroit Rock City	Kiss

Whole Lotta Love remains Led Zeppelin's only million-selling single: if the band had ever released *Stairway To Heaven* – still its most popular cut aired on American radio – as a single, it would almost certainly top both this and the all-time bestselling lists.

THE TOP 10 HEAVY METAL SINGLES OF THE 1980s IN THE USA

	Title	Artist
1	Eye Of The Tiger	Survivor
2	Keep On Loving You	REO Speedwagon
3	I Love Rock 'n' Roll	Joan Jett & The Blackhearts
4	Sweet Child O' Mine	Guns N' Roses
5	I Want To Know What Love Is	Foreigner
6	Jump	Van Halen
7	When I'm With You	Sheriff
8	Waiting For A Girl Like You	Foreigner
9	Livin' On A Prayer	Bon Jovi
10	Can't Fight This Feeling	REO Speedwagon

Sheriff's *When I'm With You* was originally released in 1983, when it peaked at US No. 61, but its reissue in 1988 resulted in a chart-topper for this Canadian rock quintet. It is interesting to note that half of this Top 10 (numbers two, five, seven, eight and 10) are rock ballads, a device often used by hard rock acts to attract a wider audience.

THE TOP 10 HEAVY METAL SINGLES OF ALL TIME IN THE USA

	Title	Artist
1	Eye Of The Tiger	Survivor
2	Keep On Loving You	REO Speedwagon
3	I Love Rock 'n' Roll	Joan Jett & The Blackhearts
4	Sweet Child O' Mine	Guns N' Roses
5	I Want To Know What Love Is	Foreigner
6	Jump	Van Halen
7	Babe	Styx
8	When I'm With You	Sheriff
9	You Ain't Seen Nothin' Yet	Bachman Turner Overdrive
10	Waiting For A Girl Like You	Foreigner

Eye Of The Tiger, which sold 2,000,000 copies, benefited not least from its exposure in the *Rocky III* movie, while the million-selling *You Ain't Seen Nothin' Yet* has continued to sell since hitting US No. 1 in 1974, thanks to President Reagan's repeated use of the phrase and song at Republican political conventions during the 1980s. Despite both entries being ballads, Foreigner's huge popularity as a hard rock act has been consistent since their chart debut in 1977.

THE TOP 10 HEAVY METAL SINGLES OF 1992 IN THE USA

	Title	Artist
1	Smells Like Teen Spirit	Nirvana
2	Under The Bridge	Red Hot Chili Peppers
3	November Rain	Guns N' Roses
4	To Be With You	Mr Big
5	Everything About You	Ugly Kid Joe
6	Don't Cry	Guns N' Roses
7	Can't Stop This Thing We Started	Bryan Adams
8	Let's Get Rocked	Def Leppard
9	The Unforgiven	Metallica
10	Have You Ever Needed Someone So Bad	Def Leppard

Seattle grunge-merchants Nirvana had the bestselling heavy metal single in the USA in 1992 with Smells Like Teen Spirit.

THE FIRST TOP 10 UK PUNK SINGLES CHART*

	Title	Artist
1	Mutant Rock	Meteors
2	Warriors	Blitz
3	Have You Got 10p (EP)	Ejected
4	Bleed For Me	Dead Kennedys
5	Religious Wars	Subhumans
6	Rising From The Dread	UK Decay
7	Run Like Hell	Peter & The Test Tube Babies
8	Suicide Bag	Action Pact
9	Beasts	Sex Gang Children
10	Gentle Murder	Mayhem

* Compiled by MRIB.

THE TOP 10 FOREIGN-LANGUAGE SINGLES IN THE UK

	Title	Artist	Language
1	Je T'aime...Moi Non Plus	Jane Birkin and Serge Gainsbourg	French
2	Rock Me Amadeus	Falco	German
3	Begin The Beguine	Julio Iglesias	Spanish
4	Chanson D'Amour	Manhattan Transfer	French
5	La Bamba	Los Lobos	Spanish
6	Come Prima/Volare	Marino Marini	Italian
7	Nessun Dorma	Luciano Pavarotti	Italian
8	Joe Le Taxi	Vanessa Paradis	French
9	Lambada	Kaoma	Portuguese
10	Dominique	Singing Nun	French

Although foreign-language hits are extremely rare in the UK (as in all English-speaking markets), the top five of this list nevertheless all reached UK No. 1, while the remainder all made the Top 10.

Although the British Punk scene was most vibrant in the late 1970s, it was not until 25 September 1982 that the first official Punk rankings for singles and albums were published (in *Sounds* and the strictly Punk publication, *Noise*). Punk remained a viable genre for a number of small independent labels until 1985 when the anger finally died down. Interesting to note that at No. 11 on the debut Punk singles chart was *Fuck The Tories*, a seminal Punk title performed by the Riot Squad.

Serge Gainsbourg and Jane Birkin, whose Je T'aime...Moi Non Plus *became the bestselling foreign language single in the UK, despite its ban by the BBC.*

THE FIRST INDIE TOP 10 SINGLES CHART

	Title	Artist	Label
1	Where's Captain Kirk?	Spizzenergi	Rough Trade
2	Daytrip To Bangor	Fiddler's Dram	Dingles
3	Mind Your Own Business	Delta Five	Rough Trade
4	White Mice	Mo-Dettes	Mode
5	California Uber Alles	Dead Kennedys	Fast
6	Transmission	Joy Division	Factory
7	Earcom Three (EP)	Various	Fast
8	We Are All Prostitutes	Pop Group	Rough Trade
9	Kamikaze	Boys	Safari
10	Silent Command	Cabaret Voltaire	Rough Trade

Now a mainstay of the British music scene, the independent chart made its first appearance in February 1980. Still compiled on a weekly basis by MRIB, the chart was initiated as a post-Punk reaction that saw hundreds of small independent record companies emerge to battle it out with the majors – with increasing success throughout the 1980s. Arguments continue to rage over what constitutes an 'indie', but the most widely accepted definition is one of default: that it is a label *not* distributed by one of the 'Big Six' record companies (CBS, EMI, PRT [now defunct], Polygram, RCA and WEA).

THE TOP 10 R & B SINGLES OF 1992 IN THE USA

	Title	Artist
1	I Will Always Love You	Whitney Houston
2	Baby Got Back	Sir Mix-A-Lot
3	End Of The Road	Boyz II Men
4	Jump	Kris Kross
5	Rump Shaker	Wreckx-N-Effect
6	Too Legit To Quit	Hammer
7	Baby-Baby-Baby	TLC
8	Ain't 2 Proud 2 Beg	TLC
9	Come And Talk To Me	Jodeci
10	Black Or White	Michael Jackson

Aside from Whitney Houston's multi-million-selling soul rendition of *I Will Always Love You*, rap rules the R & B roost, featuring in each of the remaining nine singles (even Michael Jackson's *Black Or White*, which includes a rapping bridge).

THE TOP 10 INDIE SINGLES OF ALL TIME IN THE UK

	Title	Artist	Label
1	Blue Monday	New Order	Factory
2	Love Will Tear Us Apart	Joy Division	Factory
3	This Charming Man	Smiths	Rough Trade
4	What The World Is Waiting For/Fools Gold	Stone Roses	Silvertone
5	Pump Up The Volume	M/A/R/R/S	4AD
6	World In Motion	Englandneworder	Factory
7	Only You	Yazoo	Mute
8	3 a.m. Eternal	KLF featuring The Children Of The Revolution	KLF Comms.
9	All Together Now	Farm	Produce
10	Step On	Happy Mondays	Factory

All of these titles hit No. 1 on the MRIB indie chart – the first four singles all staking a residence of more than one year on the survey, while *Blue Monday* was a chart fixture for almost five years between 1983 and 1988, when it was formally reissued (as a remix) by Factory and even hit No. 3 on the UK pop listing, subsequently becoming the bestselling 12″ single of all time. A large number of pop/dance crossover hits (from the likes of PWL's Kylie Minogue and Jason Donovan and Mute's Erasure, notably their *Abba-esque* EP) have always performed well on the indie survey, but it is the chart achievements of the more alternative indie acts that have dominated the indie scene over the past decade and help them make this all-time list.

THE TOP 10 KARAOKE TUNES

1	You've Lost That Lovin' Feelin'
2	I Will Survive
3	Like A Virgin
4	Summer Nights
5	Love Shack
6	New York, New York
7	Pretty Woman
8	Should I Stay Or Should I Go
9	It's Not Unusual
10	My Way

Source: Bellows Karaoke/Peter Frailish.

THE TOP 10 INSTRUMENTAL SINGLES OF ALL TIME IN THE UK

	Title	Artist
1	Stranger On The Shore	Mr Acker Bilk
2	Eye Level	Simon Park Orchestra
3	Telstar	Tornados
4	The Harry Lime (Third Man) Theme	Anton Karas
5	Amazing Grace	Royal Scots Dragoon Guards Band
6	Chi Mai	Ennio Morricone
7	Wonderful Land	Shadows
8	Apache	Shadows
9	Albatross	Fleetwood Mac
10	Mouldy Old Dough	Lieutenant Pigeon

If this Top 10 reveals anything, it is that non-vocal hits are more likely to be found in the 'middle-of-the-road' sector than in Rock 'n' Roll. Most of these pieces are the equivalent of ballads, with only *Apache*, possibly *Telstar*, and just possibly *Mouldy Old Dough* – which is really a novelty instrumental – qualifying as rock music. The Acker Bilk and Simon Park entries were both UK million-sellers, as noted elsewhere.

Though released in 1961, Stranger On The Shore *by Acker Bilk (originally titled* Jenny *after Bilk's daughter) remains the bestselling instrumental single of all time in the UK.*

THE TOP 10 JUKEBOX SINGLES OF ALL TIME IN THE USA*

	Title	Artist	Year
1	Crazy	Patsy Cline	1962
2	Old Time Rock 'n' Roll	Bob Seger	1979
3	Hound Dog/Don't Be Cruel	Elvis Presley	1956
4	I Heard It Through The Grapevine	Marvin Gaye	1968
5	Mack The Knife	Bobby Darin	1959
6	Rock Around The Clock	Bill Haley & His Comets	1955
7	Light My Fire	Doors	1967
8	(Sittin' On) The Dock Of The Bay	Otis Redding	1968
9	My Girl	Temptations	1965
10	New York, New York	Frank Sinatra	1980

* To October 1992.

This list was compiled by the Amusement & Music Operators Association, whose members service and operate over 250,000 jukeboxes in the USA, and is based on the estimated popularity of jukebox singles from 1950 to the present day. The list is updated every three years: 1989's chart-topper was the double A-side *Hound Dog/Don't Be Cruel*, while the Righteous Brothers' *Unchained Melody* was the highest new entry into the Top 40 in 1992 (at No. 12), due, not least, to its rebirth as the featured song in the hit movie *Ghost*.

THE TOP 10 SINGLES BY SPORTS TEAMS IN THE UK

	Title	Team	Year
1	Back Home	England World Cup Squad	1970
2	World In Motion	Englandneworder	1990
3	This Time We'll Get It Right	England World Cup Squad	1982
4	Anfield Rap (Red Machine In Full Effect)	Liverpool FC	1988
5	We Have A Dream	Scotland World Cup Squad	1982
6	Ole Ola (Muhler Brasileira)	Rod Stewart with Scotland World Cup Squad	1978
7	Ossie's Dream (Spurs Are On Their Way To Wembley)	Tottenham Hotspur FC	1981
8	Blue Is The Colour	Chelsea FC	1972
9	Snooker Loopy	Matchroom Mob with Chas & Dave	1986
10	Leeds United	Leeds United FC	1972

All these singles made the UK Top 10, and the first two were chart-topping hits. Some of the sportsmen (none of the records feature women) received professional help from the likes of New Order and Rod Stewart, while Chas & Dave, who bolstered the only non-football entry (by the Matchroom Mob of snooker professionals), also had an uncredited appearance on the Spurs single at number seven.

THE TOP 10 ONE-HIT WONDERS OF ALL TIME IN THE UK

	Title	Artist	Year
1	Eye Level	Simon Park Orchestra	1973
2	Sugar Sugar	Archies	1969
3	Grandad	Clive Dunn	1971
4	Shaddap You Face	Joe Dolce	1981
5	There's No One Quite Like Grandma	St Winifred's School Choir	1980
6	One Day At A Time	Lena Martell	1979
7	Move Closer	Phyllis Nelson	1985
8	Wand'rin' Star	Lee Marvin	1970
9	Spirit In The Sky	Norman Greenbaum	1970
10	First Time	Robin Beck	1988

These are all singles that were No. 1 hits in the UK, but which the artist utterly failed to follow with a record in the charts at any position. It is actually quite difficult to have a hit which (as in the case of all the above) sells more than 500,000 copies, and then fail to interest even a few thousand people in something with theoretically similar appeal, but clearly it can be done!

THE TOP 10 ONE-HIT WONDERS OF ALL TIME IN THE USA

	Title	Artist
1	We Are The World	USA For Africa
2	Don't Worry Be Happy	Bobby McFerrin
3	Pop Muzik	M
4	In The Year 2525 (Exordium and Terminus)	Zager & Evans
5	Miami Vice (theme)	Jan Hammer
6	Little Star	Elegants
7	Alley-Oop	Hollywood Argyles
8	He's Got The Whole World (In His Hands)	Laurie London
9	Moonglow (theme from Picnic)	Morris Stoloff
10	Get A Job	Silhouettes

All of these acts hit US No. 1 with their only American chart appearance but never followed up with any other pop chart disc. The charity ensemble USA For Africa's only single release is by far the most successful one-hit wonder, with over 4,000,000 copies sold, while numbers two to four all sold in excess of 1,000,000 – earning the artists enough to retire without another chart appearance.

10 BRITISH ONE-HIT WONDERS IN THE USA

	Title	Artist	Year
1	My Boomerang Won't Come Back	Charlie Drake	1962
2	Michelle	David and Jonathan	1966
3	Gimme Dat Ding	Pipkins	1970
4	Whole Lotta Love	C.C.S.	1971
5	Hold Your Head Up	Argent	1972
6	You're A Lady	Peter Skellern	1972
7	Tubular Bells (theme from The Exorcist)	Mike Oldfield	1974
8	Sugar Baby Love	Rubettes	1974
9	The Last Farewell	Roger Whittaker	1975
10	Jeans On	David Dundas	1976

Although all these acts had additional chart records in the UK, these hit singles remained their only successes across the pond.

10 AMERICAN ONE-HIT WONDERS IN THE UK

	Title	Artist	Year
1	The Lion Sleeps Tonight	Tokens	1961
2	You Don't Know What You've Got	Ral Donner	1961
3	Shame Shame Shame	Jimmy Reed	1964
4	Louie Louie	Kingsmen	1964
5	Step By Step	Joe Simon	1973
6	Annie's Song	John Denver	1975
7	First Impressions	Impressions	1975
8	Angie Baby	Helen Reddy	1975
9	Who'd She Coo	Ohio Players	1976
10	Stay	Jackson Browne	1978

Never again did any of these American artists find UK chart singles success, not even John Denver who landed a number of highly popular chart albums and even hit UK No. 1 with Annie's Song.

THE TOP 10 POSTHUMOUS SINGLES IN THE UK

	Title	Artist	Died	Hit year
1	Imagine	John Lennon	1980	1981
2	Reet Petite	Jackie Wilson	1984	1986
3	It Doesn't Matter Anymore	Buddy Holly	1959	1959
4	Woman	John Lennon	1980	1981
5	Way Down	Elvis Presley	1977	1977
6	I Won't Forget You	Jim Reeves	1964	1964
7	Distant Drums	Jim Reeves	1964	1966
8	Three Steps To Heaven	Eddie Cochran	1960	1960
9	Voodoo Chile	Jimi Hendrix	1970	1970
10	The Trail Of The Lonesome Pine	Laurel & Hardy	1965/ 1957	1975

Jackie Wilson's *Reet Petite* had originally been a chart hit early in his career during the 1950s, but it was the posthumous 1986 UK reissue which saw by far the greater success. The same applied to *Imagine*, which had been a more moderate hit for John Lennon when released in 1975. Excluded from this list is the 1991 reissue of Queen's *Bohemian Rhapsody*, which would be at the top if it were included: since Queen continued to exist as a group after the death of singer Freddie Mercury, the release was not strictly posthumous.

THE TOP 10 FEMALE GROUPS OF ALL TIME IN THE UK*

	Group	No. 1	Top 10	Top 20
1	Supremes	1	13	17
2	Bananarama	—	9	14
3	Three Degrees	1	5	7
4	Sister Sledge	1	4	7
5	Nolans	—	3	7
6	Bangles	1	3	5
7	Mel & Kim	—	4	4
8	Salt 'n' Pepa	—	3	4
9	Pointer Sisters	—	2	5
10	Beverley Sisters	—	2	4

* To 31 December 1992. Ranked according to total number of hits.

The Supremes also had three other Top 20 hits which have not been included because they were recorded in partnership with Motown male groups Four Tops and Temptations. However, Bananarama's charity revival of *Help!*, shared with comediennes Dawn French and Jennifer Saunders, has been included since all the participants are female.

NUMBERS QUIZ

1 Which group dialled *5-7-0-5* in 1978?

2 Who flew *Eight Miles High* in 1966?

3 How many ways did Paul Simon discover to leave your lover?

4 Who hit *Eighteen With A Bullet*?

5 Who thought that *Two Out Of Three Ain't Bad*?

6 With how many *Guns* did the Alarm shoot to fame in 1983?

7 Which group sailed on the *Seven Seas Of Rhye* for their debut hit?

8 Whose phone number was *634 5789*?

9 Which group scored with an album and a hit single titled *The Number Of The Beast*?

10 Which Minneapolis artist only uses the numerical characters '2' and '4' in place of words in his song titles?

THE 10 FEMALE SINGERS WITH THE MOST TOP 10 HITS IN THE USA AND UK*

	Artist	Hits
1	Madonna	30
2	Diana Ross (including one duet each with Marvin Gaye and Lionel Richie)	22
3=	Aretha Franklin (including one duet each with George Michael and the Eurythmics)	18
3=	Olivia Newton-John (including two duets with John Travolta and one with ELO)	18
3=	Donna Summer (including one duet with Barbra Streisand)	18
6	Connie Francis	17
7=	Brenda Lee	16
7=	Kylie Minogue (including one duet with Jason Donovan, and one with Keith Washington)	16
9=	Petula Clark	14
9=	Whitney Houston	14

* To 31 December 1992.

The hitmaking careers of some of these artists have either slowed down or ceased altogether in recent years. Only Madonna, Kylie Minogue, Diana Ross and Whitney Houston, of those listed, have had Top 10 hits so far in the 1990s, and Ms Ciccone seems likely to further widen the gap between herself and the rest of the field as the decade progresses.

THE FIRST TOP 10 UK RAP SINGLES CHART*

	Title	Artist
1	The Boomin' System	L.L. Cool J. featuring Uncle J.
2	Gangsta Gangsta	N.W.A.
3	Simba Groove/Cult Of Snap	Hi Power
4	Bonita Applebum	A Tribe Called Quest
5	Raise (63 Steps To Heaven)	Bocca Juniors
6	Superfly 1990	Curtis Mayfield & Ice T
7	Amerikkka's Most Wanted	Ice Cube
8	Steppin' To The A.M.	3rd Bass
9	100 Miles And Runnin'	N.W.A.
10	U Can't Touch This	MC Hammer

*Compiled by MRIB.

Regarded by most as a specialist, almost novelty musical fad until the late 1980s, rap simply refused to go away and has become a fully fledged and highly profitable market force. While a number of ad hoc and regional hip-hop/rap charts appeared during the 1980s, it wasn't until the advent of London's Kiss FM radio station in 1990 that MRIB began compiling, on 8 September 1990, the first UK rap singles survey for weekly broadcast on the ground-breaking dance-oriented station.

THE TOP 10 RAP SINGLES OF ALL TIME IN THE UK

	Title	Artist
1	Ice Ice Baby	Vanilla Ice
2	White Lines (Don't Don't Do It)	Grandmaster Flash & Melle Mel
3	Do The Bartman	Simpsons
4	Push It	Salt 'n' Pepa
5	Let's Talk About Sex	Salt 'n' Pepa
6	The Twist (Yo Twist)	Fat Boys with Chubby Checker
7	Wipe Out	Fat Boys featuring The Beach Boys
8	U Can't Touch This	MC Hammer
9	Rapper's Delight	Sugarhill Gang
10	Twist And Shout	Salt 'n' Pepa

Grandmaster Flash's anti-cocaine message charted on four separate occasions between 1983 and 1985, spending 43 weeks on the survey, the longest-charting rap single ever. It was released on the ground-breaking Sugarhill label which was responsible for starting the commercial rap revolution in the 1970s, not least with *Rapper's Delight*, the first disc of the genre to make the UK Top 5.

The writing on the wall: L.L. Cool J. headed the first-ever UK rap singles chart.

THE TOP 10 RAP SINGLES OF ALL TIME IN THE USA

	Title	Artist
1	Wild Thing	Tone Loc
2	Baby Got Back	Sir Mix-A-Lot
3	Jump	Kris Kross
4	Funky Cold Medina	Tone Loc
5	Ice Ice Baby	Vanilla Ice
6	Bust A Move	Young MC
7	Parents Just Don't Understand	DJ Jazzy Jeff & The Fresh Prince
8	Push It	Salt 'n' Pepa
9	It Takes Two	Rob Base & DJ E-Z Rock
10	The Breaks (Part 1)	Kurtis Blow

Young MC (Marvin Young), in addition to his appearance at number six in the list, also co-wrote numbers one and four, making him the most successful rap writer to date. Kurtis Blow's *The Breaks*, released in 1980, was the first rap single to sell over 1,000,000 copies and remains a seminal release in the history of the genre. Rap currently dominates the American music scene, with the 1992 releases at numbers two and three both shifting over 2,000,000 units each. (This list does not include marginal mainly pop-crossover acts who include rapping in their songs, such as New Kids On The Block, Technotronic or PM Dawn).

THE TOP 10 RAP SINGLES OF 1992 IN THE USA

	Title	Artist
1	Baby Got Back	Sir Mix-A-Lot
2	Jump	Kris Kross
3	Rump Shaker	Wreckx-N-Effect
4	Jump Around	House Of Pain
5	Too Legit To Quit	Hammer
6	Baby-Baby-Baby	TLC
7	Ain't 2 Proud 2 Beg	TLC
8	Come And Talk To Me	Jodeci
9	Warm It Up	Kris Kross
10	Addams Groove	Hammer

Numbers one and three were spurred to multi-million sales by concentrating their lyrics (and accompanying video clips) on the female posterior.

THE TOP 10 REGGAE SINGLES OF ALL TIME IN THE UK

	Title	Artist
1	*Israelites*	Desmond Dekker & The Aces
2	*I Don't Wanna Dance*	Eddy Grant
3	*Pass The Dutchie*	Musical Youth
4	*Red Red Wine*	UB40
5	*I Want To Wake Up With You*	Boris Gardiner
6	*Double Barrel*	Dave & Ansil Collins
7	*Don't Turn Around*	Aswad
8	*Everything I Own*	Ken Boothe
9	*Tears On My Pillow*	Johnny Nash
10	*Up Town Top Ranking*	Althia & Donna

Although he is the most successful reggae artist of all time, Bob Marley never achieved a UK No. 1 single success – his biggest hit, *Buffalo Soldier,* stopped at No. 4 in 1983, while his most fondly remembered cut, *No Woman No Cry,* peaked at No. 8. In contrast, all the singles on this list hit the top spot – *Israelites* also hitting No. 10 upon its reissue in 1975. Just missing the list is the first reggae UK chart-topper of the 1990s, Shaggy's *O Carolina,* a 1993 dancehall smash.

THE TOP 10 REGGAE SINGLES OF 1992 IN THE UK

	Title	Artist
1	*Searchin'*	China Black
2	*Boom By By*	Buju Banton
3	*Gal Wine*	Chakademus/Pliers
4	*Crying*	Neville Morrison
5	*When I See You Smile*	Singing Sweet
6	*Ah Who Say Me Done*	Cutty Ranks
7	*Murder Is A Crime*	Chakademus/Pliers
8	*No Substitute Lover*	Half Pint
9	*Heat*	General Levy
10	*To Be Poor Is A Crime*	Freddie McGregor

In contrast to the late 1970s and early 1980s, the reggae market today in Britain tends to be almost completely isolationist, with a crossover to wider or national success by a reggae single being very rare indeed. The genre can generate controversy, however: second-placed Buju Banton's extremely misogynistic single brought him into bitter conflict with feminist groups, the artist even receiving death threats at the height of the furore.

THE TOP 10 REGGAE SINGLES OF ALL TIME IN THE USA

	Title	Artist
1	*Informer*	Snow
2	*Red Red Wine*	UB40
3	*I Can See Clearly Now*	Johnny Nash
4	*Electric Avenue*	Eddy Grant
5	*The Way You Do The Things You Do*	UB40
6	*Here I Am (Come And Take Me)*	UB40
7	*Hold Me Tight*	Johnny Nash
8	*Israelites*	Desmond Dekker & The Aces
9	*Pass The Dutchie*	Musical Youth
10	*Stir It Up*	Johnny Nash

Snow's *Informer* became the first platinum certified reggae single in US chart history in March 1993 when its sales passed the million mark. *Red Red Wine* spent 40 weeks on the US chart: 15 on its first chart run to No. 34, the remainder on its way to becoming only the second reggae chart-topping single ever (behind *I Can See Clearly Now*). Bob Marley has sold more records since his death than before it, but has never cracked the Top 50 (though he did write *Stir It Up* for Johnny Nash). His son Ziggy, however, made US No. 39 with *Tomorrow People* in 1988.

Guyana-born Eddy Grant's releases feature strongly among the bestselling reggae singles of all time.

THE TOP 10 ABBA SINGLES IN THE UK

	Title	Year
1	Dancing Queen	1976
2	Knowing Me, Knowing You	1977
3	Fernando	1976
4	Super Trouper	1980
5	The Name Of The Game	1977
6	Take A Chance On Me	1978
7	Mamma Mia	1975
8	Money Money Money	1976
9	The Winner Takes It All	1980
10	Waterloo	1974

Abba are one of the biggest singles-selling groups ever in the UK. Nine of these 10 records reached No. 1, and the top eight all sold in excess of 500,000 copies each, which represents amazing consistency at a very high level. Their last year together (1982) showed a notable sales decline, at which point they split to pursue solo careers (Agnetha Fälskog and Anni-Frid 'Frida' Lyngstad) or wider musical projects such as the stage show Chess (Björn Ulvaeus and Benny Andersson).

THE TOP 10 BANANARAMA SINGLES IN THE UK

	Title	Year
1	Love In The First Degree	1987
2	Robert De Niro's Waiting	1984
3	Help!	1989
4	Cruel Summer	1983/1989
5	Shy Boy	1983
6	It Ain't What You Do, It's The Way That You Do It	1982
7	Really Saying Something	1982
8	Na Na Hey Hey Kiss Him Goodbye	1983
9	Venus	1986
10	I Want You Back	1988

Help!, co-credited to Bananarama and La Na Nee Nee Noo Noo (comediennes Dawn French and Jennifer Saunders), was a novelty version of the Beatles oldie for the 1989 Comic Relief appeal. Both It Ain't What You Do and Really Saying Something were collaborations between the group and male trio Fun Boy Three, and both of these singles also carried co-credits (the first was on Fun Boy Three's label, and listed them first).

THE TOP 10 BEACH BOYS SINGLES IN THE UK

	Title	Year
1	Good Vibrations	1966
2	Sloop John B	1966
3	God Only Knows	1966
4	Do It Again	1968
5	Cottonfields	1970
6	I Get Around	1964
7	Then I Kissed Her	1967
8	Barbara Ann	1966
9	Break Away	1969
10	Lady Lynda	1979

Good Vibrations was also a Top 20 hit when reissued a decade after its initial success, cementing its status as the Beach Boys' biggest UK seller by far. By contrast, the group's belated all-time United States top-seller, 1988's Kokomo, was only a middling British success, and registers nowhere near the Top 10 listing. The group were also co-vocalists on the Fat Boys' revival of Wipe Out in 1987; this single would appear at number eight if included here.

The three singles on Polydor originated from the group's pre-Parlophone days and were recorded in Hamburg with orchestra leader Bert Kaempfert.

THE FIRST 10 BEATLES SINGLES RELEASED IN THE UK

	Title	Label	Cat. no.
1	My Bonnie/The Saints*	Polydor	NH 66-833
2	Love Me Do/P.S. I Love You	Parlophone	R 4949
3	Please Please Me/Ask Me Why	Parlophone	R 4983
4	From Me To You/Thank You Girl	Parlophone	R 5015
5	She Loves You/I'll Get You	Parlophone	R 5055
6	I Want To Hold Your Hand/This Boy	Parlophone	R 5084
7	Why/Cry For A Shadow	Polydor	NH 52-275
8	Can't Buy Me Love/You Can't Do That	Parlophone	R 5114
9	Ain't She Sweet/If You Love Me Baby	Polydor	NH 52-317
10	A Hard Day's Night/Things We Said Today	Parlophone	R 5160

* Credited to Tony Sheridan and The Beatles, released in Germany in August 1961 and in the UK in January 1962.

THE 10 BEATLES SINGLES THAT STAYED LONGEST IN THE UK CHARTS

	Title	Year	Weeks in charts
1	She Loves You	1963–64	33
2	Twist And Shout (EP)	1963–64	32
3	I Want To Hold Your Hand	1963–64	22
4	From Me To You	1963	21
5	The Beatles' Hits (EP)	1963–64	19
6=	Love Me Do	1962–63	18
6=	Please Please Me	1963	18
8	Get Back	1969	17
9	Hey Jude	1968	16
10	Can't Buy Me Love	1964	15

These totals are based on residence in the UK Top 50 singles charts, and all refer to the original releases of these records in the 1960s; additional chart weeks acquired when EMI systematically reissued each Beatles single on its 20th anniversary in the 1980s have not been included.

THE 10 LEAST SUCCESSFUL BEATLES SINGLES IN THE UK

	Title	Year	Highest chart position
1	Sweet Georgia Brown (with Tony Sheridan)	1964	–
2	Cry For A Shadow	1964	–
3	If I Fell	1964	–
4	Twist And Shout (Live)	1977	–
5	Sgt Pepper's Lonely Hearts Club Band	1978	63
6	My Bonnie (with Tony Sheridan)	1963	48
7	Ain't She Sweet	1964	29
8	Back In The USSR	1976	19
9	Love Me Do (original release)	1962	17
10	Beatles Movie Medley	1982	10

The order of uncharted singles 1–4 is based on comparative sales.

Even the Beatles had releases which people did not buy – usually for good reasons. Most of these 10 singles are cash-ins utilizing German-recorded tracks from the group's pre-EMI days (numbers one, two, four, six and seven on the list) or LP tracks issued as singles long after they had disbanded (numbers five, eight and 10). If I Fell was an EMI export pressing which could be bought in British shops, though was given no publicity, while Love Me Do eventually became a Top 5 hit when it was reissued on its own 20th anniversary. Ironically, the most obscure of the items in the list are now high-value collectors' items because of their very obscurity and lack of success.

10 PAUL McCARTNEY HITS THAT PEAKED AT DIFFERENT POSITIONS IN THE UK TOP 10

	Title	Artist	Peak position
1	Mull Of Kintyre/Girl's School	Wings	1
2	Another Day	Paul McCartney	2
3	Band On The Run	Paul McCartney & Wings	3
4	Love Me Do	Beatles	4*
5	Hi Hi Hi/C Moon	Paul McCartney	5
6	Listen To What The Man Said	Wings	6
7	Jet	Paul McCartney & Wings	7
8	The Girl Is Mine	Michael Jackson & Paul McCartney	8
9	Waterfalls	Paul McCartney	9
10	Once Upon A Long Ago	Paul McCartney	10

* Peak position of 1982 re-entry.

McCartney has achieved a feat which eluded the Beatles, mainly because they were so successful that the great majority of their original releases all peaked at No. 1. Cliff Richard, despite logging more than 50 Top 10 hits, has peaked at every position except No. 5, meaning that McCartney is the only British performer who can truly be called a 'Top 10 artist'.

THE 10 MOST COVERED BEATLES SONGS

	Title	Written
1	Yesterday	1965
2	Something	1969
3	Eleanor Rigby	1966
4	Let It Be	1969
5	Hey Jude	1968
6	The Fool On The Hill	1967
7	The Long And Winding Road	1969
8	Michelle·	1965
9	With A Little Help From My Friends	1967
10	Day Tripper	1965

Yesterday is one of the most covered songs of all time, with the number of recorded versions now in four figures. Although most of these songs are Lennon/McCartney compositions, the number two song, *Something*, was written by George Harrison.

Kate Bush's first single Wuthering Heights *is also still her all-time bestseller, though she apparently grew sufficiently dissatisfied by it to re-record her vocal part for its later appearance on her greatest hits album.*

THE TOP 10 BEATLES SINGLES IN THE UK

	Title	Year
1	She Loves You	1963
2	I Want To Hold Your Hand	1963
3	Can't Buy Me Love	1964
4	I Feel Fine	1964
5	We Can Work It Out/ Day Tripper	1965
6	Help!	1965
7	Hey Jude	1968
8	A Hard Day's Night	1964
9	From Me To You	1963
10	Hello Goodbye	1967

The Beatles' two bestselling UK singles, both from the late 1963 'Beatlemania' period, remain among the UK's all-time Top 10 singles 30 years later. Their sales later in the 1960s were generally lower, although *Hey Jude* proved a match for the earlier mega-hits. Numbers one to five were all million-plus UK sellers; no other act has ever had more than two million-selling UK singles.

THE TOP 10 DAVID BOWIE SINGLES IN THE UK

	Title	Year
1	Space Oddity	1969/1975
2	Let's Dance	1983
3	Dancing In The Street (with Mick Jagger)	1985
4	Ashes To Ashes	1981
5	Under Pressure (with Queen)	1981
6	The Jean Genie	1972
7	Life On Mars	1973
8	Sorrow	1973
9	China Girl	1983
10	The Laughing Gnome	1973

Bowie's *Space Oddity* was a Top 5 success when first released, then an even bigger seller, reaching No. 1, upon its reissue in 1975. *The Laughing Gnome* was a 1960s recording which became a major hit after an astute reissue by Bowie's earlier record label. A particularly foolish novelty song performed in a vocal style resembling Anthony Newley's, it was a source of some embarrassment to the artist, who denounced its re-release.

THE TOP 10 KATE BUSH SINGLES IN THE UK

	Title	Year
1	Wuthering Heights	1978
2	Running Up That Hill	1985
3	Babooshka	1980
4	The Man With The Child In His Eyes	1978
5	Kate Bush On Stage (EP)	1979
6	Don't Give Up	1986
7	Wow	1979
8	Army Dreamers	1980
9	Sat In Your Lap	1981
10	Rocket Man	1991

Kate Bush is an artist who records relatively infrequently, and has only ever made one live concert tour (performances from which are captured on the *On Tour* EP). Nevertheless, she was one of the most consistently successful female vocalists of the 1980s. *Don't Give Up* was a jointly-credited duet with Peter Gabriel, and appeared on Gabriel's label rather than Bush's. *Rocket Man* came from her contribution to the *Two Rooms* tribute to the songs of Elton John and Bernie Taupin.

THE TOP 10 CHER SINGLES IN THE UK

	Title	Year
1	*I Got You Babe* (with Sonny Bono)	1965
2	*The Shoop Shoop Song (It's In His Kiss)*	1991
3	*Bang Bang (My Baby Shot Me Down)*	1966
4	*Gypsies, Tramps And Thieves*	1971
5	*Little Man* (with Sonny Bono)	1966
6	*If I Could Turn Back Time*	1989
7	*I Found Someone*	1987
8	*All I Really Want To Do*	1965
9	*All I Ever Need Is You* (with Sonny Bono)	1972
10	*Just Like Jesse James*	1990

It is sobering to consider that Cher has now had a successful singing career spanning the best part of 30 years. Her solo hits started almost simultaneously with those in duet with her first husband Sonny Bono – *All I Really Want To Do* made the Top 10 just as the duo's breakthrough hit *I Got You Babe* dropped from No. 1. Her biggest solo success, a revival of the 1960s oldie *The Shoop Shoop Song*, came from her 1991 film *Mermaids*.

THE TOP 10 DIRE STRAITS SINGLES IN THE UK

	Title	Year
1	*Private Investigations*	1982
2	*Walk Of Life*	1986
3	*Money For Nothing*	1985
4	*Sultans Of Swing*	1979
5	*Romeo And Juliet*	1981
6	*Twisting By The Pool*	1983
7	*Brothers In Arms*	1985
8	*So Far Away*	1985
9	*Your Latest Trick*	1986
10	*Calling Elvis*	1991

A band whose albums have always considerably outsold their singles, Dire Straits have amassed only 10 Top 30 hits (those in this list) in a career spanning almost 15 years. The first, *Sultans Of Swing*, 'slept' for a year on release until US success prompted its reactivation in the UK. It is worth noting that half the songs here (numbers two, three, seven, eight and nine) are taken from the album *Brothers In Arms*, which has sold 3,000,000 copies in the UK.

Dire Straits share with Adam Faith the distinction of a Top 10 single named after a Shakespeare play – Romeo And Juliet *and* As You Like It, *respectively.*

THE TOP 10 BOB DYLAN SINGLES IN THE UK

	Title	Year
1	Like A Rolling Stone	1965
2	Lay Lady Lay	1969
3	Positively 4th Street	1965
4	Rainy Day Women, Nos. 12 & 35	1966
5	The Times They Are A-Changin'	1965
6	Subterranean Homesick Blues	1965
7	Baby Stop Crying	1978
8	Knockin' On Heaven's Door	1973
9	I Want You	1966
10	Watching The River Flow	1971

Dylan has never been a particularly big singles seller in Britain, his core audience always having been album buyers from the word go. His major singles chart successes were in 1965, the year he made the perceived transition from folk artist to pop (or rock) singer, but *Like A Rolling Stone* was the only title here to exceed 250,000 UK sales. *Knockin' On Heaven's Door* was the song from the film *Pat Garrett And Billy The Kid*, in which Dylan had an acting role.

THE TOP 10 FLEETWOOD MAC SINGLES IN THE UK

	Title	Year
1	Albatross	1968/1973
2	Oh Well	1969
3	Man Of The World	1969
4	Little Lies	1987
5	Oh Diane	1982
6	Everywhere	1988
7	The Green Manalishi (With The Two-Prong Crown)	1970
8	Big Love	1987
9	Tusk	1979
10	Dreams	1977

Fleetwood Mac's three biggest sellers all came from their original Peter Green-led line-up, although Green had departed by 1973 when *Albatross* had its second successful chart run (it reached No. 1 in 1968, and No. 2 the second time around). Oddly, the mid to late period of the group's biggest American hits was their weakest in UK singles terms; far more people bought the *Fleetwood Mac* and *Rumours* albums than any of the singles taken from them.

THE TOP 10 EVERLY BROTHERS SINGLES IN THE UK

	Title	Year
1	Cathy's Clown	1960
2	All I Have To Do Is Dream/Claudette	1958
3	Walk Right Back/Ebony Eyes	1961
4	Bird Dog	1959
5	Temptation	1961
6	('Til) I Kissed You	1959
7	Wake Up Little Susie	1957
8	The Price Of Love	1965
9	When Will I Be Loved?	1960
10	So Sad/Lucille	1960

One of the most successful sibling acts of all time, Don and Phil Everly introduced a vital basic ingredient – vocal close harmony – into Rock 'n' Roll music, and were thus heavily influential on the Beatles, among others. Though they ceased to have significant hits a quarter of a century ago, the duo are still a top live attraction, and the songs in their Top 10 have become staples of 'Gold' radio.

THE TOP 10 GEORGE HARRISON SINGLES IN THE UK

	Title	Year
1	My Sweet Lord	1971
2	Got My Mind Set On You	1987
3	Give Me Love (Give Me Peace On Earth)	1973
4	Bangla Desh	1971
5	All Those Years Ago	1981
6	When We Was Fab	1988
7	Ding Dong	1974
8	You	1975
9	Blow Away	1979
10	This Is Love	1988

These 10 titles constitute all of George Harrison's solo UK chart entries. Although *My Sweet Lord* is the third all-time biggest-selling single by an ex-Beatle (after *Mull Of Kintyre* and *Imagine*), George Harrison, like Ringo Starr, fell fairly rapidly out of commercial favour in Britain, while retaining a higher chart profile in the United States. Even *My Sweet Lord* proved eventually to be a trial for him – quite literally, after he was found guilty of unconsciously plagiarizing it from the Chiffons' 1963 hit *He's So Fine*.

THE TOP 10 BUDDY HOLLY SINGLES IN THE UK

	Title	Year
1	It Doesn't Matter Anymore	1959
2	That'll Be The Day	1957
3	Peggy Sue	1957
4	Oh Boy!	1957
5	Brown-Eyed Handsome Man	1963
6	Rave On	1958
7	Maybe Baby	1958
8	Bo Diddley	1963
9	Wishing	1963
10	Baby I Don't Care	1961

Numbers two, four and seven were originally issued credited to the Crickets, of which Holly was the leader. There was no real distinction between his group and solo records of the time (the Crickets also played on the latter); it was mainly a ploy to allow simultaneous releases without apparent self-competition. Holly died on 3 February 1959, and numbers one, five and eight to 10 in the list were thus all posthumous hits.

THE TOP 10 JAM SINGLES IN THE UK

	Title	Year
1	A Town Called Malice/Precious	1982
2	Going Underground	1980
3	Start	1980
4	Beat Surrender	1982
5	The Eton Rifles	1979
6	The Bitterest Pill (I Ever Had To Swallow)	1982
7	Funeral Pyre	1981
8	Absolute Beginners	1981
9	Just Who Is The Five O'Clock Hero	1982
10	Strange Town	1979

The Jam were one of the most successful, domestically, of Britain's New Wave groups of the late 1970s, topping the UK singles chart four times (with the top four titles here) and claiming 13 Top 20 hits, all of them written by their leader, singer/guitarist Paul Weller. When Weller grew tired of the Jam's abrasive rock style and wanted to sing soul music instead, he split the group at the end of 1982 (to re-emerge with Style Council).

THE TOP 10 MICHAEL JACKSON SINGLES IN THE UK

	Title	Year
1	One Day In Your Life	1981
2	Billie Jean	1983
3	Say Say Say (with Paul McCartney)	1983
4	Don't Stop Till You Get Enough	1979
5	Beat It	1983
6	Rockin' Robin	1972
7	Black Or White	1991
8	I Just Can't Stop Loving You	1987
9	Ben	1972
10	Heal The World	1992

Despite the gigantic UK sales of Jackson's Bad and Thriller albums (or more likely, because of these successes), most of the singles taken from them, while being buoyant chart-riders, tended not to sell well enough to challenge some of his longer-term bestsellers like Ben (which continued to sell thousands each year for the best part of a decade). The major irony in this list is the top seller, which was released by Motown many years after being recorded, and quite a few years after Jackson had departed the label.

THE TOP 10 ELTON JOHN SINGLES IN THE UK

	Title	Year
1	Don't Go Breaking My Heart (with Kiki Dee)	1976
2	Sacrifice	1990
3	Rocket Man	1972
4	Nikita	1985
5	Crocodile Rock	1972
6	Daniel	1973
7	Song For Guy	1978
8	I Guess That's Why They Call It The Blues	1983
9	I'm Still Standing	1983
10	Passengers	1984

During the 1970s, Elton John's popularity in America exceeded that at home, so that US million-sellers like Bennie And The Jets, Philadelphia Freedom and Island Girl do not qualify for this Top 10. In fact, Elton did not have a solo UK No. 1 single until 1990 and Sacrifice, though his 1976 duet with Kiki Dee (which did top the chart) remains his all-time bestseller. Song For Guy is notable in spotlighting his piano playing, and has no vocal.

THE TOP 10 JONATHAN KING SINGLES IN THE UK

	Title	Name used	Year
1	Everyone's Gone To The Moon	Jonathan King	1965
2	Loop Di Love	Shag	1972
3	Una Paloma Blanca	Jonathan King	1975
4	It Only Takes A Minute	100 Ton & A Feather	1976
5	Sugar Sugar	Sakkarin	1971
6	It's The Same Old Song	Weathermen	1971
7	Hooked On A Feeling	Jonathan King	1971
8	Flirt	Jonathan King	1972
9	Lazy Bones	Jonathan King	1971
10	Let It All Hang Out	Jonathan King	1970

After starting as an ostensibly serious singer-songwriter while a Cambridge undergraduate, and scoring a worldwide 1960s hit with *Everyone's Gone To The Moon*, it became the entrepreneurial JK's speciality to cover oldies or overlooked US hits, often in a tongue-in-cheek style and frequently under a pseudonym. He got a taste of his own medicine in 1974, when a Swedish group named Blue Swede copied his arrangement of *Hooked On A Feeling*, and had a US No. 1 with it!

THE TOP 10 MADONNA SINGLES IN THE UK

	Title	Year
1	Like A Virgin	1984
2	Into The Groove	1985
3	Papa Don't Preach	1986
4	Crazy For You	1985
5	Holiday	1984
6	True Blue	1986
7	Vogue	1990
8	La Isla Bonita	1987
9	Like A Prayer	1989
10	Who's That Girl?	1987

The most successful chart artist of the 1980s, Madonna had scored 25 UK Top 10 hits, including seven No. 1s, by the end of the decade, despite the fact that she did not first make the charts until the beginning of 1984. Interestingly, her biggest seller, *Like A Virgin* (though it outsold *Into The Groove* by only just over 5,000 copies), failed to make No. 1, being held at No. 3 over Christmas 1984 by the gigantic sales of the Band Aid single and Wham!'s *Last Christmas*.

THE TOP 10 JOHN LENNON SINGLES IN THE UK

	Title	Year
1	Imagine	1975
2	Woman	1981
3	(Just Like) Starting Over	1980
4	Happy Xmas (War Is Over)	1972
5	Give Peace A Chance	1969
6	Instant Karma	1970
7	Power To The People	1971
8	Nobody Told Me	1984
9	Cold Turkey	1969
10	Mind Games	1973

John Lennon began his extra-curricular recording projects during the year before the Beatles actually split: *Give Peace A Chance* appeared in 1969, credited to the Plastic Ono Band. *Imagine* was a hit twice, the second occasion being immediately after Lennon's death, when its UK sales soared to over 1,000,000 and it reached No. 1. *Nobody Told Me* was a posthumous Top 10 chart entry just over three years after he died.

THE TOP 10 MADNESS SINGLES IN THE UK

	Title	Year
1	Baggy Trousers	1980
2	Embarrassment	1980
3	It Must Be Love	1981
4	Our House	1982
5	House Of Fun	1982
6	My Girl	1980
7	Wings Of A Dove	1983
8	Driving In My Car	1982
9	One Step Beyond	1979
10	The Return Of The Los Palmas Seven	1981

Originally known as the North London Invaders, Madness were among the most consistent of all UK hitmakers of the 1980s, scoring 20 Top 20 (and 15 Top 10) successes with their first 20 releases. Some of these (*One Step Beyond*, *It Must Be Love*) were covers of old songs, but the majority of the hits, often wryly humorous, were composed by the group.

TOP: *'The mist rolling in…' (courtesy of a dry-ice machine): Wings' 1977* Mull Of Kintyre *was the top-selling single of the 1970s and is the third bestselling single of all time in the UK.* (Redferns)
ABOVE: Sugar Sugar *by the Archies was a colossal smash worldwide, selling more than 6,000,000 copies – although the group, based on a US cartoon series, rates as a one-hit wonder in the UK.* (Redferns)

ABOVE: *With* Karma Chameleon *the bestselling single of 1983 in the UK, and their album* Colour By Numbers *ranking highly in the UK and USA, Culture Club and Boy George were a success story of the 1980s.* (Redferns)

LEFT: I Love You Love Me Love, *the bestselling single of 1973 in the UK for professional veteran Gary Glitter.* (Redferns)

BELOW: *Mercury and May in action:* Queen's Bohemian Rhapsody *was the UK's top single of 1975 and number two in 1991, while several books about the group hit the 1992 bestseller lists.* (Redferns)

ABOVE: *Banned by the Beeb – despite which Frankie Goes To Hollywood's* Relax *was the UK's second bestselling single of the 1980s and stayed on the chart for 52 weeks.* (Redferns)

LEFT: *Louis Armstrong became the oldest performer with a No. 1 single in the UK when* What A Wonderful World *topped the charts in 1968.* (Redferns)

LEFT: *Frank Sinatra has been scoring UK hits for 40 years, and is the oldest living singer to have a Top 10 hit.* (Redferns)

BELOW: *Born in 1962 and still going strong: the original Rolling Stones. The lack of cables on their guitars implies a lip-synching performance.* (Redferns)

ABOVE: *The original line-up of the Supremes, the first all-girl group to hit No. 1 in the UK, lasted from 1960 to 1969.* (Retna Pictures)

TOP: *George Michael's career spans a decade, with* Careless Whisper *making an appearance in numerous Top 10 lists and his album* Faith *topping the list of 1988 US bestsellers.* (Redferns)

LEFT: *David Bowie, an artist who has re-invented himself more than most acts have had hot albums, has sustained almost a quarter of a century of chart appearances.* (Redferns)

ABOVE: *Michael Jackson's* Thriller *holds the all-time album sales record worldwide. Note the stylishly taped fingers.* (Redferns)

OPPOSITE
TOP LEFT: *Erasure, a dominant duo in various indie rankings and noted for their successful homage EP* Abba-esque. (Redferns)

TOP RIGHT: *Rap up warm: Vanilla Ice's* Ice Ice Baby *is the bestselling rap single of all time in the UK, while his album* To The Extreme *also achieved great success on both sides of the Atlantic.* (Redferns)

BOTTOM: *Euro-Disco technologists Snap! have had a major impact on the 1990s dance singles scene.* (Retna Pictures)

LEFT: *Mick Hucknall of Simply Red, whose* Stars *was simply the bestselling album of 1991 and 1992 and is the bestselling CD of all time in the UK.* (Redferns)

BELOW: *The* South Pacific *soundtrack album was a solid seller from 1958 to 1962, scoring bally high in early LP lists.* (Ronald Grant Archive)

THE TOP 10 PAUL McCARTNEY SINGLES IN THE UK

	Title	Year
1	Mull Of Kintyre	1977
2	We All Stand Together	1984
3	Ebony And Ivory (with Stevie Wonder)	1982
4	Say Say Say (with Michael Jackson)	1983
5	Pipes Of Peace	1983
6	No More Lonely Nights	1983
7	Silly Love Songs	1976
8	Goodnight Tonight	1979
9	Let 'Em In	1976
10	With A Little Luck	1978

Down By The Lazy River, *the Osmond family group's first UK hit, led to a string of chart successes involving all possible permutations of the super-wholesome brothers and sister.*

McCartney has been by far the most commercially successful former Beatle on record, with well over 40 post-Fabs UK chart successes either to his name or that of Wings – under which guise, with various backing musicians, he operated from 1972 to 1979, and recorded numbers one, seven, eight, nine and 10 on this list, among many others.

THE TOP 10 GEORGE MICHAEL AND WHAM! SINGLES IN THE UK

	Title	Artist	Year
1	Last Christmas	Wham!	1984
2	Careless Whisper	Solo	1984
3	Freedom	Wham!	1984
4	Wake Me Up Before You Go-Go	Wham!	1984
5	A Different Corner	Solo	1985
6	I'm Your Man	Wham!	1985
7	Bad Boys	Wham!	1983
8	Don't Let The Sun Go Down On Me	With Elton John	1991
9	The Edge Of Heaven	Wham!	1986
10	Young Guns (Go For It)	Wham!	1982

By and large, George Michael's solo singles since the break-up of Wham! have not had the consistent success which the duo's records enjoyed (in the UK, anyway; the opposite is true in America). His two biggest-selling solo performances (numbers two and five above) were both made while Wham! was still operating, and the only post-split recording here is not strictly a solo effort, but a live concert performance on which Elton John (the song's writer) guested.

THE TOP 10 OSMONDS SINGLES IN THE UK*

	Title	Artist	Year
1	Long-Haired Lover From Liverpool	Little Jimmy	1972
2	Puppy Love	Donny	1972
3	Crazy Horses	Osmonds	1972
4	Paper Roses	Marie	1973
5	Why	Donny	1972
6	The Twelfth Of Never	Donny	1973
7	Let Me In	Osmonds	1973
8	Young Love	Donny	1973
9	Love Me For A Reason	Osmonds	1974
10	I'm Leaving It (All) Up To You	Donny and Marie	1974

* As a group, soloists, and in duets.

The toothy Osmond family from Salt Lake City, Utah, undertook a mini-takeover of the UK charts for a couple of years from mid-1972, finding success both as a group and via the individual efforts of the teenage Donny Osmond, the pre-teen Little Jimmy, and the family's only girl member Marie. As indicated by the list, their hits comprised both original material and revivals (especially in Donny's case) of familiar oldies.

THE TOP 10 POLICE SINGLES IN THE UK

	Title	Year
1	Don't Stand So Close To Me	1980
2	Message In A Bottle	1979
3	Every Breath You Take	1983
4	Walking On The Moon	1979
5	De Do Do Do, De Da Da Da	1980
6	Every Little Thing She Does Is Magic	1981
7	Invisible Sun	1981
8	Can't Stand Losing You	1979
9	So Lonely	1980
10	Roxanne	1979

THE FIRST 10 ELVIS PRESLEY SINGLES RELEASED IN THE USA

	Title	Label	Cat. no.
1	That's All Right Mama/Blue Moon Of Kentucky	Sun	209
2	Good Rockin' Tonight/I Don't Care If The Sun Don't Shine	Sun	210
3	You're A Heartbreaker/Milk Cow Blues Boogie	Sun	215
4	Baby Let's Play House/I'm Left, You're Right, She's Gone	Sun	217
5	I Forgot To Remember To Forget/Mystery Train	Sun	223
6	Heartbreak Hotel/I Was The One	RCA	6420
7	I Want You, I Need You, I Love You/My Baby Left Me	RCA	6540
8	Hound Dog/Don't Be Cruel*	RCA	6604
9	Love Me Tender/Any Way You Want Me	RCA	6643
10	Too Much/Playing For Keeps	RCA	6800

* Released as an official double A-side (all others are listed as A/B sides).

The trio of Sting, Andy Summers and Stuart Copeland found a very commercial niche at the end of the 1970s with a stark rock/reggae blend attached to strong, offbeat lyrics. They scored five UK chart-toppers (with numbers one to four and six on this list), and – unlike most UK New Wave groups – also went on to major success in America.

That's All Right Mama was released on 19 July 1954, with over 5,000 orders in the Memphis area following its airplay debut on 10 July on the local WHBQ radio station. Number 10 was released in January 1957, and became the fifth Elvis RCA single to sell over 1,000,000 copies.

The young Elvis Presley hung about with black musicians in Memphis and performed gospel songs at every opportunity, yet really wanted to sing just like Dean Martin. Instead, he completely revolutionized pop music the world over.

THE TOP 10 ELVIS PRESLEY SINGLES IN THE UK

	Title	Year
1	It's Now Or Never	1960
2	Jailhouse Rock	1958
3	Are You Lonesome Tonight	1961
4	Wooden Heart	1961
5	Return To Sender	1962
6	Can't Help Falling In Love	1962
7	The Wonder Of You	1970
8	Surrender	1961
9	Way Down	1977
10	All Shook Up	1957

Elvis was at his sales peak in the UK not in his 1950s heyday, but shortly after he left the army in the early 1960s. *It's Now Or Never* was his only million-seller on UK sales alone, though all the records in this list registered sales in excess of 600,000, and these 10 singles accounted for a total of 46 weeks at the top of the UK chart between them.

THE TOP 10 PRINCE SINGLES IN THE UK

	Title	Year
1	1999/Little Red Corvette	1985
2	When Doves Cry	1984
3	Gett Off	1991
4	Kiss	1986
5	Batdance	1989
6	Sexy MF/Strollin'	1992
7	Sign 'O' The Times	1987
8	Purple Rain	1984
9	U Got The Look	1987
10	Girls And Boys	1986

Prince's UK breakthrough was slower than in the United States, and his 1984 *Purple Rain* film and album, which spawned three million-selling singles in America, was a more muted success in the UK. It took the double A-side reissue of *1999* and *Little Red Corvette*, both of which had earlier been small hits in their own right, to finally give him a UK Top 3 single. Since then, he has been a chart regular, his soundtrack for the 1989 film *Batman* having provided a further boost.

10 ELVIS PRESLEY HITS THAT PEAKED AT DIFFERENT POSITIONS IN THE UK TOP 10

	Title	Peak position
1	Way Down	1
2	Heartbreak Hotel	2
3	It's Only Love/Beyond The Reef	3
4	A Big Hunk O' Love	4
5	My Boy	5
6	Too Much	6
7	Burning Love	7
8	American Trilogy	8
9	Blue Suede Shoes	9
10	Kissin' Cousins	10

Elvis is the only American act to complete this chart 'straight flush', having a great advantage over the opposition with no fewer than 55 registered Top 10 hits since *Heartbreak Hotel* made No. 2 in 1956.

THE TOP 10 QUEEN SINGLES IN THE UK

	Title	Year
1	Bohemian Rhapsody	1975/1991
2	Under Pressure (with David Bowie)	1981
3	We Are The Champions	1977
4	Radio Ga-Ga	1984
5	Killer Queen	1974
6	I Want To Break Free	1984
7	Crazy Little Thing Called Love	1979
8	Somebody To Love	1976
9	A Kind Of Magic	1986
10	Innuendo	1991

Ironically, it was Freddie Mercury's death in 1991 that resulted in Queen's achieving the UK's all-time second-bestselling single with *Bohemian Rhapsody*, which topped 2,000,000 UK sales when it returned to No. 1 16 years after its original triumph. Oddly, Queen's best-ever US seller, *Another One Bites The Dust* (1980), does not appear in the list here, having climbed to only No. 7 on the UK chart.

The only artist to have had a UK No. 1 hit single in five successive decades, Cliff has also had more UK hit singles than anybody else is likely to amass this century.

THE TOP 10 CLIFF RICHARD SINGLES WORLDWIDE

	Title	Year
1	*We Don't Talk Anymore*	1979
2	*The Young Ones*	1962
3	*Devil Woman*	1976
4	*Congratulations*	1968
5	*Living Doll*	1959
6	*The Next Time/Bachelor Boy*	1962
7	*Summer Holiday*	1963
8	*Lucky Lips*	1963
9	*Please Don't Tease*	1960
10	*Travellin' Light*	1959

Cliff Richard's bestselling singles on a global basis differ quite substantially from his UK Top 10 – for instance, the million-selling *Mistletoe And Wine* was not an international success, and *Lucky Lips* was his most successful single ever in Germany, as well as charting in the United States, thus altering the balance somewhat. The first five here have sold over 2,000,000 apiece, with *We Don't Talk Anymore* clocking up sales of 2,500,000.

THE TOP 10 CLIFF RICHARD SINGLES IN THE UK

	Title	Year
1	*The Young Ones*	1962
2	*Mistletoe And Wine*	1988
3	*The Next Time/Bachelor Boy*	1962
4	*We Don't Talk Anymore*	1979
5	*Living Doll*	1959
6	*Living Doll (with The Young Ones)*	1986
7	*Summer Holiday*	1963
8	*Travellin' Light*	1959
9	*Congratulations*	1968
10	*Daddy's Home*	1981

Cliff Richard is the only act to have had UK No. 1 singles in five decades, from the 1950s to the 1990s. Nine of these are listed here, although *Daddy's Home*, despite selling more than 500,000 copies, reached only No. 2 at Christmas 1981 because Human League's million-selling *Don't You Want Me* overtook it. *The Young Ones* entered the chart at No. 1 in January 1962 – the only time Cliff has achieved this feat.

THE TOP 10 CLIFF RICHARD DUET SINGLES IN THE UK

	Title	Duetted with
1	*Living Doll*	The Young Ones
2	*All I Ask Of You*	Sarah Brightman
3	*Throw Down A Line*	Hank Marvin
4	*She Means Nothing To Me*	Phil Everly
5	*Suddenly*	Olivia Newton-John
6	*Whenever God Shines His Light*	Van Morrison
7	*Joy Of Living*	Hank Marvin
8	*Slow Rivers*	Elton John
9	*Drifting*	Sheila Walsh
10	*Two To The Power Of Love*	Janet Jackson

The top six of these were all UK Top 20 hits, with all the others making the Top 75 apart from Cliff's 1984 duet with Janet Jackson, which was a very poor seller. This record, plus numbers four, five, six, eight and nine all had him as the second-named duettist, the single actually 'belonging' to the other artist. Band Aid II, on which Cliff performs as part of an ensemble, has not been included; if it were, it would stand at number two.

THE FIRST 10 CLIFF RICHARD SINGLES RELEASED IN THE UK

	Title	Date	Cat. no.
1	Move It/Schoolboy Crush	Aug 1958	DB 4178
2	High Class Baby/My Feet Hit The Ground	Nov 1958	DB 4203
3	Livin' Lovin' Doll/Steady With You	Jan 1959	DB 4249
4	Mean Streak/Never Mind	Apr 1959	DB 4290
5	Living Doll/Apron Strings	Jul 1959	DB 4306
6	Travellin' Light/Dynamite	Oct 1959	DB 4351
7	A Voice In The Wilderness/ Don't Be Mad At Me	Jan 1960	DB 4398
8	Fall In Love With You/ Willie And The Hand Jive	Mar 1960	DB 4431
9	Please Don't Tease/Where Is My Heart?	Jun 1960	DB 4479
10	Nine Times Out Of Ten/ Thinking Of Our Love	Sep 1960	DB 4506

Evergreen Cliff has been Britain's most enduring chart fixture, having released well over 100 successful singles since his 1958 UK No. 2 debut with *Move It* (which was, in fact, initially released as the B-side to *Schoolboy Crush*, a situation which was quickly reversed by the Columbia EMI label as *Move It*'s popularity surged).

THE TOP 10 ROLLING STONES SINGLES IN THE UK

	Title	Year
1	The Last Time	1965
2	(I Can't Get No) Satisfaction	1965
3	Honky Tonk Women	1969
4	It's All Over Now	1964
5	Get Off Of My Cloud	1965
6	Paint It Black	1966
7	Jumpin' Jack Flash	1968
8	Little Red Rooster	1964
9	Miss You	1978
10	Brown Sugar	1971

The mid-1960s were the Stones' singles-selling heyday, when the first eight of these titles reached No. 1 in the UK. Though arguably the next most popular group to the Beatles for most of that decade, their sales nonetheless rarely approached those of the Fab Four: *The Last Time* only just outsold *A Hard Day's Night*, the Beatles' eighth most successful single.

THE FIRST 10 ROLLING STONES SINGLES RELEASED IN THE UK

	Title	Date	Cat. no.
1	Come On/I Want To Be Loved	Jun 1963	F 11675
2	I Wanna Be Your Man/Stoned	Nov 1963	F 11764
3	Not Fade Away/Little By Little	Feb 1964	F 11845
4	It's All Over Now/Bad Times	Jun 1964	F 11934
5	Little Red Rooster/Off The Hook	Nov 1964	F 12014
6	The Last Time/Play With Fire	Feb 1965	F 12104
7	(I Can't Get No) Satisfaction/ The Spider And The Fly	Aug 1965	F 12220
8	Get Off Of My Cloud/ The Singer Not The Song	Oct 1965	F 12263
9	19th Nervous Breakdown/ As Tears Go By	Feb 1966	F 12331
10	Paint It Black/Long Long While	May 1966	F 12395

The first five single releases by the Stones were all cover versions (of, in order, songs by Chuck Berry, the Beatles, Buddy Holly, the Valentinos and Sam Cooke), whereas the remaining five were all Jagger/Richard compositions. All of these titles were released by Decca Records.

THE 10 LEAST SUCCESSFUL ROLLING STONES SINGLES IN THE UK

	Title	Year	Highest chart position
1	Sad Day	1973	–
2	I Don't Know Why	1975	–
3	One Hit To The Body	1986	–
4	Rock And A Hard Place	1989	63
5	Time Is On My Side (live)	1982	62
6	Waiting On A Friend	1981	50
7	Out Of Time	1975	45
8	She Was Hot	1984	42
9	Mixed Emotions	1989	36
10	She's So Cold	1980	33

The order of uncharted singles 1–3 is based on comparative sales.

Three of these singles (*Sad Day*, *I Don't Know Why* and *Out Of Time*) were oddities issued by Decca in the years after the Stones departed the company for their own label. The other entries on the list indicate that while the band are as big a live draw as ever and still have hit albums, the former selling power of their singles has largely evaporated over the last decade – in the UK at least, though less so in the United States.

THE TOP 10 DIANA ROSS SINGLES IN THE UK

	Title	Year
1	Chain Reaction	1986
2	I'm Still Waiting	1971
3	Upside Down	1980
4	When You Tell Me That You Love Me	1991
5	Theme From 'Mahogany' (Do You Know Where You're Going To?)	1976
6	Why Do Fools Fall In Love	1981
7	Ain't No Mountain High Enough	1970
8	Endless Love (duet with Lionel Richie)	1981
9	You Are Everything (duet with Marvin Gaye)	1974
10	Touch Me In The Morning	1973

This Top 10 does not include records on which Diana Ross sang as lead vocalist of the Supremes in the 1960s, but if it did, numbers five to 10 in the list would all be ousted by Supremes hits. Worth noting is the fact that three of Diana's four top UK sellers were not even Top 40 hits in the United States (*Upside Down* being the exception).

THE 10 ROLLING STONES SINGLES THAT STAYED LONGEST IN THE UK CHARTS

	Title	Year	Weeks in charts
1	The Rolling Stones (EP)	1964	20
2	Honky Tonk Women	1969	17
3	I Wanna Be Your Man	1963–64	16
4=	Not Fade Away	1964	15
4=	It's All Over Now	1964	15
6	Come On	1963	14
7=	Five By Five (EP)	1964	13
7=	The Last Time	1965	13
7=	Brown Sugar	1971	13
7=	Miss You	1978	13

These figures all refer to residence in the UK Top 50. Interestingly, five of the Stones' No. 1 hits – *(I Can't Get No) Satisfaction*, *Get Off Of My Cloud*, *Little Red Rooster*, *Jumpin' Jack Flash* and *Paint It Black* – had chart runs of between only 10 and 12 weeks, and thus failed to qualify for this list. By contrast, their first EP, *The Rolling Stones*, by far their steadiest long-term seller, never climbed above No. 20 in any of its 20 weeks on the Top 50.

THE TOP 10 SHADOWS SINGLES IN THE UK

	Title	Year
1	Wonderful Land	1962
2	Apache	1960
3	Dance On	1962
4	Foot Tapper	1963
5	Atlantis	1963
6	The Frightened City	1961
7	FBI	1961
8	Kon-Tiki	1961
9	Guitar Tango	1962
10	Man Of Mystery	1960

The world's all-time most popular small instrumental unit, the Shadows continue into the 1990s as strong album sellers, but their bestselling singles all came in the 1960–63 period just before the Beat Boom broke, when they emerged from simply backing Cliff Richard to become the role models for almost every group in the country. The top four here were all chart-toppers, and *Wonderful Land* and *Apache* both had the same writer, Jerry Lordan.

THE TOP 10 PAUL SIMON AND ART GARFUNKEL SINGLES IN THE UK*

	Title	Artist	Year
1	Bright Eyes	AG	1979
2	Bridge Over Troubled Water	S&G	1970
3	I Only Have Eyes For You	AG	1975
4	Mrs Robinson	S&G	1968
5	You Can Call Me Al	PS	1986
6	Mother And Child Reunion	PS	1972
7	The Boxer	S&G	1969
8	Homeward Bound	S&G	1966
9	Take Me To The Mardi Gras	PS	1973
10	Me And Julio Down By The Schoolyard	PS	1972

* Individually and collectively – PS: Paul Simon; AG: Art Garfunkel; S&G: Simon and Garfunkel.

Several of Simon and Garfunkel's biggest US hits, such as The Sound Of Silence and Cecilia, failed to make the UK chart, and several of Simon's major US solo successes, such as 50 Ways To Leave Your Lover, were also comparatively minor UK chartmakers. Conversely, Garfunkel's Bright Eyes, which sold more than 1,000,000 copies in the UK (more than twice the sales of the Bridge Over Troubled Water single), completely failed to make the grade in the United States.

THE TOP 10 RINGO STARR SINGLES IN THE UK

	Title	Year
1	Back Off Boogaloo	1972
2	It Don't Come Easy	1971
3	You're Sixteen	1974
4	Photograph	1973
5	Only You	1974
6	Oh My My	1976
7	Snookeroo	1975
8	A Dose Of Rock 'n' Roll	1976
9	Drowning In A Sea Of Love	1977
10	Wrack My Brain	1981

Ringo was initially the most successful former Beatle in terms of solo record success, with his first four releases (the top four here) all making the UK Top 10. In the mid-1970s, however, he rapidly fell from favour, to the extent that none of numbers six to 10 managed to reach the Top 50. He had slightly more commercial longevity in the United States, where all these titles except number nine were at least Top 40 successes.

THE TOP 10 SMITHS SINGLES IN THE UK

	Title	Year
1	Heaven Knows I'm Miserable Now	1984
2	What Difference Does It Make	1984
3	Panic	1986
4	Sheila Take A Bow	1987
5	Girlfriend In A Coma	1987
6	Ask	1986
7	Shoplifters Of The World Unite	1987
8	William, It Was Really Nothing	1984
9	This Charming Man	1983
10	The Boy With The Thorn In His Side	1985

The Smiths, a Manchester group based around the chalk-and-cheese partnership of guitarist Johnny Marr and vocalist Morrissey, were a major influence on the majority of newly emerging UK groups during the latter half of the 1980s, although before the end of the decade, despite a healthy run of hits, internal pressures had torn the Smiths themselves apart. Morrissey went on to a solo vocal career, and Marr into a variety of projects including the group Electronic.

THE TOP 10 ROD STEWART SINGLES IN THE UK

	Title	Year
1	Sailing	1975/1976
2	Maggie May	1971
3	Da Ya Think I'm Sexy?	1978
4	Baby Jane	1983
5	You Wear It Well	1972
6	I Don't Want To Talk About It/ First Cut Is The Deepest	1977
7	You're In My Heart	1977
8	The Killing Of Georgie	1976
9	Every Beat Of My Heart	1986
10	Angel/What Made Milwaukee Famous	1972

Sailing was a hit twice, reaching No. 1 on its initial outing, and then returning to No. 3 a little over a year later when the song was adopted as the theme for the hit TV series Sailor. Stewart's hits have included many covers, but the majority of his all-time biggest sellers have been originals, many of them his own compositions. Hit singles featuring him as lead singer of the Faces have not been included here.

THE TOP 10 WHO SINGLES IN THE UK

	Title	Year
1	Substitute	1966/1976
2	My Generation	1965
3	I'm A Boy	1966
4	Happy Jack	1966
5	Pinball Wizard	1969
6	Pictures Of Lily	1966
7	I Can't Explain	1965
8	I Can See For Miles	1967
9	Won't Get Fooled Again	1971
10	Anyway, Anyhow, Anywhere	1965

Substitute was the Who's largest UK seller by virtue of having been issued and charted twice – the 1966 original reaching the Top 5 (a legal battle at the time meant that three different pressings, with forced withdrawals in between, all appeared with different B-sides), and the 1976 reissue, which was the UK's first commercially-released 12″ single, climbing to No. 7.

THE TOP 10 SHEET MUSIC TITLES IN THE USA, 1900–20

	Title	Composer(s)	Year
1	Alexander's Ragtime Band	Irving Berlin	1911
2	United States Field Artillery March	John Sousa	1913
3	I Didn't Raise My Boy To Be A Soldier	Alfred Bryan & Al Pianpadosi	1915
4	When You Wore A Tulip	Weinrich & Mahoney	1914
5	Over There	George M. Cohen	1917
6	Oh Frenchy	Sam Erlich & Con Conrad	1918
7	Marine's Hymn	A. Tragina	1919
8	Oui Oui Marie	Alfred Bryan, Joe McCarthy & Fred Fisher	1918
9	Just A Baby's Prayer At Twilight	Sam Lewis, Joe Young & M. Jerome	1919
10	Rock-A-Bye My Baby With A Dixie Melody	Sam Lewis, Joe Young & Jean Schwartz	1918

Source: *The Music Exchange, New York.*

Alexander's Ragtime Band may be the biggest-selling sheet music title of all time, selling well over 1,000,000 copies in the United States. The golden era of sheet music sales was between the two World Wars when the public purchased sheet titles much as consumers buy singles today.

THE TOP 10 IMP* SHEET MUSIC TITLES IN THE UK, 1992

	Title	Composer(s)
1	Promise Me	Beverley Craven
2	Pink Panther	Henry Mancini
3	New York, New York	Betty Comden, Adolph Green, Leonard Bernstein
4	Bohemian Rhapsody	Freddie Mercury
5	As Time Goes By	Herman Hupfield
6	Cavatina	Stanley Myers
7	Chariots Of Fire	Vangelis
8	The Entertainer	Scott Joplin
9	I Just Called To Say I Love You	Stevie Wonder
10	Wind Beneath My Wings	Larry Henley, Jeff Silbar

* IMP (International Music Publications) is one of the two main sheet music title distributors in the UK.

This list is also broadly representative of the most popular titles over the past five years, with the exception of number one which, as a recent pop hit, emerged during 1991, although it is well on its way to becoming a standard. While sheet music sales up to the 1950s were the main format for consumers, often selling millions of copies, the advent of 78s, 45s and LPs quickly dominated this traditional source to the point where, today, sheet music availability and sales are minimal.

THE TOP 10 MUSIC SALES* SHEET MUSIC TITLES IN THE UK, 1992

	Title	Composer(s)
1	Everything I Do (I Do It For You)	Bryan Adams, Michael Kamen, Robert John 'Mutt' Lange
2	Love Changes Everything	Don Black, Charles Hart, Andrew Lloyd Webber
3	Unchained Melody	Alex North, Hy Zaret
4	Imagine	John Lennon
5	More Than Words	Extreme
6	All I Ask Of You	Andrew Lloyd Webber, Charles Hart, Richard Stilgoe
7	The Phantom Of The Opera	Andrew Lloyd Webber, Charles Hart, Richard Stilgoe
8	From A Distance	Julie Gold
9	Music Of The Night	Andrew Lloyd Webber, Charles Hart, Richard Stilgoe
10	Tears In Heaven	Eric Clapton, Will Jennings

* Music Sales Ltd is one of the two main sheet music title distributors in the UK. The list is also representative of the firm's bestselling sheet music titles for 1991.

Imagine and Unchained Melody have proved to be two of the most enduring pop standards and would certainly be among the 10 bestselling sheet music manuscripts of the rock era.

THE 10 MOST RECORDED SONGS IN THE USA, 1900–50

	Title	Year first recorded
1	St Louis Blues	1914
2	Tea For Two	1924
3	Body And Soul	1930
4	After You've Gone	1918
5	How High The Moon	1940
6	Blue Skies	1927
7	Dinah	1925
8	Ain't Misbehavin'	1929
9	Honeysuckle Rose	1929
10	Stardust	1929

THE 10 UK CHART SINGLES WITH THE LONGEST TITLES

	Title	Artist	Highest chart position	Year	No. of letters
1	I'm In Love With The Girl On A Certain Manchester Megastore Checkout Desk	Freshies	54	1981	60
2	If I Said You Had A Beautiful Body Would You Hold It Against Me?	Bellamy Brothers	3	1979	50
3	Gilly Gilly Ossenfeffer Katzenallen Bogen By The Sea	Max Bygraves	7	1954	45
4=	There's A Guy Works Down The Chipshop Swears He's Elvis	Kirsty MacColl	14	1981	44
4=	Have You Seen Your Mother, Baby, Standing In The Shadow?	Rolling Stones	5	1966	44
6	When The Girl In Your Arms Is The Girl In Your Heart	Cliff Richard	3	1961	41
7	I'm Gonna Sit Right Down And Write Myself A Letter	Billy Williams	22	1957	40
		Barry Manilow	36	1982	40
8=	Loving You's A Dirty Job But Someone's Got To Do It	Bonnie Tyler	73	1985	39
8=	Itsy Bitsy Teeny Weeny Yellow Polka Dot Bikini	Bryan Hyland	8	1960	39
8=	You Don't Have To Be In The Army To Fight In The War	Mungo Jerry	13	1971	39
8=	Two Pints Of Lager And A Packet Of Crisps Please	Splodgenessabounds	7	1980	39

This list includes only titles that do not contain words or phrases in brackets. It also includes only chart hits, and thus does not contain such memorable gems as Fairport Convention's 172-letter album track, Sir B. MacKenzie's Daughter's Lament For The 77th Mounted Lancers' Retreat From The Straits Of Loch Knombe In The Year Of Our Lord 1717, On The Occasion Of The Announcement Of Her Marriage To The Laird Of Kinleakie.

10 HIT SONGS BASED ON CLASSICAL MUSIC PIECES

	Title	Artist	Year	Source
1	All By Myself	Eric Carmen	1976	Rachmaninov's *Piano Concerto No. 2*
2	A Lover's Concerto	Toys	1965	J. S. Bach's *Minuet in G*
3	All Together Now	Farm	1990	Pachelbel's *Canon*
4	Alone At Last	Jackie Wilson	1960	Tchaikovsky's *Piano Concerto No. 1 in B-Flat Minor*
5	An American Tune	Paul Simon	1973	J. S. Bach's *O Sacred Head*
6	Asia Minor	Kokomo	1961	Grieg's *Piano Concerto No. 1*
7	Bumble Boogie	B. Bumble & The Stingers	1961	Rimsky-Korsakov's *Flight of the Bumble Bee*
8	Could It Be Magic	Barry Manilow	1978	Chopin's *Prelude in C Minor*
9	Hello Muddah, Hello Faddah	Allan Sherman	1963	Poncielli's *Dance of the Hours*
10	Joybringer	Manfred Mann's Earth Band	1973	Holst's 'Jupiter' from *The Planets*

The Farm's Top 10 hit with the uncredited Pachelbel borrowed hook in 1990 coincided with a less successful single released at the same time and also based on the *Canon* piece, namely Claire Hamill's *Someday We Will All Be Together*. Disco siren Donna Summer cut the original version of Barry Manilow's 1978 UK No. 25 hit, *Could It Be Magic*, in 1976. Other artists who have deemed classical music as fair pickings for pop hits include Elvis, Duane Eddy, Vince Hill, the Four Seasons and the Beach Boys.

10 UK HIT SINGLES FROM 1 TO 10 WHICH ALL MADE THE TOP 10

	Title	Artist	Top 10 chart peak
1	One	U2	7
2	Two Tribes	Frankie Goes To Hollywood	1
3	Three Times A Lady	Commodores	1
4	Four Letter Word	Kim Wilde	6
5	5–4–3–2–1	Manfred Mann	5
6	The Six Teens	Sweet	9
7	Seven Seas Of Rhye	Queen	10
8	Eighth Day	Hazel O'Connor	5
9	9 To 5	Sheena Easton	3
10	One In Ten	UB40	7

UB40's entry is entirely political: having named themselves after the official form number for claiming unemployment benefit, *One In Ten* was the band's anti-Thatcher protest – a reference to the estimate of the number of British people out of work in 1981.

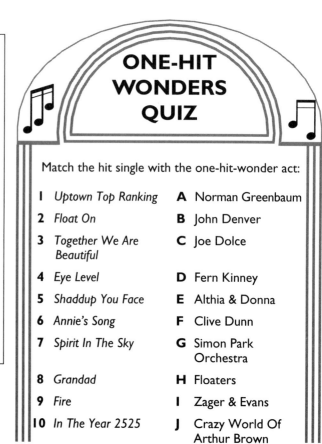

ONE-HIT WONDERS QUIZ

Match the hit single with the one-hit-wonder act:

1	Uptown Top Ranking	A	Norman Greenbaum
2	Float On	B	John Denver
3	Together We Are Beautiful	C	Joe Dolce
4	Eye Level	D	Fern Kinney
5	Shaddup You Face	E	Althia & Donna
6	Annie's Song	F	Clive Dunn
7	Spirit In The Sky	G	Simon Park Orchestra
8	Grandad	H	Floaters
9	Fire	I	Zager & Evans
10	In The Year 2525	J	Crazy World Of Arthur Brown

GUEST APPEARANCES

While the great majority of guest artists who appear on other people's records are now formally credited (indeed, the word 'featuring' is currently the most overused marketing trick in the singles business), many in the past have gone relatively unnoticed and uncredited.

One of the more intriguing mutual favours in rock history began when George Harrison played guitar with Eric Clapton's Cream, notably on the 1968 recording of the chart single, *Badge* (which they co-wrote), appearing under the pseudonym L'Angelo Mysterioso. Clapton in turn traded licks with Harrison on his memorable *While My Guitar Gently Weeps* track on *The Beatles* ('White Album') (the pair have also married the same woman, Patti Boyd, and performed a concert tour together in Japan in 1992).

Notable post-Beatle contributions by John Lennon include his guitar appearance under the name Dr Winston O'Boogie on Elton John's US chart-topping rendition of *Lucy In The Sky With Diamonds* from 1974 and as the uncredited backing singer on David Bowie's first US No. 1, *Fame*, which he also co-wrote.

Among a number of non-Stones recordings, Mick Jagger unmistakably provided backing vocals on Carly Simon's 1972 smash, *You're So Vain* (he was also rumoured, unsubstantiatedly, to be the song's lyrical subject), and can also be heard wailing on reggae star Peter Tosh's first British chart single, *(You Gotta Walk) Don't Look Back.*

Michael Jackson's most successful non-credited vocal work was for Motown label boss Berry Gordy Jr's son who released the infectious Top 10 hit *Somebody's Watching You* under the name Rockwell in 1984.

Great soul vocalists have always been as much in demand for session work as for their own recording projects: the current king of soul Luther Vandross ('The Voice') pops up on David Bowie's 1975 success *Young Americans*, provided the lead vocals on a couple of early hits by 1980s dance outfit Change (most impressively on *The Glow Of Love*) and can be discerned most recently on rocker Richard Marx's 1992 hit *Keep Coming Back.*

Workaholic Phil Collins has made dozens of musical cameos, some in his role as a drummer (for Robert Plant, Abba's Frida, Band Aid and even on Adam Ant's 1983 hit *Puss 'N Boots*), others simply as a singer (Eric Clapton, Stephen Bishop and John Martyn). Sting, another in-demand backing vocalist, helped Collins on the latter's *No Jacket Required* album and is also the high-pitched lead-in voice singing *I Want My MTV* on Dire Straits' global hit *Money For Nothing.* Mark Knopfler returned the favour, adding poetic acoustic guitar to Sting's Ivor Novello Award-winning track, *They Dance Alone,* from his 1987 album, *Soul Cages.* Knopfler has frequently guested on albums by his peers, in the capacity of producer, guitarist or vocalist (notably Bob Dylan's album *Infidels,* Joan Armatrading's *The Shouting Stage* and Randy Newman's *Land Of Dreams*) while axe-hero Jeff Beck performed lead guitar on Tina Turner's 1984 Knopfler-written hit *Private Dancer.*

Other memorable but often overlooked guest appearances include Stevie Wonder's harmonica on Chaka Khan's global chart-topper, *I Feel For You* (written by Prince), her strong backing vocals on Steve Winwood's 1986 success *Higher Love*, and the Thompson Twins' Tom Bailey (keyboards) and soul heavyweight Jennifer Holliday's contributions to Foreigner's UK/US No. 1 *I Want To Know What Love Is.* Classical Punk violinist Nigel Kennedy appeared on Kate Bush's *The Sensual World* album, Country star Ronnie Milsap provided backing vocals on Elvis Presley's 1969 hit *Don't Cry Daddy*, Bruce Hornsby's trademark piano can be heard on the Don Henley 1989 hit *The End Of The Innocence*, as can Eddie Van Halen's soaring fret-work on Michael Jackson's *Beat It.*

The largest congregation of famous guest appearances is, of course, on the historic 1984 Band Aid recording, *Do They Know It's Christmas?* For the record, the full line-up was: Bananarama, Phil Collins, Culture Club (Boy George and Jon Moss), Duran Duran, Bob Geldof, Heaven 17, Kool & The Gang (Robert Bell, James T. Taylor and Dennis Thomas), Marilyn, George Michael, Spandau Ballet, Status Quo (Rick Parfitt and Francis Rossi), Sting, U2 (Bono and Adam Clayton), Midge Ure, Jody Watley, Paul Weller and Paul Young.

ALBUMS

THE TOP 10 ALBUMS OF ALL TIME WORLDWIDE

	Title	Artist
1	Thriller	Michael Jackson
2	Saturday Night Fever	Soundtrack
3	Sgt Pepper's Lonely Hearts Club Band	Beatles
4	Grease	Soundtrack
5	Bridge Over Troubled Water	Simon and Garfunkel
6	Born In The USA	Bruce Springsteen
7	The Sound Of Music	Soundtrack
8	Rumours	Fleetwood Mac
9	Brothers In Arms	Dire Straits
10=	Dark Side Of The Moon	Pink Floyd
10=	The Bodyguard	Soundtrack

Total worldwide sales of albums have traditionally been notoriously hard to gauge, but even with the huge expansion of the album market during the 1980s, and multiple million sales of many major releases, it is not thought that anything has overtaken any of this Top 10 in recent times, the sales of most of them being between 15,000,000 and 20,000,000 globally, with *Saturday Night Fever* near 25,000,000, and the apparently uncatchable *Thriller* on 40,000,000. Both *The Bodyguard* and the 15th anniversary re-promotion of *Dark Side Of The Moon* are selling briskly and it is difficult to divide them – hence, for 1993 anyway, a temporary tied position.

THE TOP 10 ALBUMS OF ALL TIME IN THE UK

	Title	Artist
1	Sgt Pepper's Lonely Hearts Club Band	Beatles
2	Brothers In Arms	Dire Straits
3	Greatest Hits	Queen
4	Bad	Michael Jackson
5	Stars	Simply Red
6	Thriller	Michael Jackson
7	...But Seriously	Phil Collins
8	Bridge Over Troubled Water	Simon and Garfunkel
9	Greatest Hits	Simon and Garfunkel
10	Rumours	Fleetwood Mac

On the occasion of the album's 25th anniversary in 1992, EMI Records conducted new research into the sales of *Sgt Pepper* and concluded that it had sold over 4,000,000 copies in the UK, substantially more than *Brothers In Arms*, which was previously thought to have overtaken it. The Dire Straits, Queen (sales boosted hugely by Freddie Mercury's death), Simply Red and Michael Jackson *Bad* albums have all sold 3,000,000 copies, while *Thriller* hovers a mere few thousand from similar status. All the others in this list have achieved UK sales in excess of 2,500,000.

THE TOP 10 ALBUMS OF ALL TIME IN THE USA

	Title	Artist
1	Thriller	Michael Jackson
2	Rumours	Fleetwood Mac
3	Saturday Night Fever	Soundtrack
4	Dark Side Of The Moon	Pink Floyd
5	Born In The USA	Bruce Springsteen
6	Purple Rain	Prince
7	Can't Slow Down	Lionel Richie
8	Please Hammer Don't Hurt 'Em	MC Hammer
9	Dirty Dancing	Soundtrack
10	Tapestry	Carole King

Thriller's US sales are over 20,000,000, so it will take a mighty album indeed ever to catch it up. The rest of this field, all of which have sold in excess of 10,000,000 copies apiece, are well behind by comparison, with second-placed *Rumours* having sold between 13,000,000 and 14,000,000 copies, and *Saturday Night Fever* in third place, between 11,000,000 and 12,000,000. A lot of these albums were originally released before the CD age, so have benefited from 'second copy' buying, as people replace old vinyl copies with compact discs.

THE TOP 10 CDs OF ALL TIME IN THE UK

	Title	Artist
1	Stars	Simply Red
2	Brothers In Arms	Dire Straits
3	Greatest Hits	Queen
4	Bad	Michael Jackson
5	...But Seriously	Phil Collins
6	The Immaculate Collection	Madonna
7	Greatest Hits II	Queen
8	Thriller	Michael Jackson
9	Dangerous	Michael Jackson
10	We Can't Dance	Genesis

In the early 1990s, compact disc has become the major format for album releases (now joined by two new digital rivals, DCC and Mini Disc, which could have a struggle both with each other and for wide acceptance), so the emphasis among the bestsellers is on more recent releases which sold largely on CD. Brothers In Arms still outranks Stars in all-format sales, but a greater proportion of the latter's 3,000,000 sales have been on CD.

INITIALS QUIZ

Complete the act's name by matching its initials with the rest of its title:

1	Special	A	Top
2	B.B.	B	Arnold
3	10	C	40
4	C.W.	D	Proby
5	P.J.	E	King
6	P.P.	F	A.K.A.
7	S.O.S.	G	McCall
8	UB	H	cc
9	Gary U.S.	I	Band
10	ZZ	J	Bonds

THE TOP 10 ALBUMS OF 1960 IN THE UK

	Title	Artist
1	South Pacific	Soundtrack
2	Elvis Is Back	Elvis Presley
3	Down Drury Lane To Memory Lane	101 Strings
4	The Buddy Holly Story	Buddy Holly
5	Can Can	Soundtrack
6	The Twang's The Thang	Duane Eddy
7	Cliff Sings	Cliff Richard
8	Oliver!	London Cast
9	It's Everly Time	Everly Brothers
10	Me And My Shadows	Cliff Richard

At the dawn of the 1960s, albums were a tiny minority market in the UK, dominated by soundtracks and stage cast sets from films and shows, with only the very biggest pop names of the day managing to sell in quantity their LPs as well as singles. The South Pacific soundtrack was the No. 1 or No. 2 seller virtually every week of the year – as it had also been in 1959.

THE TOP 10 ALBUMS OF 1960 IN THE USA

	Title	Artist
1	The Sound Of Music	Original Cast
2	Sold Out	Kingston Trio
3	The Button-Down Mind Of Bob Newhart	Bob Newhart
4	String Along	Kingston Trio
5	Faithfully	Johnny Mathis
6	Theme From A Summer Place	Billy Vaughn
7	Nice'n'Easy	Frank Sinatra
8	Persuasive Percussion	Enoch Light & His Orchestra
9	Sentimental Sing Along With Mitch	Mitch Miller
10	G.I. Blues	Elvis Presley

The US album market was more developed than in Britain at this time, with acts like the folky Kingston Trio and singalong king Mitch Miller being among the early regular LP hitmakers, along with the more adult-oriented major pop vocalists such as Sinatra and Mathis. Elvis Presley apart, few teen-appeal artists sold albums in great numbers, however.

The West Side Story *soundtrack was the bestselling album of 1962 in the UK and USA, remaining in the Top 10 for the next two years. It was also the top album of the 1960s in the USA.*

THE TOP 10 ALBUMS OF 1961 IN THE UK

	Title	Artist
1	G.I. Blues	Elvis Presley
2	Black And White Minstrel Show	George Mitchell Minstrels
3	South Pacific	Soundtrack
4	The Shadows	Shadows
5	Another Black And White Minstrel Show	George Mitchell Minstrels
6	Listen To Cliff	Cliff Richard
7	21 Today	Cliff Richard
8	The Sound Of Music	London Cast
9	Oliver!	London Cast
10	The Button-Down Mind Of Bob Newhart	Bob Newhart

THE TOP 10 ALBUMS OF 1961 IN THE USA

	Title	Artist
1	Judy At Carnegie Hall	Judy Garland
2	Calcutta	Lawrence Welk
3	Exodus	Soundtrack
4	Stars For A Summer Night	Various
5	Camelot	Original Cast
6	Wonderland By Night	Bert Kaempfert
7	The Button-Down Mind Strikes Back	Bob Newhart
8	Blue Hawaii	Elvis Presley
9	G.I. Blues	Elvis Presley
10	Music From 'Exodus' And Other Great Themes	Mantovani

*S*outh Pacific *and* Oliver! remained in 1961 from the previous year's bestsellers, but Elvis had his biggest-selling album yet in the UK with the soundtrack from *G.I. Blues*, while the Shadows, the first rock group ever to sell LPs in large quantities, arrived with their debut set. BBC TV's *Black And White Minstrel Show* cast were also to become a fixture on the chart for a two-year period.

*T*he nature of most of these bestsellers indicates just how little influence teenage buying tastes (and thereby Rock 'n' Roll) had on the US album market at the beginning of the 1960s. Half of the Top 10 are basically orchestral offerings, of the light or soundtrack variety. The top seller, by Judy Garland, was a double live album recorded at New York's Carnegie Hall in May 1961.

THE TOP 10 ALBUMS OF 1962 IN THE UK

	Title	Artist
1	West Side Story	Soundtrack
2	Blue Hawaii	Elvis Presley
3	The Young Ones	Cliff Richard
4	Pot Luck	Elvis Presley
5	South Pacific	Soundtrack
6	The Best Of Ball, Barber And Bilk	Kenny Ball, Chris Barber and Mr Acker Bilk
7	Out Of The Shadows	Shadows
8	Black And White Minstrel Show	George Mitchell Minstrels
9	A Golden Age Of Donegan	Lonnie Donegan
10	The Shadows	Shadows

The three bestselling UK albums of 1962 were all film soundtracks, with West Side Story holding the No. 1 or 2 slot for almost the entire year. A second Shadows set joined their first, while the Lonnie Donegan and Ball, Barber and Bilk entries were compilations of old material on the low-price Golden Guinea label, which did indeed sell for a guinea (or £1.05) – about two-thirds of the price of regular albums at the time.

THE TOP 10 ALBUMS OF 1962 IN THE USA

	Title	Artist
1	West Side Story	Soundtrack
2	The First Family	Vaughn Meader
3	Modern Sounds In Country And Western Music	Ray Charles
4	Peter, Paul And Mary	Peter, Paul & Mary
5	Blue Hawaii	Elvis Presley
6	My Son The Folk Singer	Allan Sherman
7	Breakfast At Tiffany's	Henry Mancini
8	Ramblin' Rose	Nat King Cole
9	Moon River And Other Great Movie Themes	Andy Williams
10	Your Twist Party	Chubby Checker

Visible among 1962's top US albums were several burgeoning new trends: contemporary folk (Peter, Paul & Mary), the Twist (Chubby Checker) and commercial adaptation of Country music (Ray Charles, Nat 'King' Cole). At the end of the year, there was also a comedy upsurge, via Allan Sherman's musical Jewish humour, and The First Family, a soundalike parody of the Kennedys. This was a genuine cultural phenomenon, selling a reported 100,000 copies a day during December.

THE TOP 10 ALBUMS OF 1963 IN THE UK

	Title	Artist
1	With The Beatles	Beatles
2	Please Please Me	Beatles
3	West Side Story	Soundtrack
4	Summer Holiday	Cliff Richard
5	The Shadows' Greatest Hits	Shadows
6	Reminiscing	Buddy Holly
7	Meet The Searchers	Searchers
8	How Do You Like It?	Gerry & The Pacemakers
9	I'll Remember You	Frank Ifield
10	Girls! Girls! Girls!	Elvis Presley

Almost inevitably, the arrival of the Beatles and the subsequent revolution in British pop music finally ignited the UK album market. The group's debut set Please Please Me held the No. 1 slot for three-fifths of the year, selling 500,000 copies, which immediately made it the country's all-time second biggest-selling album behind South Pacific. With The Beatles, however, swept both these aside, shifting 530,000 copies in its first week on sale, and eventually topping 1,000,000 copies.

THE TOP 10 ALBUMS OF 1963 IN THE USA

	Title	Artist
1	John Fitzgerald Kennedy: A Memorial Album	Documentary
2	Days Of Wine And Roses	Andy Williams
3	The Singing Nun	The Singing Nun
4	The First Family	Vaughn Meader
5	In The Wind	Peter, Paul & Mary
6	(Moving)	Peter, Paul & Mary
7	Songs I Sing On The Jackie Gleason Show	Frank Fontaine
8	West Side Story	Soundtrack
9	Modern Sounds In Country & Western, Vol .2	Ray Charles
10	The Barbra Streisand Album	Barbra Streisand

Vaughn Meader's Kennedy satire continued to be America's top-selling album for the first two months of 1963, but by the end of the year it had been withdrawn from sale for ever following the President's assassination. The Memorial Album documentary set, based on a tribute programme broadcast by New York radio station WMCA, sold 4,000,000 copies (at 99 cents each) in the six days from 7 to 12 December.

THE TOP 10 ALBUMS OF 1964 IN THE UK

	Title	Artist
1	*Beatles For Sale*	Beatles
2	*A Hard Day's Night*	Beatles
3	*West Side Story*	Soundtrack
4	*The Rolling Stones*	Rolling Stones
5	*With The Beatles*	Beatles
6	*Please Please Me*	Beatles
7	*Wonderful Life*	Cliff Richard
8	*Moonlight And Roses*	Jim Reeves
9	*The Bachelors And 16 Great Songs*	Bachelors
10	*Stay With The Hollies*	Hollies

This was another year dominated by the Beatles, whose two top sellers from the previous year made a repeat showing (as did *West Side Story*). The Jim Reeves album was the biggest of a dozen Reeves releases which found chart success following the singer's death in a plane crash, while *Wonderful Life* gave Cliff Richard his third major film soundtrack success in as many years.

THE TOP 10 ALBUMS OF 1964 IN THE USA

	Title	Artist
1	*Meet The Beatles*	Beatles
2	*A Hard Day's Night*	Beatles
3	*The Beatles' Second Album*	Beatles
4	*Introducing The Beatles*	Beatles
5	*Something New*	Beatles
6	*People*	Barbra Streisand
7	*Honey In The Horn*	Al Hirt
8	*Hello Dolly*	Original Cast
9	*Hello Dolly*	Louis Armstrong
10	*West Side Story*	Soundtrack

The Beatles conquered America's album market in 1964 as comprehensively as they did in the singles field. *Meet The Beatles* sold more than 4,000,000 copies in the United States during the year, with the soundtrack of *A Hard Day's Night* topping 2,000,000. The two *Hello Dolly* albums, meanwhile, had only the title track in common, Louis Armstrong's LP being built around his chart-topping version of the showcase song.

THE TOP 10 ALBUMS OF 1966 IN THE UK

	Title	Artist
1	*The Sound Of Music*	Soundtrack
2	*Revolver*	Beatles
3	*Rubber Soul*	Beatles
4	*Aftermath*	Rolling Stones
5	*Pet Sounds*	Beach Boys
6	*Portrait*	Walker Brothers
7	*Take It Easy With The Walker Brothers*	Walker Brothers
8	*Mary Poppins*	Soundtrack
9	*Goin' Places*	Herb Alpert
10	*The Small Faces*	Small Faces

The *Sound Of Music*, which kept returning inexorably to the No. 1 slot through the year as it saw off shorter-lived chart-topping upstarts like the Beatles, was still the album more Britons apparently wanted to hear than any other. UK-domiciled American trio the Walker Brothers proved themselves to be strong album-sellers, while the Beach Boys' *Pet Sounds*, always critically acclaimed, was a much bigger success in the UK than the United States.

THE TOP 10 ALBUMS OF 1965 IN THE UK

	Title	Artist
1	*The Sound Of Music*	Soundtrack
2	*Beatles For Sale*	Beatles
3	*Rubber Soul*	Beatles
4	*Help!*	Beatles
5	*Mary Poppins*	Soundtrack
6	*The Rolling Stones No. 2*	Rolling Stones
7	*The Freewheelin' Bob Dylan*	Bob Dylan
8	*Bringing It All Back Home*	Bob Dylan
9	*Out Of Our Heads*	Rolling Stones
10	*Joan Baez/5*	Joan Baez

The *Sound Of Music* soundtrack, which would prove to be the second-bestselling album of the 1960s in the UK, made the first of its several annual impacts in 1965. The other big arrivals in the sales stakes were the Rolling Stones, with two of the year's bestsellers, and contemporary folk music, exemplified by Bob Dylan and Joan Baez, both of whom scored multiple simultaneous chart entries during the year.

THE TOP 10 ALBUMS OF 1965 IN THE USA

	Title	Artist
1	*Mary Poppins*	Soundtrack
2	*Beatles '65*	Beatles
3	*The Sound Of Music*	Soundtrack
4	*Whipped Cream And Other Delights*	Herb Alpert
5	*Help!*	Beatles
6	*Beatles VI*	Beatles
7	*Rubber Soul*	Beatles
8	*My Fair Lady*	Soundtrack
9	*Goldfinger*	Soundtrack
10	*Fiddler On The Roof*	Original Cast

The voice of Julie Andrews, who starred in both *Mary Poppins* and *The Sound Of Music*, rivalled those of the Beatles as the most popular of 1965. This year's list shows something of a soundtrack resurgence – including the Beatles' *Help!*, there are five film soundtracks in this Top 10. The *Goldfinger* soundtrack was the bestselling James Bond soundtrack of all, and consisted largely of instrumental music written, scored and conducted by John Barry.

THE TOP 10 ALBUMS OF 1966 IN THE USA

	Title	Artist
1	Whipped Cream And Other Delights	Herb Alpert & The Tijuana Brass
2	The Monkees	Monkees
3	If You Can Believe Your Eyes And Ears	Mamas & Papas
4	What Now My Love	Herb Alpert
5	Going Places	Herb Alpert
6	The Sound Of Music	Soundtrack
7	Ballads Of The Green Berets	Staff Sergeant Barry Sadler
8	The Mamas And The Papas	Mamas & Papas
9	Dr Zhivago	Soundtrack
10	Revolver	Beatles

Phenomenon of the year in the US album market was trumpeter Herb Alpert, who, with his mariachi-styled Tijuana Brass, sold over 8,000,000 LPs during 1966. Two new groups, the Monkees and the Mamas & Papas, showed a sign of the times by selling albums in quantities surpassing their hit singles, while Barry Sadler's album developed the right-wing patriotic themes of his freak No. 1 single and sold 2,000,000 copies.

Herb Alpert's Whipped Cream And Other Delights *topped the US bestseller list in 1966.*

THE TOP 10 ALBUMS OF 1967 IN THE UK

	Title	Artist
1	Sgt Pepper's Lonely Hearts Club Band	Beatles
2	The Sound Of Music	Soundtrack
3	Best Of The Beach Boys	Beach Boys
4	The Monkees	Monkees
5	Dr Zhivago	Soundtrack
6	More Of The Monkees	Monkees
7	Fiddler On The Roof	London Cast
8	Going Places	Herb Alpert
9	Come The Day	Seekers
10	Green, Green Grass Of Home	Tom Jones

Widely acclaimed from the time of its release as the Beatles' *meisterwerk*, *Sgt Pepper* would eventually emerge as the bestselling UK album not only of the 1960s, but of all time, with well over 4,000,000 copies shifted by the time it was finally put on to compact disc in the mid-1980s. The Monkees' UK success in 1967 was underlined by their having two of the year's top six sellers.

THE TOP 10 ALBUMS OF 1967 IN THE USA

	Title	Artist
1	Sgt Pepper's Lonely Hearts Club Band	Beatles
2	More Of The Monkees	Monkees
3	S.R.O.	Herb Alpert
4	Headquarters	Monkees
5	Magical Mystery Tour	Beatles
6	Revenge	Bill Cosby
7	The Doors	Doors
8	Pisces, Aquarius, Capricorn & Jones Ltd	Monkees
9	Sounds Like	Herb Alpert
10	Surrealistic Pillow	Jefferson Airplane

With the 'Summer of Love', *Sgt Pepper* and the Monterey Pop Festival as its foci, 1967 was the year when progressive West Coast rock began to sell albums in large numbers in the United States, via the Doors and Jefferson Airplane. On sheer numbers, though, the Beatles, Monkees and Herb Alpert's Tijuana Brass carved up the year's Top 10 between them.

THE TOP 10 ALBUMS OF 1968 IN THE UK

	Title	Artist
1	The Sound Of Music	Soundtrack
2	The Beatles ('White Album')	Beatles
3	John Wesley Harding	Bob Dylan
4	Greatest Hits	Diana Ross & The Supremes
5	This Is Soul	Various
6	Bookends	Simon and Garfunkel
7	The Hollies' Greatest	Hollies
8	Greatest Hits	Four Tops
9	The History Of Otis Redding	Otis Redding
10	Jungle Book	Soundtrack

The Sound Of Music soundtrack continued to sell with extraordinary consistency, and in fact passed the 2,000,000 UK sales mark at the beginning of October 1968. This made it the bestselling record of any kind in Britain up to this time, overtaking even the Beatles' *She Loves You*, which at 1,900,000 UK sales was the biggest-selling single.

THE TOP 10 ALBUMS OF 1968 IN THE USA

	Title	Artist
1	The Beatles ('White Album')	Beatles
2	Blooming Hits	Paul Mauriat
3	The Beat Of The Brass	Herb Alpert
4	The Graduate	Soundtrack
5	Bookends	Simon and Garfunkel
6	Disraeli Gears	Cream
7	Lady Soul	Aretha Franklin
8	Parsley, Sage, Rosemary And Thyme	Simon and Garfunkel
9	Waiting For The Sun	Doors
10	Are You Experienced?	Jimi Hendrix Experience

More heavy rock, from Cream, Hendrix and the Doors, sold in large quantities in the United States during 1968, but the year's winners were really Simon and Garfunkel, who were the main reason why 1,000,000 people bought the *Graduate* soundtrack, as well as the duo's *Bookends* album and their revitalized 1966 set *Parsley, Sage, Rosemary And Thyme*. Paul Mauriat's orchestral *Blooming Hits* was a spin-off from his hugely successful *Love Is Blue* single.

THE TOP 10 ALBUMS OF 1969 IN THE UK

	Title	Artist
1	Abbey Road	Beatles
2	Best Of The Seekers	Seekers
3	Johnny Cash At San Quentin	Johnny Cash
4	Hair	London Cast
5	Oliver!	Soundtrack
6	The Sound Of Music	Soundtrack
7	The World Of Val Doonican	Val Doonican
8	Nashville Skyline	Bob Dylan
9	The Supremes Join The Temptations	Supremes and Temptations
10	The Beatles ('White Album')	Beatles

This year was a difficult time for trend-spotting in the UK album market, since it was strong in several areas: soundtracks (including the Johnny Cash album, which was the soundtrack to a concert film made by Granada TV), compilations (Seekers, Val Doonican), and the musical *Hair*, which spun off several individual hit songs as well as providing a big-selling London cast set.

THE TOP 10 ALBUMS OF 1969 IN THE USA

	Title	Artist
1	Hair	Broadway Cast
2	Abbey Road	Beatles
3	Blood, Sweat And Tears	Blood, Sweat & Tears
4	In-A-Gadda-Da-Vida	Iron Butterfly
5	Led Zeppelin II	Led Zeppelin
6	Johnny Cash At San Quentin	Johnny Cash
7	Crosby, Stills And Nash	Crosby, Stills & Nash
8	Led Zeppelin	Led Zeppelin
9	T.C.B.	Supremes and Temptations
10	Green River	Creedence Clearwater Revival

The original broadway cast album of *Hair* dominated the 1969 US charts, also inspiring a host of hit singles in cover versions by the 5th Dimension, the Cowsills and others. It eventually sold 5,000,000 copies in the United States up to 1971. Otherwise, the chart was almost entirely rock-dominated, with both Led Zeppelin's first two albums making exceptional showings: these sold 3,000,000 apiece by the middle of 1970.

THE TOP 10 ALBUMS OF 1970 IN THE UK

	Title	Artist
1	Bridge Over Troubled Water	Simon and Garfunkel
2	Led Zeppelin II	Led Zeppelin
3	Easy Rider	Soundtrack
4	Paint Your Wagon	Soundtrack
5	Motown Chartbusters, Vol. 3	Various
6	Let It Be	Beatles
7	Abbey Road	Beatles
8	Andy Williams' Greatest Hits	Andy Williams
9	Deep Purple In Rock	Deep Purple
10	McCartney	Paul McCartney

Simon and Garfunkel's swansong prior to pursuing solo careers was not only by far 1970's biggest-selling album in the UK, but was merely getting started on several years of major sales and chart dominance. The Beatles also wound up their account in this year, with *Abbey Road* reprising its 1969 appearance alongside the final group album *Let It Be* and Paul McCartney's solo debut.

THE TOP 10 ALBUMS OF 1970 IN THE USA

	Title	Artist
1	Bridge Over Troubled Water	Simon and Garfunkel
2	Déjà Vu	Crosby, Stills, Nash & Young
3	Cosmo's Factory	Creedence Clearwater Revival
4	Woodstock	Soundtrack
5	Let It Be	Beatles
6	Led Zeppelin II	Led Zeppelin
7	Abbey Road	Beatles
8	Hey Jude	Beatles
9	McCartney	Paul McCartney
10	Blood, Sweat & Tears 3	Blood, Sweat & Tears

As the Beatles and Simon and Garfunkel, two of the biggest-selling acts of the 1960s, broke up to follow solo paths through the 1970s, they dominated the United States sellers of the first year of the new decade – the US duo with the top-selling title, and the British group with three entries (including *Abbey Road*'s second appearance), plus the first major Beatle solo release, by Paul McCartney. *Woodstock* was a triple-LP set of music from the film of the festival.

THE TOP 10 ALBUMS OF 1971 IN THE UK

	Title	Artist
1	Bridge Over Troubled Water	Simon and Garfunkel
2	Every Picture Tells A Story	Rod Stewart
3	Sticky Fingers	Rolling Stones
4	Motown Chartbusters, Vol. 5	Various
5	Electric Warrior	T. Rex
6	Ram	Paul & Linda McCartney
7	Tapestry	Carole King
8	Every Good Boy Deserves Favour	Moody Blues
9	Andy Williams' Greatest Hits	Andy Williams
10	Mud Slide Slim And The Blue Horizon	James Taylor

Bridge Over Troubled Water returned sporadically to the No. 1 slot throughout 1971 as newer chart-toppers came and went, and effortlessly registered once again as the year's top seller. Andy Williams' hits compilation also made its second annual appearance, while Carole King and James Taylor, doyens of the singer-songwriter wave which was sweeping the US album market, also scored major UK hits, though neither of their albums actually topped the chart.

THE TOP 10 ALBUMS OF 1971 IN THE USA

	Title	Artist
1	Tapestry	Carole King
2	Jesus Christ Superstar	Original UK Cast
3	Sticky Fingers	Rolling Stones
4	Pearl	Janis Joplin
5	Tea For The Tillerman	Cat Stevens
6	Mud Slide Slim And The Blue Horizon	James Taylor
7	Carpenters	Carpenters
8	All Things Must Pass	George Harrison
9	Led Zeppelin III	Led Zeppelin
10	Abraxas	Santana

Tapestry marked a remarkable career re-awakening for Carole King, who had originally been the composing half (the lyricist being her former husband Gerry Goffin) of one of the top commercial songwriting teams of the early 1960s. Her own performing talents had been largely bypassed during that era, but the success of this album – which eventually sold over 15,000,000 copies – moved her to the front rank of contemporary singer-songwriters.

THE TOP 10 ALBUMS OF 1972 IN THE UK

	Title	Artist
1	20 Dynamic Hits	Various
2	Simon And Garfunkel's Greatest Hits	Simon and Garfunkel
3	20 All-Time Hits Of The Fifties	Various
4	Never A Dull Moment	Rod Stewart
5	20 Fantastic Hits	Various
6	Bridge Over Troubled Water	Simon and Garfunkel
7	Fog On The Tyne	Lindisfarne
8	Slade Alive	Slade
9	Led Zeppelin (four symbols)	Led Zeppelin
10	American Pie	Don McLean

This was the year in which various compilations from TV mass-marketers K-Tel and Arcade arrived in Britain, to find massive success, largely via a peripheral audience of television viewers rather than pop fans. These albums collectively occupied the No. I chart slot for 18 weeks, eclipsing even the arrival of *Simon And Garfunkel's Greatest Hits*, here to join *Bridge* as a consistent chart stalwart.

THE TOP 10 ALBUMS OF 1972 IN THE USA

	Title	Artist
1	American Pie	Don McLean
2	Harvest	Neil Young
3	Led Zeppelin (four symbols)	Led Zeppelin
4	Music	Carole King
5	America	America
6	Tapestry	Carole King
7	Let's Stay Together	Al Green
8	The Concert For Bangladesh	Various
9	Chicago V	Chicago
10	Honky Chateau	Elton John

Several acts – Neil Young, Al Green and new chartmakers Don McLean and America – had their bestselling albums ever during 1972, which overall was notable for its predominance of soft-rock/singer-songwriters. Ploughing heavier turf, though, were Led Zeppelin (this album, officially untitled but for the four runic symbols, was the one which contained *Stairway To Heaven*, and thus anything but self-effacing), and the rock-with-brass fusioneers Chicago.

THE TOP 10 ALBUMS OF 1973 IN THE UK

	Title	Artist
1	Don't Shoot Me, I'm Only The Piano Player	Elton John
2	Aladdin Sane	David Bowie
3	Simon And Garfunkel's Greatest Hits	Simon and Garfunkel
4	Dark Side Of The Moon	Pink Floyd
5	We Can Make It	Peters & Lee
6	The Beatles, 1967–1970	Beatles
7	The Beatles, 1962–1966	Beatles
8	And I Love You So	Perry Como
9	Back To Front	Gilbert O'Sullivan
10	That'll Be The Day	Soundtrack

A chart of many influences, 1973's UK bestsellers veered between contemporary rock from Elton, Bowie and Pink Floyd, and 'adult' easy listening from Perry Como and the *Opportunity Knocks* winners Peters & Lee. *That'll Be The Day* was an oldies-filled compilation of material from the film starring David Essex, while the two Beatles titles were comprehensive chronological 'best of' double albums.

THE TOP 10 ALBUMS OF 1973 IN THE USA

	Title	Artist
1	Dark Side Of The Moon	Pink Floyd
2	Houses Of The Holy	Led Zeppelin
3	The Beatles, 1967–1970	Beatles
4	The Beatles, 1962–1966	Beatles
5	The World Is A Ghetto	War
6	Chicago VI	Chicago
7	No Secrets	Carly Simon
8	Talking Book	Stevie Wonder
9	Lady Sings The Blues	Soundtrack/Diana Ross
10	Seventh Sojourn	Moody Blues

Rock returned spectacularly to 1973's US bestsellers, with Carly Simon the only singer-songwriter making an appearance this time. The top-seller, Pink Floyd's *Dark Side Of The Moon*, was destined to spend the all-time record of 740 consecutive weeks (or 13½ years) on the Top 200 US album chart, over which period it would sell more than 11,000,000 copies.

THE TOP 10 ALBUMS OF 1974 IN THE UK

	Title	Artist
1	The Singles, 1969–1973	Carpenters
2	Band On The Run	Wings
3	Tubular Bells	Mike Oldfield
4	40 Greatest Hits	Elvis Presley
5	Dark Side Of The Moon	Pink Floyd
6	Diamond Dogs	David Bowie
7	Goodbye Yellow Brick Road	Elton John
8	And I Love You So	Perry Como
9	Simon And Garfunkel's Greatest Hits	Simon and Garfunkel
10	Elton John's Greatest Hits	Elton John

THE TOP 10 ALBUMS OF 1974 IN THE USA

	Title	Artist
1	John Denver's Greatest Hits	John Denver
2	Band On The Run	Wings
3	The Singles, 1969–1973	Carpenters
4	You Don't Mess Around With Jim	Jim Croce
5	Chicago VII	Chicago
6	The Sting	Soundtrack
7	Back Home Again	John Denver
8	Caribou	Elton John
9	Bachman Turner Overdrive II	Bachman Turner Overdrive
10	Goodbye Yellow Brick Road	Elton John

This was a good year for hits compilations, with the Carpenters, Elvis Presley (whose release was a double album licensed by RCA to mass-marketers Arcade) and Elton John all selling in immense quantities. Simon and Garfunkel's hits album, meanwhile, made yet another year-end showing, while the Pink Floyd and Perry Como titles repeated their 1973 success, and *Tubular Bells* marked the arrival of both the Virgin label and a new major album seller in instrumentalist Mike Oldfield.

Unusually for the US market, hits compilations (by John Denver and the Carpenters) provided two of the three biggest-selling albums of the year in 1974. Sandwiched between these two was what is still generally judged to be Paul McCartney's finest post-Beatles album, *Band On The Run*; the US pressing of this has always differed from its British equivalent by having an extra hit single, *Helen Wheels*, included on it.

The Carpenters' first singles compilation led the UK album bestsellers of 1974.

THE TOP 10 ALBUMS OF 1975 IN THE UK

	Title	Artist
1	The Best Of The Stylistics	Stylistics
2	Once Upon A Star	Bay City Rollers
3	Atlantic Crossing	Rod Stewart
4	40 Golden Greats	Jim Reeves
5	Venus And Mars	Wings
6	40 Greatest Hits	Elvis Presley
7	Elton John's Greatest Hits	Elton John
8	Horizon	Carpenters
9	Tubular Bells	Mike Oldfield
10	Perry Como's 40 Greatest Hits	Perry Como

Once again it was a year of compilations, with soft-soul group the Stylistics taking top honours with their hit singles package, and middle-of-the-road stars Jim Reeves and Perry Como following Elvis (whose album made its second consecutive year-end appearance) into the 40-track double album stakes. Bestselling 'new' album was by the Bay City Rollers, who were the year's major teenage sensation.

THE TOP 10 ALBUMS OF 1975 IN THE USA

	Title	Artist
1	Captain Fantastic And The Brown Dirt Cowboy	Elton John
2	That's The Way Of The World	Earth, Wind & Fire
3	Rock Of The Westies	Elton John
4	Physical Graffiti	Led Zeppelin
5	One Of These Nights	Eagles
6	Have You Never Been Mellow	Olivia Newton-John
7	Elton John's Greatest Hits	Elton John
8	Red Octopus	Jefferson Starship
9	AWB	Average White Band
10	Windsong	John Denver

Elton John dominated the top sellers of 1975, taking three of the Top 10 placings, including two of the top three. Captain Fantastic broke new ground on the US LP chart by being the first album ever to sell so swiftly upon release that it entered the chart at the No. 1 position. Only five months later, Elton's Rock Of The Westies repeated this feat. Jefferson Starship were a later incarnation of Jefferson Airplane, while soul group the Average White Band were indeed white, and also Scottish!

THE TOP 10 ALBUMS OF 1976 IN THE UK

	Title	Artist
1	Greatest Hits	Abba
2	20 Golden Greats	Beach Boys
3	Forever And Ever	Demis Roussos
4	A Night On The Town	Rod Stewart
5	20 Golden Greats	Glen Campbell
6	Their Greatest Hits, 1971–1975	Eagles
7	The Very Best Of Slim Whitman	Slim Whitman
8	A Night At The Opera	Queen
9	Desire	Bob Dylan
10	Wings At The Speed Of Sound	Wings

Abba's year-topping Greatest Hits package was, amazingly, released when they had had only six UK hit singles, but its success gave notice that the Swedish quartet were about to undertake a reign as the hottest act in pop music. Meanwhile, EMI launched its TV-advertised 20 Golden Greats line, which would be the most consistently successful series of its kind ever undertaken by a major UK label. Its debut release, by the Beach Boys, would eventually top 1,000,000 copies.

THE TOP 10 ALBUMS OF 1976 IN THE USA

	Title	Artist
1	Frampton Comes Alive!	Peter Frampton
2	Songs In The Key Of Life	Stevie Wonder
3	Wings At The Speed Of Sound	Wings
4	Their Greatest Hits, 1971–1975	Eagles
5	History: America's Greatest Hits	America
6	Gratitude	Earth, Wind & Fire
7	Breezin'	George Benson
8	Fleetwood Mac	Fleetwood Mac
9	A Night At The Opera	Queen
10	Presence	Led Zeppelin

Peter Frampton, whose double album Comes Alive outsold everything else in the United States in 1976, was a British (albeit US-based) singer-guitarist, a former member of UK hit groups the Herd and Humble Pie – and also a one-time schoolmate of David Bowie! Stevie Wonder's runner-up album was also a double set (with a free EP); it emulated Elton John's achievements of the previous year by debuting on the US chart at No. 1.

THE TOP 10 ALBUMS OF 1977 IN THE UK

	Title	Artist
1	Arrival	Abba
2	20 Golden Greats	Shadows
3	20 Golden Greats	Diana Ross & The Supremes
4	Rumours	Fleetwood Mac
5	A Star Is Born	Soundtrack
6	Hotel California	Eagles
7	The Sound Of Bread	Bread
8	The Johnny Mathis Collection	Johnny Mathis
9	Greatest Hits	Abba
10	Animals	Pink Floyd

Another year dominated by hits collections, though for the first time in a while a movie soundtrack also made the Top 10 in 1977 – although A Star Is Born was essentially a Barbra Streisand album. The Bread compilation The Sound Of, curiously, outsold all the US group's comparatively small number of UK hit singles added together, by a considerable margin.

THE TOP 10 ALBUMS OF 1977 IN THE USA

	Title	Artist
1	Rumours	Fleetwood Mac
2	Hotel California	Eagles
3	Boston	Boston
4	Star Wars	Soundtrack
5	A Star Is Born	Soundtrack
6	Wings Over America	Wings
7	I'm In You	Peter Frampton
8	Commodores	Commodores
9	Foreigner	Foreigner
10	Songs In The Key Of Life	Stevie Wonder

Fleetwood Mac's Rumours was by far the group's biggest-ever seller, spending an incredible seven months atop the US chart – the deliberately English spelling of the title presumably not puzzling too many American buyers. Another Anglo-American outfit, Foreigner, took their debut album into the year's top sellers, while the eponymous entry at number three by Boston was the biggest-selling debut album ever by a group, eventually topping sales of 9,000,000.

THE TOP 10 ALBUMS OF 1978 IN THE UK

	Title	Artist
1	Saturday Night Fever	Soundtrack
2	Grease	Soundtrack
3	The Album	Abba
4	Night Flight To Venus	Boney M
5	20 Golden Greats	Nat 'King' Cole
6	Rumours	Fleetwood Mac
7	Out Of The Blue	Electric Light Orchestra
8	20 Golden Greats	Buddy Holly & The Crickets
9	The War Of The Worlds	Jeff Wayne
10	The Kick Inside	Kate Bush

The RSO label's huge success in 1978, with singles by John Travolta, Olivia Newton-John, the Bee Gees and others from the films Saturday Night Fever and Grease, was reflected in the sales of its double-album soundtrack packages from each film, which collectively topped the British charts for 31 weeks. Jeff Wayne's guest-studded double-album version of H.G. Wells' The War Of The Worlds also spun off several hit singles.

THE TOP 10 ALBUMS OF 1978 IN THE USA

	Title	Artist
1	Saturday Night Fever	Soundtrack
2	Grease	Soundtrack
3	Some Girls	Rolling Stones
4	Double Vision	Foreigner
5	Running On Empty	Jackson Browne
6	Natural High	Commodores
7	The Stranger	Billy Joel
8	Stranger In Town	Bob Seger
9	News Of The World	Queen
10	Slowhand	Eric Clapton

For the first time in many years, two movie soundtrack recordings topped the year's bestsellers, though in both these cases they were replete with hit songs by major acts that were also represented in the year's singles charts. Saturday Night Fever, dominated by the Bee Gees, sold a total of 11,000,000 copies, making it the biggest-selling album ever in the United States up to this time. Grease was a slightly more modest success, shifting just 8,000,000.

THE TOP 10 ALBUMS OF 1979 IN THE UK

	Title	Artist
1	Parallel Lines	Blondie
2	Discovery	Electric Light Orchestra
3	Voulez Vous	Abba
4	Breakfast In America	Supertramp
5	The Very Best Of Leo Sayer	Leo Sayer
6	Greatest Hits, Vol. 2	Abba
7	Regatta De Blanc	Police
8	Greatest Hits, Vol. 2	Barbra Streisand
9	Spirits Having Flown	Bee Gees
10	Manilow Magic	Barry Manilow

Blondie's *Parallel Lines* was the bestselling UK album by an American group whose popularity had actually broken in Britain a year earlier, well in advance of their US chart success. Although this and the next three top sellers of the year were all new albums of original material, 1979 nevertheless marked the return of the big-selling compilation album to occupy 40 per cent of the Top 10 (Barry Manilow's entry was also a 'greatest hits' set)

THE TOP 10 ALBUMS OF 1979 IN THE USA

	Title	Artist
1	Breakfast In America	Supertramp
2	Bad Girls	Donna Summer
3	Minute By Minute	Doobie Brothers
4	Spirits Having Flown	Bee Gees
5	Blondes Have More Fun	Rod Stewart
6	Get The Knack	Knack
7	In Through The Out Door	Led Zeppelin
8	Cheap Trick At Budokan	Cheap Trick
9	The Long Run	Eagles
10	52nd Street	Billy Joel

Breakfast In America was the all-time biggest seller (and spun off the biggest hit singles) on both sides of the Atlantic for Supertramp, a British group who found rather more consistent success in the United States. Cheap Trick, an American band, sold well enough on their home territory, but had an even bigger following in Japan, which is where their live set *Cheap Trick At Budokan* was recorded.

THE TOP 10 ALBUMS OF 1980 IN THE UK

	Title	Artist
1	Super Trouper	Abba
2	Zenyatta Mondatta	Police
3	Greatest Hits	Rose Royce
4	Pretenders	Pretenders
5	Guilty	Barbra Streisand
6	Regatta De Blanc	Police
7	Flesh And Blood	Roxy Music
8	Off The Wall	Michael Jackson
9	Duke	Genesis
10	Sky 2	Sky

For no apparent reason, 1980 was notable as a year of short, often one-word, album titles. There was also a general absence of hits compilations from the biggest sellers, while the Police made their growing status felt (*Regatta De Blanc* had a second consecutive year-end showing alongside the newer *Zenyatta Mondatta*), and other major acts like Genesis, Roxy Music and Michael Jackson made their debut appearance among the annual top sellers in the UK.

THE TOP 10 ALBUMS OF 1980 IN THE USA

	Title	Artist
1	The Wall	Pink Floyd
2	Emotional Rescue	Rolling Stones
3	Against The Wind	Bob Seger
4	Glass Houses	Billy Joel
5	Guilty	Barbra Streisand
6	The River	Bruce Springsteen
7	The Game	Queen
8	The Bee Gees' Greatest	Bee Gees
9	Crimes Of Passion	Pat Benatar
10	Diana	Diana Ross

Pink Floyd's *The Wall* spent three-and-a-half months at No. 1 on the US chart, taking it some way towards emulating the group's achievement with *Dark Side Of The Moon*. The Wall eventually sold over 7,000,000 copies in the United States, against *Dark Side's* total of 11,000,000. Barbra Streisand's *Guilty* album was written and produced by the Bee Gees, themselves no strangers to the year-end US Top 10.

THE TOP 10 ALBUMS OF 1981 IN THE UK

	Title	Artist
1	Kings Of The Wild Frontier	Adam & The Ants
2	Greatest Hits	Queen
3	Face Value	Phil Collins
4	Love Songs	Cliff Richard
5	Ghost In The Machine	Police
6	Shaky	Shakin' Stevens
7	Dare	Human League
8	Double Fantasy	John Lennon and Yoko Ono
9	The Jazz Singer	Neil Diamond
10	Stars On 45	Starsound

Adam & The Ants had a spell as the UK's hottest teen audience group in 1981–82, and their first album demonstrated this appeal by becoming the year's biggest seller and capturing the year's longest spell (12 weeks) atop the chart. Queen's *Greatest Hits* compilation, issued near the end of the year, sold quickly enough to make the runner-up slot, and went on to become the fourth biggest-selling UK album of the decade.

THE TOP 10 ALBUMS OF 1981 IN THE USA

	Title	Artist
1	Hi Infidelity	REO Speedwagon
2	4	Foreigner
3	Escape	Journey
4	Tattoo You	Rolling Stones
5	Double Fantasy	John Lennon and Yoko Ono
6	Mistaken Identity	Kim Carnes
7	Paradise Theater	Styx
8	The Jazz Singer	Neil Diamond
9	Bella Donna	Stevie Nicks
10	Long Distance Voyager	Moody Blues

Rock music ruled the US album charts with a vengeance in 1981, with all the top four sellers being by rock bands, and these four titles collectively monopolizing the No. 1 slot for 35 out of 52 weeks. All the same, there was still room for two albums by female artists, while Neil Diamond's *Jazz Singer* was the soundtrack to the remake of the film of the same title, in which Diamond co-starred with Laurence Olivier.

THE TOP 10 ALBUMS OF 1982 IN THE UK

	Title	Artist
1	Love Songs	Barbra Streisand
2	The Kids From Fame	Kids From Fame
3	Complete Madness	Madness
4	The Lexicon Of Love	ABC
5	Rio	Duran Duran
6	Love Over Gold	Dire Straits
7	Dare	Human League
8	Avalon	Roxy Music
9	Pelican West	Haircut 100
10	Too-Rye-Ay	Dexy's Midnight Runners

Though Barbra Streisand's ballads collection was the year's biggest seller, followed by Madness' singles compilation at number three, most of the remainder of this Top 10 consists of new material by contemporary acts, with the ABC and Haircut 100 albums being debut efforts. The year's most unusual smash was the BBC's *The Kids From Fame*, featuring the cast from the *Fame* TV show – which was itself a spin-off from the hit 1980 movie of the same title.

THE TOP 10 ALBUMS OF 1982 IN THE USA

	Title	Artist
1	Asia	Asia
2	Beauty And The Beat	Go-Gos
3	Freeze-Frame	J. Geils Band
4	Chariots Of Fire	Soundtrack/Vangelis
5	American Fool	John Cougar
6	Built For Speed	Stray Cats
7	Mirage	Fleetwood Mac
8	Always On My Mind	Willie Nelson
9	Eye Of The Tiger	Survivor
10	Business As Usual	Men At Work

Asia were a 1980s manifestation of the late 1960s phenomenon known as the supergroup: the members (Steve Howe, Carl Palmer, Geoff Downes and John Wetton) were all celebrity players from other bands, and all British – though it was American buyers who took to the quartet's debut album in the millions, rather than their decidedly sceptical fellow-countrymen. Meanwhile, the usual Anglo-American monopoly was broken by Australian group Men At Work, whose smash album also spun off two No. 1 singles.

THE TOP 10 ALBUMS OF 1983 IN THE UK

	Title	Artist
1	Thriller	Michael Jackson
2	Let's Dance	David Bowie
3	Colour By Numbers	Culture Club
4	No Parlez	Paul Young
5	True	Spandau Ballet
6	Fantastic	Wham!
7	Business As Usual	Men At Work
8	Synchronicity	Police
9	Genesis	Genesis
10	18 Greatest Hits	Michael Jackson and Jackson 5

Michael Jackson's *Thriller*, home to an ever-growing string of hit singles, mirrored its global progress (it was the world's top-selling album by the end of the year) by becoming the bestselling UK record of the decade at that point. Its success clearly also prompted the opportunist compilation of old Jackson solo and group hits which was the year's 10th bestseller

THE TOP 10 ALBUMS OF 1983 IN THE USA

	Title	Artist
1	Thriller	Michael Jackson
2	Synchronicity	Police
3	Lionel Richie	Lionel Richie
4	Pyromania	Def Leppard
5	Flashdance	Soundtrack
6	Metal Health	Quiet Riot
7	Frontiers	Journey
8	H2O	Daryl Hall and John Oates
9	An Innocent Man	Billy Joel
10	Can't Slow Down	Lionel Richie

Michael Jackson's *Thriller*, which dominated the US charts in 1983 and early 1984 with a total of 37 weeks at No. 1, became the all-time biggest seller not only in the American record market, where it sold in excess of 20,000,000 copies, but also globally, shifting over 40,000,000. It spun off seven US Top 10 singles in a row, and far from detracting from the album's sales, the success of each one of these served to re-boost it.

THE TOP 10 ALBUMS OF 1984 IN THE UK

	Title	Artist
1	Can't Slow Down	Lionel Richie
2	The Hits Album	Various
3	Legend	Bob Marley & The Wailers
4	Make It Big	Wham!
5	Now That's What I Call Music, 3	Various
6	Thriller	Michael Jackson
7	Diamond Life	Sade
8	Now That's What I Call Music, 4	Various
9	An Innocent Man	Billy Joel
10	The Pleasuredome	Frankie Goes To Hollywood

Lionel Richie's *Can't Slow Down* was the first Motown album to top an annual chart in the UK, and in fact was the UK's biggest-selling Motown album ever. The year was also notable for the arrival of two new TV-advertised series of compilations of then recent hits by various artists (colloquially known as '*Hits*' and '*Now*'), each marketed by two or more of the major UK labels working in partnership. The early volumes of both series had massive sales – as they would continue to have through the 1980s.

THE TOP 10 ALBUMS OF 1984 IN THE USA

	Title	Artist
1	Purple Rain	Prince
2	Born In The USA	Bruce Springsteen
3	Sports	Huey Lewis & The News
4	Thriller	Michael Jackson
5	1984	Van Halen
6	Can't Slow Down	Lionel Richie
7	Footloose	Soundtrack
8	Colour By Numbers	Culture Club
9	Break Out	Pointer Sisters
10	Learning To Crawl	Pretenders

Purple Rain was the soundtrack to Prince's first starring movie, and proved to be his most successful album ever. It was also one of the fastest sellers in US record history, with a reputed 1,300,000 sales in its very first day in the shops, and 8,000,000 sold within 20 weeks. The album topped the US chart for 24 weeks, and had final sales of over 10,000,000 – though ironically this huge total was eventually overtaken by Bruce Springsteen's *Born In The USA*, which climbed to 11,000,000.

Lionel Richie's 1984 album Can't Slow Down *was the year's top seller, and the biggest-selling Motown album ever in the UK.*

THE TOP 10 ALBUMS OF 1985 IN THE UK

	Title	Artist
1	Brothers In Arms	Dire Straits
2	No Jacket Required	Phil Collins
3	Like A Virgin	Madonna
4	Born In The USA	Bruce Springsteen
5	Songs From The Big Chair	Tears For Fears
6	Now That's What I Call Music, 6	Various
7	Now – The Christmas Album	Various
8	Now That's What I Call Music, 5	Various
9	Alf	Alison Moyet
10	The Secret Of Association	Paul Young

Dire Straits' *Brothers In Arms*, spurred by spiralling sales of the CD format (it was found to be the first CD that many upwardly mobile converts to CD were buying), swept past Michael Jackson's *Thriller* album to become the biggest UK seller of the 1980s. Its sales would be over 3,000,000 by the end of the decade, making it second only to the Beatles' *Sgt Pepper* in the all-time stakes. Meanwhile, Madonna and Bruce Springsteen both made their debuts in the UK annual Top 10.

THE TOP 10 ALBUMS OF 1985 IN THE USA

	Title	Artist
1	Like A Virgin	Madonna
2	Brothers In Arms	Dire Straits
3	No Jacket Required	Phil Collins
4	We Are The World	Various
5	Miami Vice	Soundtrack
6	Songs From The Big Chair	Tears For Fears
7	Make It Big	Wham!
8	Born In The USA	Bruce Springsteen
9	Purple Rain	Prince
10	Reckless	Bryan Adams

Like A Virgin was Madonna's most successful album of the 1980s, with US sales eventually topping 7,000,000. Dire Straits' *Brothers In Arms*, which was the UK's biggest seller in the 1980s with sales of more than 3,000,000 copies, sold approximately the same number in the (much larger) American market. *We Are The World* was the album based around the USA For Africa hit, and as with the single, all its profits went to African famine aid charities.

THE TOP 10 ALBUMS OF 1986 IN THE UK

	Title	Artist
1	True Blue	Madonna
2	Brothers In Arms	Dire Straits
3	Whitney Houston	Whitney Houston
4	Graceland	Paul Simon
5	Now That's What I Call Music, 8	Various
6	A Kind Of Magic	Queen
7	Now That's What I Call Music, 7	Various
8	Silk And Steel	Five Star
9	Revenge	Eurythmics
10	The Hits Album, 5	Various

As Madonna's star magnitude grew, so her album sales climbed: *True Blue* became the UK's biggest seller of 1986 by just enough of a margin to prevent *Brothers In Arms* from pulling off a second consecutive year at the top. Paul Simon had his biggest-ever seller as a solo act with *Graceland*, and Whitney Houston's eponymous first album made the year's most impressive debut on the back of her chart-topping single *Saving All My Love For You.*

THE TOP 10 ALBUMS OF 1986 IN THE USA

	Title	Artist
1	Whitney Houston	Whitney Houston
2	True Blue	Madonna
3	Top Gun	Soundtrack
4	Live 1975–1985	Bruce Springsteen
5	Third Stage	Boston
6	5150	Van Halen
7	Dancing On The Ceiling	Lionel Richie
8	Control	Janet Jackson
9	Rapture	Anita Baker
10	Slippery When Wet	Bon Jovi

Whitney Houston's first album was the biggest-selling debut ever by a female artist, with US sales eventually topping 9,000,000. The year 1986 was also strong for girls in general, with another huge seller by Madonna, and Janet Jackson and Anita Baker also in the Top 10. Bruce Springsteen's release was a multi-album boxed set of live performances, which entered the US chart at No. 1 in its first week.

THE TOP 10 ALBUMS OF 1987 IN THE UK

	Title	Artist
1	Bad	Michael Jackson
2	The Joshua Tree	U2
3	Whitney	Whitney Houston
4	Now That's What I Call Music, 10	Various
5	The Hits Album, 6	Various
6	Tango In The Night	Fleetwood Mac
7	Now That's What I Call Music, 9	Various
8	Running In The Family	Level 42
9	Whenever You Need Somebody	Rick Astley
10	The Phantom Of The Opera	London Cast

For the first time since *Hair* almost two decades before, an original London cast album became one of the year's Top 10 sellers, in the form of Andrew Lloyd Webber's record-breaking *The Phantom Of The Opera*. Meanwhile, Michael Jackson's *Bad* broke all records by selling over 600,000 copies in the UK in its first week – one in 10 of all albums sold that week, and as many copies as the rest of the week's Top 30 put together.

THE TOP 10 ALBUMS OF 1987 IN THE USA

	Title	Artist
1	Slippery When Wet	Bon Jovi
2	Whitney	Whitney Houston
3	The Joshua Tree	U2
4	Licensed To Ill	Beastie Boys
5	Whitesnake	Whitesnake
6	Bad	Michael Jackson
7	Dirty Dancing	Soundtrack
8	Whitney Houston	Whitney Houston
9	La Bamba	Soundtrack
10	Girls Girls Girls	Motley Crue

More triumphs for Whitney Houston this year, as her second album (which debuted on the chart at No. 1) sold 5,000,000 copies, and her first almost kept pace with it. There were, unusually, two film soundtracks among the year's top sellers: *Dirty Dancing*, which contained a mixture of new songs and early 1960s period classics, and *La Bamba* featuring mostly the group Los Lobos recreating the music of the film's subject, Ritchie Valens.

THE TOP 10 ALBUMS OF 1988 IN THE UK

	Title	Artist
1	Kylie	Kylie Minogue
2	Private Collection, 1977–1988	Cliff Richard
3	Now That's What I Call Music, 13	Various
4	Bad	Michael Jackson
5	Popped In, Souled Out	Wet Wet Wet
6	Push	Bros
7	Tracy Chapman	Tracy Chapman
8	Introducing The Hardline...	Terence Trent D'Arby
9	Money For Nothing	Dire Straits
10	Tango In The Night	Fleetwood Mac

Kylie Minogue's debut release became the bestselling album ever by a female artist and the biggest-ever by an Australian act. Aged 19 at the time of her initial success, she was the youngest person ever to have a million-selling UK album, with *Kylie* eventually selling over 1,800,000 copies in the UK. Impressive debut performances were also registered in 1988 by Bros, Wet Wet Wet, Tracy Chapman and Terence Trent D'Arby.

THE TOP 10 ALBUMS OF 1988 IN THE USA

	Title	Artist
1	Faith	George Michael
2	Hysteria	Def Leppard
3	Appetite For Destruction	Guns N' Roses
4	OU812	Van Halen
5	Dirty Dancing	Soundtrack
6	Rattle And Hum	U2
7	Tracy Chapman	Tracy Chapman
8	New Jersey	Bon Jovi
9	Kick	INXS
10	Roll With It	Steve Winwood

George Michael's *Faith*, his first post-Wham! solo album, sold over 7,000,000 copies in America: proportionally a bigger success for him than it was at home, as were a series of hit singles extracted from it. Otherwise, the year's big sellers belonged mainly to the heavy rock bands, with new major sellers by Van Halen, Def Leppard and Bon Jovi, and the arrival of Guns N' Roses (with an eventual 8,000,000 seller) and Australia's INXS.

THE TOP 10 ALBUMS OF 1989 IN THE UK

	Title	Artist
1	Ten Good Reasons	Jason Donovan
2	A New Flame	Simply Red
3	...But Seriously	Phil Collins
4	Anything For You	Gloria Estefan & Miami Sound Machine
5	Enjoy Yourself	Kylie Minogue
6	The Raw And The Cooked	Fine Young Cannibals
7	Cuts Both Ways	Gloria Estefan
8	Like A Prayer	Madonna
9	Foreign Affair	Tina Turner
10	Don't Be Cruel	Bobby Brown

THE TOP 10 ALBUMS OF 1989 IN THE USA

	Title	Artist
1	Girl You Know It's True	Milli Vanilli
2	Don't Be Cruel	Bobby Brown
3	Like A Prayer	Madonna
4	The Raw And The Cooked	Fine Young Cannibals
5	Batman	Soundtrack/Prince
6	Electric Youth	Debbie Gibson
7	Rhythm Nation 1814	Janet Jackson
8	Hangin' Tough	New Kids On The Block
9	Forever Your Girl	Paula Abdul
10	Beaches	Soundtrack

Album sales boomed in the dying days of 1989, to the extent that it was not until Christmas that Jason Donovan's debut album overhauled Simply Red to become the year's biggest-selling release (and give PWL Records and the Stock Aitken Waterman production team the number one seller for the second year in a row, after Kylie Minogue's 1988 success). Phil Collins' album was not released until the end of November, but sold over 1,000,000 copies between then and the end of the year/decade.

The success of Milli Vanilli became a unique source of embarrassment in the pop music world. Having sold over 5,000,000 copies of the album *Girl You Know It's True*, the group were awarded a Grammy as the Best New Act of 1989, only to be forced to return it later when it transpired that the duo who fronted the act on TV appearances (and who had accepted the Grammy award) were merely a cosmetic front for the German-based studio act, and had played no part in the making of the record.

Milli Vanilli's album Girl You Know It's True *headed the field in the USA in 1989. Over 5,000,000 copies were sold before the two group members were revealed not to have participated at all in its recording.*

THE TOP 10 ALBUMS OF 1990 IN THE UK

	Title	Artist
1	...But Seriously	Phil Collins
2	The Essential Pavarotti	Luciano Pavarotti
3	Sleeping With The Past	Elton John
4	Only Yesterday: Greatest Hits	Carpenters
5	The Three Tenors Concert	Carreras, Domingo, Pavarotti
6	Soul Provider	Michael Bolton
7	The Very Best Of Elton John	Elton John
8	Vivaldi: The Four Seasons	Nigel Kennedy/ECO
9	Foreign Affair	Tina Turner
10	The Immaculate Collection	Madonna

In 1990, for the first time ever, classical albums sold in comparable numbers to the year's biggest-selling pop releases, with three of the Top 10 being from the classical repertoire. The twin reasons were the almost rock star appeal of violinist Nigel Kennedy, and huge media exposure for the world's three best-known tenors in concert at the time of the World Cup – for which Pavarotti's Nessun Dorma was also used as the theme to the BBC TV coverage.

THE TOP 10 ALBUMS OF 1990 IN THE USA

	Title	Artist
1	Please Hammer Don't Hurt 'Em	MC Hammer
2	To The Extreme	Vanilla Ice
3	Forever Your Girl	Paula Abdul
4	...But Seriously	Phil Collins
5	Mariah Carey	Mariah Carey
6	Wilson Phillips	Wilson Phillips
7	Soul Provider	Michael Bolton
8	Nick Of Time	Bonnie Raitt
9	Rhythm Nation 1814	Janet Jackson
10	I Do Not Want What I Haven't Got	Sinead O'Connor

This was the year when rap music crossed over to mega-sales in the United States. MC Hammer's debut album would eventually sell over 10,000,000 copies, while Vanilla Ice's first sold an astonishing 5,000,000 during its first three months on the market. Otherwise, it was also a good year for female vocalists, who (including all-girl trio Wilson Phillips) occupied six placings on this Top 10.

THE TOP 10 ALBUMS OF 1991 IN THE UK

	Title	Artist
1	Stars	Simply Red
2	Greatest Hits	Eurythmics
3	Greatest Hits II	Queen
4	Out Of Time	R.E.M.
5	Dangerous	Michael Jackson
6	The Immaculate Collection	Madonna
7	Love Hurts	Cher
8	Seal	Seal
9	From Time To Time – The Singles Collection	Paul Young
10	Waking Up The Neighbors	Bryan Adams

Simply Red's Stars snatched the year's top honours from the Eurythmics' Greatest Hits at the 11th hour, overtaking its sales rival just a day or so before Christmas. Four of the Top 10 were major artist hits compilations, while Michael Jackson's Dangerous failed to live up to the tremendous sales momentum of either his Bad or Thriller sets of the previous decade – although it, too, proved a rich source of hit singles.

THE TOP 10 ALBUMS OF 1991 IN THE USA

	Title	Artist
1	Ropin' The Wind	Garth Brooks
2	No Fences	Garth Brooks
3	Out Of Time	R.E.M.
4	Gonna Make You Sweat	C & C Music Factory
5	Time, Love And Tenderness	Michael Bolton
6	Unforgettable	Natalie Cole
7	The Immaculate Collection	Madonna
8	Metallica	Metallica
9	Use Your Illusion II	Guns N' Roses
10	Use Your Illusion I	Guns N' Roses

If any proof were needed of the status of Country singer Garth Brooks as America's biggest record seller of the early 1990s, the two albums at the top of this list each sold over 4,000,000 copies in the United States during 1991 – Ropin' The Wind achieving this figure in its first three months on sale! The remainder of the Top 10 all sold 3,000,000 copies or more, an indication of the strength of US album (or CD) sales even in the teeth of gathering economic recession.

THE TOP 10 ALBUMS OF 1992 IN THE UK

	Title	Artist
1	Stars	Simply Red
2	Back To Front	Lionel Richie
3	Diva	Annie Lennox
4	We Can't Dance	Genesis
5	Dangerous	Michael Jackson
6	Cher's Greatest Hits: 1965–1992	Cher
7	Up	Right Said Fred
8	Gold – Greatest Hits	Abba
9	Divine Madness	Madness
10	Glittering Prize '81–'92	Simple Minds

The Top 10 UK albums of 1992 divided equally between new material and compilations of earlier hits – although both Lionel Richie's and Cher's examples of the latter category shrewdly mixed in some new material among the old. Simply Red's Stars, remarkably, was the top seller for the second year running: as 1992 drew to a close its total sales had just passed the 3,000,000 mark, with some 60 per cent of those copies having crossed the counter during the previous 12 months.

THE TOP 10 ALBUMS OF 1992 IN THE USA

	Title	Artist
1	Ropin' The Wind	Garth Brooks
2	Some Gave All	Billy Ray Cyrus
3	'The Bodyguard' Original Soundtrack	Various
4	The Chase	Garth Brooks
5	Nevermind	Nirvana
6	Dangerous	Michael Jackson
7	No Fences	Garth Brooks
8	Metallica	Metallica
9	Achtung Baby	U2
10	Ten	Pearl Jam

The top four in this list all sold more than 5,000,000 copies during the year – a feat all the more remarkable for Ropin' The Wind which was actually released in 1991. Virtually unknown outside his native United States, Nashville king Garth Brooks has been a one-man two-year sales machine, credited with turning the normally insular Country music scene into a nationwide mainstream phenomenon in the 1990s. At the year's end, the soundtrack to Whitney Houston's movie The Bodyguard was selling at the rate of 1,000,000 copies a week, making it one of the fastest-selling titles of all time.

RECORDING FORMATS

On 19 February 1878, Thomas Edison obtained a patent for the Phonograph, which he named after the Greek words for 'sound-writer'. He had developed the cylindrical device the previous year at his Menlo Park, New Jersey laboratories, reciting the nursery rhyme, *Mary Had A Little Lamb* into a recording horn while rotating the cylinder, which was wrapped in tin foil, with a handle. The sound of his voice vibrated a diaphragm, which in turn was attached to a metal stylus, creating grooves (thousands of indentations) on the foil. When he reversed the procedure, the vibrating diaphragm amplified the sound of the nursery rhyme. Thus began the 'groove', although the flimsy nature of the tin foil, which meant that it lasted for only a few plays, dampened the impact of his revolutionary invention, which existed as a commercial success for 12 months.

During the next 10 years other inventors, including Alexander Graham Bell, searched for ways to improve on Edison's work, developing a wax-coated cardboard tube which slid over the cylinder. While several businessmen looked at its commercial potential, in 1893 San Francisco entrepreneur Louis Glass created the forerunner of the jukebox, installing battery-powered cylinder machines in phonograph parlours, where customers would pay a nickel to hear comedy songs, brass band recordings and vaudeville tunes. Soon after, German immigrant Emile Berliner developed a way of cutting the recording grooves onto discs, inventing the 'gramophone'. In 1901, Berliner formed the successful gramophone production enterprise, the Victor Talking Machine Company, and within five years introduced the Victrola, the first record player to include the sound reproducing horn as part of its hardware. Disc software of recordings by the vocal stars of the day (including Al Jolson and Enrico Caruso) swiftly followed as Victrolas became a hot consumer item.

The advent of radio in the United States in 1924 and the economic depression of the late 1920s temporarily halted the sales climb of discs but as electric technology advanced and the cost of turntables decreased to around $10 in the 1930s, the home entertainment market for recorded music and voice re-established itself and by 1938 78-rpm disc sales in the United States amounted to some $26,000,000.

After the Second World War, attempts were made in the United States to overcome the restriction imposed by the limited capacity of the wax blanks used for discs, which were capable of holding a maximum of four minutes of one recording, thus developing recording on tape, an innovation begun in Germany during the war. This allowed the recording of complete musical works and introduced the element of editing mistakes, or adding corrections.

The next major breakthrough, however, was led by Dr Peter Goldmark and a team of engineers at Columbia Records, who, on 21 July 1948 in New York City, unveiled the 'long-player', a 12″ microgroove disc of non-breakable vinyl that could accommodate up to 23 minutes per side of recording, reproduce a clearer sound and turn at $33\frac{1}{3}$ revolutions per minute. The following year, RCA Victor introduced the smaller five-minute 45-rpm vinyl record as hardware manufacturers began producing multi-speed turntables which could facilitate all three speeds (78s were still marketed well into the 1950s).

When Bill Haley's *Rock Around The Clock* hit US No. 1 on 9 July 1955, the Rock 'n' Roll era arrived and soon adopted the 45 'single' as its most popular format, though the proliferation in both the United States and Europe of inexpensive record and tape players allowed the dramatic growth in sales of all recorded options and led to a substantial increase in the number of record companies fuelling the popular music revolution.

Despite being initially invented by A.D. Blumlein in London in 1931, it was not until 1958 that the two-channel sound stereo format became a commercially viable alternative, though its arrival, requiring the purchase of new equipment by the consumer, took another 10 years to become the accepted standard over mono.

As the music industry boomed throughout the 1960s, the portable advantages of tape saw both audio-cassette and eight-track cartridge formats begin to challenge vinyl as significant re-recorded mediums. Eight-track was particularly popular in the United States for much of the 1970s (its much smaller UK sales figure peaking in 1974 at 6,200,000 against 14,000,000 cassette shipments), before the smaller size and superior sound quality of cassettes overwhelmed its bulkier tape cousin.

In the late 1970s, several classical labels began experimenting with the digital recording process: translating sound into a pulsed code. This in turn led electronics giants Sony and Philips to the invention of the compact disc. Debuting in Japan in 1982, and in America and Europe the following year, the 4.7-inch CD offered digitally encoded recordings read by a laser beam and decoded into the original music information. The subsequent improvements over vinyl and cassette in terms of sound quality, durability, noise and distortion reduction were considerable and brought the record industry into the digital age. Compact disc software sales in the UK rose from a cautious opening figure of 600,000 in 1983 to overtake vinyl sales in 1988 and sell over 60,000,000 annually by 1990. Together with audio-cassettes, whose popularity has risen considerably in the past 10 years with the proliferation of in-car cassette players, boom-boxes and Walkmans, CD sales now dominate on a global basis.

As the electronics and record giants attempted to persuade consumers to make two more format changes in 1992 to both DCC (Digital Compact Cassette, billed as the sound quality cassette equivalent to compact disc) and the MiniDisc (Sony's recordable and more portable format update of the CD), they should perhaps keep one eye on some other format innovations which were much hyped and shortlived: quadraphonic LPs (a four-way division of sound launched in the 1970s), CDV (Compact Disc Video singles accommodating five minutes of video film and 15 minutes of music, a few of which were released in 1987) and DAT (Digital Audio Tape, the first unsuccessful attempt to launch the cassette equivalent of CD).

Other format options, including the 7″ and 12″ picture disc singles and albums, 10″ mini-album and 3″ compact disc single have mostly been little more than marketing gimmicks dreamt up by ever hopeful record companies to boost sales. By contrast, 7″ four-track EPs were very popular in the 1960s, 12″ vinyl singles flourished in the late 1970s and 1980s, while both cassette singles and compact disc singles are currently successful format offshoots on both sides of the Atlantic.

THE TOP 10 ALBUMS OF THE 1950s IN THE USA

	Title	Artist	Release year
1	South Pacific	Soundtrack	1958
2	My Fair Lady	Original Cast	1956
3	The Music Man	Original Cast	1958
4	Gigi	Soundtrack	1958
5	Oklahoma	Soundtrack	1955
6	Calypso	Harry Belafonte	1956
7	Elvis Presley	Elvis Presley	1956
8	Love Is The Thing	Nat 'King' Cole	1957
9	Johnny's Greatest Hits	Johnny Mathis	1958
10	Love Me Or Leave Me (Soundtrack)	Doris Day	1955

Movie and musical soundtracks ruled the day until the advent of Elvis and his vocal contemporaries. *South Pacific*, one of the biggest-selling albums of all time, logged 262 weeks on the chart, 31 of them in pole position.

COMEDY QUIZ

1. Which comedian teamed with the Wonderstuff in 1991 for the hit single *Dizzy*?
2. Under what names did Peter Cook and Dudley Moore record their late 1970s trio of pornographic humour albums?
3. Which UK comedian has had more than a dozen hits, yet none of them comedy records?
4. Who had a comic hit version of the Beatles' *A Hard Day's Night*?
5. Who portrayed *Ernie (The Fastest Milkman In The West)*?
6. What bizarre phenomenon did Ray Stevens take to the top of both the UK and US charts in 1974?
7. Which comedian made *Loadsamoney (Doin' Up The House)* in 1988?
8. Who recorded *Holiday Road* for the comedy film *National Lampoon's Vacation*?
9. Which UK comic team advised *Always Look On The Bright Side Of Life*, a belated Top 3 hit in 1991, and from what film was it taken?
10. For which 1986 BBC TV comedy series did Dexy's Midnight Runners record the hit title theme?

THE TOP 10 ALBUMS OF THE 1960s IN THE UK

	Title	Artist	Release year
1	Sgt Pepper's Lonely Hearts Club Band	Beatles	1967
2	The Sound Of Music	Soundtrack	1965
3	With The Beatles	Beatles	1963
4	Abbey Road	Beatles	1969
5	South Pacific	Soundtrack	1958
6	Beatles For Sale	Beatles	1964
7	A Hard Day's Night	Beatles	1964
8	Rubber Soul	Beatles	1965
9	The Beatles ('White Album')	Beatles	1968
10	West Side Story	Soundtrack	1962

Not only did the Beatles dominate the Top 10, but three further albums by the mop-tops, *Revolver*, *Please Please Me* and *Help!*, were also the 11th, 12th and 13th bestselling albums of a decade which belonged to the most successful group in pop history.

THE TOP 10 ALBUMS OF THE 1960s IN THE USA

	Title	Artist	Release year
1	West Side Story	Soundtrack	1961
2	Meet The Beatles	Beatles	1964
3	The Sound Of Music	Soundtrack	1965
4	Sgt Pepper's Lonely Hearts Club Band	Beatles	1967
5	The Monkees	Monkees	1966
6	More Of The Monkees	Monkees	1967
7	Hair	Broadway Cast	1968
8	Whipped Cream And Other Delights	Herb Alpert & The Tijuana Brass	1965
9	Mary Poppins	Soundtrack	1964
10	John Fitzgerald Kennedy: A Memorial Album	Documentary	1963

While Beatles, Monkees and Presley discs sold huge quantities in a relatively short period of time, successful film soundtracks often stayed on the charts for years – *The Sound Of Music* eventually accrued a chart residence of more than five years.

THE TOP 10 ALBUMS OF THE 1970s IN THE UK

	Title	Artist	Release year
1	Bridge Over Troubled Water	Simon and Garfunkel	1970
2	Simon And Garfunkel's Greatest Hits	Simon and Garfunkel	1972
3	Rumours	Fleetwood Mac	1977
4	Dark Side Of The Moon	Pink Floyd	1973
5	Tubular Bells	Mike Oldfield	1973
6	Greatest Hits	Abba	1976
7	Bat Out Of Hell	Meat Loaf	1978
8	Saturday Night Fever	Soundtrack	1978
9	And I Love You So	Perry Como	1973
10	The Singles 1969–1973	Carpenters	1974

Each of the top five albums of the 1970s clocked up over 250 weeks on the British chart, with Fleetwood Mac's *Rumours* outdistancing them all with an astonishing 443 weeks on the survey. *Tubular Bells*, recorded by Mike Oldfield for a pittance, proved to be the business building block upon which Virgin label boss Richard Branson would create his Virgin empire.

THE TOP 10 ALBUMS OF THE 1970s IN THE USA

	Title	Artist	Release year
1	Rumours	Fleetwood Mac	1977
2	Saturday Night Fever	Soundtrack	1977
3	Grease	Soundtrack	1978
4	Tapestry	Carole King	1971
5	Dark Side Of The Moon	Pink Floyd	1973
6	Boston	Boston	1976
7	Frampton Comes Alive!	Peter Frampton	1976
8	Songs In The Key Of Life	Stevie Wonder	1976
9	Goodbye Yellow Brick Road	Elton John	1973
10	Hotel California	Eagles	1976

In the decade when album sales really took off (*Rumours* alone sold over 13,000,000 copies), it is notable that five of these Top 10 titles were double albums.

THE TOP 10 ALBUMS OF THE 1980s IN THE UK

	Title	Artist	Release year
1	Brothers In Arms	Dire Straits	1985
2	Bad	Michael Jackson	1987
3	Thriller	Michael Jackson	1982
4	Greatest Hits	Queen	1981
5	Kylie	Kylie Minogue	1988
6	Whitney	Whitney Houston	1987
7	Tango In The Night	Fleetwood Mac	1987
8	No Jacket Required	Phil Collins	1985
9	True Blue	Madonna	1986
10	The Joshua Tree	U2	1987

While Michael Jackson's *Thriller* was his bestselling album in most countries around the world (and, of course, the bestselling global album of all time), British buyers eventually preferred *Bad*. *Brothers In Arms* remains the top-selling UK album ever, staying in the chart for nearly four years during the mid-1980s. Fleetwood Mac is the only act to feature on the bestseller lists in two decades, following their achievement with *Rumours* in the 1970s.

THE TOP 10 ALBUMS OF THE 1980s IN THE USA

	Title	Artist	Release year
1	Thriller	Michael Jackson	1982
2	Born In The USA	Bruce Springsteen	1984
3	Dirty Dancing	Soundtrack	1987
4	Purple Rain (Soundtrack)	Prince	1984
5	Can't Slow Down	Lionel Richie	1983
6	Whitney Houston	Whitney Houston	1985
7	Hysteria	Def Leppard	1987
8	Slippery When Wet	Bon Jovi	1986
9	Appetite For Destruction	Guns N' Roses	1988
10	The Wall	Pink Floyd	1979

On 30 October 1984, *Thriller* became the first album to receive its 20th platinum sales certificate, for sales of 20,000,000 copies in the United States alone.

Although included here as a 1980s album, *The Wall* was released during the week ending 15 December 1979, but accumulated most of its sales during the following decade.

THE 10 ARTISTS WITH THE MOST CHART ALBUMS IN THE UK*

	Artist	Albums
1	Elvis Presley	95
2	James Last	56
3	Frank Sinatra	50
4	Cliff Richard	48
5	Rolling Stones	37
6	Bob Dylan	35
7	Elton John	31
8	Diana Ross	30**
9	Shirley Bassey	29
10	David Bowie	27†

* Up to 31 December 1992.

** Excluding three chart albums with the Supremes.

† Excluding two chart albums with Tin Machine.

THE FIRST 10 MILLION-SELLING ALBUMS IN THE USA

	Title	Artist	Year
1	Oklahoma	Original Cast	1949
2	South Pacific	Original Cast	1949
3	An American In Paris	Soundtrack	1952
4	Strauss Waltzes	Mantovani	1953
5	Christmas Carols	Mantovani	1953
6	Songs From 'The Student Prince'	Mario Lanza	1954
7	The Glenn Miller Story	Glenn Miller Band	1954
8	Mantovani Plays The Immortal Classics	Mantovani	1954
9	Merry Christmas	Bing Crosby	1954
10	Radio Bloopers	Kermit Schafer	1954

Albums in the traditional sense – 12″ or 10″ discs played at 33⅓ rpm – first appeared in the United States in 1948. Numbers one and nine in this Top 10 were both originally issued prior to the dates listed as boxed-set collections of 78-rpm records.

THE 10 ALBUMS THAT STAYED LONGEST AT NO. 1 IN THE US CHARTS*

	Title	Artist	Release year	Weeks at No. 1
1	Thriller	Michael Jackson	1982	37
2=	Calypso	Harry Belafonte	1956	31
2=	Rumours	Fleetwood Mac	1977	31
4=	Saturday Night Fever	Soundtrack	1978	24
4=	Purple Rain (Soundtrack)	Prince	1984	24
6	Please Hammer Don't Hurt 'Em	MC Hammer	1990	21
7	Blue Hawaii (Soundtrack)	Elvis Presley	1962	20
8=	More Of The Monkees	Monkees	1967	18
8=	Dirty Dancing	Soundtrack	1988	18
8=	Ropin' The Wind	Garth Brooks	1991	18

* Based on Billboard charts.

Some sources identify the soundtrack album of West Side Story (1961) as the longest No. 1 resident of the Billboard chart, but its 57-week stay was in a chart exclusively for stereo albums – then a relatively new phenomenon; the South Pacific soundtrack album (1958) similarly enjoyed 31 weeks in this specialist chart. Not all of the albums from the general chart had continuous No. 1 runs: in some cases, their chart-topping sojourns were punctuated by briefer stays by other records. Four of the Top 10 are film soundtracks, which suggests that a successful movie tie-in may well be an aid to sales longevity. Even as this book was going to press, another such album, that derived from the 1992 film, The Bodyguard, featuring Whitney Houston and others, was poised to enter this list, having stayed at No. 1 for 17 weeks up to 1 May 1993.

THE 10 SLOWEST UK ALBUM CHART RISES TO NO. 1

	Title	Artist	Weeks
1	My People Were Fair And Had Sky In Their Hair, But Now They're Content To Wear Stars On Their Brows	Tyrannosaurus Rex	199
2	Fame	Soundtrack	98
3	Tubular Bells	Mike Oldfield	65
4	Rumours	Fleetwood Mac	49
5	The Freewheelin' Bob Dylan	Bob Dylan	48
6=	Sleeping With The Past	Elton John	44
6=	Like A Virgin	Madonna	44
8	Circle Of One	Oleta Adams	40
9=	The Black And White Minstrel Show	George Mitchell Minstrels	36
9=	Born In The USA	Bruce Springsteen	36

The Tyrannosaurus Rex album also holds the distinction of being the album with the longest title ever to chart. It originally charted in July 1968, but had to wait until the heyday of T. Rex (the name the group were by then using) to re-chart in May 1972 as one half of a double album repackage with *Prophets, Seers And Sages, The Angels Of The Ages* when it hit UK No. 1.

THE 10 ALBUMS THAT STAYED LONGEST IN THE UK CHARTS

	Title	Artist	First year in chart
1	Rumours	Fleetwood Mac	1977
2	Bat Out Of Hell	Meat Loaf	1978
3	The Sound Of Music	Original Cast	1965
4	Greatest Hits	Queen	1981
5	Bridge Over Troubled Water	Simon and Garfunkel	1970
6	Dark Side Of The Moon	Pink Floyd	1973
7	South Pacific	Original Cast	1958
8	Greatest Hits	Simon and Garfunkel	1972
9	Face Value	Phil Collins	1981
10	Tubular Bells	Mike Oldfield	1973

The 10 longest-staying records virtually took up residence in the album charts (the Top 50, 75 or 100, depending on the years during which the charts were compiled), remaining there for periods ranging from over five years for *Tubular Bells* to the astonishing eight-and-a-half-year occupation of Fleetwood Mac's *Rumours*.

Life in the slow lane: Marc Bolan of Tyrannosaurus Rex, whose album My People Were Fair And Had Sky In Their Hair, But Now They're Content To Wear Stars On Their Brows *rose to UK No. 1 at a rate in proportion to the length of its title. (It was actually reissued as a cash-in when Bolan's more succinctly-monikered T. Rex achieved chart-topping status on a different label.)*

THE TOP 10 ALBUMS OF 1992 IN AUSTRALIA

	Title	Artist
1	Blood Sugar Sex Magik	Red Hot Chili Peppers
2	Baby Animals	Baby Animals
3	Dangerous	Michael Jackson
4	Soul Deep	Jimmy Barnes
5	Diamonds And Pearls	Prince
6	The Commitments	Soundtrack
7	Nevermind	Nirvana
8	Hepfidelity	Diesel
9	Jesus Christ Superstar	1992 Australian Cast
10	Stars	Simply Red

THE TOP 10 ALBUMS OF 1991 IN BELGIUM

	Title	Artist
1	Gert En Samson	Gert En Samson
2	On Every Street	Dire Straits
3	Dangerous	Michael Jackson
4	L'Autre	Mylene Farmer
5	Greatest Hits II	Queen
6	Waking Up The Neighbors	Bryan Adams
7	Si Ce Soir	Patrick Bruel
8	Simply The Best	Tina Turner
9	Joyride	Roxette
10	Greatest Hits	Eurythmics

Source: IFPI Belgium.

Only the bestselling album of the year was recorded by a native Belgian.

THE TOP 10 ALBUMS OF ALL TIME IN CANADA

	Title	Artist
1	Thriller	Michael Jackson
2	Rumours	Fleetwood Mac
3	Dark Side Of The Moon	Pink Floyd
4	Saturday Night Fever (Original Soundtrack)	Various
5	Brothers In Arms	Dire Straits
6	Reckless	Bryan Adams
7	Grease (Original Soundtrack)	Various
8	Led Zeppelin IV	Led Zeppelin
9	Hysteria	Def Leppard
10	Can't Slow Down	Lionel Richie

Thriller is the only album to date to receive a Double Diamond Award for sales of 2,000,000 copies. The remainder of the Top 10 have all been certified Diamond for sales over 1,000,000 units. Bryan Adams is the only Canadian artist featuring on the list, though fellow native rocker Corey Hart is just outside the Top 10 for his million-selling album Boy In The Box.

THE TOP 10 ALBUMS OF ALL TIME IN EGYPT

	Title	Artist
1	Men Gheir Lai	Abd El Wahab
2	Feeh Nas	Abd El Halim Hafez
3	Kareaa El Fingen	Abd El Halim Hafez
4	Sawah	Abd El Halim Hafez
5	Ent Omry	Om Kolthoom
6	El Atlal	Om Kolthoom
7	Ana Bastnak	Nagat
8	Batwaness Beek	Wardah
9	Asalak El Rahela	Nagat
10	Ghayrt Hayati	Mayada El Henawy

Source: IFPI – Egypt.

Abd El Wahab is the second most popular Egyptian singer of all time, behind Abd El Halim Hafez. Om Kolthoom, Nagat and Wardah complete Egypt's top five.

THE TOP 10 INTERNATIONAL ALBUMS OF ALL TIME IN FINLAND

	Title	Artist
1	Baccara	Baccara
2	Born In The USA	Bruce Springsteen
3	Joyride	Roxette
4	Brothers In Arms	Dire Straits
5	Thriller	Michael Jackson
6	Arrival	Abba
7	Foreign Affair	Tina Turner
8	Waking Up The Neighbors	Bryan Adams
9	On Every Street	Dire Straits
10	Voulez-Vous	Abba

Source: Finnish Group of the IFPI.

Curious but true to see long-forgotten Spanish female duo, Baccara, in pole position. Their 1978 eponymous effort sold 115,000 copies, outselling more traditional top titles from Dire Straits, Michael Jackson and Abba.

THE TOP 10 ALBUMS OF ALL TIME IN ISRAEL

	Title	Artist
1	The Woman In Me	David Broza
2	Hurts But Less	Yehuda Poliker
3	Sings Her Own Works	Naomi Shemer
4	Night	Shlomo Artzi
5	Rita	Rita
6	These Eyes Of Mine	Yehuda Poliker
7	Dance	Shlomo Artzi
8	A Home Loving Man	Arik Einstein
9	Like A Wildflower	Chava Alberstein
10	Ladies And Gentlemen	Mashina

Source: IFPI Israel.

THE TOP 10 ALBUMS OF ALL TIME IN THE NETHERLANDS

	Title	Artist
1	Brothers In Arms	Dire Straits
2	Money For Nothing	Dire Straits
3	Tango In The Night	Fleetwood Mac
4	Past And Present (1977–1990)	Toto
5	...But Seriously	Phil Collins
6	Labour Of Love	UB40
7	Graceland	Paul Simon
8	Once Upon A Time In The West	Ennio Morricone
9	Bad	Michael Jackson
10	Whitney	Whitney Houston

Source: NVPI.

THE TOP 10 ALBUMS OF 1991 IN GERMANY

	Title	Artist
1	Crazy World	Scorpions
2	Joyride	Roxette
3	Serious Hits...Live	Phil Collins
4	Greatest Hits	Eurythmics
5	Out Of Time	R.E.M.
6	Kuschelrock IV	Various
7	Vagabond Heart	Rod Stewart
8	The Razor's Edge	AC/DC
9	The Soul Cages	Sting
10	Live	Westernhagen

Source: Der Musikmarkt.

THE TOP 10 ALBUMS OF EACH YEAR IN ITALY, 1982–91

	Title	Artist	Year
1	La Voce Del Padrone	Franco Battiato	1982
2	L'Arca Di Noè	Franco Battiato	1983
3	Va Bene, Va Bene Così	Vasco Rossi	1984
4	La Vita E Adesso	Claudio Baglioni	1985
5	True Blue	Madonna	1986
6	C'E Chi Dice No	Vasco Rossi	1987
7	Dalla/Morandi	Lucio Dalla and Gianni Morandi	1988
8	Liberi Liberi	Vasco Rossi	1989
9	In Ogni Senso	Eros Ramazzotti	1990
10	Malinconia	Marco Masini	1991

Source: Musica Edischi.

THE TOP 10 ALBUMS OF 1991 IN PORTUGAL

	Title	Artist
1	MXMXC A.D.	Enigma
2	Out Of Time	R.E.M.
3	Waking Up The Neighbors	Bryan Adams
4	Twin Peaks	(Original TV Soundtrack)
5	Bachata Rosa	Juan Luis Guerra
6	The Very Best Of Supertramp	Supertramp
7	The Beach Boys Collection	Beach Boys
8	Innuendo	Queen
9	Mingos & Os Samurais	Rui Veloso
10	Tieta	Various

Source: Associacao Fonografica Portuguesa.

THE TOP 10 BOXED-SET ALBUMS* OF ALL TIME IN THE USA

	Title	Artist	Release year	Sales**
1	Led Zeppelin	Led Zeppelin	1990	1,000,000
2	Crossroads	Eric Clapton	1988	800,000
3	Just For The Record	Barbra Streisand	1991	470,000
4	The Complete Recordings	Robert Johnson	1990	465,000
5	Storyteller	Rod Stewart	1989	420,000
6	Biograph	Bob Dylan	1985	340,000
7	Songs Of Freedom	Bob Marley	1992	330,000
8	Pandora's Box	Aerosmith	1991	320,000
9	Boats Beaches Bars And Ballads	Jimmy Buffett	1992	280,000
10	To Be Continued ...	Elton John	1990	250,000

* CD and cassette only. ** Estimates up to 31 December 1992.

While overall back-catalogue CD sales have kept the record industry alive over the past decade, boxed-set collections in particular have proved a highly profitable and popular source of revenue. Relatively inexpensive to produce, some boxed-set compilations can begin making a profit for record companies after selling only 25,000 copies, hence the proliferation of the format. Of the titles listed here, perhaps the most surprising success is the set chronicling the early Blues roots career of Robert Johnson, widely regarded as a rewarding collection for even the most disinterested fan of the genre.

THE TOP 10 ALBUMS OF 1992 IN SPAIN

	Title	Artist
1	Aidalai	Mecano
2	Calor	Julio Iglesias
3	Dangerous	Michael Jackson
4	Viviendo De Prisa	Alejandro Sanz
5	Greatest Hits Volume II	Queen
6	On Every Street	Dire Straits
7	Sintiéndonos La Piel	Sergio Dalma
8	Tubular Bells II	Mike Oldfield
9	Llámalo Sueño	OBK
10	Física Y Química	Joaquin Sabina

Source: IFPI Spain.

Eric Clapton's career collection Crossroads *is a worthy number two among the all-time bestselling boxed sets in the USA.*

THE TOP 10 ORIGINAL CAST RECORDING ALBUMS OF ALL TIME IN THE UK

	Title	Year
1	The Phantom Of The Opera (London)	1987
2	Hair (London)	1968
3	Joseph And The Amazing Technicolor Dreamcoat (London)	1991
4	My Fair Lady (Broadway)	1958
5	The Sound Of Music (London)	1961
6	Oliver (London)	1960
7	Evita*	1977
8	Cats (London)	1981
9	Fiddler On The Roof (London)	1967
10	Jesus Christ Superstar**	1972

* A studio cast recording which outperformed the actual stage show album version released a year later.

** A studio cast recording based on the successful musical, though an original cast recording never charted.

The list belongs to Andrew Lloyd Webber who co-wrote numbers one, three, seven, eight and 10.

THE TOP 10 ORIGINAL CAST RECORDING ALBUMS OF ALL TIME IN THE USA

	Title	Year
1	My Fair Lady (Broadway)	1956
2	The Sound Of Music (Broadway)	1959
3	The Music Man (Broadway)	1958
4	The Phantom Of The Opera (London)	1988
5	Camelot (Broadway)	1961
6	West Side Story (Broadway)	1958
7	Jesus Christ Superstar*	1970
8	Fiddler On The Roof (Broadway)	1964
9	Hair (Broadway)	1968
10	Hello, Dolly! (Broadway)	1964

* Although an original Broadway cast version appeared in 1972, the album which outperformed it here was a studio cast recording made in 1970 with Deep Purple vocalist Ian Gillan playing Jesus.

The 1950s and early 1960s were clearly the golden era of musicals when cast albums regularly outperformed the burgeoning number of Rock 'n' Roll artist releases – the only cast recording titles to make the American Top 40 album chart in the 1980s were *The Phantom Of The Opera* (which has remained in the Top 200 ever since) and the Supremes-based musical, *Dreamgirls*, in 1982

THE TOP 10 CHILDREN'S ALBUMS OF ALL TIME IN THE UK

	Title	Artist
1	The Muppet Show	Muppets
2	Mary Poppins	Original Soundtrack
3	Oliver!	Original Soundtrack
4	Oliver!	Original London Cast
5	Jungle Book	Original Soundtrack
6	Teenage Mutant Ninja Turtles	Original Soundtrack
7	The Greatest Hits Of Disney	Various
8	The Muppet Show Vol. 2	Muppets
9	Chitty Chitty Bang Bang	Original Soundtrack
10	Fraggle Rock	Fraggles

The *Muppet Show* release from 1977 is the only children's album ever to hit the top of the UK chart.

THE TOP 10 CHILDREN'S ALBUMS OF ALL TIME IN THE USA

	Title	Artist
1	Mickey Mouse Disco	Various
2	Mousercise	Various
3	Children's Favorites Volume 1	Various
4	Disney's Christmas Favorites	Various
5	Children's Favorites Volume 2	Various
6	Mary Poppins	Original Soundtrack
7	The Jungle Book	Original Soundtrack
8	The Sesame Street Book And Record	Muppets
9	Chipmunk Punk	Chipmunks
10	Urban Chipmunk	Chipmunks

Released in April 1980, the *Mickey Mouse Disco* album went on to become the biggest-selling children's title of all time, notching up over 2,000,000 units, tailed closely by its follow-up release, *Mousercise*.

THE TOP 10 CDs ON CD JUKEBOXES IN THE UK, 1992

	Title	Artist
1	*Now 22*	Various
2	*Now 23*	Various
3	*Divine Madness*	Madness
4	*Gittering Prize '81–'92*	Simple Minds
5	*Maximum Rave*	Various
6	*Appetite For Destruction*	Guns N' Roses
7	*Stars*	Simply Red
8	*Ultimate Rave*	Various
9	*Nevermind*	Nirvana
10	*Back To Front*	Lionel Richie

Source: *BLMS*.

The Top 10 is based on the most-played compact discs on Arbiter Discmaster CD Jukeboxes. Approximately 3,000 have been installed in the UK and offer listeners the opportunity to select individual tracks from a range of popular CDs.

THE TOP 10 POP INSTRUMENTAL ALBUMS OF ALL TIME IN THE UK

	Title	Artist
1	*Tubular Bells*	Mike Oldfield
2	*20 Golden Greats*	Shadows
3	*Oxygene*	Jean Michel Jarre
4	*String Of Hits*	Shadows
5	*Sky 2*	Sky
6	*Chariots Of Fire*	Vangelis
7	*Tubular Bells II*	Mike Oldfield
8	*Sky*	Sky
9	*Hergest Ridge*	Mike Oldfield
10	*Moonlight Shadows*	Shadows

A handful of names have dominated the purely instrumental field for many years, the longest-established being the Shadows, who had their first No. 1 album as long ago as 1961. Mike Oldfield's *Tubular Bells*, with sales of more than 2,000,000, looks unlikely ever to be seriously challenged by another non-vocal recording – his own later *Tubular Bells II* has mustered no more than a quarter of the sales of the original.

THE TOP 10 CLASSICAL ALBUMS OF 1992 IN THE UK

	Title	Artist
1	*Essential Opera*	Various
2	*The Essential Mozart*	Various
3	*Essential Ballet*	Various
4	*Beethoven Violin Concerto*	Nigel Kennedy/Klaus Tennstedt
5	*Vivaldi: The Four Seasons*	Nigel Kennedy/ECO
6	*Pavarotti In The Park*	Luciano Pavarotti
7	*The Essential Kiri*	Kiri Te Kanawa
8	*Brahms Violin Concerto*	Nigel Kennedy/LPO/Klaus Tennstedt
9	*The Three Tenors Concert*	Carreras, Domingo, Pavarotti
10	*Tavener: The Protecting Veil*	Isserlis/Rozhdestvensky/LSO

Inevitably, the biggest classical music sellers represent the extreme populist end of the market – specifically, in 1992, several 'Essential' samplers of classic repertoire, Nigel Kennedy and the *Three Tenors*. The John Tavener work at number 10 was given a high profile when nominated alongside several rock and jazz albums in the prestigious Mercury Awards for outstanding contemporary music.

THE TOP 10 CLASSICAL ALBUMS OF ALL TIME IN THE UK

	Title	Artist
1	*The Essential Pavarotti*	Luciano Pavarotti
2	*The Three Tenors Concert*	Carreras, Domingo, Pavarotti
3	*Vivaldi: The Four Seasons*	Nigel Kennedy/ECO
4	*The Essential Mozart*	Various
5	*Essential Opera*	Various
6	*Mendelssohn/Bruch Violin Concertos*	Nigel Kennedy/ECO
7	*Brahms: Violin Concerto*	Nigel Kennedy/NPO
8	*The Essential Pavarotti, 2*	Luciano Pavarotti
9	*Essential Ballet*	Various
10	*Beethoven: Violin Concerto*	Nigel Kennedy/LPO

Sales of classical music boomed to unprecedented heights at the end of the 1980s and into the 1990s, the rider to this being that it was the records by a select band of superstars – tenors José Carreras, Placido Domingo and Luciano Pavarotti (particularly the latter, who even had a top three single with *Nessun Dorma*), and young-gun violinist Nigel Kennedy – that soared way ahead of the field as a whole. They, plus some cleverly marketed samplers in Decca's *Essential* series, inevitably fill this bestsellers chart.

THE TOP 10 COUNTRY ALBUMS OF 1992 IN THE UK

	Title	Artist
1	The Ultimate Country Collection	Various
2	Some Gave All	Billy Ray Cyrus
3	The Chase	Garth Brooks
4	The Definitive Jim Reeves	Jim Reeves
5	The Definitive Patsy Cline	Patsy Cline
6	Ingenue	k.d. lang
7	Neck And Neck	Chet Atkins and Mark Knopfler
8	Country Moods	Various
9	Come On Come On	Mary Chapin Carpenter
10	Joshua Judges Ruth	Lyle Lovett

The year's major crossover from the Country music field to pop success was made by Billy Ray Cyrus, whose *Achy Breaky Heart* was a Top 10 hit. Accordingly, his debut album also sold extremely well, in the UK outperforming *The Chase* by Garth Brooks, which in America was a multi-million-seller. New-style Country singer-songwriters k.d. lang and Mary Chapin Carpenter brought success to the contemporary sound, while Jim Reeves and Patsy Cline compilations showed that there continues to be a thriving UK market for the traditional Nashville idiom.

THE TOP 10 COUNTRY ALBUMS OF ALL TIME IN THE UK

	Title	Artist
1	Johnny Cash At San Quentin	Johnny Cash
2	20 Golden Greats	Glen Campbell
3	The Best Of John Denver	John Denver
4	40 Golden Greats	Jim Reeves
5	Images	Don Williams
6	Greatest Hits	Glen Campbell
7	The Very Best Of Slim Whitman	Slim Whitman
8	The Best Of Tammy Wynette	Tammy Wynette
9	Live In London	John Denver
10	Johnny Cash At Folsom Prison	Johnny Cash

Of Johnny Cash's two celebrated live albums recorded at two of America's most severe penal institutions, the San Quentin release holds the record for the longest-charting Country album in UK chart history with 114 weeks notched up between 1969 and 1971. Country music sales in the UK and elsewhere have never matched those in its native United States, and usually benefit only in a 'greatest hits' package: Garth Brooks, for example, America's top-selling Country artist, has sold more than 20,000,000 albums in the past four years in the USA, compared with a few hundred thousand across the whole of Europe.

THE TOP 10 COUNTRY ALBUMS OF THE 1960s IN THE USA

	Title	Artist
1	Johnny Cash At San Quentin	Johnny Cash
2	Johnny Cash At Folsom Prison	Johnny Cash
3	Greatest Hits	Patsy Cline
4	Johnny Cash's Greatest Hits Vol. 1	Johnny Cash
5	Modern Sounds In Country And Western Music	Ray Charles
6	Wichita Lineman	Glen Campbell
7	Ode To Billie Joe	Bobbie Gentry
8	Modern Sounds In Country And Western Music (Volume Two)	Ray Charles
9	Galveston	Glen Campbell
10	The Return Of Roger Miller	Roger Miller

Traditionally an R & B performer, Ray Charles' foray into Country music yielded two of the bestselling genre albums of the decade, which between them logged more than 97 weeks on the pop album chart. Johnny Cash is the most successful artist to perform in penal institutions, selling more than 4,000,000 copies of numbers one and two. Patsy Cline's appearance at number three shows the strange limitations of the pop album charts in the United States: despite selling over 2,000,000 units, this title never made the mainstream albums surveys, and succeeded only on the Country charts.

THE TOP 10 COUNTRY ALBUMS OF THE 1970s IN THE USA

	Title	Artist
1	Stardust	Willie Nelson
2	Greatest Hits	Waylon Jennings
3	Waylon & Willie	Waylon Jennings and Willie Nelson
4	Wanted: The Outlaws	Waylon Jennings, Jessi Colter, Tompall Glaser and Willie Nelson
5	Million Mile Reflections	Charlie Daniels Band
6	Kenny	Kenny Rogers
7	Back Home Again	John Denver
8	Behind Closed Doors	Charlie Rich
9	The Gambler	Kenny Rogers
10	We Must Believe In Magic	Crystal Gayle

The decade belonged to Country legends Willie Nelson and Waylon Jennings.

THE TOP 10 COUNTRY ALBUMS OF THE 1980s IN THE USA

	Title	Artist
1	Always And Forever	Randy Travis
2	Feels So Right	Alabama
3	Mountain Music	Alabama
4	Storms Of Life	Randy Travis
5	The Closer You Get	Alabama
6	Anne Murray's Greatest Hits	Anne Murray
7	Always On My Mind	Willie Nelson
8	Roll On	Alabama
9	Greatest Hits	Ronnie Milsap
10	Willie Nelson's Greatest Hits (And Some That Will Be)	Willie Nelson

Randy Travis paved the way for the explosion of 'New Country' that took place in 1990 with the advent of Garth Brooks, Clint Black and Billy Ray Cyrus, while Alabama proved to be the most popular Country group of all time, notching up nine million-selling albums during the 1980s, of which numbers two and three each sold more than 3,000,000 copies.

THE TOP 10 COUNTRY ALBUMS OF 1992 IN THE USA

	Title	Artist
1	Ropin' The Wind	Garth Brooks
2	Some Gave All	Billy Ray Cyrus
3	The Chase	Garth Brooks
4	No Fences	Garth Brooks
5	Beyond The Season	Garth Brooks
6	Wynonna	Wynonna
7	Garth Brooks	Garth Brooks
8	For My Broken Heart	Reba McEntire
9	Brand New Man	Brooks & Dunn
10	It's All About To Change	Travis Tritt

Garth Brooks' absolute domination of the Country field makes him the biggest-selling artist ever of the genre. His five album releases from the past three years had sold over 27,000,000 copies in the United States by the end of 1992, an extraordinary tally boosted by his festive Christmas album, *Beyond The Season*.

THE TOP 10 COUNTRY ALBUMS OF ALL TIME IN THE USA

	Title	Artist
1	No Fences	Garth Brooks
2	Ropin' The Wind	Garth Brooks
3	Some Gave All	Billy Ray Cyrus
4	Garth Brooks	Garth Brooks
5	Always And Forever	Randy Travis
6	Feels So Right	Alabama
7	Mountain Music	Alabama
8	Storms Of Life	Randy Travis
9	The Closer You Get	Alabama
10	Anne Murray's Greatest Hits	Anne Murray

All of these albums have sold more than 3,000,000 copies each in the United States alone, but Garth Brooks is in a league of his own. Exploding onto the Country scene in 1990, he sold over 20,000,000 albums in under two years and is the first Country artist to sell 10,000,000 copies of one album (*No Fences*). By the end of 1992 he added two more multi-platinum releases to the three listed here, namely *The Chase* and his Christmas-themed *Beyond The Season*.

THE TOP 10 GREATEST HITS ALBUMS OF ALL TIME IN THE UK

	Title	Artist
1	Greatest Hits	Queen
2	Simon And Garfunkel's Greatest Hits	Simon and Garfunkel
3	Abba's Greatest Hits	Abba
4	Money For Nothing	Dire Straits
5	Greatest Hits II	Queen
6	The Immaculate Collection	Madonna
7	The Singles, 1969–1973	Carpenters
8	20 Golden Greats	Beach Boys
9	Legend	Bob Marley & The Wailers
10	Private Collection, 1977–1988	Cliff Richard

Some of the biggest of these hits compilations have achieved truly immense sales in the UK – far more, in many cases, than the hit singles they anthologize. All the albums here have sold at least 1,500,000 copies, while Queen's *Greatest Hits* (its sales boosted by Freddie Mercury's death) has topped 3,000,000, and Simon and Garfunkel's compilation is on 2,500,000.

THE FIRST TOP 10 UK HEAVY METAL ALBUMS CHART*

	Title	Artist
1	Pictures At Eleven	Robert Plant
2	Killers	KISS
3	Wiped Out	Raven
4	Aldo Nova	Aldo Nova
5	Turn Out The Lights	Bernie Tormé
6	The Number Of The Beast	Iron Maiden
7	Metal On Metal	Anvil
8	Asia	Asia
9	The Eagle Has Landed	Saxon
10	Special Forces	.38 Special

* Compiled by MRIB.

Like the first heavy metal singles chart, the album chart first appeared on 10 July 1982.

THE TOP 10 HEAVY METAL ALBUMS OF ALL TIME IN THE UK

	Title	Artist
1	Bat Out Of Hell	Meat Loaf
2	Led Zeppelin II	Led Zeppelin
3	Hysteria	Def Leppard
4	Led Zeppelin IV	Led Zeppelin
5	Eliminator	ZZ Top
6	Appetite For Destruction	Guns N' Roses
7	Slippery When Wet	Bon Jovi
8	Back In Black	AC/DC
9	The Number Of The Beast	Iron Maiden
10	Paranoid	Black Sabbath

Bat Out Of Hell only ever peaked at UK No. 9, but logged an impressive 416 weeks on the chart, an achievement split over two decades. Between 1969 and 1979, Led Zeppelin hit UK No. 1 with each of their eight albums from Led Zeppelin II right up to In Through The Out Door.

THE TOP 10 HEAVY METAL ALBUMS OF 1992 IN THE UK

	Title	Artist
1	Nevermind	Nirvana
2	Adrenalize	Def Leppard
3	Fear Of The Dark	Iron Maiden
4	Greatest Hits II	Queen
5	Ten	Pearl Jam
6	Angel Dust	Faith No More
7	III Sides To Every Story	Extreme
8	Metallica	Metallica
9	Use Your Illusion I	Guns N' Roses
10	Use Your Illusion II	Guns N' Roses

In 1992 the heavy rock album scene was largely dominated by the established giants of the genre like Iron Maiden, Def Leppard, Guns N' Roses and Metallica, but top sales actually went to the newer US band Nirvana, whose gritty, sleazy sound was a major influence upon acts on both sides of the Atlantic. No fewer than five of the nine bands featured in the Top 10 played at the Wembley Stadium tribute concert for Freddie Mercury, including, obviously, the surviving members of Queen.

THE TOP 10 HEAVY METAL ALBUMS OF THE 1970s IN THE UK

	Title	Artist
1	Bat Out Of Hell	Meat Loaf
2	Led Zeppelin II*	Led Zeppelin
3	Led Zeppelin IV	Led Zeppelin
4	Paranoid	Black Sabbath
5	Led Zeppelin III	Led Zeppelin
6	Blue For You	Status Quo
7	In Rock	Deep Purple
8	Physical Graffiti	Led Zeppelin
9	Billion Dollar Babies	Alice Cooper
10	Live And Dangerous	Thin Lizzy

* Released in November 1969, Led Zeppelin II remained on the UK chart well into 1972 – a total of 138 weeks.

THE TOP 10 HEAVY METAL ALBUMS OF THE 1980s IN THE UK

	Title	Artist
1	Hysteria	Def Leppard
2	Eliminator	ZZ Top
3	Appetite For Destruction	Guns N' Roses
4	Slippery When Wet	Bon Jovi
5	Bat Out Of Hell	Meat Loaf
6	Back In Black	AC/DC
7	The Number Of The Beast	Iron Maiden
8	Deadringer	Meat Loaf
9	Misplaced Childhood	Marillion
10	1987	Whitesnake

(Opposite) *The Red Hot Chili Peppers, whose* Blood Sugar Sex Magik *was one of the top-selling heavy metal albums of 1992 in the USA.*

THE TOP 10 HEAVY METAL ALBUMS OF THE 1970s IN THE USA

	Title	Artist
1	Boston	Boston
2	Van Halen	Van Halen
3	Double Vision	Foreigner
4	Don't Look Back	Boston
5	Bat Out Of Hell	Meat Loaf
6	Foreigner	Foreigner
7	Infinity	Journey
8	In Through The Out Door	Led Zeppelin
9	Pieces Of Eight	Styx
10	Point Of Know Return	Kansas

THE TOP 10 HEAVY METAL ALBUMS OF THE 1980s IN THE USA

	Title	Artist
1	Hysteria	Def Leppard
2	Appetite For Destruction	Guns N' Roses
3	Slippery When Wet	Bon Jovi
4	Escape	Journey
5	Pyromania	Def Leppard
6	Hi Infidelity	REO Speedwagon
7	Eliminator	ZZ Top
8	1984	Van Halen
9	New Jersey	Bon Jovi
10	4	Foreigner

 THE TOP 10 HEAVY METAL ALBUMS OF 1992 IN THE USA

	Title	Artist
1	Nevermind	Nirvana
2	Metallica	Metallica
3	Ten	Pearl Jam
4	Blood Sugar Sex Magik	Red Hot Chili Peppers
5	Adrenalize	Def Leppard
6	Use Your Illusion I	Guns N' Roses
7	Use Your Illusion II	Guns N' Roses
8	Waking Up The Neighbors	Bryan Adams
9	No More Tears	Ozzy Osbourne
10	The Southern Harmony And Musical Companion	Black Crowes

While all of these albums have sold over 3,000,000 copies each, Boston's achievement with over 9,000,000 sales to date of their debut album remains an extraordinary rock feat. Largely ignored by British rock fans, the band is led by MIT graduate Tom Scholz who recorded their eponymous debut album mostly in his basement studio in Boston. The band has issued only three albums in 16 years.

Each of these albums has sold more than 5,000,000 copies, during a decade in which sales of heavy metal were at an all-time high as middle America and radio finally embraced the rock genre en masse.

Seattle became the centre of heavy metal activity in 1992 with the advent of grunge rock led by the equally anarchic Nirvana and Pearl Jam. Their multi-platinum success began a band-signing frenzy by record companies eager to capitalize on the sudden and unexpected focus on the Seattle music scene.

THE TOP 10 HEAVY METAL ALBUMS OF ALL TIME IN THE USA

	Title	Artist
1	Hysteria	Def Leppard
2	Boston	Boston
3	Appetite For Destruction	Guns N' Roses
4	Slippery When Wet	Bon Jovi
5	Escape	Journey
6	Pyromania	Def Leppard
7	Hi-Infidelity	REO Speedwagon
8	Eliminator	ZZ Top
9	Van Halen	Van Halen
10	1984	Van Halen

All of these albums have sold more than 6,000,000 copies each in the United States alone, with *Hysteria* now approaching 10,000,000 – a particularly remarkable achievement for Def Leppard, the British band whose line-up has suffered a death (Steve Clark in 1991) and whose long-time drummer, Rick Allen, continues to perform with the band despite losing his left arm in a 1984 car accident.

THE TOP 10 ORIGINAL SOUND-TRACK ALBUMS OF ALL TIME IN THE UK*

	Title	Year
1	The Sound Of Music	1965
2	Saturday Night Fever	1978
3	Grease	1978
4	Dirty Dancing	1987
5	South Pacific	1958
6	West Side Story	1961
7	The Bodyguard	1992
8	Top Gun	1986
9	A Star Is Born	1977
10	Fame	1980

* To 31 January 1993.

The Beatles' *A Hard Day's Night* and *Help!* albums have been excluded from this list because only one side of each contained the films' soundtrack songs, the remainder in each case being made up of new non-movie material. If included, they would stand at numbers six and 10, and *A Star Is Born* and *Fame* would disappear. *The Bodyguard* was still the UK's top-selling album when this list was compiled, and could eventually climb higher.

THE TOP 10 INDIE ALBUMS OF 1992 IN THE UK

	Title	Artist
1	Boss Drum	Shamen
2	Pop! The First 20 Hits	Erasure
3	Copper Blue	Sugar
4	Going Blank Again	Ride
5	Doppelganger	Curve
6	Screamadelica	Primal Scream
7	Bleach	Nirvana
8	Dry	P.J. Harvey
9	Slanted And Enchanted	Pavement
10	Fontanelle	Babes In Toyland

The year's bestselling independently distributed albums gave a fairly accurate overview of the cutting edge of young rock music, with most of these records being, in fact, big sellers in the mainstream market. If there is a trend to be spotted, it seems to be towards ever-shorter album titles by ever-shorter group names.

THE TOP 10 INDIE ALBUMS OF ALL TIME IN THE UK

	Title	Artist	Label
1	The Innocents	Erasure	Mute
2	Circus	Erasure	Mute
3	Signing Off	UB40	Graduate
4	Upstairs At Eric's	Yazoo	Mute
5	Substance	New Order	Factory
6	Hatful Of Hollow	Smiths	Rough Trade
7	Violator	Depeche Mode	Mute
8	The Smiths	Smiths	Rough Trade
9	Technique	New Order	Factory
10	The Stone Roses	Stone Roses	Silvertone

Though both Kylie Minogue and Jason Donovan have performed well on the UK independent charts over the years (their releases being issued by independent label, PWL), their major success has always been on the mainstream pop surveys, hence their absence from this list. Similarly, although UB40's *Signing Off* album was issued by their debut label, Graduate, all their later releases were licensed through Virgin.

THE TOP 10 JAZZ ALBUMS OF 1992 IN THE UK

	Title	Artist
1	Jazz On A Summer's Day	Various
2	The Antidote	Ronny Jordan
3	We Are In Love	Harry Connick Jr
4	Blue Light, Red Light	Harry Connick Jr
5	The Best Of Donald Byrd	Donald Byrd
6	Mad About The Boy	Dinah Washington
7	Doo Bop	Miles Davis
8	Five Guys Named Moe	London Stage Cast
9	Secret Story	Pat Metheny
10	When Harry Met Sally	Soundtrack/Harry Connick Jr

Pianist/vocalist Harry Connick Jr dominates the 1992 jazz bestsellers much as he did the previous two years' charts – and with mostly the same albums. Many of the other entries are compilations of vintage material, with *Jazz On A Summer's Day* rounding up three decades' worth of jazz tracks which crossed over to pop success in their day.

THE TOP 10 MAINSTREAM JAZZ ALBUMS OF ALL TIME IN THE USA

	Title	Artist
1	Time Out Featuring Take Five	Dave Brubeck Quartet
2	Hello Dolly	Louis Armstrong
3	Getz & Gilberto	Stan Getz and Joao Gilberto
4	Sun Goddess	Ramsey Lewis
5	Jazz Samba	Charlie Byrd and Stan Getz
6	Bitches Brew	Miles Davis
7	The In Crowd	Ramsey Lewis Trio
8	Time Further Out	Dave Brubeck Quartet
9	Mack The Knife – Ella In Berlin	Ella Fitzgerald
10	Exodus To Jazz	Eddie Harris

Dave Brubeck's *Time Out* album spent 86 weeks in the American Top 40 between 1960 and 1962, an unprecedented achievement for a jazz album during that era and due, not least, to the huge popularity of the track featured in its full title, *Take Five*, which hit US No. 25 on the pop chart. The quartet comprised Brubeck (b. David Warren) on piano, Joe Morello (drums), Eugene Wright (bass) and Paul Desmond (alto sax).

THE TOP 10 MODERN JAZZ ALBUMS OF ALL TIME IN THE USA

	Title	Artist
1	Breezin'	George Benson
2	Breathless	Kenny G
3	Duotones	Kenny G
4	Silhouette	Kenny G
5	Winelight	Grover Washington Jr
6	Simple Pleasures	Bobby McFerrin
7	In Flight	George Benson
8	Feels So Good	Chuck Mangione
9	Head Hunters	Herbie Hancock
10	Morning Dance	Spyro Gyra

In each case, these predominantly jazz fusion albums succeeded beyond the specialist jazz market due to successful hit singles. Though George Benson went on to substantial success in the R & B, pop and even big band markets, his early albums were a jazz/R & B blend which, in the case of *Breezin'*, yielded the Top 10 hit, *This Masquerade*. Jazz vocal Grammy award winner Bobby McFerrin's album, *Simple Pleasures*, soared to platinum sales status (over 1,000,000 copies) following the crossover success of his global hit, *Don't Worry Be Happy*. Kenny G (Gorelick), America's most popular saxophonist, is the only jazz fusion artist to secure three double platinum albums (2,000,000 sales each), while his *Breathless* album had topped 3,000,000 by spring 1993.

THE TOP 10 NEW AGE ALBUMS OF ALL TIME IN THE USA

	Title	Artist
1	Watermark	Enya
2	Shepherd Moons	Enya
3	December	George Winston
4	Winter Into Spring	George Winston
5	Deep Breakfast	Ray Lynch
6	Autumn	George Winston
7	Reflections Of A Passion	Yanni
8	Summer	George Winston
9	Dancing With The Lion	Andreas Vollenweider
10	Nouveau Flamenco	Ottmar Liebert

What started out in the early 1980s as an eclectic and obscure new form of mainly instrumental mood music blossomed into the fully-fledged and profitable New Age genre that warranted its own chart in the United States, beginning on 29 October 1988. Of the early protagonists, George Winston became the most successful artist with a series of seasonal themed albums which sold over 1,000,000 copies each. When Enya became the first New Age act to secure a hit single (*Orinoco Flow (Sail Away)*) in 1989, she quickly outsold her contemporaries: by the end of 1992, her *Watermark* album had logged nearly 200 weeks on the US New Age chart, while her second effort, *Shepherd Moons*, spent the entire year at No. 1.

THE TOP 10 RAP ALBUMS OF 1992 IN THE USA

	Title	Artist
1	Totally Krossed Out	Kris Kross
2	Too Legit To Quit	Hammer
3	Mack Daddy	Sir Mix-A-Lot
4	Oooooooohhh...On The TLC Trip	TLC
5	Naughty By Nature	Naughty By Nature
6	3 Years, 5 Months And 2 Days In The Life Of Arrested Development	Arrested Development
7	Music For The People	Marky Mark & The Funky Bunch
8	Death Certificate	Ice Cube
9	Cypress Hill	Cypress Hill
10	Dead Serious	Das EFX

THE TOP 10 RAP ALBUMS OF ALL TIME IN THE UK

	Title	Artist
1	Please Hammer Don't Hurt 'Em	MC Hammer
2	3 Feet High And Rising	De La Soul
3	Licence To Ill	Beastie Boys
4	Greatest Hits	Salt 'n' Pepa
5	To The Extreme	Vanilla Ice
6	3 Years, 5 Months And 2 Days In The Life Of Arrested Development	Arrested Development
7	Rap Trax	Various
8	A Salt With A Deadly Pepa	Salt 'n' Pepa
9	Hip Hop And Rapping In The House	Various
10	De La Soul Is Dead	De La Soul

All of these albums are by American acts. The most successful domestic rapper is Rebel MC who has scored two Top 30 UK albums to date. A serious rap act from either country has yet to hit the top of the British album survey.

THE TOP 10 RAP ALBUMS OF ALL TIME IN THE USA

	Title	Artist
1	Please Hammer Don't Hurt 'Em	MC Hammer
2	To The Extreme	Vanilla Ice
3	Licence To Ill	Beastie Boys
4	Totally Krossed Out	Kris Kross
5	Bigger And Deffer	L.L. Cool J.
6	Loc'ed After Dark	Tone Loc
7	He's The DJ, I'm The Rapper	D.J. Jazzy Jeff & The Fresh Prince
8	Raising Hell	Run DMC
9	Stone Cold Rhymin'	Young MC
10	Mama Said Knock You Out	L.L. Cool J.

THE TOP 10 RAP ACTS OF ALL TIME IN THE UK

1	Hammer (aka MC Hammer)
2	De La Soul
3	Salt 'n' Pepa
4	Run DMC
5	Public Enemy
6	L.L. Cool J.
7	Vanilla Ice
8	Beastie Boys
9	Grandmaster Flash & The Furious Five
10	Rebel MC

Based on total album sales.

This is an all-American line-up with the exception of Rebel MC. De La Soul have proved more popular abroad than in their home territory: in the UK their first two albums logged 68 weeks on the chart, a considerable achievement given the usual fleeting chart appearance which befalls a large number of rap albums, most notably those by hard-core rap terrorists Public Enemy and N.W.A.

On 7 March 1987, number three became the first rap album to top the American album chart. MC Hammer's bestselling album spent 21 weeks in No. 1 position in 1990, though, as with many a follow-up project, his next release, 1991's *Too Legit To Quit*, failed to come anywhere near what will probably be his career apex. All of the albums listed here have sold over 2,000,000 copies in the United States alone, with Atlanta teen-rap duo Kris Kross being the most successful genre act of 1992, shifting over 4,000,000 copies of their debut release.

THE TOP 10 REGGAE ACTS OF ALL TIME IN THE UK

1	UB40
2	Bob Marley & The Wailers
3	Aswad
4	Eddy Grant
5	Maxi Priest
6	Black Uhuru
7	Third World
8	Steel Pulse
9	Johnny Nash
10	Gregory Isaacs

Based on total album sales.

UB40 have charted more albums, 13 in all, than any other reggae act, although Bob Marley, even in his absence, moved closer in 1992 with the release of the exemplary career-chronicling boxed set, *Songs Of Freedom*.

THE TOP 10 REGGAE ALBUMS OF ALL TIME IN THE UK

	Title	Artist
1	Legend	Bob Marley & The Wailers
2	The Best Of UB40 Volume 1	UB40
3	Labour Of Love	UB40
4	Exodus	Bob Marley & The Wailers
5	Signing Off	UB40
6	Labour Of Love Volume II	UB40
7	Kaya	Bob Marley & The Wailers
8	Killer On The Rampage	Eddy Grant
9	Confrontation	Bob Marley & The Wailers
10	Uprising	Bob Marley & The Wailers

As the godfather of reggae, Bob Marley's chart achievements are clearly unmatched. His 1984 greatest hits collection, *Legend*, spent an unprecedented 129 weeks on the UK survey. UB40 have been the dominant British reggae outfit since their 1980 album chart debut with *Signing Off*, one of 11 Top 20 releases for the Birmingham-based band during the subsequent decade.

Released in 1984 on the third anniversary of his death, Bob Marley's Legend *has since sustained its ranking as the all-time bestselling reggae album in both the UK and USA.*

THE TOP 10 REGGAE ALBUMS OF ALL TIME IN THE USA

	Title	Artist
1	Legend	Bob Marley & The Wailers
2	Labour Of Love	UB40
3	Killer On The Rampage	Eddy Grant
4	Conscious Party	Ziggy Marley & The Melody Makers
5	Bonafide	Maxi Priest
6	As Raw As Ever	Shabba Ranks
7	Rastaman Vibration	Bob Marley & The Wailers
8	Exodus	Bob Marley & The Wailers
9	The Youth Of Today	Musical Youth
10	I Can See Clearly Now	Johnny Nash

Reggae has rarely been commercially successful in the United States, although the latent success of Bob Marley's *Legend* and the late 1980s popularity of UB40 has seen recent awareness of the genre increase. Shabba Ranks, who offers a hard 'raggamuffin' reggae/rap 'toasting' (competitive rap conversation) style, has proved to be the most successful new artist of the 1990s, selling over 500,000 copies of his debut Epic album in 1991.

THE FIRST TOP 10 UK PUNK ALBUMS CHART*

	Title	Artist
1	Christ The Album	Crass
2	Punk And Disorderly – Further Charges	Various
3	City Baby Attacked By Rats	G.B.H.
4	Oi Oi, That's Your Lot	Various
5	We Are…The League	Anti-Nowhere League
6	The Wild Ones	Cockney Rejects
7	Troops Of Tomorrow	Exploited
8	Hear Nothing, See Nothing, Say Nothing	Discharge
9	Fresh Fruit For Rotting Vegetables	Dead Kennedys
10	He Who Dares Wins	Theatre Of Hate

* Compiled by MRIB.

Like the first Punk singles chart, the album chart first appeared on 25 September 1982.

THE TOP 10 SOUL ALBUMS OF 1992 IN THE USA

	Title	Artist
1	'The Bodyguard' Original Soundtrack	Various
2	Dangerous	Michael Jackson
3	Cooleyhighharmony	Boyz II Men
4	Unforgettable	Natalie Cole
5	C.M.B.	Color Me Badd
6	Emotions	Mariah Carey
7	Funky Divas	En Vogue
8	MTV Unplugged (7-track EP)	Mariah Carey
9	Spellbound	Paula Abdul
10	The Comfort Zone	Vanessa Williams

Despite being the least successful of his last three releases, Michael Jackson's Dangerous still managed to stay on the US chart throughout the year and sell over 4,000,000 copies. It was the bestselling soul venture of the year right up to December when the Whitney Houston-led predominantly soul-style Bodyguard soundtrack began a lightning sales surge approaching 5,000,000 copies.

THE TOP 10 SKA ALBUMS OF ALL TIME IN THE UK

	Title	Artist
1	One Step Beyond	Madness
2	The Specials	Specials
3	Just Can't Stop It	Beat
4	More Specials	Specials
5	Wha'ppen	Beat
6	This Is Ska	Various
7	Too Much Pressure	Selecter
8	This Are 2-Tone	Various
9	The Specials Singles	Specials
10	Club Ska '67	Various

Although they subsequently moved into a more mainstream pop arena, Madness began their chart career as a ska-based combo at the beginning of the major UK ska revival in the late 1970s. Their first hit single, The Prince, appeared on the now legendary 2-Tone label, the creation of Jerry Dammers who proved to be the driving force of latter-day ska as leader of the Specials (aka The Specials AKA), by far the most popular UK ska group ever.

The Whitney Houston-dominated soundtrack album The Bodyguard *topped the US soul album bestsellers in 1992 and is the first album to enter the UK soundtrack Top 10 since* Dirty Dancing.

THE TOP 10 ABBA ALBUMS IN THE UK

	Title	Year
1	*Greatest Hits*	1976
2	*Arrival*	1976
3	*Greatest Hits Vol. 2*	1979
4	*The Album*	1978
5	*Super Trouper*	1980
6	*Voulez-Vous*	1979
7	*Gold – Abba's Greatest Hits*	1992
8	*The Singles: The First Ten Years*	1982
9	*The Visitors*	1981
10	*Abba*	1976

All but number 10 hit UK No. 1 for the Swedish superstars of the 1970s, their most dominant year being 1976. With the success of Erasure's *Abba-esque* EP (and the subsequent novelty success of the parody quartet, Bjorn Again), Abba saw their fourth *Greatest Hits* collection, *Gold*, make the top spot in 1992.

THE TOP 10 BEACH BOYS ALBUMS IN THE UK

	Title	Year
1	*20 Golden Greats*	1976
2	*The Very Best Of The Beach Boys*	1983
3	*Best Of The Beach Boys*	1966
4	*Pet Sounds*	1966
5	*Summer Dreams*	1990
6	*Best Of The Beach Boys, Vol. 2*	1967
7	*Summer Days (And Summer Nights)*	1966
8	*The Beach Boys' Greatest Hits*	1970
9	*20:20*	1969
10	*The Beach Boys Today*	1966

Compilations, of which the Beach Boys have had an awful lot – mostly concentrating on their earlier surf/cars/sunshine repertoire – dominate this list. Their *20 Golden Greats* was the first album in EMI's TV-advertised compilation series, and its huge success launched a marketing trend which has never gone away. The group's critically acclaimed *Pet Sounds* remains their bestselling 'real' album in the UK.

THE TOP 10 JOAN ARMATRADING ALBUMS IN THE UK

	Title	Year
1	*Walk Under Ladders*	1981
2	*Me Myself I*	1980
3	*Show Some Emotion*	1977
4	*Joan Armatrading*	1976
5	*Track Record*	1983
6	*The Key*	1983
7	*To The Limit*	1978
8	*Secret Secrets*	1985
9	*The Very Best Of Joan Armatrading*	1991
10	*The Shouting Stage*	1988

THE FIRST 10 BEATLES ALBUMS RELEASED IN THE UK

	Title	Label	Cat. no.
1	*Please Please Me*	Parlophone	PCS 3042
2	*With The Beatles*	Parlophone	PCS 3045
3	*The Beatles' First**	Polydor	236-201
4	*A Hard Day's Night*	Parlophone	PCS 3058
5	*Beatles For Sale*	Parlophone	PCS 3062
6	*Help!*	Parlophone	PCS 3071
7	*Rubber Soul*	Parlophone	PCS 3075
8	*Revolver*	Parlophone	PCS 7009
9	*A Collection Of Beatles Oldies (But Goldies)*	Parlophone	PCS 7016
10	*Sgt Pepper's Lonely Hearts Club Band*	Parlophone	PCS 7027

* *Bandwagon compilation release from their early German recordings.*

THE 10 BEATLES ALBUMS THAT STAYED LONGEST IN THE UK CHARTS

	Title	Weeks in charts
1	Sgt Pepper's Lonely Hearts Club Band	164
2	The Beatles, 1962–1966	148
3	The Beatles, 1967–1970	113
4	Abbey Road	83
5	Please Please Me	74
6	Let It Be	60
7	With The Beatles	53
8	Beatles For Sale	48
9	Rubber Soul	45
10	A Hard Day's Night	43

Some of the earliest albums in this list would have had their chart stays extended had the published chart of the time been more extensive. In 1963, when *Please Please Me* and *With The Beatles* were released, the UK album chart was only a Top 20, but by the early 1970s when the 2nd- and 3rd-placed compilations appeared, it had been extended to a Top 50. However, all the early releases picked up in 1987 when their CD reissues charted.

The Beatles' albums dominated the bestseller lists for more than 10 years with Sgt Pepper's Lonely Hearts Club Band *the all-time number one in the UK.*

THE 10 LONGEST BEATLES TRACKS

	Title	Duration min	sec
1	Revolution No. 9	8	15
2	I Want You (She's So Heavy)	7	49
3	Hey Jude	7	11
4	It's All Too Much	6	27
5=	A Day In The Life	5	3
5=	Within You Without You	5	3
7	While My Guitar Gently Weeps	4	46
8	I Am The Walrus	4	35
9	Helter Skelter	4	30
10	You Know My Name (Look Up The Number)	4	20

Most of the Beatles' lengthy tracks come from their later recording days; in the earlier 1960s, they largely clocked in at between two and three minutes. Apart from *Hey Jude* (still the longest No. 1 single ever) and *You Know My Name* (the B-side of *Let It Be*), the tracks listed here are found on the albums from *Sgt Pepper* onwards, with the widely reviled *Revolution No. 9*, the group's attempt at an avant-garde sound collage on *The Beatles* ('White Album'), emerging as their lengthiest opus. It is also the track most Beatles fans skip over.

THE TOP 10 BEATLES ALBUMS IN THE UK

	Title	Year
1	Sgt Pepper's Lonely Hearts Club Band	1967
2	With The Beatles	1963
3	The Beatles, 1962–1966	1973
4	The Beatles, 1967–1970	1973
5	Abbey Road	1969
6	Beatles For Sale	1964
7	A Hard Day's Night	1964
8	Rubber Soul	1965
9	The Beatles ('White Album')	1968
10	Revolver	1966

Research by EMI into the sales of *Sgt Pepper* following its 1987 CD release indicated that, after more than a quarter of a century (and including sales from the said CD), it remains Britain's bestselling album, having sold over 4,100,000 copies. Worth noting: the two 1973 compilations and the 'White Album' were all doubles, selling at almost twice the price of a standard LP.

THE TOP 10 BEE GEES ALBUMS IN THE UK

	Title	Year
1	Saturday Night Fever (Soundtrack)	1978
2	Spirits (Having Flown)	1979
3	The Very Best Of The Bee Gees	1990
4	Bee Gees' Greatest	1979
5	E.S.P.	1987
6	Best Of The Bee Gees	1969
7	Bee Gees First	1967
8	Idea	1968
9	One	1989
10	Horizontal	1968

Saturday Night Fever is included atop this list because even though the Bee Gees did not perform every track on the soundtrack package, it was the source of several of their biggest-selling singles (Night Fever, Stayin' Alive), and the trio also wrote most of the songs performed on the album by others. Purists who insist that, as a 'various artists' set, it is not a valid inclusion here, should mentally move everything else up a slot and install the group's 1969 album Odessa at number 10.

THE TOP 10 DAVID BOWIE ALBUMS IN THE UK

	Title	Year
1	The Rise And Fall Of Ziggy Stardust And The Spiders From Mars	1972
2	Hunky Dory	1972
3	Aladdin Sane	1973
4	Let's Dance	1983
5	Pinups	1973
6	Scary Monsters And Super Creeps	1980
7	Changesbowie	1990
8	Changesonebowie	1976
9	Diamond Dogs	1974
10	The Very Best Of David Bowie	1981

Although it never made the top spot, number one spent 176 weeks on the UK album chart: from 1972–74, in 1981 and upon its CD release in 1990. There is no place in this list for Bowie's more recent Tin Machine project albums which have proved to be a commercial disaster.

THE TOP 10 MARC BOLAN AND T. REX ALBUMS IN THE UK

	Title	Year
1	Electric Warrior	1971
2	Bolan Boogie	1972
3	The Best Of The 20th Century Boy	1985
4	The Ultimate Collection	1991
5	The Slider	1972
6	Prophets, Seers And Sages, The Angels Of The Ages/ My People Were Fair And Had Sky In Their Hair But Now They're Content To Wear Stars On Their Brows*	1972
7	T. Rex	1971
8	Tanx	1973
9	The Best Of T. Rex	1971
10	A Beard Of Stars	1970

* My People... charted originally in 1968 and re-charted as one half of a double package in 1972.

The 1968 Tyrannosaurus Rex album My People... has the distinction of being the longest title of any single or album in UK chart history.

THE TOP 10 CARPENTERS ALBUMS IN THE UK

	Title	Year
1	The Singles 1969–1973	1974
2	Only Yesterday	1990
3	Now And Then	1973
4	Horizon	1975
5	Close To You	1971
6	The Singles 1974–1978	1978
7	A Kind Of Hush	1976
8	Voice Of The Heart	1983
9	Yesterday Once More	1984
10	The Carpenters	1971

American harmony duo the Carpenters have charted more albums (nine) in Britain since their demise (Karen Carpenter died on 4 February 1983) than when they were recording (eight).

THE TOP 10 ERIC CLAPTON ALBUMS IN THE UK

	Title	Year
1	The Cream Of Eric Clapton*	1987
2	August	1986
3	Journeyman	1989
4	Unplugged	1992
5	461 Ocean Boulevard	1974
6	Just One Night	1980
7	No Reason To Cry	1976
8	Behind The Sun	1985
9	Money And Cigarettes	1983
10	Time Pieces – The Best Of Eric Clapton	1982

* Also features tracks by Cream.

Despite 19 solo album releases, Clapton has yet to make UK No. 1, although as a member of both Cream and Blind Faith he made the top spot with *Goodbye* and *Blind Faith*.

THE TOP 10 ELVIS COSTELLO ALBUMS IN THE UK

	Title	Year
1	Armed Forces	1979
2	Get Happy	1980
3	Punch The Clock	1983
4	The Best Of Elvis Costello – The Man	1985
5	This Year's Model	1978
6	Spike	1989
7	Almost Blue	1981
8	Imperial Bedroom	1982
9	Mighty Like A Rose	1991
10	Trust	1981

Costello, who has also released records under his real name, Declan MacManus, issued his debut album, the seminal *My Aim Is True*, on the Stiff label in 1977. On all the albums listed here, with the exception of numbers six and nine, Costello was backed by his long-time musical sidemen, The Attractions.

Elvis Costello has collaborated with many other artists on record in his time, including Paul McCartney, George Jones and more recently the classical Brodsky Quartet.

Remaining faithful to their musical style and unique visual identity, the Cure achieved steady album sales throughout the 1980s.

THE TOP 10 CURE ALBUMS IN THE UK

	Title	Year
1	Standing On A Beach – The Singles	1986
2	Disintegration	1989
3	Wish	1992
4	Kiss Me Kiss Me Kiss Me	1987
5	The Head On The Door	1986
6	Mixed Up	1990
7	Pornography	1982
8	The Top	1984
9	Entreat	1991
10	Faith	1981

Wish, which was released on lead singer Robert Smith's 33rd birthday (21 April 1992), became the Cure's first chart-topping album after 14 previous attempts, but stayed on the UK survey for only 13 weeks.

THE TOP 10 DEPECHE MODE ALBUMS IN THE UK

	Title	Year
1	Violator	1990
2	The Singles '81–'85	1985
3	Black Celebration	1986
4	Speak And Spell	1981
5	Songs Of Faith And Devotion*	1993
6	Some Great Reward	1984
7	Construction Time Again	1983
8	A Broken Frame	1982
9	101	1989
10	Music For The Masses	1987

* Still charted as of May 1993.

All of Depeche Mode's singles and albums have been released on Daniel Miller's Mute label, and have helped the company to become one of the leading independent forces in the UK record industry.

THE TOP 10 DOORS ALBUMS IN THE UK

	Title	Year
1	The Doors (Original Soundtrack)	1991
2	Best Of The Doors	1991
3	Morrison Hotel	1970
4	Waiting For The Sun	1968
5	The Doors	1991
6	In Concert	1991
7	L.A. Woman	1971
8	Alive, She Cried	1983
9	Live At The Hollywood Bowl	1987
10	Weird Scenes Inside The Goldmine	1972

The most successful UK sales period for the Doors was in April 1991 when three albums (numbers one, two and five) were all simultaneously launched around the premiere of Oliver Stone's biographical movie, The Doors.

THE TOP 10 DEEP PURPLE ALBUMS IN THE UK

	Title	Year
1	Deepest Purple	1980
2	Deep Purple In Rock	1970
3	Fireball	1971
4	Machine Head	1972
5	Burn	1974
6	Who Do We Think We Are	1973
7	Stormbringer	1974
8	Perfect Strangers	1984
9	24 Carat Purple	1975
10	Made In Japan	1973

After Led Zeppelin, Purple were Britain's bestselling heavy rockers of the 1970s, and can lay claim to being one of the world's first major bands in the heavy metal style, propelled in their case by ace guitar-riffer Ritchie Blackmore. Top of this list is a TV-advertised compilation, while 24 Carat Purple also anthologized earlier singles. The group split in the mid-1970s but re-formed in 1984 and recorded Perfect Strangers.

THE TOP 10 NEIL DIAMOND ALBUMS IN THE UK

	Title	Year
1	The Jazz Singer	1980
2	The Greatest Hits, 1966–1992	1992
3	20 Golden Greats	1978
4	Love At The Greek	1977
5	12 Greatest Hits	1974
6	Beautiful Noise	1976
7	You Don't Bring Me Flowers	1979
8	Moods	1972
9	Primitive	1984
10	I'm Glad You're Here With Me Tonight	1977

The Jazz Singer album featured the soundtrack from the 1980 remake of the film, in which Neil Diamond starred and for which he wrote the songs. Numbers two, three and five in the list are hits compilations, including a comparatively recent two-CD package which actually made No. 1 on the UK album chart – a feat never previously achieved by Diamond in more than 25 years of recording.

THE TOP 10 BOB DYLAN ALBUMS IN THE UK

	Title	Year
1	Blonde On Blonde	1966
2	Bringing It All Back Home	1965
3	Bob Dylan's Greatest Hits	1967
4	Nashville Skyline	1969
5	John Wesley Harding	1968
6	Highway 61 Revisited	1965
7	Street Legal	1978
8	The Freewheelin' Bob Dylan	1963
9	Desire	1976
10	New Morning	1970

Bob Dylan's sales heyday in Britain was in the mid and late 1960s, when he was one of the first artists to sell large quantities of albums rather than singles. Titles such as Blonde On Blonde and Bringing It All Back Home continue to sell healthily as catalogue CDs, with a lot of original fans replacing their worn-out vinyl copies! By contrast, Dylan has placed only two albums in the UK Top 10 in the past 10 years.

THE TOP 10 ELECTRIC LIGHT ORCHESTRA ALBUMS IN THE UK

	Title	Year
1	Out Of The Blue	1977
2	A New World Record	1976
3	Discovery	1979
4	Time	1981
5	Xanadu (Original Film Soundtrack)*	1980
6	E.L.O.'s Greatest Hits (Jet label)	1979
7	Secret Messages	1983
8	The Greatest Hits (Telstar label)	1989
9	Balance Of Power	1986
10	Three Light Years	1979

* Recorded with Olivia Newton-John (side 1), E.L.O. (side 2).

The double album *Out Of The Blue*, which secured global advance orders of 4,000,000 copies prior to its release in 1977, spawned four UK Top 20 hit singles and proved to be the commercial apex for the band formed by Jeff Lynne in 1972. E.L.O. Part 2 formed in 1991 (incredibly, without Lynne) and released one unremarkable self-titled flop.

THE TOP 10 EVERLY BROTHERS ALBUMS IN THE UK

	Title	Year
1	It's Everly Time	1960
2	A Date With The Everly Brothers	1961
3	Walk Right Back With The Everlys	1975
4	The Fabulous Style Of The Everly Brothers	1960
5	The Everly Brothers' Original Greatest Hits	1970
6	Living Legends	1977
7	Love Hurts	1982
8	The Everly Brothers Reunion Concert	1984
9	Golden Hits Of The Everly Brothers	1962
10	The Everly Brothers	1984

Major album-sellers at the beginning of the 1960s, the Everly Brothers scored mainly in later years with compilations based around their hit singles (numbers three, six and seven were TV-advertised packages), though *Reunion Concert* was a double live album of their Royal Albert Hall comeback, and the eponymously titled *The Everly Brothers* was a 1984 set of contemporary material.

THE TOP 10 BRYAN FERRY AND ROXY MUSIC ALBUMS IN THE UK

	Title	Year
1	Street Life	1986
2	Flesh And Blood	1980
3	Avalon	1982
4	Boys And Girls	1985
5	These Foolish Things	1973
6	The Ultimate Collection	1988
7	Manifesto	1979
8	For Your Pleasure	1973
9	Another Time, Another Place	1974
10	Stranded	1973

Numbers two, three, seven, eight and 10 were recorded by Roxy Music, four, five and nine were Bryan Ferry solo albums, while one and six were released by Bryan Ferry & Roxy Music.

Most of Bryan Ferry's solo albums have shown a strong penchant for personalized cover versions, Ferry apparently saving the not inconsiderable fruits of his own songwriting mainly for his parallel career in Roxy Music.

THE TOP 10 FLEETWOOD MAC ALBUMS IN THE UK

	Title	Year
1	Rumours	1977
2	Tango In The Night	1982
3	Greatest Hits*	1988
4	Mirage	1982
5	Tusk	1979
6	Fleetwood Mac**	1968
7	Behind The Mask	1990
8	Then Play On	1969
9	Mr Wonderful	1968
10	Fleetwood Mac	1976

* Warner Bros. label: not to be confused with the 1972 Greatest Hits compilation (CBS label).

** Blue Horizon label: not to be confused with number 10 (Reprise label).

One of the world's bestselling albums of all time, *Rumours* spent 443 weeks on the British chart during the 1970s and 1980s. It is interesting to note that all the top five Fleetwood Mac albums featured Lindsey Buckingham who clearly had the golden touch: the band were never as successful as they were with him in the line-up (1974–87), acting as multi-instrumentalist, writer, singer and producer.

THE TOP 10 GENESIS ALBUMS IN THE UK

	Title	Year
1	Invisible Touch	1986
2	We Can't Dance	1991
3	Genesis	1983
4	Duke	1980
5	Abacab	1981
6	A Trick Of The Tail	1976
7	And Then There Were Three	1978
8	Selling England By The Pound	1973
9	3 Sides Live	1982
10	Wind And Wuthering	1977

Having not released an album in five years (due not least to Phil Collins' solo career and production duties and Mike Rutherford's extra-curricular activity, Mike & The Mechanics), Genesis released two titles in the space of 12 months: November 1991's million-selling *We Can't Dance*, closely followed by 1992's less successful *Live – The Way We Walk*. Including their early albums featuring Peter Gabriel as lead vocalist, the band has now issued 17 titles in 20 years.

THE TOP 10 JIMI HENDRIX ALBUMS IN THE UK

	Title	Year
1	Are You Experienced?	1967
2	Smash Hits	1968
3	Axis: Bold As Love	1967
4	Cry Of Love	1971
5	Band Of Gypsies	1970
6	Electric Ladyland	1968
7	Hendrix In The West	1972
8	The Jimi Hendrix Concerts	1982
9	Rainbow Bridge	1971
10	The Ultimate Experience	1992

Literally dozens of Jimi Hendrix compilations, collections of out-takes, film soundtracks, unofficial collaborations and all other possible excuses for an album have constantly assailed the market during the two decades since the guitarist's death. Rather fittingly, with only a couple of exceptions, none of them has sold comparably to the groundbreaking original albums released (or in preparation for subsequent issue, like *Cry Of Love*) in Hendrix's own lifetime.

On the basis that people still listen to some of his records trying to figure out how he could possibly have done what he did with the guitar, there are some folk who seriously believe that Jimi Hendrix was an extra-terrestrial visitor, presumably recalled to his starship on that fateful day in 1970.

THE TOP 10 PETER GABRIEL ALBUMS IN THE UK

	Title	Year
1	So	1986
2	Peter Gabriel (3)	1980
3	Peter Gabriel (4)	1982
4	Us	1992
5	Peter Gabriel (1)	1977
6	Shaking The Tree – Golden Greats	1990
7	Peter Gabriel Plays Live	1983
8	Peter Gabriel (2)	1978
9	Passion	1989
10	Birdy – Music From The Film	1985

In typically eccentric manner, Gabriel decided to release his first four albums under the same eponymous title. The success of *So* was due not least to the popularity of his biggest hit single, *Sledgehammer*.

THE TOP 10 HOLLIES ALBUMS IN THE UK

	Title	Year
1	20 Golden Greats	1978
2	Hollies' Greatest	1968
3	Stay With The Hollies	1964
4	The Hollies Sing Dylan	1969
5	Hollies Live Hits	1977
6	Hollies	1965
7	Evolution	1967
8	Would You Believe	1966
9	For Certain Because	1966
10	All The Hits And More	1988

Three of the above are compilation albums with selections from the Hollies' lengthy list of hit singles: *20 Golden Greats* was a TV-advertised package, while *All The Hits And More* was a comparatively recent set which sold mainly on CD. However, unlike many of their contemporaries, the group also consistently made hit albums during their 1960s/70s heyday, as several of the titles above indicate.

THE TOP 10 IRON MAIDEN ALBUMS IN THE UK

	Title	Year
1	The Number Of The Beast	1982
2	Seventh Son Of A Seventh Son	1988
3	Piece Of Mind	1983
4	No Prayer For The Dying	1990
5	Live After Death	1985
6	Powerslave	1984
7	Iron Maiden	1980
8	Somewhere In Time	1986
9	Fear Of The Dark	1992
10	Killers	1981

Iron Maiden's legion of loyal fans has always ensured that the band's albums debut high and fast: 1992's *Fear Of The Dark* entered at UK No. 1, speeding out of the Top 75 in just five weeks, the fastest chart demise of a chart-topping album in that year. Utterly irrelevant footnote: lead singer Bruce Dickinson, who joined the line-up in 1981, is also an accomplished fencer, ranked No. 7 in the UK in 1989.

THE TOP 10 ELTON JOHN ALBUMS IN THE UK

	Title	Year
1	The Very Best Of Elton John	1990
2	Goodbye Yellow Brick Road	1973
3	Elton John's Greatest Hits	1974
4	Don't Shoot Me I'm Only The Piano Player	1973
5	Sleeping With The Past	1989
6	Too Low For Zero	1983
7	Captain Fantastic And The Brown Dirt Cowboy	1975
8	Caribou	1974
9	Breaking Hearts	1984
10	Honky Chateau	1972

Including 1992's *The One*, Elton John has secured 31 chart titles and has had an album on the UK survey every year since his eponymous debut effort scored in 1970.

THE TOP 10 BUDDY HOLLY ALBUMS IN THE UK

	Title	Year
1	20 Golden Greats	1978
2	The Buddy Holly Story	1959
3	Buddy Holly's Greatest Hits	1967
4	Reminiscing	1963
5	True Love Ways	1989
6	The Buddy Holly Story, Vol. 2	1960
7	Showcase	1964
8	The Chirping Crickets	1958
9	Buddy Holly	1958
10	That'll Be The Day	1961

Only the albums at numbers eight and nine in this list were released during Holly's lifetime. Others, like *Reminiscing* and *Showcase*, were assembled from previously unreleased material in the years following his death. The rest represent the many hits compilations that have appeared through the years, with *20 Golden Greats* and *True Love Ways* having been TV-promoted.

THE TOP 10 MICHAEL JACKSON ALBUMS IN THE UK

	Title	Year
1	Bad	1987
2	Thriller	1982
3	Dangerous	1991
4	Off The Wall	1979
5	The Best Of Michael Jackson	1981
6	The Michael Jackson Mix	1987
7	Farewell My Summer Love	1984
8	Ben	1973
9	One Day In Your Life	1981
10	Got To Be There	1972

Britain is one of the few countries where *Bad* has outsold the all-time global bestselling album, *Thriller*. Numbers five, seven, eight, nine and 10 were all released on the Motown label and merit inclusion simply because, since 1979, when he signed a solo deal with Epic, Jackson has released only three original studio albums, a moderate workload which has clearly paid off for the self-proclaimed 'King of Pop'.

Singer/composer/pianist Reg Dwight had abundant talent but reckoned his name was going to get him nowhere. Casting about for a more charismatic alternative, he alighted on Elton Dean of Soft Machine and appropriated half of his.

THE TOP 10 TOM JONES ALBUMS IN THE UK

	Title	Year
1	Live At The Talk Of The Town	1967
2	Delilah	1968
3	Green, Green Grass Of Home	1967
4	Tom Jones Live In Las Vegas	1969
5	20 Greatest Hits	1975
6	13 Smash Hits	1967
7	This Is Tom Jones	1969
8	Tom	1970
9	Help Yourself	1968
10	I Who Have Nothing	1970

In 1967, his peak year, the Welsh crooner scored three Top 10 albums including number one, which went on to log 90 weeks on the UK chart, subsequently becoming one of the bestselling live albums of the decade.

THE TOP 10 MARK KNOPFLER AND DIRE STRAITS ALBUMS IN THE UK

	Title	Year
1	Brothers In Arms	1985
2	Money For Nothing	1988
3	Love Over Gold	1982
4	Makin' Movies	1980
5	Alchemy – Dire Straits Live	1984
6	Dire Straits	1978
7	On Every Street	1991
8	Communiqué	1979
9	Missing...Presumed Having A Good Time*	1990
10	Local Hero (Original Film Soundtrack)**	1983

* Released by the Notting Hillbillies.

** Released by Mark Knopfler.

As originator, writer, producer, lead guitarist and lead vocalist of Dire Straits, Knopfler has been one of the most consistent and successful home-grown exports of the past 15 years as the band's albums have earned dozens of gold and platinum awards worldwide. The albums listed here have together spent over 1,000 weeks on the UK chart, with *Makin' Movies* alone residing on the survey for nearly five years. Aside from production work for the likes of Bob Dylan and Randy Newman, Knopfler has also recorded a handful of film scores (including *Cal*, *Comfort And Joy* and *The Princess Bride*), a Grammy Award-winning album with Nashville veteran Chet Atkins (*Neck And Neck*) and was the driving force behind the low-key 1990 club band, the Notting Hillbillies.

Keith Moon of the Who reputedly remarked that Jimmy Page's proposed New Yardbirds would 'go down like a lead Zeppelin'. Actually, the new band went down rather well in the 1970s, but Moon's musing proved useful nonetheless!

THE TOP 10 LED ZEPPELIN ALBUMS IN THE UK

	Title	Year
1	Led Zeppelin II	1969
2	Led Zeppelin (four symbols)	1971
3	Led Zeppelin	1969
4	Led Zeppelin III	1970
5	Physical Graffiti	1975
6	In Through The Out Door	1979
7	The Song Remains The Same	1976
8	Presence	1976
9	Houses Of The Holy	1973
10	Coda	1982

All except numbers three and 10 made UK No. 1, while their debut album spent 18 months on the chart. Persistent rumours of a Led Zeppelin reunion have been strong enough to fuel the successful release of out-takes albums and greatest hits retrospectives, including *Remasters* and the *Led Zeppelin* boxed set (not to be confused with number three), both issued in 1990. The *'four symbols'* album from 1971 continues to be a strong back-catalogue item, containing the *Stairway To Heaven* track so synonymous with the band, but which was never released as a single in the UK.

THE TOP 10 JOHN LENNON ALBUMS IN THE UK

	Title	Year
1	*Imagine*	1971
2	*The John Lennon Collection*	1982
3	*Double Fantasy*	1980
4	*Shaved Fish*	1975
5	*Rock 'n' Roll*	1975
6	*Milk And Honey*	1984
7	*Walls And Bridges*	1974
8	*Mind Games*	1973
9	*John Lennon And The Plastic Ono Band*	1971
10	*Sometime In New York City*	1972

Paradoxically, while universally acclaimed by rock critics, Lennon's albums have always fallen short of the commercial popularity attained by Paul McCartney's releases – which, in contrast, have been generally slammed by observers. *Imagine* is, of course, the exception, spending three weeks short of two years on the UK chart.

THE TOP 10 BARRY MANILOW ALBUMS IN THE UK

	Title	Year
1	*Manilow Magic*	1979
2	*Barry Live In Britain*	1982
3	*Barry*	1980
4	*If I Should Love Again*	1981
5	*Even Now*	1978
6	*A Touch More Magic*	1983
7	*I Wanna Do It With You*	1982
8	*Songs 1975–1990*	1990
9	*One Voice*	1979
10	*2.00 am, Paradise Cafe*	1984

This smooth-voiced romantic balladeer was the top seller on the UK easy-listening market through the late 1970s and the 1980s, occupying the niche once filled by Andy Williams and Engelbert Humperdinck. He had a string of hit singles, too, and of the albums above, numbers one, three and eight are all compilations of those hits. The jazzy *2.00 am, Paradise Cafe*, meanwhile, revealed a largely unknown side of Manilow's vocal style.

THE TOP 10 MADNESS ALBUMS IN THE UK

	Title	Year
1	*Complete Madness*	1982
2	*One Step Beyond*	1979
3	*Absolutely*	1980
4	*Divine Madness*	1992
5	*Madness 7*	1981
6	*The Rise And Fall*	1982
7	*Keep Moving*	1984
8	*Mad Not Mad*	1985
9	*Utter Madness*	1986
10	*Madstock*	1992

The 'Nutty Boys' were signed to Stiff Records for their first six releases, but lost their Top 10 touch with three subsequent albums on their own Zarjazz label between 1985 and 1988. Their reunion in 1992 prompted renewed chart success with their No. 1 *Divine Madness* retrospective collection and the release of the live *Madstock* album in November of that year.

THE TOP 10 BOB MARLEY ALBUMS IN THE UK

	Title	Year
1	*Legend*	1984
2	*Exodus*	1977
3	*Kaya*	1978
4	*Confrontation*	1983
5	*Uprising*	1980
6	*Rastaman Vibration*	1976
7	*Live/Live At The Lyceum**	1975/1981
8	*Survival*	1979
9	*Babylon By Bus*	1978
10	*Songs Of Freedom*	1992

* *The album, Live, was reissued in 1981 as Live At The Lyceum.*

Four albums have charted since Marley's death in 1981 at the age of 36, most notably the Top 10 definitive 1992 boxed set, *Songs Of Freedom*.

THE TOP 10 JOHNNY MATHIS ALBUMS IN THE UK

	Title	Year
1	The Johnny Mathis Collection	1977
2	Tears And Laughter	1980
3	You Light Up My Life	1978
4	Celebration	1981
5	Unforgettable: A Musical Tribute (with Natalie Cole)	1983
6	That's What Friends Are For (with Deniece Williams)	1978
7	When Will I See You Again	1975
8	I Only Have Eyes For You	1976
9	I'm Coming Home	1975
10	Rhythms And Ballads Of Broadway	1960

Although silk-voiced balladeer Mathis had been selling albums in Britain ever since 1958, in the wake of his first UK Top 10 single, his sales soared notably during the 1970s, a new wave of popularity coinciding with the general expansion of album sales at the time. Both numbers one and two were compilations of earlier singles and popular LP tracks, while *Unforgettable* consisted of songs associated with Nat 'King' Cole.

THE TOP 10 JONI MITCHELL ALBUMS IN THE UK

	Title	Year
1	Blue	1971
2	Ladies Of The Canyon	1970
3	Court And Spark	1974
4	The Hissing Of Summer Lawns	1975
5	Don Juan's Reckless Daughter	1978
6	Hejira	1976
7	Mingus	1979
8	Chalk Mark In A Rain Storm	1988
9	Night Ride Home	1991
10	Wild Things Run Fast	1982

Canadian singer-songwriter Joni Mitchell, like her countryman Neil Young, has traditionally been a critics' and aficionados' favourite, rather than a regular hitmaker, since her early songs (like *Both Sides Now*) first brought her to notice in the late 1960s. The two top titles (also the two earliest) on this list, remain her only UK Top 10 albums, though she now has over 20 years' worth of LP chart entries to her credit.

THE TOP 10 PAUL McCARTNEY ALBUMS IN THE UK

	Title	Year
1	Band On The Run	1973
2	Wings At The Speed Of Sound	1976
3	Venus And Mars	1975
4	All The Best!	1987
5	Tug Of War	1982
6	McCartney	1970
7	Ram	1971
8	Wings' Greatest Hits	1978
9	Give My Regards To Broad Street	1984
10	Flowers In The Dirt	1989

Since 1970, each of Paul McCartney's 23 albums (including 1993's *Off The Ground*) has charted, with numbers one, three, five, seven, nine and 10 making the top spot. Having signed a long-term contract with the EMI Records group in 1992, it is likely that McCartney's entire British recording career, from the Beatles through Wings and into his solo releases, will remain with one music corporation.

THE TOP 10 MOODY BLUES ALBUMS IN THE UK

	Title	Year
1	On The Threshold Of A Dream	1969
2	To Our Children's Children's Children	1969
3	Every Good Boy Deserves Favour	1971
4	A Question Of Balance	1970
5	In Search Of The Lost Chord	1968
6	Seventh Sojourn	1972
7	Octave	1978
8	Long Distance Voyager	1981
9	Days Of Future Passed	1967
10	The Present	1983

Originally an R & B group (*Go Now*, etc), the Moody Blues became, after their 1967 conceptual album *Days Of Future Passed* (containing their most famous song, *Nights In White Satin*), the essence of progressive, semi-classical 'cosmic' rock. This was a genre held in high disregard by the end of the 1970s – which has not stopped the Moodies from recording successfully in more or less the same style until the present day.

THE TOP 10 VAN MORRISON ALBUMS IN THE UK

	Title	Year
1	The Best Of Van Morrison	1990
2	Enlightenment	1990
3	Avalon Sunset	1989
4	Beautiful Vision	1982
5	Hymns To The Silence	1991
6	Inarticulate Speech Of The Heart	1983
7	Irish Heartbeat	1988
8	Into The Music	1979
9	Wavelength	1978
10	Poetic Champions Compose	1987

Although Morrison has proved to be a consistent seller of back-catalogue, his UK album chart achievements are meagre. It was not until his 16th solo release, *The Best Of Van Morrison*, that the Belfast-born ex-Them member finally cracked the Top 10.

THE TOP 10 ROY ORBISON ALBUMS IN THE UK

	Title	Year
1	The Legendary Roy Orbison	1988
2	The Best Of Roy Orbison	1975
3	Mystery Girl	1989
4	In Dreams	1963
5	Oh, Pretty Woman	1964
6	King Of Hearts	1992
7	There Is Only One Roy Orbison	1965
8	The Orbison Way	1966
9	The Classic Roy Orbison	1966
10	A Black And White Night	1989

The top two releases here were both TV-advertised hits collections, while *Mystery Girl* was the album of new material that Orbison had just completed prior to his sudden death. Other posthumous successes were *A Black And White Night*, the soundtrack to a guest-studded late 1980s TV special, and *King Of Hearts*, which the singer's widow Barbara Orbison completed from unfinished tapes and previously uncollected singles.

THE TOP 10 PINK FLOYD ALBUMS IN THE UK

	Title	Year
1	Dark Side Of The Moon	1973
2	Wish You Were Here	1975
3	Meddle	1971
4	The Wall	1979
5	Atom Heart Mother	1970
6	Animals	1977
7	The Final Cut	1983
8	A Momentary Lapse Of Reason	1987
9	Ummagumma	1969
10	Obscured By Clouds (Original Film Soundtrack)	1972

Despite spending over 300 weeks on the UK chart and being one of the bestselling albums ever, *Dark Side Of The Moon* never made UK No. 1, peaking instead at No. 2. Following Roger Waters' acrimonious departure from the group in 1986, Floyd's album success has been severely diminished, while his solo career has similarly failed to recall the heady days of *Dark Side Of The Moon* and *The Wall*.

THE TOP 10 MIKE OLDFIELD ALBUMS IN THE UK

	Title	Year
1	Tubular Bells	1973
2	Hergest Ridge	1974
3	Ommadawn	1975
4	Crises	1983
5	Tubular Bells II	1992
6	Five Miles Out	1982
7	Incantations	1978
8	Discovery	1984
9	Exposed	1979
10	QE2	1980

Having failed to regain the top spot since *Hergest Ridge* in 1974, Oldfield finally returned to UK No. 1 in September 1992 with the Trevor Horn co-produced soundalike follow-up to the multi-platinum *Tubular Bells*. It is interesting to note that Richard Branson's Virgin empire was built on the staggering five-year chart streak of the innovative original album, yet *Tubular Bells II* was Oldfield's first product not to be released by Virgin since he was signed by Warner Brothers in 1991 specifically to produce the *Bells* sequel.

THE TOP 10 OSMOND FAMILY ALBUMS IN THE UK

	Title	Member	Year
1	Portrait Of Donny	Donny	1972
2	The Plan	Osmonds	1973
3	Too Young	Donny	1972
4	Our Best To You	Osmonds	1974
5	Alone Together	Donny	1973
6	Crazy Horses	Osmonds	1972
7	A Time For Us	Donny	1973
8	The Osmonds Live	Osmonds	1972
9	I'm Leaving It Up To You	Donny and Marie	1974
10	Killer Joe	Little Jimmy	1973

The toothsome, wholesome Osmonds dominated teen-appeal music in the UK from 1972 to 1974, scoring not only as a harmony rock group, but via various spin-offs: Donny had a parallel teen-balladeer career, sister Marie sang pop/Country music, and they worked together as a middle-of-the-road duo. Youngest brother Jimmy was recorded solo apparently as a gag (to judge by the recordings), but he too joined in the family's general chart domination.

THE FIRST 10 ELVIS PRESLEY ALBUMS RELEASED IN THE USA

	Title	Label	Cat. no.
1	Elvis Presley	RCA	LPM 1254
2	Elvis	RCA	LPM 1382
3	Loving You (Original Soundtrack)	RCA	LPM 1515
4	Elvis' Christmas Album	RCA	LOC 1035
5	Elvis' Golden Records	RCA	LPM 1701
6	King Creole (Original Soundtrack)	RCA	LPM 1884
7	For LP Fans Only	RCA	LPM 1990
8	A Date With Elvis	RCA	LPM 2011
9	50,000,000 Elvis Fans Can't Be Wrong: Elvis' Golden Records Vol. 2	RCA	LPM 2075
10	Elvis Is Back	RCA	LPM 2231

Elvis Presley, the debut release, was issued in May 1956 and hogged the top spot for 10 weeks. Elvis Is Back was the first Elvis album to be issued simultaneously in mono and stereo (the latter with a different catalogue number: LPS 2231).

THE TOP 10 PRINCE ALBUMS IN THE UK

	Title	Year
1	Purple Rain: Music From The Motion Picture	1984
2	Diamonds And Pearls	1991
3	Lovesexy	1988
4	Sign O' The Times	1987
5	Parade: Music From 'Under The Cherry Moon'	1986
6	Batman	1989
7	Symbol	1992
8	Around The World In A Day	1985
9	1999	1984
10	Graffiti Bridge	1990

Prince's first UK chart album, Purple Rain, is still his most successful and earned him the 'Best Original Score' Oscar at the 1985 Academy Awards. A workaholic, reclusively based at his own Paisley Park recording studio in Minneapolis, Prince has released at least one album per year for the past five years.

THE TOP 10 ELVIS PRESLEY ALBUMS IN THE UK

	Title	Date
1	40 Greatest Hits	1974
2	Blue Hawaii	1961
3	G.I. Blues	1960
4	Presley – The All-Time Greatest Hits	1987
5	Elvis' Golden Records	1958
6	From The Heart – His Greatest Love Songs	1992
7	Elvis Is Back	1960
8	Moody Blue	1977
9	Love Songs	1979
10	Elvis: NBC TV Special	1969

Elvis' 40 Greatest was a TV-advertised double-LP anthology of hit singles, sales of which doubled three years after its release when Presley died. Most of these albums are compilations, several of them posthumous (the two Love Songs sets being completely different), while Blue Hawaii and G.I. Blues are the soundtrack recordings from two of his most popular post-army film musicals.

THE TOP 10 QUEEN ALBUMS IN THE UK

	Title	Year
1	Greatest Hits	1981
2	Greatest Hits II	1991
3	Innuendo	1991
4	The Works	1984
5	A Kind Of Magic	1986
6	A Night At The Opera	1975
7	The Miracle	1989
8	Sheer Heart Attack	1974
9	Live Magic	1986
10	Jazz	1978

Even prior to Freddie Mercury's death, Queen managed to notch up eight chart-topping UK albums, and, as is traditional with a major rock death, the group's back-catalogue and label compilations flooded the chart in 1992. A Mercury solo retrospective, The Freddie Mercury Album (which contained his prophetic 1984 debut solo hit, Love Kills), also made the Top 5 in the same year.

THE TOP 10 CHRIS REA ALBUMS IN THE UK

	Title	Year
I	The Road To Hell	1989
2	Auberge	1991
3	New Light Through Old Windows	1988
4	Dancing With Strangers	1987
5	On The Beach	1986
6	God's Great Banana Skin	1992
7	Shamrock Diaries	1985
8	Wired To The Moon	1984
9	Chris Rea	1982
10	Deltics	1979

Despite scoring with the 1978 hit *Fool If You Think It's Over*, Rea had to wait until 1987 to achieve his first Top 10 album success (number four). Since then, he has been a Top 5 regular, although 1992's *God's Great Banana Skin* faltered at No. 4, preventing a hat-trick of consecutive No. 1s which began with *The Road To Hell* – the title track of which was inspired by the London orbital motorway, the M25.

THE TOP 10 R.E.M. ALBUMS IN THE UK

	Title	Year
I	Out Of Time	1991
2	Automatic For The People	1992
3	The Best Of R.E.M.	1991
4	Green	1988
5	Document	1987
6	Fables Of The Reconstruction	1985
7	Life's Rich Pageant	1986
8	Dead Letter Office	1987
9	Eponymous	1988
10	Reckoning	1984

R.E.M. (Rapid Eye Movement)'s breakthrough album came with the Grammy Award-winning *Out Of Time*. Despite enormous critical and financial success, the band resolutely refuses to leave its longtime home base in Athens, Georgia.

THE TOP 10 CLIFF RICHARD ALBUMS IN THE UK

	Title	Year
I	Private Collection, 1977–1988	1988
2	Love Songs	1981
3	Always Guaranteed	1987
4	Summer Holiday	1963
5	The Young Ones	1961
6	40 Golden Greats	1977
7	Stronger	1989
8	From A Distance – The Event	1990
9	Wired For Sound	1981
10	Rock 'n' Roll Juvenile	1979

Among performers who first found success in the 1950s, Cliff Richard is unique in still having a high-selling contemporary profile in the 1990s, when album sales are considerably higher. Hence, only two of his chart-topping early albums survive in sales terms alongside the more recent material – the soundtracks from his two most successful films, which continue to sell buoyantly today as budget-priced CDs.

THE TOP 10 JIM REEVES ALBUMS IN THE UK

	Title	Year
I	40 Golden Greats	1975
2	Distant Drums	1966
3	Moonlight And Roses	1964
4	The Best Of Jim Reeves	1965
5	Twelve Songs Of Christmas	1964
6	According To My Heart	1969
7	Jim Reeves' Golden Records	1971
8	The Definitive Jim Reeves	1992
9	Good'n'Country	1964
10	Gentleman Jim	1964

After Country balladeer Jim Reeves died in a plane crash in mid 1964, the charts immediately filled with his albums: he sold more LPs in Britain than anyone that year apart from the Beatles. Subsequently, albums of unreleased material and various hits compilations have preserved Reeves as an active record-seller into the present decade.

THE FIRST 10 CLIFF RICHARD ALBUMS RELEASED IN THE UK

	Title	Date	Cat. no.
I	Cliff	Apr 1959	SX 1147
2	Cliff Sings	Nov 1959	SX 1192
3	Me And My Shadows	Oct 1960	SX 1261
4	Listen To Cliff	Apr 1961	SX 1320
5	21 Today	Oct 1961	SX 1368
6	The Young Ones (Original Soundtrack)	Dec 1961	SX 1384
7	32 Minutes And 17 Seconds With Cliff Richard	Sep 1962	SX 1431
8	Summer Holiday (Original Soundtrack)	Jan 1963	SX 1472
9	Cliff's Hit Album	Jul 1963	SX 1512
10	When In Spain	Sep 1963	SX 1541

Cliff has charted 47 albums in 33 years since his 1959 debut, all of them released either on the Columbia (EMI) label or, post-1972, on the main EMI label.

THE FIRST 10 ROLLING STONES ALBUMS RELEASED IN THE UK

	Title	Date	Cat. no.
1	The Rolling Stones	Apr 1964	LK 4605
2	The Rolling Stones No. 2	Jan 1965	SKL 4661
3	Out Of Our Heads	Oct 1965	SKL 4733
4	Aftermath	Apr 1966	SKL 4786
5	Big Hits (High Tide And Green Grass)	Nov 1966	TXS 101
6	Between The Buttons	Jan 1967	SKL 4852
7	Their Satanic Majesties Request	Dec 1967	TXS 103
8	Beggars Banquet	Dec 1968	SKL 4955
9	Through The Past Darkly (Big Hits Vol. 2)	Sep 1969	SKL 5019
10	Let It Bleed	Dec 1969	SKL 5025

All released on Decca Records, numbers one, two, four and 10 all topped the UK album chart.

THE TOP 10 ROLLING STONES ALBUMS IN THE UK

	Title	Year
1	The Rolling Stones No .2	1965
2	Aftermath	1966
3	Rolled Gold – The Very Best Of The Rolling Stones	1975
4	Let It Bleed	1969
5	Sticky Fingers	1971
6	Some Girls	1978
7	Emotional Rescue	1980
8	Exile On Main Street	1972
9	The Rolling Stones	1964
10	Tattoo You	1981

The Stones' second release is still their all-time bestseller, at around 500,000 copies in the UK, but otherwise most stages of the band's career are represented among their top titles. While they may not still have their 1960s pre-eminence, higher general album sales in the 1980s have boosted some later releases proportionately.

THE 10 ROLLING STONES ALBUMS THAT STAYED LONGEST IN THE UK CHARTS

	Title	Weeks in charts
1	The Rolling Stones	51
2	Rolled Gold – The Very Best Of The Rolling Stones	50
3	Big Hits (High Tide And Green Grass)	43
4=	The Rolling Stones No. 2	37
4=	Through The Past Darkly (Big Hits Vol. 2)	37
6=	Let It Bleed	29
6=	Tattoo You	29
8	Aftermath	28
9=	Sticky Fingers	25
9=	Some Girls	25

As with the Beatles' albums, the long-stay scores of some early Rolling Stones albums were inhibited by the shorter chart of their day. The 1965 album *Out Of Our Heads*, which just missed this Top 10 with a 24-week stay, was issued when only a UK Top 20 LP chart existed, but in reality it continued to sell for longer than *Tattoo You*, *Some Girls* and certain other albums.

ROLLING STONES QUIZ

1. Who replaced Brian Jones as the Stones' rhythm guitarist?

2. What was the band's first UK chart-topper?

3. Which reggae star is the only artist other than the Stones to chart on Rolling Stones records?

4. Who wrote the group's first UK Top 20 hit, *I Wanna Be Your Man*?

5. Who is the only member of the band to have served in the Royal Air Force?

6. With which band did Ron Wood play prior to joining the Stones?

7. Which of the following has not had a child by Mick Jagger: Marianne Faithfull, Marsha Hunt, Jerry Hall?

8. Under what names do Jagger and Richards produce records?

9. Which member formally announced he was quitting the band in January 1993?

10. Which Stone's extra-curricular musical outfit is called the X-Pensive Winos?

THE TOP 10 DIANA ROSS ALBUMS IN THE UK

	Title	Year
1	Diana & Marvin*	1974
2	20 Golden Greats	1979
3	Greatest Hits 2	1976
4	Touch Me In The Morning	1973
5	Portrait	1983
6	Diana Ross	1976
7	Love Songs	1982
8	Diana	1980
9	Eaten Alive	1985
10	I'm Still Waiting	1971

* Recorded with Marvin Gaye.

Including 1991's *The Force Behind The Power* (which was far more popular in the UK than in the United States), Ms Ross has made the UK albums chart on no fewer than 31 occasions, excluding her recordings with the Supremes in the 1960s.

THE TOP 10 SIMON AND GARFUNKEL ALBUMS IN THE UK

	Title	Year
1	Bridge Over Troubled Water	1970
2	Simon And Garfunkel's Greatest Hits	1972
3	The Simon And Garfunkel Collection	1981
4	Bookends	1968
5	Sounds Of Silence	1966
6	Parsley, Sage, Rosemary And Thyme	1966
7	The Definitive Simon And Garfunkel	1991
8	The Graduate (Soundtrack)	1968
9	The Concert In Central Park	1982
10	Wednesday Morning, 3 a.m.	1964

Simon and Garfunkel's top two albums were also the two biggest sellers of the 1970s, and remain among the 20 bestselling albums of all time in the UK. *The Graduate* soundtrack contains some non-Simon and Garfunkel music (background music by Dave Grusin), but even allowing for this and the three compilations, the duo only ever made 10 legitimate albums, so the 1967 Allegro label budget set *Simon And Garfunkel*, containing their 1950s tracks recorded as Tom & Jerry, would be at number 11. Originally priced at around 65p, it is now a very expensive collectors' item.

THE TOP 10 SHADOWS ALBUMS IN THE UK

	Title	Year
1	20 Golden Greats	1977
2	String Of Hits	1979
3	The Shadows	1961
4	The Shadows' Greatest Hits	1963
5	Out Of The Shadows	1962
6	Moonlight Shadows	1986
7	Reflections	1990
8	Dance With The Shadows	1964
9	Simply Shadows	1987
10	The Sound Of The Shadows	1965

A UK musical institution ever since they first stepped out from behind Cliff Richard as a hit instrumental act in their own right in 1960, the Shadows were, from the outset, always strong album sellers – their debut set is still their number three all-time bestseller – and have seen this market grow for them in the 1980s and 1990s long after the hit singles have melted away.

THE TOP 10 SIMPLE MINDS ALBUMS IN THE UK

	Title	Year
1	Once Upon A Time	1985
2	Sparkle In The Rain	1984
3	Glittering Prize '81–'92	1992
4	New Gold Dream (81, 82, 83, 84)	1982
5	Street Fighting Years	1989
6	Live In The City Of Light	1987
7	Real Life	1991
8	Sons And Fascinations/Sisters Feelings Call*	1981
9	A Life In The Day	1979
10	Celebration	1982

* Released as a '2-in-1' double album package.

THE TOP 10 FRANK SINATRA ALBUMS IN THE UK

	Title	Year
1	My Way	1969
2	20 Golden Greats	1978
3	Portrait Of Sinatra	1977
4	Songs For Swinging Lovers	1956
5	Come Fly With Me	1958
6	Strangers In The Night	1966
7	New York, New York (Greatest Hits)	1986
8	Come Dance With Me	1959
9	Frank Sinatra's Greatest Hits	1968
10	Greatest Hits, Vol. 2	1970

Sinatra was the biggest and most consistent album-seller of all during the 1950s, albeit when the LP market was but a fraction of its later size. Nonetheless, his biggest 1950s sellers (numbers four, five and eight in this list) continue actively even today on CD. His *20 Golden Greats* was a TV-promoted compilation of 1950s Capitol label hits; the other four compilations listed are all of 1960s/70s reprise material.

THE TOP 10 SMITHS ALBUMS IN THE UK

	Title	Year
1	The Smiths	1984
2	Hatful Of Hollow	1984
3	The Queen Is Dead	1986
4	Meat Is Murder	1985
5	Strangeways Here We Come	1987
6	The World Won't Listen	1987
7	Best Of The Smiths Vol. 1	1992
8	Rank	1988
9	Best Of The Smiths Vol. 2	1992
10	Louder Than Bombs*	1987

* Import.

Numbers six, seven, nine and 10 are all retrospective compilations.

THE TOP 10 BRUCE SPRINGSTEEN ALBUMS IN THE UK

	Title	Year
1	Born In The USA	1984
2	The River	1980
3	Tunnel Of Love	1987
4	Born To Run	1975
5	Darkness On The Edge Of Town	1978
6	Human Touch	1992
7	Nebraska	1982
8	The Wild, The Innocent And The E. Street Shuffle	1985
9	Lucky Town	1992
10	Live 1975–1985	1986

Born In The USA – the first of three UK No. 1 albums for Bruce Springsteen – was dramatically more successful than any of his other releases, staying on the chart for over two years (by contrast, his 1992 chart-topper, Human Touch, left the survey after only four months).

THE TOP 10 STATUS QUO ALBUMS IN THE UK

	Title	Year
1	Blue For You	1976
2	12 Gold Bars	1980
3	Hello	1973
4	On The Level	1975
5	1982	1982
6	Rocking All Over The Years	1990
7	In The Army Now	1986
8	Quo	1974
9	From The Makers Of...	1982
10	Just Supposin'	1980

Numbers one, three, four and five all made the top spot on the albums chart. The best years may be behind the veteran blue-jean rockers: 1992's Live Alive Quo release peaked at a lowly No. 37.

Status Quo, who had their first hit in the late 1960s, have been rockin' all over the world and through the years since.

THE TOP 10 CAT STEVENS ALBUMS IN THE UK

	Title	Year
1	Teaser And The Firecat	1971
2	Greatest Hits	1975
3	Catch Bull At Four	1972
4	Tea For The Tillerman	1970
5	Buddha And The Chocolate Box	1974
6	The Very Best Of Cat Stevens	1990
7	Foreigner	1973
8	Matthew And Son	1967
9	Izitso	1977
10	Mona Bone Jakon	1970

Cat Stevens is one of the few artists in rock history to have three names: in addition to his rock persona, Stevens was born Steven Georgiou (the son of a Greek restaurateur) and changed his name again in 1978 to Yusef Islam, renouncing his considerable musical success and devoting himself to the Muslim faith.

THE TOP 10 ROD STEWART ALBUMS IN THE UK

	Title	Year
1	Atlantic Crossing	1975
2	Every Picture Tells A Story	1971
3	Rod Stewart's Greatest Hits	1979
4	The Best Of Rod Stewart*	1989
5	A Night On The Town	1976
6	Never A Dull Moment	1972
7	Sing It Again Rod	1973
8	Blondes Have More Fun	1978
9	Smiler	1974
10	Footloose And Fancy Free	1977

*   Warner Bros. label: not to be confused with the similarly titled 1977 Mercury album.

This Top 10 does not include Rod's six chart albums recorded with the Faces between 1970 and 1977, none of which was successful enough to make the list.

THE TOP 10 SUPERTRAMP ALBUMS IN THE UK

	Title	Year
1	Breakfast In America	1979
2	Crime Of The Century	1974
3	Famous Last Words	1982
4	The Autobiography Of Supertramp	1986
5	Paris	1980
6	Even In The Quietest Moments	1977
7	Crisis? What Crisis?	1975
8	Brother Where You Bound	1985
9	Greatest Hits	1992
10	Free As A Bird	1987

UK band Supertramp found the largest market for their layered, harmonic rock in the US, but despite constant critical griping in the UK, they managed to sell copious quantities of most of their album output at home. A reunion is on the cards for 1994.

THE TOP 10 TALKING HEADS ALBUMS IN THE UK

	Title	Year
1	Little Creatures	1985
2	Stop Making Sense	1984
3	Naked	1988
4	Once In A Lifetime – Sand In The Vaseline	1992
5	Remain In Light	1980
6	True Stories	1986
7	Speaking In Tongues	1983
8	The Name Of This Band Is Talking Heads	1982
9	Fear Of Music	1979
10	More Songs About Buildings And Food	1975

From their inception Talking Heads brought an intelligence and wry humour to the uncertain world of the US New Wave, and as a result managed to long outlast it. Leader David Byrne continues in similar style as a soloist.

THE TOP 10 JETHRO TULL ALBUMS IN THE UK

	Title	Year
1	Stand Up	1969
2	Aqualung	1971
3	Benefit	1970
4	Thick As A Brick	1972
5	This Was	1968
6	Living In The Past	1972
7	Songs From The Wood	1977
8	A Passion Play	1973
9	Broadsword And The Beast	1982
10	Crest Of A Knave	1987

Ian Anderson-led Jethro Tull, one of Britain's longest-surviving rock bands, was formed in 1967 and has secured 24 chart albums in 25 years of recording. Stand Up, their only UK No. 1 album, was also the first release on the Chrysalis label formed in 1968 by the band's agents, Terry Ellis and Chris Wright.

THE TOP 10 UB40 ALBUMS IN THE UK

	Title	Year
1	The Best Of UB40 Vol. 1	1987
2	Labour Of Love	1983
3	Signing Off	1980
4	Labour Of Love Vol. II	1989
5	Present Arms	1981
6	Rat In The Kitchen	1986
7	Baggaradim	1985
8	Geffrey Morgan	1984
9	UB44	1982
10	UB40	1988

UB40 confounded the supposed wisdom that reggae-based acts can't sell albums. The West Midlands-based outfit found that their exceptional consistency in the singles charts also transferred to the longer format – although their biggest-selling album was a compilation of their most successful singles.

(Opposite) *Ian Anderson (and support) of Jethro Tull, possibly the most successful group to be named after an eighteenth-century agricultural writer and inventor.*

THE TOP 10 U2 ALBUMS IN THE UK

	Title	Year
1	The Joshua Tree	1987
2	The Unforgettable Fire	1984
3	War	1983
4	U2 Live: Under A Blood Red Sky	1987
5	Achtung Baby	1991
6	Rattle And Hum	1988
7	October	1981
8	Wide Awake In America*	1985
9	Boy	1981
10	The Joshua Tree Singles	1988

* Import.

U2's status rose steadily through the 1980s, until by 1987 their most successful release The Joshua Tree not only spun off two US No. 1 singles, but also became one of the UK's top-selling albums of the decade.

Ireland's U2 became one of the top-selling album acts of the 1980s, as well as winning countless awards such as the Grammy shown here.

As the driving force behind both the Jam and the Style Council (which he formed with Mick Talbot in 1984 following the Jam's demise), Paul Weller has been a UK chart regular since the Jam's debut album, *In The City*, made the Top 20 in 1977. He began a third period in his career with the launch of his first self-titled solo album on the Go! Discs label in September 1992.

Roger Daltrey and Pete Townshend of the Who represent a solid rock career stretching back to the early 1960s, when they were originally known as the High Numbers.

THE TOP 10 PAUL WELLER ALBUMS IN THE UK

	Title	Group	Year
1	Café Bleu	Style Council	1984
2	Snap	Jam	1983
3	The Gift	Jam	1982
4	Our Favourite Shop	Style Council	1985
5	Sound Affects	Jam	1980
6	Dig The New Breed	Jam	1982
7	Setting Sons	Jam	1979
8	The Singular Adventures Of The Style Council	Style Council	1989
9	Greatest Hits	Jam	1991
10	All Mod Cons	Jam	1978

THE TOP 10 WHO ALBUMS IN THE UK

	Title	Year
1	Who's Next	1971
2	The Story Of The Who	1976
3	Live At Leeds	1970
4	Quadrophenia	1973
5	A Quick One	1966
6	My Generation	1965
7	Tommy	1969
8	Face Dances	1981
9	Who Are You	1978
10	Who's Better Who's Best	1988

Upon close inspection, the Who's mighty reputation as a major rock band looks fragile: the group's albums have spent a total of only 203 weeks on the UK chart compared to the 688 weeks notched up by the Rolling Stones over a similar time period. The Who's only UK No. 1 was, curiously, 1970's *Live At Leeds*, while *Tommy*, which many regard as the definitive rock opera, spent a mere nine weeks on the chart in 1969 and has never re-charted.

THE TOP 10 STEVIE WONDER ALBUMS IN THE UK

	Title	Year
1	Hotter Than July	1980
2	Songs In The Key Of Life	1976
3	Innervisions	1973
4	Talking Book	1973
5	Woman In Red: Selections From The Motion Picture Soundtrack	1984
6	Fulfillingness' First Finale	1974
7	In Square Circle	1985
8	Original Musiquarium Vol. 1	1982
9	Journey Through The Secret Life Of Plants	1979
10	Love Songs – 16 Classic Hits	1984

As with many R & B acts, Wonder's album chart achievements are linked to his hit singles performance: *Hotter Than July* spawned four Top 10 hits, including Bob Marley's *Masterblaster (Jammin')*, and album sales benefited accordingly.

THE TOP 10 ANDY WILLIAMS ALBUMS IN THE UK

	Title	Year
1	Andy Williams' Greatest Hits	1970
2	Reflections	1978
3	Home Loving Man	1971
4	Can't Help Falling In Love	1970
5	Almost There	1965
6	Solitaire	1973
7	Love, Andy	1968
8	Honey	1968
9	Love Theme From The Godfather	1972
10	Greatest Love Classics	1984

In the late 1960s and early 1970s, with a popular weekly TV show to keep his profile high, and an acute sense for covering the strongest ballads of the day, crooner Andy Williams was both an impressive singles and album seller. Most of the albums in his Top 10 were collections of such cover versions, with the top seller being an anthology of his own hit singles.

THE TOP 10 YES ALBUMS IN THE UK

	Title	Year
1	Going For The One	1977
2	The Yes Album	1971
3	Tales From The Topographic Oceans	1973
4	Close To The Edge	1972
5	90125	1983
6	Fragile	1971
7	Relayer	1974
8	Yessongs	1973
9	Drama	1980
10	Tormato	1978

The title of number five was derived from its catalogue number.

THE TOP 10 NEIL YOUNG ALBUMS IN THE UK

	Title	Year
1	Harvest	1972
2	After The Goldrush	1970
3	Harvest Moon	1992
4	Rust Never Sleeps	1979
5	Ragged Glory	1990
6	American Stars'n'Bars	1977
7	Freedom	1979
8	Weld	1991
9	Trans	1983
10	Time Fades Away	1973

Despite two-and-a-half decades of critical appreciation which have made Young, a Canadian, one of rock music's grand old men of the 1990s, he has never been (except for occasional commercial forays with Crosby, Stills & Nash) a particularly consistent hitmaker in his own right, with just one major chart single, *Heart Of Gold* in 1972, and one chart-topping album with that song's parent LP *Harvest* – by far his bestselling record.

THE TOP 10 FRANK ZAPPA ALBUMS IN THE UK

	Title	Year
1	Hot Rats	1970
2	Burnt Weeny Sandwich	1970
3	Weasels Ripped My Flesh	1970
4	Sheik Yerbouti	1979
5	We're Only In It For The Money	1968
6	Tinsel Town Rebellion	1981
7	Ship Arriving Too Late To Save A Drowning Witch	1982
8	Joe's Garage, Act 1	1979
9	Chunga's Revenge	1970
10	You Are What You Is	1981

The idiosyncratic Zappa has spent almost three decades as a thorn in the sides of establishments both musical and political, but has generally found critical acclaim along with controversy, if not consistent commercial success – *Hot Rats* is the only Top 10 album he ever had. Numbers two, three and five in this list were credited to his original band the Mothers Of Invention, with the rest issued under his own name.

COMPOSERS AND PRODUCERS

THE TOP 10 UK HITS COMPOSED BY BURT BACHARACH

	Title	Charting artist(s)
1	*Walk On By*	Average White Band, D Train, Stranglers, Sybil, Dionne Warwick
2	*Anyone Who Had A Heart*	Cilla Black, Mary May, Dionne Warwick
3	*Magic Moments*	Perry Como, Ronnie Hilton
4	*Make It Easy On Yourself*	Walker Brothers
5	*Tower Of Strength*	Gene McDaniels, Frankie Vaughan
6	*Trains And Boats And Planes*	Burt Bacharach, Billy J. Kramer & The Dakotas
7	*The Story Of My Life*	Alma Cogan, Dave King, Michael Holliday
8	*On My Own*	Patti LaBelle & Michael McDonald
9	*I'll Never Fall In Love Again*	Bobbie Gentry
10	*Raindrops Keep Fallin' On My Head*	Sacha Distel, Bobbie Gentry, B.J. Thomas

Trains And Boats And Planes remains Bacharach's only major hit single as a performer in either the UK or United States, making UK No. 4 for the writer in 1965. Bacharach & David became the first songwriting team to achieve consecutive UK No. 1 hits back in 1958 when *The Story Of My Life* was replaced at the top (a position it was to hold for eight weeks) by Perry Como's version of *Magic Moments*.

THE TOP 10 US HITS COMPOSED BY BURT BACHARACH

	Title	Charting artist(s)
1	*That's What Friends Are For*	Dionne Warwick & Friends
2	*Raindrops Keep Fallin' On My Head*	B.J. Thomas
3	*(They Long To Be) Close To You*	B.T. Express, Jerry Butler & Brenda Lee Eager, Carpenters
4	*This Guy's In Love With You/ This Girl's In Love With You*	Herb Alpert, Dionne Warwick
5	*Arthur's Theme (Best That You Can Do)*	Christopher Cross
6	*I Say A Little Prayer*	Glen Campbell & Anne Murray, Aretha Franklin, Dionne Warwick
7	*On My Own*	Patti LaBelle & Michael McDonald
8	*Walk On By*	Average White Band, Gloria Gaynor, Isaac Hayes, Sybil, Dionne Warwick
9	*Baby It's You*	Shirelles, Smith
10	*Alfie*	Cilla Black, Cher, Eivets Rednow*, Dionne Warwick

* *A pseudonym of Stevie Wonder.*

American hit veteran Burt Bacharach has succeeded primarily as one-half of two separate songwriting teams. In the 1960s his partnership with Hal David provided hit material for the likes of Dionne Warwick, Herb Alpert and the Drifters, while his marriage to Carole Bayer-Sager spawned dozens of more recent hits, among them numbers one, five and seven.

THE TOP 10 UK HITS COMPOSED BY JEFF BARRY AND ELLIE GREENWICH

	Title	Charting artist(s)
1	Sugar Sugar	Archies, Sakkarin
2	Leader Of The Pack	Shangri-Las (four times), Twisted Sister
3	Then I Kissed Her/Then He Kissed Me	Beach Boys/Crystals
4	Do Wah Diddy Diddy	Manfred Mann
5	Tell Laura I Love Her	Ricky Valance
6	Montego Bay	Amazulu, Bobby Bloom, Freddie Notes & The Rudies, Sugar Cane
7	Baby, I Love You	Dave Edmunds, Ramones, Ronettes
8	River Deep Mountain High	Ike & Tina Turner, Supremes & The Four Tops
9	Be My Baby	Ronettes
10	Remember (Walkin' In The Sand)	Shangri-Las

Do Wah Diddy Diddy, the biggest Barry and Greenwich hit by a UK act, was originally recorded with little commercial success by the songwriters themselves under the name the Raindrops.

THE TOP 10 US HITS COMPOSED BY JEFF BARRY AND ELLIE GREENWICH

	Title	Charting artist(s)
1	Sugar Sugar	Archies, Wilson Pickett
2	Da Doo Ron Ron	Shaun Cassidy, Crystals, Ian Matthews
3	Chapel Of Love	Dixie Cups, Bette Midler
4	Do Wah Diddy Diddy	Exciters, Manfred Mann
5	Leader Of The Pack	Shangri-Las, Twisted Sister
6	Be My Baby	Cissy Houston, Andy Kim, Ronettes
7	I Honestly Love You	Olivia Newton-John
8	Baby, I Love You	Andy Kim, Ronettes
9	Remember (Walkin' In The Sand)	Aerosmith, Louise Goffin, Shangri-Las
10	Hanky Panky	Tommy James & The Shondells

Another married songwriting team with early 1960s roots in the infamous Brill Building, the early work of Barry and Greenwich was produced by Phil Spector with whom they wrote *River Deep Mountain High* in 1966. Its poor US chart performance (a No. 88 peak) hurt Spector so deeply that he quit the music business.

THE TOP 10 UK HITS COMPOSED BY MIKE BATT

	Title	Charting artist(s)
1	Bright Eyes	Art Garfunkel
2	Wombling Merry Christmas	Wombles
3	A Winter's Tale	David Essex
4	Remember You're A Womble	Wombles
5	The Wombling Song	Wombles
6	Summertime City	Mike Batt with the New Edition
7	Please Don't Fall In Love	Cliff Richard
8	I Feel Like Buddy Holly	Alvin Stardust
9	Banana Rock	Wombles
10	Minuetto Allegretto	Wombles

In addition to being the musical 'mastermind' behind the hugely popular mid-1970s children's TV characters, The Wombles, Batt has also been a successful soundtrack composer and writer of pop ballads, the most notable of which, *Bright Eyes*, the main theme for the animated movie, *Watership Down*, combined both elements to great effect for Art Garfunkel who took it to UK No. 1 in 1979.

THE TOP 10 UK HITS WRITTEN BY DON BLACK

	Title	Charting artist(s)
1	Ben	Michael Jackson, Marti Webb
2	Love Changes Everything	Michael Ball
3	Take That Look Off Your Face	Marti Webb
4	Walk Away	Matt Monro
5	Anyone Can Fall In Love	Anita Dobson
6	Sam	Olivia Newton-John
7	I'll Put You Together Again	Hot Chocolate
8	Always There	Marti Webb
9	Thunderball	Tom Jones
10	For Mama	Matt Monro

Currently best known as the lyricist for two of Andrew Lloyd Webber's most recent musical productions, *Aspects Of Love* and *Sunset Boulevard*, London-born Don Black's songwriting success dates back to the 1960s, notably with Matt Monro's fourth UK Top 10 hit, *Walk Away*, in 1964. In addition to number nine, Black was also responsible (with John Barry) for two other James Bond themes, *Diamonds Are Forever* and *The Man With The Golden Gun*. His biggest UK success has been *Ben* – the bestselling single ever written about a rat!

THE TOP 10 US HITS WRITTEN BY DON BLACK

	Title	Charting artist(s)
1	To Sir With Love	Lulu, Herbie Mann
2	Ben	Michael Jackson
3	Born Free	Hesitations, Roger Williams
4	Sam	Olivia Newton-John
5	Walk Away	Matt Monro
6	Thunderball	Tom Jones
7	True Grit	Glen Campbell
8	For Mama	Connie Francis, Jerry Vale
9	Diamonds Are Forever	Shirley Bassey
10	Downtown	One 2 Many

Never far away from a hit film theme during the 1960s and 1970s, Black's biggest US hit was also Lulu's greatest American success: the title theme to the 1967 movie, *To Sir With Love*, which spent five weeks atop the US survey and sold more than 2,000,000 copies. Numbers one, three, five, six, seven and nine all proved successful US hits from major films, while Black also wrote the lyrics (to Quincy Jones' music) to the popular Matt Monro theme from *The Italian Job* (*On Days Like These*). His most recent US chart composition was that for One 2 Many in 1989.

THE TOP 10 UK HITS COMPOSED BY FELICE AND BOUDLEAUX BRYANT

	Title	Charting artist(s)
1	All I Have To Do Is Dream	Glen Campbell & Bobbie Gentry, Everly Brothers
2	Wake Up Little Susie	Everly Brothers, King Brothers
3	Hey Joe	Frankie Laine
4	Bird Dog	Everly Brothers
5	She Wears My Ring	Solomon King
6	Love Hurts	Jim Capaldi
7	Bye Bye Love	Everly Brothers, Webb Pierce
8	Willie Can	Beverley Sisters, Alma Cogan
9	Let's Think About Living	Bob Luman
10	Hawkeye	Frankie Laine

Aside from the obvious Everly Brothers hits, the UK list is significantly different from the Bryants' US ranking, due not least to American 1950s vocalist Frankie Laine, who took *Hey Joe* to the top of the UK survey in 1953 long before the pair had achieved the same feat in their home country.

THE TOP 10 US HITS COMPOSED BY FELICE AND BOUDLEAUX BRYANT

	Title	Charting artist(s)
1	All I Have To Do Is Dream	Glen Campbell & Bobbie Gentry, Richard Chamberlain, Everly Brothers (twice), Andy Gibb & Victoria Principal, Nitty Gritty Dirt Band
2	Wake Up Little Susie	Everly Brothers, Simon and Garfunkel
3	Bye Bye Love	Everly Brothers, Webb Pierce
4	Bird Dog	Everly Brothers
5	Problems	Everly Brothers
6	Love Hurts	Jim Capaldi, Nazareth
7	Devoted To You	Everly Brothers, James Taylor and Carly Simon
8	Mexico	Bobby Moore
9	Let's Think About Living	Bob Luman
10	Raining In My Heart	Buddy Holly, Leo Sayer

Barely known outside the publishing world, Felice and Boudleaux Bryant married in 1945 and began writing together (though a number of their hits were credited solely to Boudleaux), eventually linking up with the Everly Brothers for whom they wrote a string of unforgettable pop classics which are still covered to this day and are featured in many TV commercials.

THE TOP 10 UK HITS COMPOSED BY NICKY CHINN AND MIKE CHAPMAN

	Title	Charting artist(s)
1	Blockbuster	Sweet
2	Can The Can	Suzi Quatro
3	Lonely This Christmas	Mud
4	Tiger Feet	Mud
5	Devil Gate Drive	Suzi Quatro
6	Co-Co	Sweet
7	Mickey	Toni Basil
8	Hell Raiser	Sweet
9	Some Girls	Racey
10	Ballroom Blitz	Sweet

Nicky Chinn and Mike Chapman rank as one of the UK's foremost songwriting teams of the 1970s and beyond.

As 'house' writers for Mickie Most's RAK stable of pop acts during the 1970s, Chinn and Chapman were the most successful UK-based writers of the decade, churning out hits for the Sweet (on RCA), Mud, Suzi Quatro, Racey, New World and the Arrows among others. All the songs listed here made either No. 1 or No. 2 on the UK chart. Mike Chapman went on to find more success as a producer for, among others, Blondie, the Knack and Rod Stewart, and also co-wrote (with Holly Knight), Tina Turner's Top 5 smash, *The Best*.

SONGWRITERS QUIZ

Which individual songwriters were responsible for composing the following hits by other acts?

1 *Red Red Wine* (UB40).

2 *All The Young Dudes* (Mott The Hoople).

3 *By The Time I Get To Phoenix* (Glen Campbell).

4 *Both Sides Now* (Judy Collins).

5 *Living Doll* (Cliff Richard).

6 *Blowin' In The Wind* (Peter, Paul & Mary).

7 *I Will Always Love You* (Whitney Houston)

8 *Fire* (Pointer Sisters).

9 *Daydream Believer* (Monkees).

10 *Jealous Guy* (Roxy Music).

THE TOP 10 UK HITS COMPOSED BY VINCE CLARKE

	Title	Charting artist(s)
1	Only You	Flying Pickets, Yazoo
2	Sometimes	Erasure
3	Stop*	Erasure
4	A Little Respect	Erasure
5	Don't Go	Yazoo
6	Blue Savannah	Erasure
7	Never Never	Assembly
8	Drama!	Erasure
9	The Circus	Erasure
10	Oh L'amour	Dollar

* *The main song featured on Erasure's Crackers International EP.*

While Vince Clarke is best known as one-half of UK hit-making duo Erasure, he was also responsible for writing a couple of early Depeche Mode hits (*Just Can't Get Enough* and *New Life*), was the creative force behind the ad hoc outfit the Assembly and was Alison Moyet's partner in Yazoo, during which time he wrote *Only You*, which has sold well over 1,000,000 copies as a No. 2 hit for Yazoo and a Christmas No. 1 acappella smash for the Flying Pickets.

One of the most successful British songwriting teams of the 1960s, Cook and Greenaway began writing together as members of the Kestrels. Their first collaboration, *You've Got Your Troubles*, took them less than 30 minutes to write but has been covered more than 150 times and is held off the top of this list only by the double success of *Something's Gotten Hold Of My Heart* and what became Coca-Cola's advertising anthem, *I'd Like To Teach The World To Sing (I'd Like To Buy The World A Coke)*. Cook and Greenaway also scored a couple of UK hits under the performing pseudonym, David and Jonathan (a name suggested by producer George Martin's wife).

THE TOP 10 UK HITS COMPOSED BY ROGER COOK AND ROGER GREENAWAY

	Title	Charting artist(s)
1	Something's Gotten Hold Of My Heart	Marc Almond featuring Gene Pitney, Gene Pitney
2	I'd Like To Teach The World To Sing	New Seekers
3	You've Got Your Troubles	Fortunes
4	Melting Pot	Blue Mink
5	Something Tells Me (Something Is Gonna Happen Tonight)	Cilla Black
6	The Way It Used To Be	Engelbert Humperdinck
7	Banner Man	Blue Mink
8	Softly Whispering I Love You	Congregation, Paul Young
9	I Was Kaiser Bill's Batman	Whistling Jack Smith
10	Freedom Come, Freedom Go	Fortunes

In addition to writing two of the Monkees' biggest international hits, it is generally forgotten that Diamond also penned Lulu's third Top 10 UK hit in 1967, *The Boat That I Row*, which was never a hit by any artist in his home country.

THE TOP 10 UK HITS COMPOSED BY NEIL DIAMOND

	Title	Charting artist(s)
1	Red Red Wine	Jimmy James & The Vagabonds, Tony Tribe, UB40
2	I'm A Believer	Monkees
3	A Little Bit Me, A Little Bit You	Monkees
4	Cracklin' Rosie	Neil Diamond
5	I Am...I Said	Neil Diamond
6	You Don't Bring Me Flowers	Barbra Streisand & Neil Diamond
7	The Boat That I Row	Lulu
8	Sweet Caroline (Good Times Never Seemed So Good)	Neil Diamond
9	Song Sung Blue	Neil Diamond
10	Beautiful Noise	Neil Diamond

Well known as a hit performer, Diamond's songwriting catalogue has also been richly mined by dozens of artists, most surprisingly by UB40 whose reggae interpretation of his 1968 solo flop (US No. 62) *Red Red Wine* finally hit US No. 1, taking no less than four years to do so (the British band's version was originally released in the United States in 1984).

THE TOP 10 US HITS COMPOSED BY NEIL DIAMOND

	Title	Charting artist(s)
1	Red Red Wine	Vic Dana, Neil Diamond, UB40 (twice)
2	I'm A Believer	Neil Diamond, Monkees
3	You Don't Bring Me Flowers	Barbra Streisand & Neil Diamond
4	Cracklin' Rosie	Neil Diamond
5	Song Sung Blue	Neil Diamond
6	Love On The Rocks	Neil Diamond
7	Sweet Caroline (Good Times Never Seemed So Good)	Neil Diamond, Bobby Womack
8	Holly, Holy	Neil Diamond, Junior Walker & The All-Stars
9	A Little Bit Me, A Little Bit You	Monkees
10	I Am...I Said	Neil Diamond

THE TOP 10 UK HITS COMPOSED BY BOB DYLAN

	Title	Charting artist(s)
1	Knockin' On Heaven's Door	Eric Clapton, Bob Dylan, Guns N' Roses
2	Mr Tambourine Man	Byrds
3	Mighty Quinn (Quinn The Eskimo)	Manfred Mann
4	If You Gotta Go, Go Now	Manfred Mann*
5	All I Really Want To Do	Byrds, Cher
6	All Along The Watchtower	Jimi Hendrix Experience (twice)
7	Like A Rolling Stone	Bob Dylan
8	Blowin' In The Wind	Peter, Paul & Mary, Stevie Wonder
9	Lay Lady Lay	Bob Dylan
10	I'll Be Your Baby Tonight	Robert Palmer & UB40

* Fairport Convention also had a hit in 1969 with a French version of the song, Si Tu Dois Partir.

The strength of Dylan's songs is demonstrated by the wide variety of acts that have succeeded with cover versions from his catalogue. Other artists just outside the Top 10 who have relied on Robert Zimmerman's songwriting skill include Brian Auger, Bryan Ferry and even Siouxsie & The Banshees.

THE TOP 10 US HITS COMPOSED BY BOB DYLAN

	Title	Charting artist(s)
1	Blowin' In The Wind	Peter, Paul & Mary, Stevie Wonder
2	Mr Tambourine Man	Byrds
3	Lay Lady Lay	Bob Dylan, Ferrante & Teicher, Isley Brothers
4	Like A Rolling Stone	Bob Dylan
5	Rainy Day Women, Nos. 12 & 35	Bob Dylan
6	Don't Think Twice	Peter, Paul & Mary, Wonder Who?
7	It Ain't Me Babe	Johnny Cash, Turtles
8	Mighty Quinn (Quinn The Eskimo)	Manfred Mann
9	Knockin' On Heaven's Door	Bob Dylan
10	All I Really Want To Do	Byrds, Cher

A much-covered songwriter, with hundreds of his titles recorded by other artists, often as album tracks, Dylan material has also proved successful for the likes of Jimi Hendrix (All Along The Watchtower), Rod Stewart (Forever Young) and Olivia Newton-John (If Not For You).

THE TOP 10 UK HITS COMPOSED BY KENNY GAMBLE AND LEON HUFF

	Title	Charting artist(s)
1	Don't Leave Me This Way	Communards, Thelma Houston, Harold Melvin & The Bluenotes
2	If You Don't Know Me By Now	Harold Melvin & The Bluenotes, Simply Red
3	Now That We've Found Love	Heavy D & The Boyz, Third World
4	When Will I See You Again	Three Degrees
5	Show You The Way To Go	Jacksons
6	I'm Gonna Make You Love Me	Supremes & The Temptations
7	Love Train	O'Jays
8	Take Good Care Of Yourself	Three Degrees
9	Me And Mrs Jones	Freddie Jackson, Billy Paul
10	You'll Never Find Another Love Like Mine	Lou Rawls

Only a No. 28 success for them in the US, Show You The Way To Go hit UK No. 1 in 1977 courtesy of the Jacksons, who scored their first UK chart-topper under their new name (changed from the Jackson 5 after their break from Motown). Number four on this list is allegedly Prince Charles' favourite pop hit ever.

THE DECLINE OF THE SONGWRITER

Noted by some as yet another poor year in terms of the quality of its music, 1992's top-selling album was released in 1991 (Simply Red's *Stars*) while 18 of the Top 100 bestselling singles of the year were cover versions: former classic hits such as Andrew Gold's *Never Let Her Slip Away* and Johnny Bristol's *Hang On In There Baby* given a 1990s update, often in a dance vein, often by second-rate acts unable to secure hits with their own original material. Undercover, the group responsible for regurgitating *Never Let Her Slip Away*, is entirely devoted to releasing cover material without even a pretence that it might be worthwhile to explore new creative avenues. Yet the band was nominated for a Brit Award for Best New Act in 1992, itself another indication of the dangerously low creative depths to which the UK record industry has plunged.

Perhaps part of the problem lies in the decline in recognition of the importance of the songwriter in the record-making process. Although the Beatles established a new trend whereby an act would write its own material, and Bob Dylan began the singer-songwriter revolution, a great number of recording stars during the 1960s and 1970s, aware of their own limitations as writers of songs, were heavily reliant upon the distinct skills of songwriters, in the same way that successful writers realized their short-comings as singers. Over the past 10 years or so, a number of factors have, however, led to the decline of the songwriter's craft, particularly in the UK.

While many artists (and music publishers) have recognized that they can make more money by recording their own compositions, instantly dispensing with the need to employ the services of a writer who is possibly more skilled at this art, the astonishing advances in technology have perhaps had an even greater impact on the substandard quality of so much of today's pop music. In addition to hiding an artist's musical shortcomings, studio innovations have concentrated our attention on the 'sound' of a record as opposed to its songwriting qualities, a deviation which has become so prevalent that the UK charts are full of singles which are little more than a rhythmic collection of beeps. This unfortunate trend, fuelled by the growth of specialist dance markets, has squeezed out the most important element of any song that is likely to be remembered: that of melody, the basic building tool employed by the great songwriting teams of even the recent past.

Rhythm has largely replaced composition and the UK record companies are largely to blame, believing that songwriting is the least important factor in signing and recording a new artist and that sound and image are enough to sell most acts. Many major labels have short-sightedly been content to secure a stream of forgettable low-selling electronic-based hit singles instead of nurturing real talent and finding, for example, a great singer whose vocal potential can be married with the skills of a songwriter.

The rise in importance of music video during the 1980s has also contributed to the redundancy of the composer. Hits are now sold on visual wizardry rather than moments of musical magic, once again giving image the edge over substance.

While there will always be exceptions, artists who brilliantly combine skills of songwriting *and* performance, it may be that the British record industry needs a few more bankrupt years before it recognizes that the most essential foundation for any lasting career is a song.

THE TOP 10 US HITS COMPOSED BY KENNY GAMBLE AND LEON HUFF

	Title	Charting artist(s)
1	If You Don't Know Me By Now	Harold Melvin & The Bluenotes, Simply Red
2	Don't Leave Me This Way	Communards, Thelma Houston
3	Me And Mrs Jones	Dramatics, Billy Paul
4	Love Train	O'Jays
5	TSOP (The Sound Of Philadelphia)	MFSB
6	I'm Gonna Make You Love Me	Madeline Bell, Supremes & The Temptations, Dee Dee Warwick
7	When Will I See You Again	Three Degrees
8	You'll Never Find Another Love Like Mine	Lou Rawls
9	Usa Ta Be My Girl	O'Jays
10	Only The Strong Survive	Jerry Butler

Through a succession of Philadelphia-based labels in the 1960s, including Crimson, Gamble Records and Neptune, up to their early 1970s stable, Philadelphia International, Kenny Gamble and Leon Huff created their very own 'Philly sound', best exemplified by the self-explanatory number five. Many of their classic R & B hits continue to be covered today, not least by Simply Red who hit US No. 1 in 1989 with their cover of the classic ballad, *If You Don't Know Me By Now*.

10 OF THE MOST SUCCESSFUL UK SONGWRITING TEAMS

	Team	Significant charting artists
1	John Lennon & Paul McCartney	Beatles, Cilla Black, Rolling Stones
2	Barry, Maurice & Robin Gibb	Bee Gees, Barbra Streisand, Dionne Warwick
3	Mike Stock, Matt Aitken & Pete Waterman	Rick Astley, Jason Donovan, Kylie Minogue
4	Nicky Chinn & Mike Chapman	Mud, Suzi Quatro, Sweet
5	Elton John & Bernie Taupin	Kate Bush, Elton John, George Michael
6	Mick Jagger & Keith Richards	Marianne Faithfull, Melanie, Rolling Stones
7	Roger Greenaway & Roger Cook	Blue Mink, Drifters, Fortunes
8	Annie Lennox & Dave Stewart	Eurythmics
9	Neil Tennant & Chris Lowe	Liza Minnelli, Pet Shop Boys, Dusty Springfield
10	Barry Mason & Les Reed	Drifters, Engelbert Humperdinck, Tom Jones

While it is impossible definitively to rank Britain's most successful songwriters, this list represents, in reasonable order, 10 of the more prominent teams over the past 40 years. All of them have won at least one Ivor Novello Award, the ultimate songwriting trophy for a British writer.

Mick Jagger and Keith Richards appear in the Top 10 UK songwriting teams both for Stones songs and those recorded by others.

THE TOP 10 UK HITS COMPOSED BY THE GIBB BROTHERS

	Title	Charting artist(s)
1	Night Fever	Bee Gees
2	You Win Again	Bee Gees
3	Chain Reaction	Diana Ross
4	Massachusetts	Bee Gees
5	I've Gotta Get A Message To You	Bee Gees
6	To Love Somebody*	Bee Gees, Michael Bolton, Nina Simone, Jimmy Somerville
7	Saved By The Bell**	Robin Gibb (twice)
8	Don't Forget To Remember†	Bee Gees
9	Heartbreaker	Dionne Warwick
10	Tragedy	Bee Gees

* Written by Barry and Robin Gibb.

** Written by Robin Gibb.

† Written by Barry and Maurice Gibb.

Six of these 10 made UK No. 1 (including Robin Gibb's 1969 solo departure at number seven), with *Chain Reaction* being perhaps the most interesting. Peaking at a poor US No. 95 on its original release in 1985, it became one of the bestselling singles of the year in Britain, and Diana Ross' first No. 1 since 1971. Spurred by its UK success, it was remixed and reissued in the States the following year but still failed to climb higher than No. 66. The timeless quality of the brothers Gibb material continues to this day with Michael Bolton's 1992 hit treatment of their 1967 chestnut, *To Love Somebody*.

THE TOP 10 US HITS COMPOSED BY THE GIBB BROTHERS

	Title	Charting artist(s)
1	Stayin' Alive	Bee Gees
2	Night Fever	Bee Gees
3	Shadow Dancing*	Andy Gibb
4	Islands In The Stream	Kenny Rogers and Dolly Parton
5	Too Much Heaven	Bee Gees
6	Grease**	Frankie Valli
7	Emotion†	Samantha Sang
8	Tragedy	Bee Gees
9	I Just Want To Be Your Everything**	Andy Gibb
10	How Deep Is Your Love	Bee Gees

* Written by the Gibb trio with Andy Gibb.

** Written by Barry Gibb.

† Written by Barry and Robin Gibb.

To illustrate the extent of Barry, Maurice and Robin Gibb's songwriting success, there is no room for *Heartbreaker* (Dionne Warwick), *Woman In Love* (Barbra Streisand), *If I Can't Have You* (Yvonne Elliman), *Love Is (Thicker Than Water)* (Andy Gibb), *Hold On To My Love* (Jimmy Ruffin) or dozens of other Bee Gees hits, all written by the most successful trio of brothers in pop history.

The top eight in this list all sold over 2,000,000 copies each in the United States alone.

10 OF THE MOST SUCCESSFUL US SONGWRITING TEAMS

	Team	Significant charting artists
1	Gerry Goffin & Carole King	Animals, Little Eva, James Taylor
2	Burt Bacharach & Hal David	Gene Pitney, B.J. Thomas, Dionne Warwick
3	Brian Holland, Lamont Dozier & Eddie Holland	Four Tops, Supremes, Temptations
4	Bob Crewe & Bob Gaudio	Four Seasons, Tremeloes, Walker Brothers
5	Jeff Barry & Ellie Greenwich	Archies, Manfred Mann, Ronettes
6	Jerry Leiber & Mike Stoller	Coasters, Aretha Franklin, Elvis Presley
7	Jimmy Jam & Terry Lewis	Human League, Janet Jackson, Alexander O'Neal
8	Barry Mann & Cynthia Weil	Mama Cass, Righteous Brothers, Linda Ronstadt
9	Kenny Gamble & Leon Huff	Harold Melvin & The Bluenotes, O'Jays, Three Degrees
10	Bernard Edwards & Nile Rodgers	Chic, Diana Ross, Sister Sledge

Other prominent American songwriting partnerships include Doc Pomus & Mort Shuman (Coasters, Dion, Drifters), Billy Steinberg & Tom Kelly (Bangles, Whitney Houston, Madonna), Felice & Boudleaux Bryant (Everly Brothers), Antonio 'L.A.' Reid & Kenneth 'Babyface' Edmonds (Bobby Brown, Whitney Houston, Karyn White), Nick Ashford & Valerie Simpson (Marvin Gaye, Chaka Khan, Diana Ross), Neil Sedaka & Howard Greenfield (Captain & Tennille, Connie Francis, Neil Sedaka) and Thom Bell & Linda Creed (Detroit Spinners, Johnny Mathis, Stylistics).

THE TOP 10 UK HITS COMPOSED BY GERRY GOFFIN AND CAROLE KING

	Title	Charting artist(s)
1	The Locomotion	Little Eva, Kylie Minogue, Dave Stewart & Barbara Gaskin, Vernons Girls
2	I'm Into Something Good	Herman's Hermits
3	It Might As Well Rain Until September	Carole King
4	Halfway To Paradise	Billy Fury
5	Take Good Care Of My Baby	Smokie, Bobby Vee
6	Will You Love Me Tomorrow	Melanie, Shirelles
7	I Want To Stay Here	Steve & Eydie
8	Don't Bring Me Down	Animals
9	Up On The Roof	Julie Grant, Kenny Lynch
10	Oh No Not My Baby	Manfred Mann, Rod Stewart

A substantially different list from the US ranking of their hits, it exemplifies the international depth of Goffin and King's extensive catalogue. Although they divorced in 1967, both continued successful solo songwriting careers (not least for Carole King with her *Tapestry* album) and occasionally reunited professionally, notably on two cuts for King's under-rated 1989 album, *City Streets*.

THE TOP 10 US HITS COMPOSED BY GERRY GOFFIN AND CAROLE KING

	Title	Charting artist(s)
1	Go Away Little Girl	Happenings, Steve Lawrence, Donny Osmond
2	The Locomotion	Grand Funk, Little Eva, Kylie Minogue
3	Will You Love Me Tomorrow	Roberta Flack, Four Seasons, Dave Mason, Melanie, Shirelles, Dana Valery
4	Up On The Roof	Cryin' Shames, Drifters, Laura Nyro, James Taylor
5	Take Good Care Of My Baby	Bobby Vee, Bobby Vinton
6	One Fine Day	Chiffons, Rita Coolidge, Julie, Carole King
7	I'm Into Something Good	Earl-Jean, Herman's Hermits
8	Hey Girl	Donny Osmond, Freddie Scott, Bobby Vee
9	Pleasant Valley Sunday	Monkees
10	I Can't Stay Mad At You	Skeeter Davis

A nother creative and personal partnership which flourished during the 1960s, Goffin and King were part of the legendary early decade songwriting house, New York's Brill Building where they initially earned $50 a week as staff writers. Numbers one and two are among an elite group of songs which have hit US No. 1 in versions recorded by two different artists in separate decades.

THE TOP 10 UK HITS COMPOSED BY ALBERT HAMMOND

	Title	Charting artist(s)
1	Nothing's Gonna Stop Us Now	Starship
2	When I Need You	Leo Sayer
3	Don't Turn Around	Aswad
4	One Moment In Time	Whitney Houston
5	The Air That I Breathe	Hollies
6	Little Arrows	Leapy Lee
7	Make Me An Island	Joe Dolan
8	Room In Your Heart	Living In A Box
9	Gimme Dat Ding	Pipkins
10	Freedom Come Freedom Go	Fortunes

L ike its US counterpart, this list shows the great variety in Hammond's work, ranging from the infectious pure pop of number nine to the anthemic ballad quality of *One Moment In Time*, which was used as the official theme to the 1988 Olympic Games. Aswad took their reggae version of Hammond's *Don't Turn Around* (which he co-wrote with Diane Warren) to the top of the UK chart in 1988.

THE TOP 10 US HITS COMPOSED BY ALBERT HAMMOND

	Title	Charting artist(s)
1	Nothing's Gonna Stop Us Now	Starship
2	When I Need You	Leo Sayer
3	One Moment In Time	Whitney Houston
4	It Never Rains In Southern California	Albert Hammond
5	To All The Girls I've Loved Before	Julio Iglesias & Willie Nelson
6	The Air That I Breathe	Hollies
7	Gimme Dat Ding	Pipkins
8	Little Arrows	Leapy Lee
9	Through The Storm	Aretha Franklin & Elton John
10	I'm A Train	Albert Hammond

T he 1990 recipient of the Ivor Novello Special Award For International Achievement, British-born Hammond grew up in Gibraltar but is now resident in the United States, where he has had the majority of his success. To write hits for artists ranging from Leapy Lee to Aretha Franklin is no mean achievement!

THE TOP 10 UK HITS COMPOSED BY HOLLAND, DOZIER AND HOLLAND

	Title	Charting artist(s)
1	*You Can't Hurry Love*	Phil Collins, Supremes
2	*You Keep Me Hangin' On*	Roni Hill, Supremes, Vanilla Fudge, Kim Wilde
3	*Baby Love*	Honey Bane, Supremes (twice)
4	*Reach Out I'll Be There*	Four Tops (twice), Gloria Gaynor
5	*Band Of Gold*	Freda Payne, Sylvester
6	*This Old Heart Of Mine*	Isley Brothers, Rod Stewart, Rod Stewart featuring Ronald Isley
7	*There's A Ghost In My House*	R. Dean Taylor, Fall
8	*Where Did Our Love Go*	Donnie Elbert, Manhattan Transfer, Supremes
9	*I Can't Help Myself*	Donnie Elbert, Four Tops (twice)
10	*Give Me Just A Little More Time*	Chairman Of The Board, Kylie Minogue

Their songwriting talent endures: Kylie Minogue recently took *Give Me Just A Little More Time* back into the UK Top 10, while Lamont Dozier co-wrote Phil Collins' 1988 Motown-retro hit, *Two Hearts*.

LYRICS QUIZ

In which hit songs do the following lyrics appear?

1 Her hair is Harlow gold, her lips a sweet surprise.
2 I see people walking through my head, one of them's got a gun, to shoot the other one.
3 For forty days and forty nights, the law was on her side.
4 Out on the wily windy moors, we'd roll and fall in green.
5 Don't let this glad expression, give you the wrong impression.
6 Nothing really matters, anyone can see, nothing really matters, nothing really matters to me.
7 And now she's looking for a downtown man, that's what I am.
8 Open up your eyeballs, pretending that you're Al Green, Al Green.
9 You could look into my eyes under the moonlight, the serious moonlight.
10 The five years we've been together have been such good times.

THE TOP 10 US HITS COMPOSED BY HOLLAND, DOZIER AND HOLLAND

	Title	Charting artist(s)
1	*You Keep Me Hangin' On*	Jackie De Shannon, Wilson Pickett, Supremes, Vanilla Fudge (twice), Kim Wilde
2	*Please Mr Postman**	Carpenters, Gentle Persuasion, Marvelettes
3	*Baby Love*	Supremes
4	*You Can't Hurry Love*	Phil Collins, Supremes
5	*I Can't Help Myself*	Donnie Elbert, Four Tops, Bonnie Pointer
6	*Where Did Our Love Go*	Donnie Elbert, J. Geils Band, Supremes
7	*Reach Out I'll Be There*	Four Tops, Gloria Gaynor, Diana Ross, Merrilee Rush
8	*How Sweet It Is (To Be Loved By You)*	Marvin Gaye, James Taylor, Junior Walker & The All-Stars
9	*Come See About Me*	Nella Dodds, Supremes, Junior Walker & The All-Stars
10	*Stop! In The Name Of Love*	Hollies, Margie Joseph, Supremes

* *Written by Brian Holland with Robert Bateman and Fred Gorman.*

No Holland/Dozier/Holland, no Motown: when brothers Brian and Eddie teamed with Lamont Dozier in the early 1960s, they effectively forged the early Motown sound, turning into a hit songwriting and production machine for, among others, the Supremes and the Four Tops until they split up into separate writing entities in 1968.

THE TOP 10 UK HITS COMPOSED BY JIMMY JAM AND TERRY LEWIS

	Title	Charting artist(s)
1	Dub Be Good To Me/ Just Be Good To Me	Beats International/ S.O.S. Band
2	The Best Things In Life Are Free	Janet Jackson & Luther Vandross
3	What Have You Done For Me Lately	Janet Jackson
4	Saturday Love	Cherrelle with Alexander O'Neal (twice)
5	Let's Wait Awhile	Janet Jackson
6	Criticize	Alexander O'Neal
7	Human	Human League
8	Fake/Fake '88 Remix	Alexander O'Neal
9	When I Think Of You	Janet Jackson
10	I Didn't Mean To Turn You On	Robert Palmer

When UK dance combo Beats International re-grooved the S.O.S. Band's 1984 hit *Just Be Good To Me* into *Dub Be Good To Me*, Jimmy Jam and Terry Lewis achieved their first UK chart-topper. This list is markedly different from the songwriting team's US ranking, due not least to the appeal of Alexander O'Neal's records in Europe, where his record label has seen fit to remix and re-release a number of Jam and Lewis nuggets, often to the chagrin of soul purists.

THE TOP 10 US HITS COMPOSED BY JIMMY JAM AND TERRY LEWIS

	Title	Charting artist(s)
1	Miss You Much	Janet Jackson
2	Romantic	Karyn White
3	Escapade	Janet Jackson
4	Love Will Never Do	Janet Jackson
5	Human	Human League
6	When I Think Of You	Janet Jackson
7	I Didn't Mean To Turn You On	Cherrelle, Robert Palmer
8	Rub You The Right Way	Johnny Gill
9	Nasty	Janet Jackson
10	What Have You Done For Me Lately	Janet Jackson

The most successful American R & B songwriting team of the 1980s, Jimmy Jam and Terry Lewis have been a chart fixture in the United States since the ex-Time members formed their multi-platinum Flyte Tyme songwriting and production partnership in 1982. They are largely responsible for the career achievements of Janet Jackson, having written and co-produced most of her hits from her *Control* album onwards.

THE TOP 10 UK HITS COMPOSED BY LEIBER AND STOLLER

	Title	Artist(s)
1	Jailhouse Rock	Elvis Presley
2	Stand By Me	Ben E. King, John Lennon, *et al*
3	Hound Dog	Elvis Presley
4	Don't	Elvis Presley
5	King Creole	Elvis Presley
6	Charlie Brown	Coasters
7	Searchin'	Coasters, Hollies
8	Spanish Harlem	Aretha Franklin, Jimmy Justice
9	Yakety Yak	Coasters
10	Poison Ivy	Coasters, Paramounts

Some of Leiber and Stoller's big US hit songs like *Kansas City* and *Love Potion No. 9* never had a sizeable hit version in the UK, even though both are regarded as Rock 'n' Roll standards in this country. The writers received a bonus, however, when Elvis' title song from *King Creole* was issued as a UK single (which it wasn't in the US) and reached No. 2.

THE TOP 10 US HITS COMPOSED BY LEIBER AND STOLLER

	Title	Artist(s)
1	Hound Dog	Elvis Presley
2	Jailhouse Rock	Elvis Presley
3	Stand By Me	Ben E. King, John Lennon, *et al*
4	Spanish Harlem	Ben E. King, Aretha Franklin
5	Don't	Elvis Presley
6	On Broadway	Drifters, George Benson
7	Kansas City	Wilbert Harrison, Trini Lopez
8	Love Potion No. 9	Clovers, Searchers
9	Searchin'/Young Blood	Coasters
10	Yakety Yak	Coasters

Jerry Leiber and Mike Stoller wrote not only some of Elvis Presley's best 1950s material, but also a string of successes for several of the major black groups of the late 1950s and early 1960s, like the Drifters, Clovers and Coasters – the latter being long-term protégés of the songwriting duo. Because the Coasters' *Searchin'* and *Young Blood* were coupled on the same single, they are kept together on this list because, obviously, they sold equally.

THE TOP 10 UK HITS COMPOSED BY JOHN LENNON AND PAUL McCARTNEY

	Title	Charting artist(s)
1	She Loves You	Beatles
2	I Want To Hold Your Hand	Beatles
3	Can't Buy Me Love	Beatles, Ella Fitzgerald
4	I Feel Fine	Beatles
5	We Can Work It Out	Beatles, Stevie Wonder
6	Help!	Bananarama & La Nee Nee Noo Noo, Beatles, Tina Turner
7	Day Tripper	Beatles, Otis Redding
8	Hey Jude	Beatles, Wilson Pickett
9	Let It Be	Beatles, Ferry Aid
10	A Hard Day's Night	Beatles, Peter Sellers

The most successful non-Beatles Lennon and McCartney song is *A World Without Love*, a No. 1 hit for Peter & Gordon in 1964, which is their 14th most successful composition behind *Get Back, Hello Goodbye* and *Ticket To Ride*.

THE TOP 10 US HITS COMPOSED BY JOHN LENNON AND PAUL McCARTNEY

	Title	Charting artist(s)
1	I Want To Hold Your Hand	Beatles, Boston Pops Orchestra
2	Hey Jude	Beatles, Wilson Pickett
3	She Loves You	Beatles
4	Can't Buy Me Love	Beatles
5	Come Together	Aerosmith, Beatles, Ike & Tina Turner
6	Get Back	Beatles with Billy Preston, Billy Preston*
7	I Feel Fine	Beatles
8	Help!	Beatles
9	A Hard Day's Night	Beatles, Ramsey Lewis Trio
10	Let It Be	Joan Baez, Beatles

* In addition to accompanying the Beatles on the original version, Preston also charted with a solo version in 1978.

I Want To Hold Your Hand remains the biggest-selling Lennon and McCartney composition in the United States, selling just under 5,000,000 copies in 1964; it was also their first American hit. Covers of their compositions have continued up to the present day, with successful versions of *I Saw Her/Him Standing There* (Tiffany), *Happiness Is A Warm Gun* (World Party) and *Strawberry Fields Forever* (Candy Flip) all released in the past five years.

THE TOP 10 NON-LENNON AND McCARTNEY UK HITS COMPOSED BY PAUL McCARTNEY

	Title	Charting artist(s)
1	Mull Of Kintyre	Wings
2	Pipes Of Peace	Paul McCartney
3	Ebony And Ivory	Paul McCartney with Stevie Wonder
4	We All Stand Together	Paul McCartney & The Frog Chorus (twice)
5	Let 'Em In	Billy Paul, Wings
6	No More Lonely Nights	Paul McCartney
7	Say Say Say	Paul McCartney & Michael Jackson
8	Another Day	Paul McCartney
9	Live And Let Die	Guns N' Roses, Wings (twice)
10	Come And Get It	Badfinger

Number one was actually released as a double A-side with *Girl's School*, but *Mull Of Kintyre* was clearly the primary reason for the record's massive success. One of McCartney's earliest non-Lennon partnership compositions was the number 10 entry, his 1970 song *Come And Get It*, recorded by the Apple signing Badfinger. It was written by McCartney for inclusion in *The Magic Christian*, a film based on the Terry Southern novel and starring Peter Sellers and Ringo Starr (among many others, from Spike Milligan and Yul Brynner to Racquel Welch and John Cleese).

THE TOP 10 NON-LENNON AND McCARTNEY US HITS COMPOSED BY PAUL McCARTNEY

	Title	Charting artist(s)
1	Ebony And Ivory	Paul McCartney with Stevie Wonder
2	Say Say Say	Paul McCartney & Michael Jackson
3	Silly Love Songs	Wings
4	My Love	Paul McCartney & Wings
5	Coming Up (Live At Glasgow)	Paul McCartney
6	With A Little Luck	Wings
7	Uncle Albert/Admiral Halsey	Paul & Linda McCartney
8	Band On The Run	Paul McCartney & Wings
9	Live And Let Die	Guns N' Roses, Wings
10	Goodnight Tonight	Wings

Although either Lennon or McCartney often wrote Beatles songs independently of each other, they were always credited together, so that Paul McCartney's solo success as a songwriter dates entirely from his post-Beatles period. All 10 hits listed here sold over 1,000,000 copies in the United States, with *Ebony And Ivory* spending seven weeks in the No. 1 position.

THE TOP 10 NON-LENNON AND McCARTNEY UK HITS COMPOSED BY JOHN LENNON

	Title	Charting artist(s)
1	Imagine	Randy Crawford, John Lennon & Plastic Ono Band (three times)
2	Happy Xmas (War Is Over)	John & Yoko & Plastic Ono Band with the Harlem Community Choir (six times)
3	(Just Like) Starting Over	John Lennon
4	Jealous Guy	John Lennon (twice), Roxy Music
5	Woman	John Lennon
6	Instant Karma	John Ono Lennon & Plastic Ono Band
7	Nobody Told Me	John Lennon
8	Power To The People	John Lennon & Plastic Ono Band & Yoko Ono
9	Cold Turkey	John Lennon
10	Fame	David Bowie

Although *Give Peace A Chance* was Lennon's first UK solo hit (reaching No. 2 in 1969), it was credited as a co-composition with McCartney, a hangover from their Beatles partnership. Aside from *Happy Xmas (War Is Over)*'s achievement of making the chart on six separate occasions, perhaps the most interesting item here is *Jealous Guy* which Roxy Music recorded as a tribute to Lennon, and which spent two weeks at No. 1 in March 1981, just two months after *Imagine* had topped the UK survey following Lennon's murder.

THE TOP 10 NON-LENNON AND McCARTNEY US HITS COMPOSED BY JOHN LENNON

	Title	Charting artist(s)
1	(Just Like) Starting Over	John Lennon
2	Fame	David Bowie
3	Woman	John Lennon
4	Whatever Gets You Thru The Night	John Lennon with Plastic Ono Nuclear Band
5	Imagine	John Lennon & Plastic Ono Band, Tracie Spencer
6	Instant Karma	John Ono Lennon & Plastic Ono Band
7	Nobody Told Me	John Lennon
8	#9 Dream	John Lennon
9	Watching The Wheels	John Lennon
10	Power To The People	John Lennon & Plastic Ono Band & Yoko Ono

The most notable success for another artist in Lennon's shortlived solo songwriting career is *Fame*, which sold over 1,000,000 copies in the United States and earned David Bowie his first American No. 1. Co-written by Lennon and Bowie with Carlos Alomar, the single also featured Lennon on backing vocals.

10 LENNON AND McCARTNEY SONGS NEVER RECORDED (OR NEVER RELEASED) BY THE BEATLES

	Title	Artist	Year
1	A World Without Love	Peter & Gordon	1964
2	Bad To Me	Billy J. Kramer & The Dakotas	1963
3	Goodbye*	Mary Hopkin	1969
4	I'm In Love	Fourmost	1963
5	It's For You	Cilla Black	1964
6	Like Dreamers Do	Applejacks	1964
7	One And One Is Two	Strangers with Mike Shannon	1964
8	That Means A Lot	P.J. Proby	1965
9	Thingummybob	Black Dyke Mills Band	1968
10	Tip Of My Tongue	Tommy Quickly	1963

* *Written by McCartney alone as a UK follow-up to Hopkin's debut hit,* Those Were The Days.

It is likely that the Beatles recorded demos of some of these songs, but none of them ever saw the light of day as an official Beatles cut. Of the 10 listed here, numbers one, two, three, four, five, six and eight were all UK chart hits, with *Bad To Me* memorable as a chart-topper for Billy J. Kramer.

THE TOP 10 UK HITS COMPOSED BY BARRY MANN AND CYNTHIA WEIL

	Title	Charting artist(s)
1	You've Lost That Lovin' Feelin'	Cilla Black, Hall & Oates, Righteous Brothers (four times), Telly Savalas
2	We Gotta Get Out Of This Place	Angelic Upstarts, Animals
3	I'm Gonna Be Strong	Gene Pitney
4	Don't Know Much	Linda Ronstadt featuring Aaron Neville
5	Looking Through The Eyes Of Love	Partridge Family, Gene Pitney
6	Saturday Night At The Movies	Drifters
7	I Just Can't Help Believing	Elvis Presley
8	Somewhere Out There	Linda Ronstadt & James Ingram
9	Walkin' In The Rain	Partridge Family, Walker Brothers
10	Come On Over To My Place	Drifters (twice)

One of America's most successful songwriting teams over the past three decades, Mann and Weil were married in 1961 and have continued to churn out hits as recent as Linda Ronstadt's 1989 smash, *Don't Know Much*. While they are on record as saying that the Animals' version of *We Gotta Get Out Of This Place* (originally penned for the Righteous Brothers) is their least favourite cover, they may not have heard the Punk version recorded in 1980 by the Angelic Upstarts which reached No. 65 in the UK charts.

THE TOP 10 US HITS COMPOSED BY BARRY MANN AND CYNTHIA WEIL

	Title	Charting artist(s)
1	You've Lost That Lovin' Feelin'	Long John Baldry & Kathi McDonald, Roberta Flack & Donny Hathaway, Hall & Oates, Righteous Brothers, Dionne Warwick
2	Never Gonna Let You Go	Sergio Mendes
3	Don't Know Much	Linda Ronstadt featuring Aaron Neville
4	I Love How You Love Me*	Paris Sisters, Bobby Vinton
5	Sometimes When We Touch**	Dan Hill
6	He's So Shy†	Pointer Sisters
7	(You're My) Soul And Inspiration	Donny & Marie Osmond, Righteous Brothers
8	Running With The Night§	Lionel Richie
9	Here You Come Again	Dolly Parton
10	On Broadway#	George Benson, Drifters

* Co-written by Mann and Larry Kobler.   ** Co-written by Mann and Dan Hill.
† Co-written by Weil and Tom Snow.   § Co-written by Weil and Lionel Richie.
\# Co-written by Mann and Weil with Leiber and Stoller.

One of the bestselling singles of all time, *You've Lost That Lovin' Feelin'* (which they co-wrote with producer Phil Spector) is also one of the most covered – eight different acts have taken the ballad into either the US or UK singles charts since the Righteous Brothers scored with the original in 1965, while hundreds of other artists have attempted versions on album releases.

THE TOP 10 UK HITS COMPOSED BY TONY MACAULAY

	Title	Charting artist(s)
1	Don't Give Up On Us	David Soul
2	Baby, Now That I've Found You	Foundations
3	You Won't Find Another Fool Like Me	New Seekers
4	Let The Heartaches Begin	Long John Baldry
5	Silver Lady	David Soul
6	Love Grows (Where My Rosemary Goes)	Edison Lighthouse
7	Build Me Up Buttercup	Foundations
8	Kissin' In The Back Row Of The Movies	Drifters
9	Going In With My Eyes Open	David Soul
10	Sorry Suzanne	Hollies

Among Britain's least known but most successful songwriters, Macaulay has also penned hits for Gladys Knight & The Pips, Marmalade and Scott Walker and often collaborated with Rogers Cook and Greenaway. All of the top nine on this list made either UK No. 1 or No. 2.

THE TOP 10 UK HITS COMPOSED BY GEORGE MICHAEL

	Title	Charting artist(s)
1	Last Christmas	Wham! (three times)
2	Careless Whisper	George Michael
3	Wake Me Up Before You Go-Go	Wham!
4	Everything She Wants	Wham!
5	Freedom	Wham!
6	I'm Your Man	Wham!
7	A Different Corner	George Michael
8	Bad Boys	Wham!
9	Faith	George Michael
10	The Edge Of Heaven	Wham!

The million-plus selling *Last Christmas* was held off the top spot in December 1984 only by the unique sales of the Band Aid single, but its enduring appeal saw it re-chart in both 1985 and 1986. Each of these titles hit either UK No. 1 or No. 2 for the still young songwriter who looks most likely to become Britain's most successful composer in the final decade of the century (not least since the court battle with his recording label, Sony, prevents him from recording during much of 1992–93, leaving writing as his main focus).

Legendary American songwriter Doc Pomus wrote many of his hits, particularly those for Elvis Presley, with Mort Shuman. The pair joined Hill & Range Publishing as staff writers through another Presley hit composer, Otis Blackwell.

THE TOP 10 US HITS COMPOSED BY GEORGE MICHAEL

	Title	Charting artist(s)
1	I Want Your Sex	George Michael
2	Careless Whisper	Wham! featuring George Michael
3	Faith	George Michael
4	Wake Me Up Before You Go-Go	Wham!
5	One More Try	George Michael
6	Everything She Wants	Wham!
7	Freedom	Wham!
8	Father Figure	George Michael
9	Monkey	George Michael
10	Praying For Time	George Michael

It is ironic that Michael's only 2,000,000-selling single in the United States (*I Want Your Sex*) is his only composition in the top nine listed here not to make it to No. 1 (it peaked at No. 2 in 1987). Together with Phil Collins, Michael is Britain's most successful songwriting export over the past 10 years.

THE TOP 10 UK HITS COMPOSED BY DOC POMUS

	Title	Charting artist(s)
1	Can't Get Used To Losing You	Beat, Andy Williams
2	A Teenager In Love	Dion & The Belmonts, Craig Douglas, Marty Wilde
3	Save The Last Dance For Me	Drifters (twice), Ben E. King
4	Surrender	Elvis Presley
5	Sweets For My Sweet	Searchers
6	Little Children	Billy J. Kramer & The Dakotas
7	She's Not You	Elvis Presley
8	A Mess Of Blues	Elvis Presley
9	Kiss Me Quick	Elvis Presley
10	Suspicion	Elvis Presley, Terry Stafford

THE TOP 10 US HITS COMPOSED BY DOC POMUS

	Title	Charting artist(s)
1	Save The Last Dance For Me	DeFranco Family, Drifters, Dolly Parton
2	Young Blood	Bad Company, Coasters, Bruce Willis
3	Surrender	Elvis Presley
4	Can't Get Used To Losing You	Andy Williams
5	This Magic Moment	Drifters, Jay & The Americans
6	Suspicion	Terry Stafford
7	Marie's The Name (His Latest Flame)	Elvis Presley
8	Teenager In Love	Dion & The Belmonts
9	She's Not You	Elvis Presley
10	Go, Jimmy, Go	Jimmy Clanton

THE TOP 10 UK HITS COMPOSED BY PRINCE

	Title	Charting artist(s)
1	Nothing Compares 2 U	Sinead O'Connor
2	I Feel For You	Chaka Khan
3	Little Red Corvette	Prince (three times)
4	Kiss	Art Of Noise featuring Tom Jones, Prince & The Revolution
5	When Doves Cry/Pray*	Prince, MC Hammer
6	1999	Prince (twice)
7	Manic Monday	Bangles
8	Purple Rain	Prince & The Revolution
9	Batdance	Prince
10	Let's Go Crazy	Prince & The Revolution

* *MC Hammer's hit* Pray *used the rhythm track from* When Doves Cry.

Somewhat ironically, despite having notched up over 30 UK singles chart entries, this prolific artist has yet to secure a UK No. 1 as a songwriter *and* performer. His most successful compositions to date remain the two famous cover versions of old Prince album cuts.

THE TOP 10 US HITS COMPOSED BY PRINCE

	Title	Charting artist(s)
1	When Doves Cry/Pray	Prince, MC Hammer
2	Nothing Compares 2 U	Sinead O'Connor
3	Kiss	Art Of Noise featuring Tom Jones, Prince & The Revolution
4	I Feel For You	Chaka Khan
5	Let's Go Crazy	Prince & The Revolution
6	Batdance	Prince
7	Purple Rain	Prince & The Revolution
8	I Wanna Be Your Lover	Prince
9	Little Red Corvette	Prince
10	Cream	Prince & The New Power Generation

The first eight songs in this list all sold over 1,000,000 copies, while the first seven have all peaked at either No. 1 or No. 2 in the United States. Prince is a prolific writer, constantly penning material for his stable of artists at Paisley Park, his Minneapolis recording empire. He also crops up occasionally under songwriting pseudonyms, notably as 'Christopher' on *Manic Monday*, the Bangles' 1986 hit, and as 'Alexander Nevermind' on Sheena Easton's 1985 smash, *Sugar Walls*.

THE TOP 10 UK HITS COMPOSED BY LIONEL RICHIE

	Title	Charting artist(s)
1	Hello	Lionel Richie
2	Three Times A Lady	Commodores
3	All Night Long (All Night)	Lionel Richie
4	We Are The World	USA For Africa
5	Easy	Commodores (twice), Faith No More
6	Still	Commodores
7	Endless Love	Diana Ross & Lionel Richie
8	Truly	Lionel Richie
9	Dancing On The Ceiling	Lionel Richie
10	Say You, Say Me	Lionel Richie

Two of Richie's biggest hits have also been the love themes from moderately successful films: number seven accompanied the Brooke Shields movie of the same name, while number 10 was featured in the 1985 picture, *White Nights*.

THE TOP 10 US HITS COMPOSED BY LIONEL RICHIE

	Title	Charting artist(s)
1	We Are The World	USA For Africa
2	Endless Love	Diana Ross & Lionel Richie
3	All Night Long (All Night)	Lionel Richie
4	Three Times A Lady	Commodores
5	Lady	Kenny Rogers
6	Say You, Say Me	Lionel Richie
7	Hello	Lionel Richie
8	Truly	Lionel Richie
9	Still	Commodores
10	Dancing On The Ceiling	Lionel Richie

While Richie's first songwriting success was as co-author of the Temptations' 1974 hit *Happy People*, he went on to become one of the most successful writers of the past 20 years. *We Are The World*, which he co-wrote with Michael Jackson, is the biggest-selling single ever in the United States, with over 8,000,000 copies sold, while *Endless Love* stayed atop the US chart for nine weeks in 1981.

THE TOP 10 UK HITS COMPOSED BY NEIL SEDAKA

	Title	Charting artist(s)
1	Stupid Cupid*	Connie Francis
2	Breaking Up Is Hard To Do*	Partridge Family, Neil Sedaka (twice)
3	Oh! Carol*	Neil Sedaka (twice)
4	Solitaire	Carpenters, Andy Williams
5	Happy Birthday, Sweet Sixteen*	Neil Sedaka
6	Where The Boys Are*	Connie Francis
7	Little Devil*	Neil Sedaka (twice)
8	Calendar Girl*	Neil Sedaka
9	I Go Ape*	Neil Sedaka
10	Breakin' In A Brand New Broken Heart*	Connie Francis

*   Co-written with his early songwriting partner, Howard Greenfield.

Sedaka's enduring appeal as both a songwriter and performer is still evident 33 years after he first charted in the UK with *I Go Ape* – his *Greatest Hits* collection making the album survey in 1992.

THE TOP 10 US HITS COMPOSED BY NEIL SEDAKA

	Title	Charting artist(s)
1	Breaking Up Is Hard To Do*	Neil Sedaka (twice)
2	Love Will Keep Us Together**	Captain & Tennille (twice)
3	Laughter In The Rain	Neil Sedaka
4	Bad Blood	Neil Sedaka
5	Lonely Night (Angel Face)	Captain & Tennille
6	Where The Boys Are	Connie Francis
7	Calendar Girl	Neil Sedaka
8	Oh! Carol	Neil Sedaka
9	Breakin' In A Brand New Broken Heart	Connie Francis
10	Happy Birthday, Sweet Sixteen	Neil Sedaka

*   Sedaka himself succeeded with two different versions of his own composition when he updated the up-tempo 1962 US chart-topper in 1975, this time as a sweet, slow-paced ballad.

** The Captain & Tennille (Carpenters soundalikes) scored a second time with a Spanish language version of the same song, Por Amor Viviremos.

THE TOP 10 UK HITS COMPOSED BY BRUCE SPRINGSTEEN

	Title	Charting artist(s)
1	Dancing In The Dark	Big Daddy, Bruce Springsteen
2	Because The Night	Patti Smith Group
3	Pink Cadillac	Natalie Cole
4=	I'm On Fire*	Bruce Springsteen
4=	Born In The USA*	Bruce Springsteen
6	Blinded By The Light	Manfred Mann's Earth Band
7	Cover Me	Bruce Springsteen (twice)
8	My Hometown	Bruce Springsteen
9	Tougher Than The Rest	Bruce Springsteen
10	Born To Run	Bruce Springsteen

*   Released as a double A-side.

Certainly the most bizarre cover version of a Springsteen song was *Dancing In The Dark* recorded by the wacky American close harmony group Big Daddy in 1985. *Because The Night* was a rare occasion when Springsteen teamed up with another writer. He and Patti Smith penned the song which went on to become a global hit for her group in 1978.

THE TOP 10 US HITS COMPOSED BY BRUCE SPRINGSTEEN

	Title	Charting artist(s)
1	Fire	Pointer Sisters, Bruce Springsteen
2	Blinded By The Light	Manfred Mann's Earth Band
3	Dancing In The Dark	Bruce Springsteen
4	Born In The USA/ Banned In The USA	Bruce Springsteen Luke & The 2 Live Crew
5	Hungry Heart	Bruce Springsteen
6	Glory Days	Bruce Springsteen
7	Pink Cadillac	Natalie Cole
8	I'm On Fire	Bruce Springsteen
9	Cover Me	Bruce Springsteen
10	This Little Girl	Gary U.S. Bonds

In addition to his own hits, Springsteen's songs have proved to be fertile cover material, even in the rap field: Luke & The 2 Live Crew used the rhythm track from *Born In The USA* to Top 20 effect in 1990.

THE TOP 10 UK HITS COMPOSED BY ROD TEMPERTON

	Title	Charting artist(s)
1	Boogie Nights	Heatwave, La Fleur
2	Stomp	Brothers Johnson
3	Thriller	Michael Jackson
4	Give Me The Night	George Benson, Mirage
5	Off The Wall	Michael Jackson
6	Rock With You	Michael Jackson
7	Always And Forever	Heatwave
8	Love X Love	George Benson
9	Baby Come To Me	Patti Austin & James Ingram
10	Sweet Freedom	Michael McDonald

UK-born Rod Temperton, now resident in California, was a former keyboard player and songwriter with UK soul/disco combo Heatwave. His most extraordinary achievement has been the composition of *Thriller*, which most assume was written by Michael Jackson. *Boogie Nights*, in addition to its British success, sold over 2,000,000 copies in the United States, while Temperton has also written hits for Aretha Franklin, Manhattan Transfer, Donna Summer and Herbie Hancock among others.

THE TOP 10 UK HITS COMPOSED BY DIANE WARREN

	Title	Charting artist(s)
1	Nothing's Gonna Stop Us Now	Starship
2	Don't Turn Around	Aswad
3	Rhythm Of The Night	DeBarge
4	If I Could Turn Back Time	Cher
5	I Get Weak	Belinda Carlisle
6	How Can We Be Lovers	Michael Bolton
7	Just Like Jesse James	Cher
8	Time, Love And Tenderness	Michael Bolton
9	Who Will You Run To	Heart
10	Blame It On The Rain	Milli Vanilli (twice)

Although Warren's songs have not yielded the same degree of success in the UK (her compositions are the epitome of the 'adult contemporary' style which is so much more popular on American radio), *Don't Turn Around* (co-written with Albert Hammond) is the exception: a UK No. 1 for Aswad in 1988, the song has never been a hit in her home country, despite a Neil Diamond cover in 1990.

THE TOP 10 US HITS COMPOSED BY DIANE WARREN

	Title	Charting artist(s)
1	Look Away	Chicago
2	Nothing's Gonna Stop Us Now	Starship
3	Love Will Lead You Back	Taylor Dayne
4	When I See You Smile	Bad English
5	Blame It On The Rain	Milli Vanilli
6	I Get Weak	Belinda Carlisle
7	If I Could Turn Back Time	Cher
8	How Can We Be Lovers	Michael Bolton
9	Rhythm Of The Night	DeBarge
10	If You Asked Me To	Celine Dion, Patti Labelle

America's most successful female songwriter since Carole King, Los Angeles-based Diane Warren has dominated the US chart with her compositions (co-written with such composers as Michael Bolton, David Foster and Albert Hammond) for the past 10 years. The top four on this list have all been certified gold, while all of the Top 10 have made it into the US Top 5.

The timeless epic *MacArthur Park*, which Webb was inspired to write after taking several lunchtime walks with his girlfriend in the Los Angeles park, proved its longevity when, in 1978 (10 years after actor Richard Harris first took it into the US Top 5), Donna Summer recorded a full-length eight-minute disco version – which went one better than Harris' success, topping the US survey for three weeks.

THE TOP 10 US HITS COMPOSED BY JIMMY WEBB

	Title	Charting artist(s)
1	MacArthur Park	Four Tops, Richard Harris, Waylon Jennings, Donna Summer
2	Wichita Lineman	Glen Campbell, Sergio Mendes & Brasil '66
3	Galveston	Glen Campbell, Roger Williams
4	Up-Up And Away	5th Dimension, Johnny Mann Singers, Hugh Masekela
5	Worst That Could Happen	Brooklyn Bridge
6	By The Time I Get To Phoenix	Glen Campbell, Glen Campbell & Anne Murray, Isaac Hayes, Mad Lads
7	All I Know	Art Garfunkel
8	Honey Come Back	Glen Campbell
9	Where's The Playground Susie	Glen Campbell
10	Do What You Gotta Do	Nina Simone, Bobby Vee

THE TOP 10 UK ALBUMS COMPOSED BY ANDREW LLOYD WEBBER

	Title	Charting artist(s)
1	The Phantom Of The Opera	Original London Cast
2	Joseph And The Amazing Technicolor Dreamcoat	Original London Cast (1991)
3	Evita	Studio Cast
4	Aspects Of Love	Original London Cast
5	Variations	Andrew Lloyd Webber featuring Julian Lloyd Webber
6	Michael Crawford Performs Andrew Lloyd Webber	Michael Crawford
7	Requiem	Sarah Brightman, Placido Domingo, Paul Miles-Kingston, Winchester Cathedral Choir & The English Chamber Orchestra
8	Cats	Original London Cast
9	Jesus Christ Superstar	Studio Cast
10	Lloyd Webber Plays Lloyd Webber	Julian Lloyd Webber

THE TOP 10 UK HITS COMPOSED BY NORMAN WHITFIELD

	Title	Charting artist(s)
1	I Heard It Through The Grapevine	Marvin Gaye (twice), Gladys Knight & The Pips, Slits
2	War	Bruce Springsteen, Edwin Starr
3	Wherever I Lay My Hat (That's My Home)	Paul Young
4	Car Wash	Gwen Dickey, Rose Royce (twice)
5	Too Busy Thinking 'Bout My Baby	Marvin Gaye, Mardi Gras
6	Papa Was A Rollin' Stone	Temptations (twice), Was (Not Was)
7	Really Saying Something	Bananarama with Fun Boy Three
8	It Should've Been Me	Yvonne Fair
9	Ball Of Confusion	Temptations
10	Just My Imagination (Running Away With Me)	Temptations

Two Norman Whitfield songs in particular have performed better in the UK than in his native United States: number three provided Paul Young with his first UK solo hit, while number seven launched the career of UK trio Bananarama in 1982. One hopes that Whitfield has never heard the Punk version of I Heard It Through The Grapevine 'performed' by the Slits.

THE TOP 10 US HITS COMPOSED BY NORMAN WHITFIELD

	Title	Charting artist(s)
1	I Heard It Through The Grapevine	California Raisins, Creedence Clearwater Revival, King Curtis, Marvin Gaye, Gladys Knight & The Pips, Roger
2	War	Bruce Springsteen, Edwin Starr
3	I Can't Get Next To You	Al Green, Temptations
4	Just My Imagination (Running Away With Me)	Temptations
5	Papa Was A Rollin' Stone	Temptations, Undisputed Truth, Wolf
6	I Wish It Would Rain	Gladys Knight & The Pips, Temptations
7	Car Wash	Rose Royce
8	Ball Of Confusion	Temptations
9	Ain't Too Proud To Beg	Rick Astley, Rolling Stones, Temptations
10	Cloud Nine	Temptations, Mongo Santamaria

One of the first in-house Motown writers and producers, Whitfield co-wrote Marvin Gaye's first Top 10 hit, Pride And Joy, in 1963. He went on to create further hits for the Temptations and Gaye before leaving Motown. During the 1970s, having established his own Whitfield label, he wrote and produced a string of hits for Rose Royce, notably for the soundtrack to the movie, Car Wash.

THE TOP 10 US HITS PRODUCED BY PETER ASHER

	Title	Charting artist
1	Blue Bayou	Linda Ronstadt
2	You've Got A Friend	James Taylor
3	Don't Know Much	Linda Ronstadt featuring Aaron Neville
4	Somewhere Out There	Linda Ronstadt & James Ingram
5	When Will I Be Loved	Linda Ronstadt
6	Fire And Rain	James Taylor
7	Handy Man	James Taylor
8	It's So Easy	Linda Ronstadt
9	After All	Cher & Peter Cetera
10	Lonely Boy	Andrew Gold

First hitting the pop scene in 1964 as one-half of Peter & Gordon, UK-born production veteran Peter Asher, a long-time California resident, has had a distinguished production career, steering the chart paths of both Ronstadt (whose *Blue Bayou* sold more than 2,000,000 copies) and Taylor and producing other hits for 10,000 Maniacs, Manfred Mann and Diana Ross among others. Asher also runs a management company whose roster includes Ronstadt and Randy Newman.

THE TOP 10 UK HITS PRODUCED BY THOM BELL

	Title	Charting artist
1	You Make Me Feel Brand New	Stylistics
2	I'm Stone In Love With You	Johnny Mathis, Stylistics
3	Rockin' Roll Baby	Stylistics
4	Ghetto Child	Detroit Spinners
5	Let's Put It All Together	Stylistics
6	Could It Be I'm Falling In Love	Detroit Spinners
7	Betcha By Golly Wow	Stylistics
8	The Rubberband Man	Detroit Spinners
9	Didn't I (Blow Your Mind This Time)	Delfonics (twice)
10	I'm Doin' Fine Now	New York City

Bell has achieved a very rare chart feat with the double Top 10 appearance of *I'm Stone In Love With You*. In addition to co-writing this hit (with Linda Creed and Anthony Bell), Bell produced two different versions of the same song: the Sylistics original made UK No. 9 in 1972, while Mathis hit No. 10 with the second Bell version in 1975.

THE TOP 10 US HITS PRODUCED BY THOM BELL

	Title	Charting artist
1	Then Came You	Dionne Warwick & The Spinners
2	You Make Me Feel Brand New	Stylistics
3	The Rubberband Man	Spinners
4	Betcha By Golly Wow	Stylistics
5	I'll Be Around	Spinners
6	Could It Be I'm Falling In Love	Spinners
7	They Just Can't Stop It (Games People Play)	Spinners
8	Break Up To Make Up	Stylistics
9	Mama Can't Buy You Love	Elton John
10	Didn't I (Blow Your Mind This Time)	Delfonics

One of only a handful of producers whose sound can be instantly recognized, veteran soul producer Thom Bell cut his teeth with fellow Philadelphia-based producers Gamble and Huff during the 1960s. Subsequently teaming up with songwriter Linda Creed, Bell usually co-wrote the hits he produced, most successfully with the Detroit Spinners (known in the United States as the Spinners). His most recent success came in 1990 with his production of James Ingram's US No. 1 ballad, *I Don't Have The Heart*.

THE TOP 10 US HITS PRODUCED BY MIKE CHAPMAN

	Title	Charting artist
1	Hot Child In The City	Nick Gilder
2	My Sharona	Knack
3	Kiss You All Over	Exile
4	Rapture	Blondie
5	Heart Of Glass	Blondie
6	The Tide Is High	Blondie
7	Stumblin' In	Suzi Quatro & Chris Norman
8	Close My Eyes Forever	Lita Ford with Ozzy Osbourne
9	Love Touch	Rod Stewart
10	The Warrior	Scandal featuring Patti Smith

Successful in the UK with Nicky Chinn as songwriters and producers of many of the pure pop hits of the 1970s by the Sweet, Mud, Smokie and Suzi Quatro, Mike Chapman has also been a million-selling producer in the United States for more than 10 years. Each of the top seven in this list has passed the 1,000,000 mark, with *Hot Child In The City* selling over twice that number.

THE TOP 10 UK HITS PRODUCED BY BERNARD EDWARDS AND NILE RODGERS

	Title	Charting artist
1	Let's Dance	David Bowie
2	Like A Virgin*	Madonna
3	A View To A Kill*	Duran Duran
4	Wild Boys*	Duran Duran
5	Upside Down	Diana Ross
6	China Girl*	David Bowie
7	Modern Love*	David Bowie
8	Material Girl*	Madonna
9	I Want Your Love	Chic
10	Good Times	Chic

* *Produced by Nile Rodgers.*

Two notable hits produced by Edwards and Rodgers which fared better in the UK than in their native United States are *Why* by Carly Simon (1982) and Sheila B. Devotion's 1979 Top 20 success, *Spacer*. One of the best examples of their early Chic-style material which proved universally unsuccessful was an eponymous solo album they wrote and produced for sometime Chic vocalist Norma Jean in 1978.

THE TOP 10 US HITS PRODUCED BY TOM DOWD

	Title	Charting artist
1	Do Ya Think I'm Sexy?	Rod Stewart
2	Tonight's The Night	Rod Stewart
3	I Shot The Sheriff	Eric Clapton
4	Spanish Harlem*	Aretha Franklin
5	You're In My Heart	Rod Stewart
6	Bridge Over Troubled Water*	Aretha Franklin
7	Good Lovin'	Young Rascals
8	Day Dreaming*	Aretha Franklin
9	Rock Steady*	Aretha Franklin
10	Layla	Derek & The Dominos (twice)

* *Co-produced with Arif Mardin.*

New York-born Dowd started his career in the late 1950s as an engineer with Atlantic Records, and moved up to produce hits for Aretha Franklin and the Young Rascals in the 1960s before linking with Eric Clapton in 1972 for the classic *Layla*. His biggest-selling productions came via a highly successful union with Rod Stewart, whose *Do Ya Think I'm Sexy?* sold over 2,000,000 copies in the United States alone.

THE TOP 10 US HITS PRODUCED BY BERNARD EDWARDS AND NILE RODGERS

	Title	Charting artist
1	Le Freak	Chic
2	Like A Virgin*	Madonna
3	Upside Down	Diana Ross
4	Let's Dance*	David Bowie
5	Good Times	Chic
6	Addicted To Love**	Robert Palmer
7	We Are Family	Sister Sledge
8	Roam*	B52s
9	Angel*	Madonna
10	Dance, Dance, Dance (Yowsah, Yowsah, Yowsah)	Chic

*   Produced by Nile Rodgers.

** Produced by Bernard Edwards.

Originally pairing in 1972 in rock-fusion trio the Big Apple Band, Edwards and Rodgers were the founding members, writers and producers of seminal 1970s disco outfit Chic. Following successful projects with Sister Sledge and Diana Ross, they split to pursue solo production careers with rock's top artists, occasionally reuniting to record less successful Chic material. In addition to the million-selling tracks listed here, they have also produced a prodigious body of work for Duran Duran, Jody Watley, ABC, the Thompson Twins, Mick Jagger, Aretha Franklin, Jeff Beck, the Power Station (of which Edwards was a member), and the Honeydrippers (whose line-up included Rodgers) among many others.

THE TOP 10 UK HITS PRODUCED BY TREVOR HORN

	Title	Charting artist
1	Relax	Frankie Goes To Hollywood
2	Two Tribes	Frankie Goes To Hollywood
3	Video Killed The Radio Star	Buggles
4	Belfast Child	Simple Minds
5	The Power Of Love	Frankie Goes To Hollywood
6	Crazy	Seal
7	Double Dutch	Malcolm McLaren
8	Mirror Mirror (Mon Amour)	Dollar
9	The Look Of Love	ABC
10	Give Me Back My Heart	Dollar

One-half of UK duo Buggles, British-born Horn was largely responsible for the Frankie Goes To Hollywood phenomenon of the early 1980s, producing their three No. 1 hits. Relax, which sold more than 2,000,000 copies and spent an entire year on the UK chart, was underpinned by his unmistakable synthesized studio trickery, techniques which have also hallmarked other Horn-produced hits including Grace Jones' Slave To The Rhythm, the Art Of Noise's Close To The Edit and Yes' US chart-topper, Owner Of A Lonely Heart. His most recent chart project was co-producing Mike Oldfield's Tubular Bells II album in 1992.

THE TOP 10 US ALBUMS PRODUCED BY JIMMY JAM AND TERRY LEWIS

	Title	Charting artist
1	Control	Janet Jackson
2	Janet Jackson's Rhythm Nation 1814	Janet Jackson
3	Mo' Money (Original Soundtrack)	Various
4	Heartbreak	New Edition
5	Crash	Human League
6	Hearsay	Alexander O'Neal
7	High Priority	Cherrelle
8	Alexander O'Neal	Alexander O'Neal
9	Affair	Cherrelle
10	My Gift To You	Alexander O'Neal

Although Jam and Lewis have production credits on dozens of hit albums (including those by Karyn White, Change, Johnny Gill, Ralph Tresvant, Herb Alpert, Morris Day, S.O.S. Band, Force M.D.s, Cheryl Lynn, Sounds Of Blackness, Bell Biv DeVoe, Patti Austin, Color Me Badd, Patti Labelle and Shabba Ranks), this list identifies only those albums which were wholly produced by the Minneapolis hit factory team. As producers, Jam and Lewis have also scored a string of US No. 1 hit singles, not least with George Michael for whom they remixed his cut Monkey in 1988.

THE TOP 10 UK HITS PRODUCED BY QUINCY JONES

	Title	Charting artist
1	Billie Jean	Michael Jackson
2	We Are The World	USA For Africa
3	I Just Can't Stop Loving You	Michael Jackson featuring Siedah Garrett
4	Leave Me Alone	Michael Jackson
5	Beat It	Michael Jackson
6	Don't Stop 'Til You Get Enough	Michael Jackson
7	Bad	Michael Jackson
8	The Way You Make Me Feel	Michael Jackson
9	She's Out Of My Life	Michael Jackson
10	Yah Mo B There	James Ingram with Michael McDonald (three times)

In addition to his ground-breaking production work for top-flight singers, Jones has also scored and produced nearly 50 film soundtracks.

THE TOP 10 US HITS PRODUCED BY QUINCY JONES

	Title	Charting artist
1	We Are The World	USA For Africa
2	Billie Jean	Michael Jackson
3	Rock With You	Michael Jackson
4	Beat It	Michael Jackson
5	Don't Stop 'Til You Get Enough	Michael Jackson
6	Baby, Come To Me	Patti Austin & James Ingram
7	The Girl Is Mine	Michael Jackson & Paul McCartney
8	I Just Can't Stop Loving You	Michael Jackson featuring Siedah Garrett
9	It's My Party	Lesley Gore
10	She's Out Of My Life	Michael Jackson

Although his most successful commercial work has been with Michael Jackson, Quincy Jones is a veteran producer whose lengthy credits stretch back to Leslie Gore's version of It's My Party in 1963. In addition to producing the bestselling US single of all time (number one) and the bestselling global album of all time (Thriller), Jones has also produced hits for the Brothers Johnson, George Benson, Donna Summer, Tevin Campbell, Aretha Franklin, Ray Charles, Chaka Khan, Diana Ross and himself, among dozens of top artists.

Although Quincy Jones's greatest successes in a career as a producer that spans more than 30 years have been with Michael Jackson, he has been responsible for a huge catalogue of hit records.

RIGHT: Hysteria *by British group Def Leppard, seen here on stage, is remarkably the bestselling heavy metal album of all time in the USA.* (Retna Pictures)

BELOW: *Harry Belafonte's 1956 album* Calypso *equals Fleetwood Mac's* Rumours *with 31 weeks at US No. 1, while his 1957 Christmas hit* Mary's Boy Child *was the second single to sell a million copies in the UK.* (Retna Pictures)

BELOW RIGHT: *With* Ropin' The Wind *the top US album of both 1991 and 1992 and with* No Fences *the bestselling Country album ever, Garth Brooks has rapidly established his pre-eminence as the Country singer of the 1990s.* (Redferns)

RIGHT: *You wear it well: Rod Stewart, in striking red ensemble, was one of the most consistent album stars of the 1970s.* (Redferns)

BELOW: *The Bee Gees have been churning out hits for more than 25 years, with the Gibb brothers also scoring highly as composers.* (Redferns)

OPPOSITE
TOP LEFT: *As well as topping the list of all-time bestselling rap albums in the UK and USA, MC Hammer makes an almost monotonous appearance in two dozen Top 10 lists.* (Redferns)

TOP RIGHT: *W. Axl Rose of Guns N' Roses, one of the highest profile bands of recent years with top-selling albums and singles, blockbusting concerts and even bestselling T-shirts.* (Redferns)

BOTTOM: *Thank you for the music: although disbanded in 1982, super-group Abba were back in the album charts 10 years later.* (Redferns)

OPPOSITE
ABOVE: *New Kids On The Block's* Hangin' Tough *album and video and their triumphant tours placed them among the highest-earning groups in the world, although this success was short-lived.* (Redferns)

BELOW: *With box-office rental income approaching $100,000,000 in North America alone,* Grease *(1978) is the highest-earning musical film of all time.* (The Kobal Collection)

ABOVE LEFT: *With 30 years in the business, Bob Dylan has achieved innumerable hits as both performer and songwriter.* (Redferns)

ABOVE: *His consistent album sales and sell-out concert appearances rank Bruce Springsteen as one of the highest achievers throughout the 1980s.* (Redferns)

LEFT: *Lennon and McCartney at the keyboard: their joint compositions were the bedrock of the success of the Beatles and many other artists.* (Retna Pictures)

OPPOSITE: The Phantom Of The Opera, *outstanding as one of the longest-running shows both in the West End and on Broadway, also tops the list of original cast recordings in the UK.* (Clive Barda)

TOP: *With a string of bestselling albums during the 1970s and 1980s, veteran Country singer/songwriter Willie Nelson has received 17 gold and nine platinum albums as well as many other awards.* (Retna Pictures)

LEFT: *Releasing solo album and single smashes throughout the 1980s, Phil Collins, the drummer who began singing in Genesis only because he could sound passably like the departed Peter Gabriel, has won the greatest haul of Brit Awards.* (Redferns)

Prince, a major force as both songwriter and performer throughout the 1980s, also ranks prominently among artists inspiring collectable records and pop memorabilia. (Redferns)

THE TOP 10 UK HITS PRODUCED BY JEFF LYNNE

	Title	Charting artist
1	*Xanadu*	Olivia Newton-John & E.L.O.
2	*Got My Mind Set On You*	George Harrison
3	*You Got It*	Roy Orbison
4	*Don't Bring Me Down*	E.L.O.
5	*Livin' Thing*	E.L.O.
6	*Hold On Tight*	E.L.O.
7	*Wild West Hero*	E.L.O.
8	*Mr Blue Sky*	E.L.O.
9	*Roll Over Beethoven*	E.L.O.
10	*Shine A Little Love*	E.L.O

As the creator, songwriter, lead vocalist and producer of the Electric Light Orchestra, Lynne logged up 14 UK Top 10 hits between 1972 and 1981. Following the band's demise, Lynne became an increasingly hot item as a writer/producer, notably rejuvenating the careers of George Harrison and Roy Orbison, both of whom joined him in 1988 in the first incarnation of the Traveling Wilburys, along with Bob Dylan and Tom Petty.

THE TOP 10 US HITS PRODUCED BY JEFF LYNNE

	Title	Charting artist
1	*Got My Mind Set On You*	George Harrison
2	*Don't Bring Me Down*	E.L.O.
3	*Telephone Line*	E.L.O.
4	*Free Fallin'*	Tom Petty
5	*Xanadu*	Olivia Newton-John & E.L.O.
6	*Shine A Little Love*	E.L.O.
7	*You Got It*	Roy Orbison
8	*Can't Get It Out Of My Head*	E.L.O.
9	*Evil Woman*	E.L.O.
10	*Hold On Tight*	E.L.O.

In addition to producing the last albums recorded by both Del Shannon and Roy Orbison prior to their deaths, Lynne has also overseen projects for Randy Newman, Duane Eddy and fellow Traveling Wilbury, Tom Petty, notably his 1989 million-selling *Full Moon Fever* album.

THE TOP 10 US HITS PRODUCED BY ARIF MARDIN

	Title	Charting artist
1	*People Got To Be Free*	Rascals
2	*Against All Odds (Take A Look At Me Now)*	Phil Collins
3	*From A Distance*	Bette Midler
4	*Jive Talkin'*	Bee Gees
5	*Pick Up The Pieces*	Average White Band
6	*Wind Beneath My Wings*	Bette Midler
7	*Spanish Harlem**	Aretha Franklin
8	*I Feel For You*	Chaka Khan
9	*Until You Come Back To Me (That's What I'm Gonna Do)*	Aretha Franklin
10	*Bridge Over Troubled Water**	Aretha Franklin

* *Co-produced with Tom Dowd.*

Turkish-born Mardin earned his first production spurs with the Rascals in 1965 at Atlantic Records, where he has remained ever since. One of the most successful producers of all time, all 10 of these titles are million-sellers. Among the dozens of artists who have also benefited from his studio skills are Hall & Oates, Brook Benton, Howard Jones, Culture Club, Carly Simon, Dusty Springfield, Judy Collins and Roberta Flack.

THE TOP 10 UK HITS PRODUCED BY GIORGIO MORODER

	Title	Charting artist
1	Take My Breath Away	Berlin
2	I Feel Love	Donna Summer (twice)
3	Call Me	Blondie
4	Flashdance...What A Feeling	Irene Cara
5	No More Tears (Enough Is Enough)	Barbra Streisand and Donna Summer
6	Together In Electric Dreams	Giorgio Moroder & Phil Oakey
7	Love's Unkind	Donna Summer
8	Never Ending Story	Limahl
9	Love To Love You Baby	Donna Summer
10	MacArthur Park	Donna Summer

Although he began his chart career in 1972 as the co-author of Chicory Tip's chart-topper, *Son Of My Father*, Moroder found substantial production success as the composer and producer of film soundtracks and themes, including Berlin's *Take My Breath Away* from *Top Gun* and *Never Ending Story* from the film of the same name sung by former Kajagoogoo vocalist, Limahl. Moroder also revived the Three Degrees' career in 1979 (with *The Runner*) and kick-started Freddie Mercury's solo sojourn with the 1984 Top 10 hit *Love Kills*, taken from the *Metropolis* movie soundtrack.

THE TOP 10 US HITS PRODUCED BY GIORGIO MORODER

	Title	Charting artist
1	Bad Girls	Donna Summer
2	Hot Stuff	Donna Summer
3	Flashdance...What A Feeling	Irene Cara
4	Call Me	Blondie
5	MacArthur Park	Donna Summer
6	No More Tears (Enough Is Enough)	Barbra Streisand and Donna Summer
7	Love To Love You Baby	Donna Summer
8	Dim All The Lights	Donna Summer
9	On The Radio	Donna Summer
10	I Feel Love	Donna Summer

It was in Germany in 1973 that Munich-based producer/songwriter Giorgio Moroder first got together with Donna Summer to record the first of 16 US chart hits which dominated the disco explosion of the mid-1970s, 10 of them selling over 1,000,000 copies (numbers one and two shifted more than 2,000,000 units). His main production success aside from Summer was with film themes: he won Oscars for *Midnight Run* and *Flashdance,* while Blondie's *Call Me* was featured in the Richard Gere movie, *American Gigolo.*

THE TOP 10 UK HITS PRODUCED BY MICKIE MOST

	Title	Charting artist
1	House Of The Rising Sun	Animals (three times)
2	I'm Into Something Good	Herman's Hermits
3	You Sexy Thing	Hot Chocolate (twice)
4	So You Win Again	Hot Chocolate
5	We Gotta Get Out Of This Place	Animals
6	My Sentimental Friend	Herman's Hermits
7	Sunshine Superman	Donovan
8	No Doubt About It	Hot Chocolate
9	Dance With The Devil	Cozy Powell
10	Silhouettes	Herman's Hermits

One of Britain's most successful producers of the past 30 years, Most discovered the Animals and Herman's Hermits in the 1960s before going on to establish his own RAK label in the 1970s (signing, though not producing, acts including Racey, Mud, Suzi Quatro and Kim Wilde). Among the dozens of other hits produced by him are *Tobacco Road* (Nashville Teens), *Whole Lotta Love* (CCS), *Journey* (Duncan Browne), *The Boat That I Row* (Lulu) and *Hi-Ho Silver Lining* (Jeff Beck), which charted on no less than three occasions, though never getting higher than No. 14.

THE TOP 10 US HITS PRODUCED BY MICKIE MOST

	Title	Charting artist
1	To Sir With Love	Lulu
2	Mrs Brown You've Got A Lovely Daughter	Herman's Hermits
3	House Of The Rising Sun	Animals (three times)
4	I'm Henry VIII, I Am	Herman's Hermits
5	Mellow Yellow	Donovan
6	You Sexy Thing	Hot Chocolate
7	There's A Kind Of Hush	Herman's Hermits
8	Every 1's A Winner	Hot Chocolate
9	Sunshine Superman	Donovan
10	Can't You Hear My Heartbeat	Herman's Hermits

Curiously, Most's biggest US production success came with the million-selling title theme from the film *To Sir With Love* which was released only as a B-side in the UK, and therefore never a British hit for Lulu. In addition to producing most of the US chart entries by the Hermits and the Animals, Most also secured 10 American hits for Scottish folk singer Donovan between 1966 and 1969.

THE TOP 10 UK HITS PRODUCED BY RICHARD PERRY

	Title	Charting artist
1	*Without You*	Nilsson
2	*When I Need You*	Leo Sayer
3	*I Only Have Eyes For You*	Art Garfunkel
4	*Automatic*	Pointer Sisters
5	*You Make Me Feel Like Dancing*	Leo Sayer
6	*You're So Vain*	Carly Simon
7	*You're Sixteen*	Ringo Starr
8	*Rhythm Of The Night*	DeBarge
9	*Jump (For My Love)*	Pointer Sisters
10	*Nobody Does It Better*	Carly Simon

THE TOP 10 US HITS PRODUCED BY RICHARD PERRY

	Title	Charting artist
1	*Without You*	Nilsson
2	*You're So Vain*	Carly Simon
3	*When I Need You*	Leo Sayer
4	*You Make Me Feel Like Dancing*	Leo Sayer
5	*You're Sixteen*	Ringo Starr
6	*Slow Hand*	Pointer Sisters
7	*Photograph*	Ringo Starr
8	*Nobody Does It Better*	Carly Simon
9	*Fire*	Pointer Sisters
10	*He's So Shy*	Pointer Sisters

After being introduced to Harry Nilsson at a party hosted by Phil Spector in 1968, Perry went on to produce Nilsson's album *Nilsson Schmilsson* (which spawned the global No. 1, *Without You*). He has also been responsible for hits by Barbra Streisand (*Stoney End*), Jeffrey Osbourne (*You Should Be Mine*) and Julio Iglesias and Willie Nelson (*To All The Girls I've Loved Before*).

Brooklyn-born Perry's first production stint was an unlikely collaboration with Captain Beefheart, before going on to join Warner Brothers Records as an in-house producer during the 1960s. Establishing his own Planet label in the following decade, Perry produced an impressive string of Top 5 hits, most consistently for the Pointer Sisters. All of the cuts listed here reached either US No. 1 or No. 2 and all sold over 1,000,000 American copies.

Mickie Most was one of the top producers of the 1960s and 1970s, responsible for transatlantic million-selling hits with the Animals, Lulu, Herman's Hermits and Donovan, as well as the multifarious acts on his own 1970s-launched RAK label.

THE TOP 10 UK HITS PRODUCED BY PHIL SPECTOR

	Title	Charting artist	Year
1	Unchained Melody	Righteous Brothers	1965
2	You've Lost That Lovin' Feelin'	Righteous Brothers	1965
3	River Deep, Mountain High	Ike & Tina Turner	1966
4	Then He Kissed Me	Crystals	1963
5	To Know Him Is To Love Him	Teddy Bears	1958
6	Be My Baby	Ronettes	1963
7	Da Doo Ron Ron	Crystals	1963
8	Instant Karma	John Ono Lennon & Plastic Ono Band	1970
9	Baby, I Love You	Ronettes	1964
10	Baby, I Love You	Ramones	1980

Most of Phil Spector's biggest-selling productions are from the period during the 1960s when he was running his own Philles label. Number five pre-dates this, being the first record he made, while still a teenager (he was also a member of the group). Co-productions have not been included, thus excluding George Harrison's *My Sweet Lord* which he co-produced with the ex-Beatle, and which would otherwise top this and the US list opposite.

PHIL SPECTOR

Unique among his peers, both as the architect of the Wall of Sound and as an enigmatic and elusive character off the record, producer Phil Spector was born on 26 December 1940 in the Bronx, New York. Moving to Los Angeles in 1953 with his mother (his father died in 1949) he attended Fairfax High School where he won a talent contest in 1956, performing Lonnie Donegan's *Rock Island Line*.

Two years later, Spector secured a recording deal with Era Records as one-third of the vocal trio the Teddy Bears (with Annette Bard and Marshall Lieb) and enjoyed his first No. 1 hit, *To Know Him Is To Love Him*, which Spector wrote, inspired by the epitaph on his father's grave. After a handful of less successful recordings, the band split and he began working in New York as an apprentice producer for Lester Sill who was co-ordinating recordings for the songwriting duo Leiber and Stoller. His first hit productions were with the Coasters and notably Ray Peterson's *Corrina, Corrina* in November 1960. One month later, Ben E. King's classic *Spanish Harlem*, co-written by Jerry Leiber and Spector, began its rise into the American Top 10 and initiated a parallel career for Spector, writing and/or producing scores of hits over the next 10 years, and becoming the most successful and envied maestro of his era in the American record industry.

In September 1961, Sill and Spector formed their own Philles record label. His first signing was the all-female black quintet from Brooklyn, the Crystals. Two Top 20 hits later (and with Spector now running the label on his own) the 22-year-old self-made millionaire scored the first Philles chart-topper with the Crystals' *He's A Rebel*, written by Gene Pitney. Though not in the group, the lead vocal was actually sung by Darlene Love who was the featured singer in Spector's next creation, Bob B. Soxx & The Blue Jeans whose *Zip-A-Dee-Doo-Dah* became the next Philles Top 10 success in the States. Spinning Love off into a three-hit solo run, Spector's next empire-building signing, the Ronettes in 1963, included his wife-to-be Veronica 'Ronnie' Bennett. Their first and biggest success was *Be My Baby*, co-written by Spector with Ellie Greenwich and Jeff Barry.

Producing all of the Philles output, Spector had now established his innovative recording techniques, over-dubbing a multitude of instrumental and vocal tracks, literally building a 'wall of sound' around the simplest of classic pop melodies. Although the majority of the label's acts were R & B-based, Spector broadened the songs' appeal by projecting them at a teen market, crossing racial and international barriers. In producing these unique recordings, Spector used the finest session musicians available, including Leon Russell, Dr John, Glen Campbell and Sonny Bono, all of whom went on to

THE TOP 10 US HITS PRODUCED BY PHIL SPECTOR

	Title	Charting artist	Year
1	You've Lost That Lovin' Feelin'	Righteous Brothers	1965
2	Unchained Melody	Righteous Brothers (twice)	1965
3	Instant Karma	John Ono Lennon & Plastic Ono Band	1970
4	To Know Him Is To Love Him	Teddy Bears	1958
5	He's A Rebel	Crystals	1962
6	Be My Baby	Ronettes	1963
7	The Long And Winding Road	Beatles	1970
8	Imagine	John Lennon/Plastic Ono Band	1971
9	Da Doo Ron Ron	Crystals	1963
10	I Love How You Love Me	Paris Sisters	1961

The aural architect of the 'Wall of Sound', Spector's first hit was behind the controls and in the line-up of the Teddy Bears smash, *To Know Him Is To Love Him* in 1958. He went on to write and produce dozens of hits on his own Philles label (among them the Crystals, Righteous Brothers, Bob B. Soxx, Ronettes and Ike & Tina Turner). It was the Beatles' manager Allen Klein who pulled the reclusive Spector out of retirement in the late 1960s, principally to produce the *Let It Be* sessions. This led to brief but highly successful separate unions with John Lennon (*Imagine*) and George Harrison (*All Things Must Pass*), including the million-plus selling *My Sweet Lord*, which hit US No. 1 for four weeks.

subsequent solo success, and also employed Jack Nitzsche as his in-house arranger.

One of the few Philles commercial failures was *Phil Spector's Christmas* album, the seminal seasonal collection he created from his stable of acts in 1963. Its release date of 22 November coincided with the assassination of John F. Kennedy, and the jolly upbeat Santa songs jarred badly with the gloom that hung over the USA that Christmas. Following the label's demise in 1967, the album became a prized collectors' item until its reissue in the 1970s and subsequent annual re-packaging and re-release ever since.

Perhaps Spector's creative and certainly his commercial apex was with the Righteous Brothers' *You've Lost That Lovin' Feelin'*. Conducting the backing band for all the acts that appeared on a bill including the Ronettes at the Cow Palace in San Francisco in the spring of 1964, Spector was so impressed by the performance of Bobby Hatfield and Bill Medley that he bought their recording contract from Moonglow and signed the Righteous Brothers as the first white act to appear on Philles. Co-credited with writing the song with Cynthia Weil and Barry Mann, Spector built his ultimate 'wall' and saw his instant classic top both the US and UK charts in 1965 (despite the disc's being voted a 'miss' by all four panellists on BBC Television's *Juke Box Jury*).

His last signing to the label was Ike & Tina Turner, for whom Spector created the unforgettable *River Deep, Mountain High* in 1966. Although it was a Top 3 hit in Britain, its failure to rise above No. 88 in his home country was such a profound dis-

appointment to him that he effectively quit the business and began dismantling the Philles label. Increasingly embittered, his growing eccentricity saw him retreat to his guarded home in Hollywood. Reclusive ever since, his subsequent production outings were initially Beatles-related, honing, at John Lennon's request, the *Let It Be* sessions and subsequent solo albums by both Lennon (*Imagine*) and George Harrison (*Bangladesh*). Thereafter, his credits have been sparse but have included Cher, Dion, Leonard Cohen (*Death Of A Ladies Man* LP) and the Ramones (*End Of The Century* LP). (During his work on the band's track *Rock 'n' Roll High School*, the perfectionist Spector reportedly spent 10 hours alone listening to the song's opening chord.)

While his production and songwriting legacy (which also includes *Unchained Melody, My Sweet Lord, Da Doo Ron Ron, I Love How You Love Me, Then He Kissed Me* and *Baby I Love You*) speaks for itself (and continues to assure him of substantial royalty income), perhaps it is best left for Spector himself to assess the impact of his work (as he did in a November 1969 interview in *Rolling Stone*): 'I could tell you I'm the greatest f***in' record producer who ever lived.'

THE STOCK AITKEN WATERMAN PHENOMENON

On 14 April 1990, Stock Aitken Waterman saw their 100th singles chart entry, Pat & Mick's *Use It Up And Wear It Out*, enter the UK survey, a total all the more remarkable in that this century was scored in just seven years. The hitmaking trio dominated the UK record industry in the 1980s as songwriters, producers, owners of their own recording studio and heads of their own independent label, PWL (Pete Waterman Limited). With Waterman fulfilling the most prominent role as SAW spokesman, DJ (on Radio City), creator and co-host of the long-running late night TV dance show, *The Hitman And Her*, magazine columnist and outspoken self-promoting pop analyst, Mike Stock and Matt Aitken took more of a backseat role creating the musical machine which drove the unit to becoming the most successful writing and production team in UK recording history.

Stock and Aitken's first hit collaboration was at the Proto label in 1984 where, following their own unsuccessful single *The Upstroke* released under the name Agents Aren't Aeroplanes, they linked with disco singer Hazell Dean for a string of hits, including their first songwriting smash, *Whatever I Do (Wherever I Go)*. Industry veteran Waterman, who had previously worked as a freelance dance product promoter and producer working on hits for Susan Cadogan and the Gull Records label, and been a disco columnist for the *Record Business* trade paper in the late 1970s, was invited to form a permanent writing and production team with Stock and Aitken, and the trio's first assignment was for Dead Or Alive led by Pete Burns. On 9 March 1985, they secured their first UK chart-topper (and US hit) with the group's *You Spin Me Round (Like A Record)*.

Thereafter, the trio concocted a rapid-fire armoury of infectious, uptempo pop dance confections for Dean, Dead Or Alive, Sinitta, Princess, Bananarama, Mel & Kim and Samantha Fox. They also became increasingly in demand as re-mixers and producers for dozens of acts that were equally reliant on production techniques. SAW even scored two Top 20 hits under their own name in 1987. With their writing and production of Rick Astley's 1987 solo debut, *Never Gonna Give You Up*, however, their success went truly international as its UK No. 1 status was repeated around the world, also giving them their first American chart-topper.

Forming their PWL label in 1987, their first entirely home-made, self-written and produced label hit also marked the beginning of their most fruitful artist relationship: Kylie Minogue's *I Should Be So Lucky* began its chart rise to UK No. 1 on 23 January 1988 and opened a three-year period of total Stock Aitken Waterman chart domination.

Revolving their song productions around an insistent synthesizer-driven dance-friendly rhythm track which barely changed from hit to hit, and employing catchy lightweight pop lyrics, SAW amassed scores of Top 30 entries for the likes of Big Fun, Sonia, Brother Beyond, Donna Summer, Pat & Mick, Cliff Richard and the Reynolds Girls.

The trio's two biggest acts, both personally groomed by and entirely reliant upon SAW's hit formula were Kylie, whose first 10 hits, nine of them written by SAW and all produced by them, all lodged in the Top 5, an unprecedented achievement by a female artist; and Jason Donovan, her *Neighbours* soap star colleague and PWL label-mate, who hit the top spot with *Too Many Broken Hearts* and *Sealed With A Kiss* in 1989 and also scored SAW's biggest seller, the ballad *Especially For You,* in duet with Kylie in January of that year. Both artists also secured a run of multi-platinum albums, all conceived, largely written and entirely produced by the trio.

Despite constant criticism by the music press who viewed their hit factory as nothing more than a mechanical pop-spewing machine, SAW's chart success was accompanied by a slew of awards, most notably their three-year consecutive win of the Songwriter of the Year trophy at the annual Ivor Novello Awards for 1987, 1988 and 1989. In his acceptance speech for the last of these wins, Waterman somewhat staggeringly compared their achievements to those of Lennon & McCartney. Their achievements have, however, often been more charitable, not least in their re-recordings of *Do They Know It's Christmas?* for Band Aid II in 1989 and *Ferry Cross The Mersey*, organized by Waterman and recorded by Liverpudlian acts the same year to help the families of the Liverpool Football Club Hillsborough disaster, both of which were produced by SAW and reached UK No. 1.

Having been responsible for over 10,000,000 singles sales in the UK alone in the past 10 years and amassing small fortunes, not least via their All Boys publishing company, Matt Aitken quietly split from the trio in 1992, while Stock and Waterman continued to notch up hits at a less prodigious pace (they also parted ways with Donovan in 1991). Having also formed PWL International, many of their more recent non-Kylie successes have been secured via licensing deals for dance hits already recorded in Europe. Love them or loathe them, Pete Waterman's prophecy that SAW have been the Motown of the 1980s, however sacrilegious to pop purists, has certainly rung true commercially.

THE TOP 10 UK HITS WRITTEN AND PRODUCED BY STOCK AITKEN WATERMAN

	Title	Charting artist
1	*Especially For You*	Kylie Minogue and Jason Donovan
2	*Never Gonna Give You Up*	Rick Astley
3	*I Should Be So Lucky*	Kylie Minogue
4	*Respectable*	Mel & Kim
5	*Too Many Broken Hearts*	Jason Donovan
6	*When You Come Back To Me*	Jason Donovan
7	*Hand On Your Heart*	Kylie Minogue
8	*Got To Be Certain*	Kylie Minogue
9	*Wouldn't Change A Thing*	Kylie Minogue
10	*Je Ne Sais Pas Pourquoi*	Kylie Minogue

With total UK singles sales now well over the 10,000,000 mark, it is ironic that for all the uptempo pop dance confection that has made Stock Aitken Waterman the most prolific and successful UK songwriting (and production) team of the 1980s, their most popular outing to date has been a ballad.

THE TOP 10 US HITS PRODUCED BY STOCK AITKEN WATERMAN

	Title	Charting artist
1	*Never Gonna Give You Up*	Rick Astley
2	*This Time I Know It's For Real*	Donna Summer
3	*Together Forever*	Rick Astley
4	*Venus*	Banarama
5	*The Loco-Motion*	Kylie Minogue
6	*I Heard A Rumour*	Bananarama
7	*It Would Take A Strong Man*	Rick Astley
8	*You Spin Me Round (Like A Record)*	Dead Or Alive
9	*Brand New Lover*	Dead Or Alive
10	*That's What Love Can Do*	Boy Krazy

Despite logging scores of hits in their native UK, Stock Aitken Waterman have achieved only moderate success in the United States, and even this, more as producers than writers. Of this list, only number one sold more than 1,000,000 copies, while number two is the only other title to be certified gold for sales exceeding 500,000. Number 10, a Top 10 hit in February 1993 – the trio's first such success since number two scored in 1989 – evicted Kylie Minogue's *I Should Be So Lucky* from their personal US Top 10.

PERFORMANCE

10 ACTS FOR WHOM THE BEATLES OPENED

1	Joe Brown
2	Bruce Chanel
3	Shane Fenton & The Fentones
4	Frank Ifield
5	Chris Montez
6	Little Richard
7	Tommy Roe
8	Royal Showband
9	Helen Shapiro
10	Gene Vincent

On their way up, between their early Hamburg years and their first tour as bill-toppers in 1963, the Beatles paid their dues as support act to a wide variety of talent. The Fabs supported Helen Shapiro, Chris Montez and Tommy Roe on UK package tours in 1962 and 1963, while the majority of the other acts listed here headlined a Liverpool bill on which the Beatles were the local support act, often only for one show. Shane Fenton (born Bernard Jewry), incidentally, transmogrified himself into Alvin Stardust in 1974.

Liza Minnelli's 15 Radio City concerts in 1991 clocked up a record $3,826,916 in ticket sales.

THE TOP 10 GROSSING ACTS AT ONE VENUE, WORLDWIDE, 1991

	Act	Venue	No. of shows	Gross ticket sales ($)
1	Liza Minnelli	Radio City Music Hall, New York, USA	15	3,826,916
2	Grateful Dead	Madison Square Garden, New York, USA	9	3,747,519
3	Grateful Dead, Little Feat	Giants Stadium, New Jersey, USA	2	2,924,925
4	Walden Woods Benefit: Don Henley, Billy Joel, Sting, Jimmy Buffett, Bonnie Raitt	Madison Square Garden, New York, USA	3	2,903,800
5	Billy Joel	Palacio De Los Deportes, Mexico City, Mexico	4	2,772,853
6	New Kids On The Block, Biscuit	Wembley Arena, Wembley, UK	9	2,618,304
7	New Kids On The Block	Skydome, Toronto, Canada	2	2,433,467
8	Summer XS: INXS, Hothouse Flowers, Deborah Harry, Jesus Jones, Roachford, Jellyfish	Wembley Stadium, Wembley, UK	1	2,358,198
9	Guns N' Roses, Skid Row	Alpine Valley Music Theater, Wisconsin, USA	2	2,050,560
10	Grateful Dead	Boston Garden, Massachusetts, USA	6	2,039,659

Source: *Amusement Business.*

Minnelli's extraordinary total, due not least to her lengthy residence at the venue, included nine sell-out performances, with a top ticket price of $50.

THE 10 BIGGEST GROSSING US TOURS OF 1992*

	Act	Gross receipts ($)
1	U2	61,258,890
2	Neil Diamond	44,952,131
3	Metallica	40,022,751
4	Guns N' Roses	36,794,259
5	Genesis	30,368,945
6	Bruce Springsteen	29,010,690
7	Elton John	28,180,879
8	Grateful Dead	27,683,418
9	Eric Clapton	20,469,308
10	Hammer	20,304,239

* All of the tours were predominantly North American, though gross figures do reflect receipts from some international portions of the acts' itineraries.

Source: Amusement Business.

THE TOP 10 CLASSICAL COMPOSERS IN PERFORMANCE, 1992

	Composer	Performances
1	Ludwig van Beethoven	50
2	Wolfgang Amadeus Mozart	33
3	Joseph Haydn	29
4	Gustav Mahler	25⅕
5=	Antonin Dvorák	20¼
5=	Peter Tchaikovsky	20¼
7	Johannes Brahms	20
8	Dmitri Shostakovich	16
9	Jean Sibelius	15
10	Franz Schubert	12

David Chesterman has been writing to The Times every year since 1952, reporting on the 10 composers whose symphonies have been most performed at the Royal Albert, Royal Festival, Barbican and Queen Elizabeth Halls and at St John's, Smith Square, London. His analysis is based on the number of times each composer's work is played, with individual movements counted as fractions of the whole symphony. In 1990 Beethoven took a temporary back seat when Mozart outperformed him – for only the third time in 40 years, the 1991 celebration of the bicentenary of his death resulting in even more concerts featuring his work. Beethoven regained his pre-eminence in 1992, with his 7th Symphony alone performed nine times. In 1991 Dvorák, who had ranked 5th in 1989 but was not even in the Top 10 in 1990, regained his position, maintaining it in 1992, while Sergei Prokofiev and Anton Bruckner, both in the 1991 list, dropped out in 1992. No English composer has ever made the Top 10 but, to apply the jargon of pop music, Ralph Vaughan Williams (11th in 1992) is 'bubbling under'.

THE 10 BIGGEST GROSSING US TOURS OF ALL TIME*

	Act	Year**	No. of shows	Gross receipts ($)
1	Rolling Stones	1989	46	70,426,073
2	U2	1992	60	61,258,890
3	New Kids On The Block	1990	133	50,584,801
4	Neil Diamond	1992	79	44,952,131
5	Paul McCartney	1990	46	44,930,681
6	Billy Joel	1990	91	41,670,038
7	Metallica	1992	62	40,022,751
8	Guns N' Roses	1992	50	36,794,259
9	Grateful Dead	1991	79	35,243,237
10	Who	1989	34	34,874,576

* For tours reported up to 1 December 1992. All of the tours were predominantly North American, though gross figures do reflect receipts from some international portions of the acts' itineraries.

** Peak year of tours extending over more than one year.

The Grateful Dead's non-stop touring sojourn between 1986 and 1992 has netted the band a staggering total of $164,335,410 in the United States alone, easily making them the highest-earning live rock act of all time. Not surprisingly, the San Francisco band took a rest in the autumn of 1992 to let band leader Gerry Garcia recover from exhaustion.

Source: Amusement Business.

THE FIRST 10 ACTS TO PERFORM AT THE BAND AID CONCERT

1	Status Quo
2	Paul Weller
3	Bob Geldof & The Boomtown Rats
4	Adam Ant
5	INXS
6	Ultravox
7	Spandau Ballet
8	Elvis Costello
9	Nik Kershaw
10	B.B. King

Status Quo took the stage at 12.01 p.m. on 13 July 1985, to begin the historic 16-hour fund-raising rock extravaganza, Live Aid. The event was broadcast live to an estimated 2 billion people around the world from the two venues at Wembley Stadium, London, and the JFK Stadium in Philadelphia, USA, and raised over $70,000,000 for hunger relief in Africa. Phil Collins made rock history by playing a set at Wembley, flying immediately to Philadelphia and performing a second set in the States, the first time an artist had ever played two gigs on different continents on the same day.

THE 10 LARGEST CONCERT VENUES IN THE UK

	Venue	Capacity
1	Wembley Stadium, London	72,000*
2	Milton Keynes Bowl	45,000
3	Scottish Exhibition & Conference Centre, Glasgow	28,600*
4	Birmingham International Arena	19,000*
5	London Olympia	18,000
6	Edinburgh Exhibition & Trade Centre	15,500*
7	London (Docklands) Arena	12,600
8	Wembley Arena, London	12,000
9	Manchester G-Mex	9,000
10=	King's Hall, Belfast	7,000
10=	Queen's Hall, Bradford	7,000

* Shared seating and standing capacity.

The common theme shared by the majority of these venues is the severe lack of parking space.

Wembley Stadium, the UK's top concert venue, with a capacity crowd of 72,000.

THE 10 LARGEST CONCERT VENUES IN THE USA

	Venue	Capacity
1	Rose Bowl, Pasadena, California	104,696
2	Pontiac Silverdome, Pontiac, Michigan	100,000
3	Ohio State University Stadium, Columbus, Ohio	86,071
4	Cleveland Municipal Stadium, Cleveland, Ohio	80,032
5=	Georgia Dome, Atlanta, Georgia*	80,000
5=	Legion Field, Birmingham, Alabama	80,000
7	Arrowhead Stadium, Kansas City, Missouri	78,097
8	Camp Randall Stadium, University of Wisconsin, Madison, Wisconsin	77,280
9	Giants Stadium, East Rutherford, New Jersey	76,891
10	Texas Stadium, Irving, Texas	73,855

* *The indoor Georgia Dome opened in October 1992 with a concert by U2.*

10 GREAT ROCK FESTIVALS

	Festival/venue (major acts)	Date	Estimated attendance
1	Monterey/Monterey, California (Jimi Hendrix, Who, Janis Joplin)	16–18 Jun 1969	60,000
2	Stones In The Park/Hyde Park, London (Rolling Stones)	5 Jul 1969	250,000
3	Woodstock/Whitelake, near Bethel, New York (Crosby Stills Nash & Young, Joe Cocker, Jimi Hendrix)	15–17 Aug 1969	300,000
4	Watkins Glen/Watkins Glen Raceway, New York (Allman Brothers, Grateful Dead, Band)	28 Jul 1973	600,000
5	Simon and Garfunkel In Central Park/ Central Park, New York (Paul Simon and Art Garfunkel)	19 Sep 1981	400,000
6	US Festival '83/Devore, California (David Bowie, Clash, Van Halen)	28–30 May 1983	500,000
7	Live Aid/Wembley Stadium, London & JFK Stadium, Philadelphia (Madonna, U2, Phil Collins)	13 Jul 1985	162,000
8	Farm Aid I/Champaign, Illinois (Willie Nelson, John Mellencamp, Neil Young)	22 Sep 1985	100,000
9	The Wall/Potzdamer Platz, Berlin, Germany (Roger Waters, Bryan Adams, Joni Mitchell)	21 Jul 1990	200,000
10	Rock In Rio II/Maracana Stadium, Rio de Janeiro, Brazil (George Michael, Guns N' Roses, Prince)	18–25 Jan 1991	670,000

Although attended by just 60,000 people, number one is generally regarded as the first major rock festival and heralded the 'Summer of Love' which also witnessed Mick Jagger releasing 3,000 butterflies in Hyde Park (number two) and the staging of the legendary Woodstock. Simon and Garfunkel reunited for a massive free concert in Central Park in 1981; number six was the second and last three-day US rock festival organized by Apple Computers co-founder Steve Wozniak; Live Aid, attended by only 162,000 at the two venues, became the most-watched global TV broadcast ever, seen by an estimated 2 billion people; Farm Aid was Country superstar Willie Nelson's response to Live Aid and became an annual festival devoted to raising funds for American farmers; ex-Pink Floyd's Roger Waters staged a spectacular rock musical of his composition, *The Wall*, in celebration of the dismantling of the Berlin Wall in 1990, while number 10 was the second Rock In Rio festival (the first was in 1985), a non-charity event which drew even larger crowds than the original.

THE 10 LONGEST-RUNNING BBC RADIO MUSIC PROGRAMMES

	Programme	First broadcast
1	Choral Evensong	7 Oct 1926
2	Desert Island Discs	29 Jan 1942
3	Composer Of The Week (originally This Week's Composer)	2 Aug 1943
4	Friday Night Is Music Night	25 Sep 1953
5	Talking About Music	13 Jan 1954
6	Record Review	5 Oct 1957
7	Sing Something Simple	3 Jul 1959
8	Your Hundred Best Tunes (originally The Hundred Best Tunes)	22 Nov 1959
9	Jazz Record Requests	12 Dec 1964
10	Midweek Choice	16 Dec 1964

Music In Our Time (first broadcast 26 March 1965) and the BBC Lunchtime Concert, Live From St John's, Smith Square (8 December 1969) are the only two other programmes that have been running since before the 1970s. In addition to these, one annual musical event, The Proms, has a long pedigree, having been first broadcast on 13 August 1927.

One of the longest-standing radio music presenters is Humphrey Lyttelton: his first show was broadcast in 1950, he went on to present The Jazz Scene and continues to front The Best Of Jazz on Radio 2 on Monday nights.

Alan Keith has been presenting Your Hundred Best Tunes *on Radio 2 since 1959.*

THE TOP 10 RADIO STATIONS IN THE USA

	Station	City	Format	Audience
1	WINS	New York	News	2,345,700
2	WHTZ	New York	Contemporary Hit Radio	2,185,600
3	WPLJ	New York	Contemporary Hit Radio	1,978,800
4	WRKS	New York	Urban Contemporary	1,893,100
5	WCBS-FM	New York	Gold (oldies)	1,892,800
6	WXRK	New York	Classic Rock	1,881,400
7	WLTW	New York	Adult Contemporary	1,788,200
8	WCBS	New York	News	1,787,700
9	KIIS AM & FM	Los Angeles	Contemporary Hit Radio	1,663,200
10	WBLS	New York	Urban Contemporary	1,658,100

Source: Radio & Records/Arbitron, as at May 1992.

The audience figure is for average daily listenership (measured as 'cume' – the cumulative audience, or number of different people listening during a specified period of time).

In New York alone there are now 433 legal broadcasting stations (over four times the total number in the United Kingdom), of which 260 are on the FM wavelength.

THE TOP 10 FORMATS ON US RADIO, 1991

	Format	AM	No. of stations FM	total
1	Country	1,391	1,212	2,603
2	Adult Contemporary	831	1,516	2,347
3	Religious	590	514	1,104
4	Oldies	599	421	1,020
5	Contemporary Hit Radio/Top 40	119	726	845
6	MOR (Middle of the Road)	450	100	550
7	Rock/AOR (Adult Oriented Rock)	65	474	539
8	News	276	254	530
9	News and Talk	470	59	529
10	Variety/Diverse*	122	405	527

* *Stations with four or more formats, typically public broadcasting stations.*

In the radio-crazy United States there are 4,889 AM and 6,189 FM stations of which the vast majority – a total of 9,448 – are commercial. Classical music is the 11th most popular format, accounting for 428 stations.

THE 10 MOST PERFORMED BMI SONGS OF ALL TIME IN THE USA

	Title	Composer(s)
1	*Yesterday*	Lennon & McCartney
2	*Never My Love*	Donald & Richard Addrisi
3	*By The Time I Get To Phoenix*	Jim Webb
4	*Gentle On My Mind*	John Hartford
5	*You've Lost That Lovin' Feelin'*	Phil Spector, Barry Mann & Cynthia Weil
6	*More*	Norman Newell, Nino Oliviero, Riz Ortalani and Marcello Ciorcioloni
7	*Georgia On My Mind*	Hoagy Carmichael & Stuart Gorrell
8	*Bridge Over Troubled Water*	Paul Simon
9	*Something*	George Harrison
10	*Mrs Robinson*	Paul Simon

Source: BMI (up to 1992).

This list represents the most broadcast songs of all time on American radio and television, for those titles represented by the BMI (Broadcast Music Incorporated). The first five songs have all been broadcast over 5,000,000 times in the United States alone – *Yesterday*, in 1989, becoming the first song to reach this figure. The last five songs in this list have all been aired over 4,000,000 times.

THE 10 MOST FREQUENTLY BROADCAST WORKS ON BBC RADIO 3, 1992

	Work	Composer	No. of broadcasts
1	*Dumbarton Oaks Concerto*	Stravinsky	56
2	*Clarinet Concerto No. 2*	Weber	52
3	*Bransle De Post*	Susato	48
4	*Viennese Musical Clock*	Kodaly	44
5	*String Quartet*	Ravel	22
6	*Sunday Morning*	Britten	16
7	*Der Freischutz*	Weber	15
8=	*Cello Concerto*	Elgar	14
8=	*Marriage Of Figaro Overture*	Mozart	14
8=	*Quartet Movement (allegro assai) for Strings*	Schubert	14

THE TOP 10 SINGLES OF ALL TIME IN THE UK BANNED BY THE BBC

	Title	Artist
1	Relax	Frankie Goes To Hollywood
2	Je T'aime...Moi Non Plus	Jane Birkin and Serge Gainsbourg
3	Tell Laura I Love Her	Ricky Valance
4	God Save The Queen	Sex Pistols
5	I Want Your Sex	George Michael
6	Magic Roundabout	Jasper Carrott
7	Hi Hi Hi	Wings
8	Wet Dream	Max Romeo
9	Big Seven	Judge Dread
10	Big Six	Judge Dread

Until recent years, BBC radio was prone to keep records off the airwaves if (a) their melody was a desecration of a classical piece (though, oddly, *Nut Rocker* never succumbed), (b) their lyrics were deemed offensive because of a concern with sex, drugs, death or politics, or (c) they mentioned commercial trade names, which was reckoned to be against the BBC's charter. Most of those on the list were adjudged to be in category (b) – and yet they all became Top 10 hits regardless. (A sign of the changing times: George Michael's disc was banned only from daytime play, but permitted after the 9 p.m. 'watershed'.)

DJs & RADIO QUIZ

1 Which ex-DJ in 1993 became programme controller of Virgin 1215?
2 Who is the self-proclaimed 'Hairy Cornflake'?
3 Which legendary American DJ appeared in the Rock 'n' Roll movie, *American Graffiti*?
4 What was the first commercial radio station to broadcast in the UK?
5 Which ex-Radio 1 female DJ is related to Keith Chegwin?
6 With which Radio 1 DJ do you associate the characters Mr Angry, Easylife and Sid The Manager?
7 Who is the only knighted disc jockey?
8 Who hosts the Classical Chart Countdown on Classic FM?
9 Which weekday programme features the popular 'Our Tune' segment?
10 Which two DJs scored with their parody version of C.W. McCall's *Convoy* in 1976 under the pseudonym Laurie Lingo & The Dipsticks?

THE FIRST 10 RECORDS PLAYED ON BBC RADIO 1

	Title	Artist
1	Flowers In The Rain	Move
2	Massachusetts	Bee Gees
3	Even The Bad Times Are Good	Tremeloes
4	Fakin' It	Simon and Garfunkel
5	The Day I Met Marie	Cliff Richard
6	You Can't Hurry Love	Supremes
7	The Last Waltz	Engelbert Humperdinck
8	Baby, Now That I've Found You	Foundations
9	Good Times	Eric Burdon & The Animals
10	A Banda	Herb Alpert & The Tijuana Brass

Radio 1 was launched on Saturday, 30 September 1967, at 7 a.m., with the Tony Blackburn Show. These are the first 10 of the 26 records that Blackburn played that morning on a show produced by future Radio 1 controller Johnny Beerling. All were then current UK Top 20 hits, apart from the Simon and Garfunkel and Herb Alpert titles, neither of which charted, despite this notable media exposure. The 12-string guitar played by Roy Wood of the Move on *Flowers In The Rain* was sold for £1,870 at Christie's, London, on 7 May 1992, the cachet of its association with this notable 'first' undoubtedly enhancing its price.

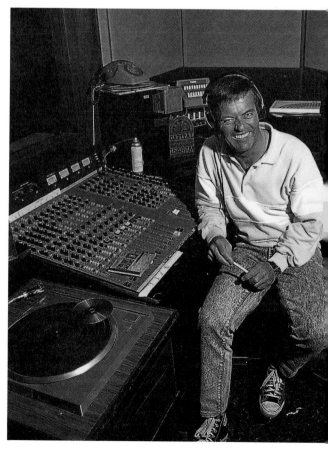

Tony Blackburn, the disc jockey who launched Radio 1 on 30 September 1967, now spins music from that same period on London's oldies station Capital Gold.

THE FIRST 10 RECORDS PLAYED ON CLASSIC FM

	Composer/piece	Conductor/orchestra
1	Georg Friedrich Handel, *Zadok the Priest*	Robert King/The King's Consort
2	Carl Maria von Weber, *Invitation to the Dance*	Hamish Milne (soloist)
3	Serge Prokofiev, *Symphony No. 1 in D Major*, Opus 25	Yoel Levi/Atlanta Symphony Orhestra
4	Alessandro Marcello, *Concerto in D Minor for Oboe, Strings and Continuo*	Ian Watson/English Chamber Orchestra
5	Mikhail Ippolitov-Ivanov, *Procession of the Sardar*	Leopold Stokowski/National Philharmonic Orchestra
6	Johann Sebastian Bach, *Suite No. 1 in G Major for Solo Cello*	Yuri Turovsky (soloist)
7	Benjamin Britten, *Matinées Musicales*, Opus 24	Sir Adrian Boult/London Philharmonic Orchestra
8	Marc-Antoine Charpentier, *Prelude to a* Te Deum *in D Major*	Peter Hurford/Michael Laird Brass Ensemble
9	Manuel de Falla, *Ritual Fire Dance*	Bramwell Tovey/Royal Philharmonic Orchestra
10	Wolfgang Amadeus Mozart, 'Der Vogelfanger bin ich ya', aria from *The Magic Flute*	Nikolaus Harnoncourt/Anton Scharinger (soloist)/ Orchestra of the Zurich Opera House

The 10 pieces in the list (plus one further item, Henry Purcell's *Abdelazer* performed by Raymond Leppard and the English Chamber Orchestra) represent the first hour's broadcasting on Classic FM, the nationwide independent classical music radio station that went on air at 6.00 a.m. on Monday 7 September 1992.

THE TOP 10 COMPOSERS ON CLASSIC FM

	Composer	Works played	Total plays*
1	Wolfgang Amadeus Mozart	306	681
2	Johann Sebastian Bach	190	500
3	Ludwig van Beethoven	186	476
4	Georg Friedrich Handel	121	400
5	Frederic Chopin	213	380
6	Peter Tchaikovsky	132	373
7	Franz Schubert	126	339
8	Antonio Vivaldi	174	335
9	Franz Liszt	96	293
10	Antonin Dvořák	93	287

* 7 September to 31 December 1992.

THE FIRST 10 'BREAKFAST' DJs ON BBC RADIO 1

1	Tony Blackburn
2	Noel Edmonds
3	Dave Lee Travis
4	Mike Read
5	Mike Smith
6	Simon Mayo
7–10	To be announced...

Since its inception in 1967, only six DJs have occupied the much coveted 'Breakfast' slot on Fab FM. As of 1992, the only surviving DJs still broadcasting on Radio 1 are the current breakfast incumbent Simon Mayo and Dave Lee Travis.

THE TOP 10 SONGS ON *YOUR HIT PARADE*, 1935–58

	Title	Composer	Year
1	*Too Young*	Sid Lippman	1951
2	*White Christmas*	Irving Berlin	1942
3	*Because Of You*	Arthur Hammerstein & Dudley Wilson	1951
4	*You'll Never Know*	Harry Warren	1943
5	*I'll Be Seeing You*	Sammy Fain	1938
6	*Now Is The Hour*	Dorothy Stewart & Clement Scott	1946
7	*Peg O' My Heart*	Fred Fisher	1947
8	*People Will Say We're In Love*	Richard Rodgers	1943
9	*A Tree In The Meadow*	Bille Reid	1948
10	*Some Enchanted Evening*	Richard Rodgers	1949

Your Hit Parade, a popular syndicated US radio programme featuring the most successful sheet-music sales on a weekly basis, began broadcasting in 1935.

THE 10 MOST REQUESTED RECORDS ON *DESERT ISLAND DISCS*

	Composer	Work
1	Ludwig van Beethoven	'O Freunds, nicht diese Tone' (choral) from *Symphony* No. 9
2	Claude Debussy	*Claire de Lune*
3	Edward Elgar	*Pomp and Circumstance*, March No. 1
4	Richard Wagner	'Liebestod' from *Tristan und Isolde*
5	George Gershwin	*Rhapsody in Blue*
6	Johann Christian Bach/ Charles François Goundod	*Ave Maria*
7	Felix Mendelssohn	'Nocturne' from *A Midsummer Night's Dream*
8	Ludwig van Beethoven	*Symphony* No. 5
9	Georg Friedrich Handel	'Hallelujah Chorus' from *Messiah*
10	Giuseppi Verdi	'Dies Irae' from *Requiem*

The Beethoven at number one has been requested by more than 60 'castaways' in the programme's 50-year history.

THE FIRST 10 ARTISTS TO FEATURE IN A COCA-COLA RADIO COMMERCIAL

	Act	Jingle	Year
1	McGuire Sisters	*Pause For A Coke*	1958
2	Limelighters	*Things Go Better With Coke*	1963
3=	Four Seasons	*Things Go Better With Coke*	1965
3=	Freddie & The Dreamers	*Things Go Better With Coke*	1965
3=	Jan and Dean	*Things Go Better With Coke*	1965
3=	Jay & The Americans	*Things Go Better With Coke*	1965
3=	Tom Jones	*Things Go Better With Coke*	1965
3=	Shirelles	*Things Go Better With Coke*	1965
9=	Petula Clark	*Things Go Better With Coke*	1966
9=	Lee Dorsey	*Things Go Better With Coke*	1966
9=	Everly Brothers	*Things Go Better With Coke*	1966
9=	Marvin Gaye	*Things Go Better With Coke*	1966
9=	Gary Lewis & The Playboys	*Things Go Better With Coke*	1966
9=	Little Milton	*Things Go Better With Coke*	1966
9=	Roy Orbison	*Things Go Better With Coke*	1966
9=	Supremes	*Things Go Better With Coke*	1966

Coke radio ads continue to employ such artists as Michael McDonald, Kim Carnes, Devo, Elton John and New Kids On The Block, but this list reads like a who's who of pop music in the 1960s.

THE TOP 10 BMI 'MILLION-AIRS'

	Songwriter(s)	No. of Million-Airs
1	Lennon & McCartney	26
2	Barry Gibb	22
3	Paul Simon	15
4	Norman Gimbel	12
5	Holland, Dozier, Holland	10
6	Barry Mann	9
7	Cynthia Weil	8
8=	Gerry Goffin	7
8=	Daryl Hall	7
8=	Carole Bayer-Sager	7
8=	Gamble & Huff	7
8=	John & Taupin	7

In the repertoire of more than 1,500,000 songs in the BMI (Broadcast Music Incorporated) nearly 1,000 have achieved 'Million-Air' status, that is, titles that have been broadcast over 1,000,000 times in the United States. With each song averaging three minutes, this is equal to more than 50,000 hours of broadcasting, or 5.7 years of continuous airplay. It is estimated that, at any given time, there is a Lennon & McCartney composition being played on at least one US radio station – a graphic reminder of the partnership's colossal and ongoing royalty income.

THE 10 MOST PERFORMED SONGS IN THE UK BY BRITISH SONGWRITERS, 1962–71

	Title	Year	Songwriter(s)
1	My Sweet Lord	1971	George Harrison
2	Yellow River	1970	Jeff Christie
3	Ob-La-Di, Ob-La-Da	1969	John Lennon, Paul McCartney
4	Congratulations	1968	Bill Martin, Phil Coulter
5	Puppet On A String	1967	Bill Martin, Phil Coulter
6	Michelle	1966	John Lennon, Paul McCartney
7	I'll Never Find Another You	1965	Tom Springfield
8	Can't Buy Me Love	1964	John Lennon, Paul McCartney
9	She Loves You	1963	John Lennon, Paul McCartney
10	Stranger On The Shore	1962	Mr Acker Bilk

Source: PRS.

In an era dominated by the Beatles, there were also two big British Eurovision entries which became the most performed UK songs of their years: Cliff Richard came second with *Congratulations* in 1968 while Sandie Shaw's *Puppet On A String* won the Song For Europe competition in the previous year.

THE 10 MOST PERFORMED SONGS IN THE UK BY BRITISH SONGWRITERS, 1972–81

	Title	Year	Songwriter(s)
1	You Drive Me Crazy	1981	Ronnie Harwood
2	Together We Are Beautiful	1980	Ken Leray
3	Bright Eyes	1979	Mike Batt
4	Night Fever	1978	Barry Gibb, Maurice Gibb, Robin Gibb
5	Don't Cry For Me Argentina	1977	Tim Rice, Andrew Lloyd Webber
6	Save Your Kisses For Me	1976	Tony Hiller, Martin Lee, Lee Sheriden
7	I'm Not In Love	1975	Graham Gouldman, Eric Stewart
8	Wombling Song	1974	Mike Batt
9	Get Down	1973	Gilbert O'Sullivan
10	Beg, Steal Or Borrow	1972	Graeme Hall, Tony Cole, Steve Wolfe

Source: PRS.

Despite being the most performed songs of the era, numbers one and 10 are perhaps least remembered: *You Drive Me Crazy* was a No. 2 hit for Shakin' Stevens while *Beg, Steal Or Borrow* made the Top 3 for the New Seekers in 1972.

THE 10 MOST PERFORMED SONGS IN THE UK BY BRITISH SONGWRITERS, 1982–91

	Title	Year	Songwriter(s)*
1	I'm Too Sexy	1991	Fred Fairbrass, Rob Manzoli, Richard Fairbrass
2	Blue Savannah	1990	Andy Bell, Vince Clarke
3	This Time I Know It's For Real	1989	Mike Stock, Matt Aitken, Pete Waterman, (Donna Summer)
4	I Should Be So Lucky	1988	Mike Stock, Matt Aitken, Pete Waterman
5	Never Gonna Give You Up	1987	Mike Stock, Matt Aitken, Pete Waterman
6	Chain Reaction	1986	Barry Gibb, Maurice Gibb, Robin Gibb
7	Easy Lover	1985	Phil Collins, (Philip Bailey), (Nathan East)
8	Careless Whisper	1984	George Michael, Andrew Ridgeley
9	Every Breath You Take	1983	Gordon Sumner**
10	Golden Brown	1982	Jet Black, Hugh Cornwall, David Greenfield, (Jean-Jacques Burnell)

*   Writers listed in brackets are non-UK co-composers.   ** aka Sting.

Source: PRS.

Each year the Performing Right Society – the UK licensing agency responsible for collecting broadcast and performance royalties for songs written by British songwriters – assesses the most performed songs of the year for a subsequent presentation at the annual Ivor Novello Awards. Their listing is based on airplay data from radio and television broadcasters and the frequency of airplay in discos, clubs and other public performance outlets.

THE 10 MOST-WATCHED MUSIC PROGRAMMES ON BRITISH TELEVISION, 1992

	Programme	Channel	Broadcast date*	Audience
1	Top Of The Pops	BBC1	6 Feb	9,649,000
2	The Freddie Mercury Tribute	BBC2	20 Apr	6,994,000
3	Michael Jackson: The Dangerous Tour In Bucharest	BBC1	22 Nov	5,316,000
4	Rock Bottom	BBC2	31 Aug	4,913,000
5	Tom Jones – The Right Time	ITV	6 Jun	4,665,000
6	Tina Turner: The Girl From Nutbush	BBC1	25 Feb	4,136,000
7	Wet Wet Wet: In Concert	BBC1	16 Apr	3,717,000
8	Queen In Concert: A Tribute To Freddie Mercury (1982)	Channel 4	11 Jan	3,322,000
9	The Chart Show	ITV	7 Mar	2,962,000
10	The Michael Jackson Special	BBC2	13 Jul	2,927,000

* Peak audience only for regularly broadcast series, such as the weekly Top Of The Pops.

Source: AGB/BARB; 1 Jan–30 Nov 1992.

Jimmy (now Sir Jimmy) Savile hosts the first-ever Top Of The Pops *on 1 January 1964 – from a studio in a converted Manchester church!*

THE 10 HIGHEST-RATED NETWORKED MUSIC TV SERIES IN THE USA, 1950–90

	Programme	Year	% of TV audience*
1	Stop The Music	1951	34.0
2	Your Hit Parade	1958	33.6
3	The Perry Como Show	1956	32.6
4	Name That Tune	1958	26.7
5	The Dean Martin Show	1966	24.8
6	The Sonny & Cher Hour	1973	23.3
7	The Partridge Family	1972	22.6
8	The Glen Campbell Goodtime Hour	1968	22.5
9	The Johnny Cash Show	1969	21.8
10	Cher	1975	21.3

* Percentage of American households with TV sets watching the broadcast: the total of households rose from 3,800,000 in 1950 to 92,100,000 in 1990.

THE 10 HIGHEST-RATED NETWORKED MUSIC TV SHOWS IN THE USA, 1980–90

	Show	Broadcast date	% of TV audience*
1	The Grammy Awards	28 Feb 84	30.8
2	American Music Awards	16 Jan 84	27.4
3	American Music Awards	28 Jan 85	25.8
4=	American Music Awards	17 Jan 83	24.4
4=	Country Music Awards	11 Oct 82	24.4
6	The Grammy Awards	27 Feb 80	23.9
7	The Grammy Awards	26 Feb 85	23.8
8	Country Music Awards	13 Oct 80	22.9
9	Country Music Awards	10 Oct 83	22.6
10	American Music Awards	26 Jan 87	22.2

* Percentage of American households with TV sets watching the broadcast.

Pure rock/pop music series such as *American Bandstand* and *Soul Train* have never managed to penetrate the annual Top 20 highest audience share lists in the United States, where the market has always preferred middle-of-the-road music quiz programmes or variety-style broadcasts hosted by a famous music artist. With the dawn of MTV in the 1980s, the four major US networks have largely ignored music programming, with the exception of one-off music specials or concerts and the annual music award broadcasts, such as those for the Grammys, American Music Awards and Country Music Awards.

The Grammy Awards is primarily a music industry voting affair, while the American Music Awards is based on votes cast by the public and therefore tends to be a more teen-oriented broadcast. Among the plethora of annual music awards shows, which dominate US network music programming and prove far more popular than, say, *Soul Train* or *Casey Kasem's American Top 10* weekly programmes, the American viewing audience can also choose from the *MTV Music Awards* (broadcast on cable), the *Jukebox Music Awards*, the *International Rock Awards*, the *Billboard Music Awards*, the *Rock Music Awards* and the *Annual Country Music Awards*, a rival to the more successful *Country Music Awards* listed here.

10 MUSIC ACTS THAT HAVE HAD THEIR OWN US TELEVISION SERIES

	Act	Year first broadcast
1	Archies*	1968
2	Beatles*	1965
3	Glen Campbell	1969
4	David Cassidy (The Partridge Family)	1970
5	Donny & Marie Osmond	1976
6	MC Hammer*	1990
7	Jackson 5*	1971
8	KISS*	1978
9	Monkees	1966
10	Sonny & Cher**	1971

* Cartoon series   ** Cher also hosted her own series.

Two of these acts were specifically created for start-up television series: Filmation Studios were commissioned by CBS Television in 1967 to produce an animated Saturday morning show featuring the Archies, a fictional rock group based on the comic book characters created by John Goldwater in 1942. With songs mostly written by hit songwriting duo Jeff Barry and Ellie Greenwich, *The Archies* made its US TV debut on 14 September 1968 and proved so popular that it launched a hit singles career which climaxed with the global chart-topper *Sugar Sugar*. The Monkees were a similar TV-led creation originated by writer/producer/director Bob Rafelson who devised a pilot show based around a Beatles-type group using Richard Lester's *A Hard Day's Night* film as its framework. Among the 437 hopefuls who turned up at the auditions: Stephen Stills (of Crosby, Stills, Nash & Young), songwriter Paul Williams – and cult leader and murderer Charles Manson.

THE FIRST 10 ACTS TO APPEAR ON *SOUL TRAIN*

1	Gladys Knight & The Pips
2	Bobby Hutton
3	Honeycones
4	Eddie Kendrick
5	Watts 103rd Street Band
6	Carla Thomas
7	General Cook
8	Chairman Of The Board
9	Rufus Thomas
10	Laura Lee

Soul Train, conceived and hosted by Don Cornelius, made its American television broadcast debut on 17 August 1972, and quickly became the definitive soul/disco/dance showcase for R & B acts. The programme, which has also spawned the annual Soul Train Music Awards, recently celebrated its 20th anniversary of weekly broadcasts.

THE FIRST 10 ACTS TO APPEAR ON *AMERICAN BANDSTAND*

	Act	Song performed	Date
1	Billy Williams	*I'm Gonna Sit Right Down And Write Myself A Letter*	5 Aug 57
2	Chordettes	*Just Between You And Me*	5 Aug 57
3	Dale Hawkins	*Susie Q*	6 Aug 57
4	Don Rondo	*White Silver Sands*	6 Aug 57
5	Paul Anka	*Diana*	7 Aug 57
6	Lee Andrews & The Hearts	*Long Lonely Nights*	9 Aug 57
7	Gene Vincent & His Blue Caps	*Lotta Lovin'/Wear My Ring*	12 Aug 57
8	Four Coins	*Shangri-La*	12 Aug 57
9	Jodi Sands	*With All My Heart*	13 Aug 57
10	Sal Mineo	*Start Movin'/Lasting Love*	13 Aug 57

Notable as the first pop music TV programme, *American Bandstand*, hosted by Dick Clark, began nationwide American broadcasting on 67 stations on 5 August 1957. A five show per week long-lasting series, it usually included two or three artists performing live in the studio, mixed with the audience dancing to the audio tracks of the latest hottest pop hits.

THE FIRST 10 ACTS TO APPEAR ON *OH BOY!*

1	Marty Wilde
2	Dallas Boys
3	John Barry Seven
4	Lord Rockingham's XI
5	Cherry Wainer with Red Price
6	Neville Taylor & The Cutters
7	Vernon Girls
8	Bernice Reading
9	Dudley Heslop
10	Kerry Martin

Hosted by Jack Good, *Oh Boy!*, which was broadcast by ITV live from the Hackney Empire in London every Saturday at 6 p.m., debuted on 15 June 1958 with these artists. Notable as the first entirely Rock 'n' Roll orientated British TV show, it also contributed to the early success of Cliff Richard who appeared on the programme 20 times before it was axed on 30 May 1959.

THE FIRST 10 SONGS ON *TOP OF THE POPS*

	Title	Artist
1	*I Only Want To Be With You*	Dusty Springfield
2	*I Wanna Be Your Man*	Rolling Stones
3	*24 Hours From Tulsa*	Gene Pitney
4	*Glad All Over*	Dave Clark Five
5	*Don't Talk To Him*	Cliff Richard & The Shadows
6	*Stay*	Hollies
7	*She Loves You*	Beatles
8	*Hippy Hippy Shake*	Swinging Blue Jeans
9	*You Were Made For Me*	Freddie & The Dreamers
10	*I Want To Hold Your Hand*	Beatles

Top Of The Pops was first broadcast from a BBC TV Manchester studio on 1 January 1964 and presented by Jimmy Savile. All the featured records were from that week's UK Top 20. Five of them were served by film clips and/or dance sequences, while Dusty Springfield, the Rolling Stones, the Dave Clark Five, the Hollies and the Swinging Blue Jeans were present in the studio to lip-synch their songs.

THE 10 SINGLES REVIEWED BY THE BEATLES ON *JUKE BOX JURY*

	Title	Artist	Hit or miss	Highest chart position
1	I Could Write A Book	Chants	Hit (4–0)	–
2	Kiss Me Quick	Elvis Presley	Hit (4–0)	14
3	Hippy Hippy Shake	Swinging Blue Jeans	Hit (4–0)	2
4	Did You Have A Happy Birthday	Paul Anka	Miss (0–4)	–
5	The Nitty Gritty	Shirley Ellis	Miss (0–4)	–
6	I Can't Stop Talking About You	Steve Lawrence and Eydie Gorme	Hit (3–1)*	–
7	Do You Really Love Me Too	Billy Fury	Hit (4–0)	13
8	There, I've Said It Again	Bobby Vinton	Miss (0–4)	34
9	Love Hit Me	Orchids	Miss (1–3)**	–
10	I Think Of You	Merseybeats	Hit (4–0)	5

* *Dissenting vote from John who said, 'They're getting on a bit – I don't like it.'*   ** *The dissenting vote was from Ringo who thought it wouldn't sell.*

The four Beatles appeared on BBC television's *Juke Box Jury* on 7 December 1963, the first time a group had constituted the entire panel. They discussed and voted upon the likely hit potential of 10 singles introduced by DJ David Jacobs, and were accurate in their predictions on seven of the records.

THE TOP 10 SINGLES OF TV THEME TUNES IN THE UK

	Title	Artist	Programme
1	Stranger On The Shore	Mr Acker Bilk	Stranger On The Shore
2	Eye Level	Simon Park Orchestra	Van Der Valk
3	The Wombling Song	Wombles	The Wombles
4	The Army Game	TV Cast	The Army Game
5	Something Tells Me	Cilla Black	The Cilla Black Show
6	I Could Be So Good For You	Dennis Waterman	Minder
7	Staccato's Theme	Elmer Bernstein	Johnny Staccato
8	Theme From Harry's Game	Clannad	Harry's Game
9	Doina De Jale	Gheorghe Zamfir	Light Of Experience
10	Miami Vice Theme	Jan Hammer	Miami Vice

These themes, equally divided between instrumentals and vocal, cover more than 30 years of British TV shows. All those listed here were Top 5 hits following exposure on the programme concerned, and the top two not only both reached No. 1 on the chart, but also each sold over 1,000,000 in the UK. One or two of the records have also decidedly outgrown their parent shows – who today still recalls the 1961 children's drama series *Stranger On The Shore?*

THE FIRST 10 ARTISTS TO APPEAR IN PEPSI-COLA COMMERCIALS

1	Michael Jackson
2	Lionel Richie
3	Glenn Frey
4	Robert Palmer
5	Linda Ronstadt
6	Tina Turner
7	David Bowie
8	Gloria Estefan
9	MC Hammer
10	Ray Charles

Though Pepsi featured many celebrities in their TV advertising as early as the 1950s (when James Dean was a Pepsi spokesman), it was not until their signing of Michael Jackson in 1985 that their commercials began a new era of big-event music marketing. The current Ray Charles campaign in the United States has been so successful (with its vocal backing line 'Uh-Uh' becoming a nationwide catchphrase) that he was voted 'Most Persuasive Celebrity Spokesman' in 1992. He is also the only performer to have made TV commercials for both Coke and Pepsi.

THE FIRST 10 ARTISTS TO FEATURE IN A COCA-COLA TELEVISION COMMERCIAL

	Artist	Jingle	Year
1	McGuire Sisters	*Pause For A Coke*	1958
2=	Brothers Four*	*Refreshing New Feeling*	1960
2=	Anita Bryant	*Refreshing New Feeling*	1960
2=	Connie Francis	*Refreshing New Feeling*	1960
5=	Fortunes	*Things Go Better With Coke*	1963
5=	Limelighters*	*Things Go Better With Coke*	1963
7	Ray Charles	*Things Go Better With Coke*	1969
8=	Bobby Goldboro	*It's The Real Thing*	1971
8=	New Seekers*	*It's The Real Thing*	1971
10	Dottie West*	*It's The Real Thing (Country Sunshine)*	1972

* Artist provided only the audio soundtrack for the commercial.

Today's pop audience assumes that the inclusion of George Michael, Elton John or Paula Abdul in Coke commercials is a new phenomenon. Coke has in fact featured music artists in its promotion since the turn of the century, when they enlisted the support of popular opera stars. Going on to sponsor music TV shows in the 1950s for the likes of Eddie Fisher and Mario Lanza, the company has always had close musical ties, including 1980s ads featuring the Thompson Twins, Robert Plant, Chuck Berry and even Julio Iglesias.

THE FIRST 10 'OLDIES' USED ON LEVI'S TV COMMERCIALS IN THE UK

	Title	Artist
1	*I Heard It Through The Grapevine*	Marvin Gaye
2	*Wonderful World*	Sam Cooke
3	*Stand By Me*	Ben E. King
4	*When A Man Loves A Woman*	Percy Sledge
5	*C'Mon Everybody*	Eddie Cochran
6	*Mannish Boy*	Muddy Waters
7	*Be My Baby*	Ronettes
8	*Ain't Nobody Home*	B.B. King
9	*Can't Get Enough*	Bad Company
10	*The Joker*	Steve Miller Band

In 1986, Levi's jeans began to use hit records from the past as the soundtracks to their UK TV commercials, a practice which has been continued ever since. This soon proved beneficial not only to jeans sales, but to the fortunes of the singles which were reissued to capitalize on this exposure. Ben E. King and Steve Miller reached No. 1 (as did the 11th track used, the Clash's *Should I Stay Or Should I Go?*), and only the Ronettes' single failed completely – through *not* being reissued.

THE FIRST 10 MUSIC VIDEOS BROADCAST BY MTV (USA)

	Title	Artist
1	Video Killed The Radio Star	Buggles
2	You Better Run	Pat Benatar
3	She Won't Dance With Me	Rod Stewart
4	You Better You Bet	Who
5	Little Susie's On The Up	PhD
6	We Don't Talk Anymore	Cliff Richard
7	Brass In Pocket	Pretenders
8	Time Heals	Todd Rundgren
9	Take It On The Run	REO Speedwagon
10	Rockin' The Paradise	Styx

Source: MTV.

This varied line-up inaugurated the world's first 24-hour music video network on 1 August 1981. What makes this list all the more interesting is that it may be the only occasion that Cliff Richard has ever been featured on MTV (this song remains his only major hit in the United States). Six of the 10 are British acts, there are no R & B videos (a policy that MTV persevered with until the explosion of Michael Jackson's *Thriller* project) and little-known British duo, PhD, who have never secured a US chart record, make an incongruous appearance at number five.

THE FIRST 10 MUSIC VIDEOS BROADCAST ON MTV EUROPE

	Title	Artist
1	Money For Nothing	Dire Straits
2	Fake	Alexander O'Neal
3	U Got The Look	Prince with Sheena Easton
4	It's A Sin	Pet Shop Boys
5	I Wanna Dance With Somebody (Who Loves Me)	Whitney Houston
6	I Want Your Sex	George Michael
7	Who's That Girl	Madonna
8	I Really Didn't Mean It	Luther Vandross
9	Misfit	Curiosity Killed The Cat
10	Higher And Higher	Jackie Wilson

MTV Europe began its pan-European broadcasting on 1 August 1987 with a most appropriate video clip by Dire Straits featuring the opening lyrics, sung by its co-writer, Sting: *I Want My MTV*. Now an integral part of our cultural landscape, MTV Europe celebrated its fifth anniversary in 1992 with a party at the House of Commons.

10 MUSIC ACTS THAT HAVE HAD THEIR OWN BRITISH TELEVISION SERIES

	Act	Year first broadcast
1	Cilla Black	1968
2	Marc Bolan	1977
3	John Denver	1973
4	Lonnie Donegan	1958
5	David Essex	1988
6	Jools Holland	1982
7	Lulu	1965
8	Cliff Richard	1970
9	Leo Sayer	1978
10	Scott Walker	1969

Several of these music celebrities have hosted more than one series: Cilla Black (*Cilla, Surprise, Surprise, Blind Date*), Jools Holland (*The Tube, Juke Box Jury*), Lulu (*Stramash, The Whole Scene Going, Three Of A Kind, Lulu*), Cliff Richard (a number of different musical variety show series which regularly featured Olivia Newton-John) and Leo Sayer (who returned for a second *Leo Sayer* BBC TV series in 1983). American Country singer John Denver's TV series was curiously first broadcast in the UK: his weekly live BBC television *The John Denver Show* preceded his US variety shows, premiering from the Shepherds Bush Green studios on 29 April 1973.

THE TOP 10 ELVIS PRESLEY FILM SONGS IN THE UK*

	Title	Film	Year
1	Jailhouse Rock	Jailhouse Rock	1957
2	Wooden Heart	G.I. Blues	1960
3	Return To Sender	Girls! Girls! Girls!	1962
4	Can't Help Falling In Love	Blue Hawaii	1961
5	Teddy Bear	Loving You	1957
6	King Creole	King Creole	1958
7	Let's Have A Party	Loving You	1957
8	Hard Headed Woman	King Creole	1958
9	I Just Can't Help Believing	Elvis – That's The Way It Is	1970
10	Always On My Mind	Elvis On Tour	1972

* Based on UK sales.

Elvis' film-extracted singles from 1963–69, which actually formed the bulk of his releases during this period, ironically sold much less well than those from the 1950s, when his recording career was paramount, or from the 1970s, when he was concentrating on live performance. The title song from his first film, *Love Me Tender*, though a multi-million seller in the United States, was a much smaller hit in Britain, and would fall at No. 14 if this list were extended.

THE 10 HIGHEST-GROSSING ELVIS PRESLEY FILMS

	Film	Year	Gross ($)
1	Viva Las Vegas	1964	5,500,000
2	Blue Hawaii	1961	4,700,000
3	Love Me Tender	1956	4,500,000
4	G.I. Blues	1960	4,300,000
5	Jailhouse Rock	1957	4,000,000
6	Loving You	1957	3,700,000
7	Girls! Girls! Girls!	1962	3,600,000
8	Tickle Me	1965	3,400,000
9	Roustabout	1964	3,300,000
10	Girl Happy	1965	3,200,000

Presley's most successful cinema period broadly mirrored his initial spell as the world's biggest-selling pop star, although, interestingly, his biggest-grossing movie of all was screened precisely when this initial success was waning, courtesy of the Beatles. The explanation is almost certainly that in *Viva Las Vegas* he had, uniquely, a major-name leading lady – Ann-Margret – with screen dynamism to match Elvis's, as well as a huge fan following of her own.

THE 10 OSCAR-WINNING SONGS OF THE 1940s

Year	Title	Film
1940	When You Wish Upon A Star	Pinocchio
1941	The Last Time I Saw Paris	Lady Be Good
1942	White Christmas	Holiday Inn
1943	You'll Never Know	Hello Frisco, Hello
1944	Swinging On A Star	Going My Way
1945	It Might As Well Be Spring	State Fair
1946	On The Atcheson, Topeka And The Sante Fe	The Harvey Girls
1947	Zip-A-Dee-Doo-Dah	Song Of The South
1948	Buttons And Bows	The Paleface
1949	Baby, It's Cold Outside	Neptune's Daughter

The 'Best Song' category was introduced into the Academy Awards in 1934, when it was won by *The Continental* from the film *The Gay Divorcee*. The other winners of the 1930s were: 1935 – *Lullaby Of Broadway* (*Gold Diggers Of 1935*); 1936 – *The Way You Look Tonight* (*Swing Time*); 1937 – *Sweet Leilani* (*Waikiki Wedding*); 1938 – *Thanks For The Memory* (*Big Broadcast Of 1938*); and 1939 – *Over The Rainbow* (*The Wizard Of Oz*).

THE 10 OSCAR-WINNING SONGS OF THE 1950s

Year	Title	Film
1950	Mona Lisa	Captain Carey USA
1951	In The Cool, Cool Of The Evening	Here Comes The Groom
1952	High Noon	High Noon
1953	Secret Love	Calamity Jane
1954	Three Coins In The Fountain	Three Coins In The Fountain
1955	Love Is A Many-Splendored Thing	Love Is A Many-Splendored Thing
1956	Whatever Will Be, Will Be	The Man Who Knew Too Much
1957	All The Way	The Joker Is Wild
1958	Gigi	Gigi
1959	High Hopes	A Hole In The Head

Most of these songs, like the majority of Oscar-winning movie themes, went on to become big hit singles in both the UK and USA. Frank Sinatra dominated in the 1950s, performing the songs from 1954, 1957 and 1959.

Audrey Hepburn strumming Moon River *from* Breakfast At Tiffany's, *winner of the 1961 Oscar for Best Song.*

THE 10 OSCAR-WINNING SONGS OF THE 1960s

Year	Title	Film
1960	Never On A Sunday	Never On A Sunday
1961	Moon River	Breakfast At Tiffany's
1962	Days Of Wine And Roses	Days Of Wine And Roses
1963	Call Me Irresponsible	Papa's Delicate Condition
1964	Chim Chim Cheree	Mary Poppins
1965	The Shadow Of Your Smile	The Sandpiper
1966	Born Free	Born Free
1967	Talk To The Animals	Dr Doolittle
1968	The Windmills Of Your Mind	The Thomas Crown Affair
1969	Raindrops Keep Falling On My Head	Butch Cassidy And The Sundance Kid

Both Noel Harrison's *The Windmills Of Your Mind* and B. J. Thomas' *Raindrops Keep Falling On My Head* hit the US Top 10, while French crooner Sacha Distel's cover version of the 1969 Oscar-winner charted no less than five times in the UK, all in one year, 1970.

THE 10 OSCAR-WINNING SONGS OF THE 1970s

Year	Title	Film
1970	For All We Know	Lovers And Other Strangers
1971	Theme From 'Shaft'	Shaft
1972	The Morning After	The Poseidon Adventure
1973	The Way We Were	The Way We Were
1974	We May Never Love Like This Again	The Towering Inferno
1975	I'm Easy	Nashville
1976	Evergreen	A Star Is Born
1977	You Light Up My Life	You Light Up My Life
1978	Last Dance	Thank God It's Friday
1979	It Goes Like It Goes	Norma Rae

THE 10 OSCAR-WINNING SONGS OF THE 1980s

Year	Title	Film
1980	Fame	Fame
1981	Up Where We Belong	An Officer And A Gentleman
1982	Arthur's Theme (Best That You Can Do)	Arthur
1983	Flashdance	Flashdance
1984	I Just Called To Say I Love You	The Woman In Red
1985	Say You, Say Me	White Nights
1986	Take My Breath Away	Top Gun
1987	(I've Had) The Time Of My Life	Dirty Dancing
1988	Let The River Run	Working Girl
1989	Under The Sea	The Little Mermaid

Barbra Streisand became the first artist since Frank Sinatra to win two Oscar song awards in the same decade, with *The Way We Were* and *Evergreen*, both of which went on to become huge international hits. Isaac Hayes' memorable *Theme From 'Shaft'*, in addition to being a rare 'non-ballad' winner, became an influential milestone in both film and TV theme music, often copied but never equalled throughout the rest of the decade.

Award winners in the 1990s are: 1990 – *Sooner Or Later (I Always Get My Man)* from *Dick Tracy*; 1991 – *Beauty And The Beast* from the Disney film of the same name; and 1992 – *Whole New World* from *Aladdin*. Of the winning songs of the 1980s only the one from *The Little Mermaid* did not make the Top 10 in both the UK and US singles charts.

Fame, from the film of the same name, won the Best Song Oscar in 1980.

THE TOP 10 JAMES BOND FILM THEMES IN THE UK

	Title	Artist	Film
1	A View To A Kill	Duran Duran	Same
2	The Living Daylights	a-ha	Same
3	Licence To Kill	Gladys Knight	Same
4	Nobody Does It Better	Carly Simon	The Spy Who Loved Me
5	For Your Eyes Only	Sheena Easton	Same
6	Live And Let Die	Paul McCartney & Wings	Same
7	You Only Live Twice	Nancy Sinatra	Same
8	The James Bond Theme	John Barry	Dr No
9	Goldfinger	Shirley Bassey	Same
10	Casino Royale	Herb Alpert's Tijuana Brass	Same

Not all the James Bond themes have been major hits. Although all 10 in this list reached the Top 30, only the first six made the Top 10, and there has never been a Bond-associated No. 1 hit. Themes from certain of the films (*The Man With The Golden Gun*, *Moonraker* and *On Her Majesty's Secret Service*) failed to chart at all, even though major artists (Lulu, Shirley Bassey and Louis Armstrong) were involved.

ROCK AND THE MOVIES

The appearance of Bill Haley & His Comets performing *(We're Gonna) Rock Around The Clock* in the 1955 movie *The Blackboard Jungle* was the fuse that lit the Rock 'n' Roll fire. Rock has maintained its close ties with the film industry ever since.

Initially prevalent as a musical comedy medium, both Elvis Presley and Cliff Richard substantially widened their pop appeal via a succession of lightweight but often lucrative romantic Rock 'n' Roll vehicles. Elvis's early pictures included *Love Me Tender* (1956), *Loving You* (1957), *Jailhouse Rock* (1957) and *King Creole* (1957); Cliff's first entry into celluloid was his part as Bongo Herbert in *Expresso Bongo* (1959), followed by the successful *The Young Ones* (1961), *Summer Holiday* (1963) and *Wonderful Life* (1964, filmed in the Canary Islands with his regular backing band, the Shadows).

While the Beatles continued this Rock 'n' Roll film tradition with *A Hard Day's Night* and *Help!*, it was not until the late 1960s that live concert footage made up an entire film. *Woodstock*, a lengthy documentary chronicling the legendary August 1969 Music and Art Festival, captured the spirit, size and musical history that was made by the likes of Joe Cocker, Jimi Hendrix, Crosby, Stills, Nash & Young, Santana and the Who. The documentary concert movie, filmed for general release in cinemas, became a regular event in the 1970s, and included: *Born To Boogie* (1972, the T. Rex movie directed by Ringo Starr), *Abba: The Movie* (1977), *Celebration At Big Sur* (1971, a Woodstock copy), *The Concert For Bangladesh* (1972), *Gimme Shelter* (1970, the 1969 Rolling Stones Altamont concert), *The Kids Are Alright* (1979, the Who), *Pink Floyd At Pompeii* (1971) and most notably, *The Last Waltz* (1978, directed by Martin Scorsese and capturing the Band's final concert appearance). The rockumentary/documentary is still alive today as witnessed by recent live film cinematic releases by U2 (*Rattle And Hum*), Madonna (*Truth Or Dare*) and the Rolling Stones (*Steel Wheels Tour* 1989–90, released in 1992 as the first IMAX wide-screen rock film).

Aside from the artistic assumption made by a great number of rock artists that they can also act, among them David Bowie, Mick Jagger, Sting, Phil Collins, Tina Turner, Debbie Harry, Adam Ant, Prince and Lyle Lovett, the remaining, and most successful area where the two industries meet has been via the soundtrack. Some of the biggest-selling albums of all time have been simply the vinyl spin-offs from movies, from *The Sound Of Music* and *South Pacific* through *Saturday Night Fever* and *Grease* right up to the more recent multi-platinum soundtrack to *The Bodyguard*. The latter is a good example of the increasing synergy employed by the major entertainment conglomerates (many of which now include both music and film divisions) where the accompanying music, previously an afterthought, is now often an integral part of the film package, even to the point of supplying the film's title, as in the case of such films as *Pretty Woman* and *Stand By Me*.

ROCK & THE MOVIES QUIZ

1. Who took the lead role in the films *That'll Be The Day* and *Stardust*?

2. What was the Beatles' first movie?

3. Who played Ace in the film version of the Who's *Quadrophenia*?

4. Which of the following movies has David Bowie *not* appeared in: *Into The Night*, *The Hunger*, *The Man Who Sold The World*, *The Last Temptation Of Christ*, *The Man Who Fell To Earth*, *Merry Christmas, Mr Lawrence*?

5. Which group was largely responsible for providing the music to the hit film *Saturday Night Fever*?

6. What actor wrote and sang the 1975 winner of the 'Best Song' Oscar, *I'm Easy* from the film *Nashville*?

7. Who took the lead role in the 1978 biopic, *The Buddy Holly Story*?

8. What was the title of Paul McCartney's feature-length movie in 1985?

9. Who played 'The Jazz Singer' in the 1980 film of this title?

10. In which film, for which she also secured a Top 5 hit with its theme, did Tina Turner star?

THE TOP 10 MUSICAL FILMS OF ALL TIME

	Film	Year
1	Grease	1978
2	The Sound Of Music	1965
3	Saturday Night Fever	1977
4	American Graffiti	1973
5	The Best Little Whorehouse In Texas	1982
6	Mary Poppins	1964
7	Fiddler On The Roof	1971
8	Annie	1982
9	A Star Is Born	1976
10	Flashdance	1983

Traditional musicals (films in which the cast actually sing) and films in which a musical soundtrack forms a major component of the film are included. Several other musical films have also each earned in excess of $30,000,000 in North American rentals, among them *Coalminer's Daughter* (1980), *The Rocky Horror Picture Show* (1975), *Footloose* (1984), *The Blues Brothers* (1980) and *Purple Rain* (1984), but it would appear that the era of the blockbuster musical film is over.

THE TOP 10 MUSIC VIDEOS OF 1992 IN THE UK

	Title	Artist
1	Greatest Flix 2	Queen
2	Moving Picture Book	Simply Red
3	We Will Rock You	Queen
4	Divine Madness	Madness
5	Box Of Flix	Queen
6	Greatest Hits	ZZ Top
7	The Three Tenors Concert	Carreras, Domingo, Pavarotti
8	Queen Live At Wembley	Queen
9	Kylie's Greatest Hits	Kylie Minogue
10	Queen's Greatest Flix	Queen

Queen dominated the market in music video sales during 1992, perhaps inevitably following the death of Freddie Mercury and the consequently even higher profile which the group's music achieved. The *Greatest Flix* releases and *Box Of Flix* (a three-tape boxed set) were compilations of promo clips for Queen singles, while the other two tapes both captured vintage live performances.

THE TOP 10 MUSIC VIDEOS OF ALL TIME IN THE UK

	Title	Artist
1	The Three Tenors Concert	Carreras, Domingo, Pavarotti
2	Queen's Greatest Flix	Queen
3	Kylie: The Video	Kylie Minogue
4	Making Michael Jackson's 'Thriller'	Michael Jackson
5	The Immaculate Collection	Madonna
6	Greatest Flix 2	Queen
7	U2: Rattle And Hum	U2
8	Pavarotti In The Park	Luciano Pavarotti
9	Hangin' Tough	New Kids On The Block
10	The Legend Continues	Michael Jackson

Music video sales in the UK reached a peak in the late 1980s, since when the format has marked time: as sell-through video continued to grow, music titles seemed to succumb early to recessionary pressures, and failed to move with it. One of the exceptions, amazingly, was a classical release – the visual version of the three tenors' Milan concert on the eve of the 1990 World Cup matched the success of the audio version, being consistently one of the biggest-selling videos for some three years.

THE TOP 10 MUSIC VIDEOS OF ALL TIME IN THE USA

	Title	Artist
1	Hangin' Tough – Live	New Kids On The Block
2	Hangin' Tough	New Kids On The Block
3	Step By Step	New Kids On The Block
4	Moonwalker	Michael Jackson
5	Garth Brooks	Garth Brooks
6	Justify My Love	Madonna
7	Video Anthology 1978–1988	Bruce Springsteen
8	This Is Garth Brooks	Garth Brooks
9	In Concert	Carreras, Domingo, Pavarotti
10	Hammer Time	MC Hammer

Source: *RIAA*.

While the Recording Industry Association of America's sales certifications for music videos began only in 1986, it is likely that *The Making Of Michael Jackson's 'Thriller'* (1984) is the only earlier video that would appear in this list. It would struggle, however, to match the New Kids' phenomenal music video achievements: numbers one, two and three have all sold more than 1,000,000 copies each, compared to *Moonwalker's* 800,000 units. As sales of music videos in the United States began a dramatic decline in 1992, only Country superstar Garth Brooks currently seems able to shift more than 300,000 units.

THE TOP 10 MUSIC VIDEOS OF 1992 IN THE USA

	Title	Artist
1	This Is Garth Brooks	Garth Brooks
2	Billy Ray Cyrus	Billy Ray Cyrus
3	The Judds: Their Final Concert	Judds
4	Jump	Kris Kross
5	Greatest Hits	ZZ Top
6	Soul And Passion	Michael Bolton
7	MTV Unplugged + 3	Mariah Carey
8	Achtung Baby	U2
9	Unplugged	Eric Clapton
10	Live At The El Mocambo	Stevie Ray Vaughan & Double Trouble

THE 10 LONGEST-RUNNING MUSICALS OF ALL TIME ON BROADWAY

	Show	Performances
1	A Chorus Line (1979–90)	6,137
2	Cats (1982–)	4,274*
3	42nd Street (1980–89)	3,486
4	Grease (1972–80)	3,388
5	Fiddler On The Roof (1964–72)	3,242
6	Hello Dolly! (1964–71)	2,844
7	My Fair Lady (1956–62)	2,717
8	Annie (1977–83)	2,377
9	Les Misérables (1987–)	2,360*
10	Man Of La Mancha (1965–71)	2,328

* *Still running; total at 31 December 1992.*

Off Broadway, the musical show *The Fantasticks* by Tom Jones and Harvey Schmidt has been performed continuously at the Sullivan Street Playhouse, New York, since 3 May 1960 – a total of more than 13,500 performances.

THE 10 LONGEST-RUNNING MUSICALS OF ALL TIME IN THE UK

	Show	Performances
1	The Black And White Minstrel Show	6,464
2	Me And My Girl	5,524
3	Cats	4,871*
4	Oliver!	4,125
5	Starlight Express	3,635*
6	Jesus Christ, Superstar	3,357
7	Les Misérables	2,932*
8	Evita	2,900
9	Phantom Of The Opera	2,671*
10	The Sound Of Music	2,386

* *Still running; total at 31 December 1992.*

The *Black And White Minstrel Show* total includes both the original 10-year run (1962–72) and the 1973 revival. *Me And My Girl* opened at the Victoria Palace on 16 December 1937 and, apart from a brief closure in 1939, ran until 29 June 1940, by which time it had achieved 1,646 performances. Revivals in 1941, 1945–46, 1949–50 and 1985–16 January 1993 boosted the total to make it the UK's longest-running musical comedy of all time. Total performances of *Oliver!* include runs at different theatres from 1960–66, 1967–68, 1977–80 and 1983–84. On 12 May 1989 *Cats*, which opened in 1981, became the longest continuously running musical in British theatre history. In 1991 *My Fair Lady*, formerly at number 10 with 2,281 performances, was relegated from the list when the continuing run of *Les Misérables* overtook it, and the subsequent entry of *Phantom Of The Opera* displaced *Salad Days* (2,283 performances).

THE 10 OPERAS MOST FREQUENTLY PERFORMED AT THE ROYAL OPERA HOUSE, COVENT GARDEN, 1833–1992

	Opera	Composer	First performance	Total
1	La Bohème	Giacomo Puccini	2 Oct 1897	485
2	Carmen	Georges Bizet	27 May 1882	478
3	Aïda	Giuseppi Verdi	22 Jun 1876	446
4	Faust	Charles Gounod	18 Jul 1863	428
5	Rigoletto	Giuseppi Verdi	14 May 1853	423
6	Don Giovanni	Wolfgang Amadeus Mozart	17 Apr 1834	365
7	Norma	Vincenzo Bellini	12 Jul 1833	353
8	Tosca	Giacomo Puccini	12 Jul 1900	342
9	La Traviata	Giuseppi Verdi	25 May 1858	339
10	Madama Butterfly	Giacomo Puccini	10 Jul 1905	325

The total number of performances is up to 31 July 1992. The records are complete back to 1847, but for the two operas premiered earlier, the figure is based on the best available evidence.

THE 10 OPERAS MOST FREQUENTLY PERFORMED AT THE ROYAL OPERA HOUSE, COVENT GARDEN, 1946–92*

	Opera	Composer	First performance	Total
1	La Bohème	Giacomo Puccini	15 Oct 1948	277
2	Carmen	Georges Bizet	14 Jan 1947	269
3	Aïda	Giuseppi Verdi	29 Sep 1948	253
4	Tosca	Giacomo Puccini	18 Nov 1950	218
5=	Rigoletto	Giuseppi Verdi	31 Oct 1947	194
5=	Le Nozze di Figaro	Wolfgang Amadeus Mozart	22 Jan 1949	194
7	Die Zauberflöte	Wolfgang Amadeus Mozart	20 Mar 1947	188
8	La Traviata	Giuseppi Verdi	6 Apr 1948	173
9	Madama Butterfly	Giacomo Puccini	17 Jan 1950	171
10	Der Rosenkavalier	Richard Strauss	22 Apr 1947	161

* Royal Opera at Royal Opera House only, excluding performances on tour and performances by visiting companies.

Contrasting with the Royal Opera House's 'all-time' list, this Top 10 for performances from 1946 to 1992 gives a view of modern taste. During this period La Bohème has risen from 2nd to 1st place while Carmen (which once held 1st place) fell to 3rd but has recently climbed to 2nd; Rigoletto has similarly moved up one place. Le Nozze di Figaro, Die Zauberflöte and Der Rosenkavalier do not appear at all in the all-time list. Mozart's Don Giovanni has left the Top 10 altogether, and Charles Gounod's Faust, number four in the all-time list with 428 performances, and Vincenzo Bellini's Norma, number seven with 353, do not even feature in the post-war Top 20.

A scene from Bizet's Carmen. *Although among the Royal Opera House's most performed operas, it has consistently been beaten into second place by* La Bohème.

THE 10 LARGEST OPERA HOUSES IN THE WORLD

	Opera house	Location	seating	Capacity standing	total
1	The Metropolitan Opera	New York, USA	3,800	265	4,065
2	Cincinnati Opera	Cincinnati, USA	3,630	–	3,630
3	Lyric Opera of Chicago	Chicago, USA	3,563	–	3,563
4	San Francisco Opera	San Francisco, USA	3,176	300	3,476
5	The Dallas Opera	Dallas, USA	3,420	–	3,420
6	Canadian Opera Company	Toronto, Canada	3,167	–	3,167
7	Los Angeles Music Center Opera	Los Angeles, USA	3,098	–	3,098
8	San Diego Opera	San Diego, USA	2,992	84	3,076
9	Seattle Opera	Seattle, USA	3,017	–	3,017
10	L'Opéra de Montréal	Montreal, Canada	2,874	–	2,874

THE 10 LARGEST OPERA HOUSES IN EUROPE

	Opera house	Location	seating	Capacity standing	total
1	Opera Bastille	Paris, France	2,716	–	2,716
2	Gran Teatre del Liceu	Barcelona, Spain	2,700	–	2,700
3	English National Opera	London, UK	2,356	75	2,431
4	Staatsoper	Vienna, Austria	1,709	567	2,276
5	Teatro alla Scala	Milan, Italy	2,015	150	2,165
6	Bol'Shoy Theatre	Moscow, Russia	2,153	*	2,153
7	The Royal Opera House	London, UK	2,067	42	2,109
8	Bayerische Staatsoper	Munich, Germany	1,773	328	2,101
9	Bayreuth Festspielhaus	Bayreuth, Germany	1,925	–	1,925
10	Teatro Comunale	Florence, Italy	1,890	–	1,890

* Standing capacity unspecified.

THE 10 LARGEST OPERA HOUSES IN THE REST OF THE WORLD*

	Opera house	Location	seating	Capacity standing	total
1	Teatro Colon	Buenos Aires, Argentina	2,467	–	2,467
2	Teatro Municipal	Rio de Janeiro, Brazil	2,357	–	2,357
3	Victoria State Opera	Melbourne, Australia	2,000	–	2,000
4	State Opera of South Australia	Adelaide, Australia	1,837	–	1,837
5	Opera Nacional	Mexico City, Mexico	1,750	–	1,750
6	Australian Opera	Sydney, Australia	1,547	22	1,569
7	Nissei Theatre	Tokyo, Japan	1,238	–	1,238
8=	Teatro Municipal	Santiago, Chile	1,200	–	1,200
8=	Egyptian Opera House	Cairo, Egypt	1,200	–	1,200
10	New Israeli Opera	Tel Aviv, Israel	830	–	830

* Excluding North America and Europe.

THE 10 LONGEST OPERAS PERFORMED AT THE ROYAL OPERA HOUSE, COVENT GARDEN

	Opera	Composer	Running time* hr:min
1	Götterdämmerung	Richard Wagner	6:00
2	Die Meistersinger von Nürnberg	Richard Wagner	5:40
3	Siegfried	Richard Wagner	5:25
4	Tristan und Isolde	Richard Wagner	5:19
5	Die Walküre	Richard Wagner	5:15
6	Parsifal	Richard Wagner	5:09
7	Donnerstag aus Licht	Karlheinz Stockhausen	4:42
8	Lohengrin	Richard Wagner	4:26
9	Der Rosenkavalier	Richard Strauss	4:25
10	Don Carlo	Giuseppe Verdi	4:19

* Including intervals.

AWARDS AND FAVOURITES

THE 10 ACTS WITH MOST PLATINUM ALBUMS IN THE USA

	Artist	Platinum albums
1	Elvis Presley	28
2	Barbra Streisand	20
3	Chicago	17
4=	Beatles	16
4=	Rolling Stones	16
6=	Paul McCartney	12
6=	Linda Ronstadt	12
8=	AC/DC	11
8=	Neil Diamond	11
8=	Billy Joel	11
8=	Kenny Rogers	11
8=	Bruce Springsteen	11
8=	Led Zeppelin	11

Source: *RIAA.; to October 1992.*

This award, made by the Recording Industry Association of America, the trade association of record companies in the United States, confirms a minimum sale of 1,000,000 copies of an album.

THE 10 GROUPS WITH MOST PLATINUM ALBUMS IN THE USA

	Artist	Platinum albums
1	Chicago	17
2=	Beatles	16
2=	Rolling Stones	16
4=	AC/DC	11
4=	Led Zeppelin	11
6	KISS	10
7=	Aerosmith	9
7=	Alabama	9
7=	Rush	9
10=	Credence Clearwater Revival	8
10=	Earth Wind & Fire	8
10=	Heart	8
10=	Journey	8
10=	Pink Floyd	8
10=	REO Speedwagon	8

Source: *RIAA.; to October 1992.*

THE 10 FEMALE ARTISTS WITH MOST PLATINUM ALBUMS IN THE USA

	Artist	Platinum albums
1	Barbra Streisand	20
2	Linda Ronstadt	12
3	Madonna	9
4=	Pat Benatar	6
4=	Olivia Newton-John	6
6	Amy Grant	5
7	Anne Murray	4
8=	Whitney Houston	3
8=	Reba McEntire	3
8=	Donna Summer	3

Source: *RIAA; to October 1992.*

The most recent female artist to receive a platinum award on this list is Madonna for her October 1992 album *Erotica*.

THE 10 MALE ARTISTS WITH MOST PLATINUM ALBUMS IN THE USA

	Artist	Platinum albums
1	Elvis Presley	28
2	Paul McCartney	12
3=	Neil Diamond	11
3=	Billy Joel	11
3=	Kenny Rogers	11
3=	Bruce Springsteen	11
7=	Willie Nelson	9
7=	Prince	9
7=	Bob Seger	9
7=	Rod Stewart	9

Source: *RIAA.; to October 1992.*

THE 10 ACTS WITH MOST GOLD ALBUMS IN THE USA

	Artist	Gold albums
1	Elvis Presley	60
2	Rolling Stones	34
3	Barbra Streisand	30
4	Elton John	26
5	Beatles	25
6	Neil Diamond	23
7	Bob Dylan	21
8	Kenny Rogers	20
9=	Frank Sinatra	19
9=	Chicago	19

Source: RIAA; to October 1992.

This award, made by the Recording Industry Association of America, confirms a minimum sale of 500,000 copies of an album. The RIAA began certification for gold records in 1958, when the *Oklahoma* Original Soundtrack was awarded the first such honour.

Elvis Presley receives one of his record-breaking 60 gold discs.

THE 10 FEMALE ARTISTS WITH MOST GOLD ALBUMS IN THE USA

	Artist	Gold albums
1	Barbra Streisand	30
2	Linda Ronstadt	16
3	Olivia Newton-John	13
4=	Anne Murray	11
4=	Donna Summer	11
6=	Aretha Franklin	10
6=	Reba McEntire	10
8=	Pat Benatar	9
8=	Madonna	9
10=	Amy Grant	8
10=	Helen Reddy	8

Source: RIAA; to October 1992.

THE 10 GROUPS WITH MOST GOLD ALBUMS IN THE USA

	Artist	Gold albums
1	Rolling Stones	34
2	Beatles	25
3	Chicago	19
4	Kiss	18
5	Beach Boys	17
6	Jefferson Airplane/Starship*	16
7	Rush	15
8=	AC/DC	14
8=	Alabama	14
8=	Jethro Tull	14
8=	Santana	14

* Includes awards for Jefferson Airplane, Jefferson Starship and Starship (the evolution in the band's name).

Source: RIAA; to October 1992.

THE 10 MALE ARTISTS WITH MOST GOLD ALBUMS IN THE USA

	Artist	Gold albums
1	Elvis Presley	60
2	Elton John	26
3	Neil Diamond	23
4	Bob Dylan	21
5	Kenny Rogers	20
6	Frank Sinatra	19
7=	Paul McCartney*	17
7=	Willie Nelson	17
7=	Andy Williams	17
7=	Hank Williams Jr	17

* Includes awards for Wings but not with the Beatles.

Source: RIAA; to October 1992.

THE FIRST 10 RECIPIENTS OF THE ASCAP 'SONGWRITER OF THE YEAR' AWARD

	Songwriter	Year
1	Lionel Richie	1984
2	Lionel Richie	1985
3	Lionel Richie	1986
4	Narada Michael Walden	1987
5	Jimmy Jam and Terry Lewis	1988
6=	Debbie Gibson	1989
6=	Bruce Springsteen	1989
8	Diane Warren	1990
9	Diane Warren	1991
10	Jimmy Jam and Terry Lewis	1992

The first Annual Pop Awards Dinner organized by ASCAP (the American Society of Composers, Authors & Publishers) was held on 3 May 1984 at the Beverly Wilshire Hotel, Beverly Hills, and was hosted by Burt Bacharach's longtime songwriting partner and ASCAP president Hal David. Together with the BMI, ASCAP is responsible for licensing and collecting performance royalties for the great majority of American songwriters and publishers and its prestigious 'Songwriter of the Year' award is an acknowledgement of the most successful American composer of the year.

THE FIRST 10 RECIPIENTS OF THE BRITS 'OUTSTANDING CONTRIBUTION TO BRITISH MUSIC' AWARD

	Artist	Date
1	John Lennon	24 Feb 82
2	Beatles	8 Feb 83
3	George Martin	21 Feb 84
4	Police	11 Feb 85
5	Wham! and Elton John	10 Feb 86
6	Eric Clapton	9 Feb 87
7	Who	8 Feb 88
8	Cliff Richard	13 Feb 89
9	Queen	9 Feb 90
10	Status Quo	10 Feb 91

The Outstanding Contribution Award is the highest honour bestowed by the Brits Awards committee, which inaugurated the annual ceremony in 1982 at Grosvenor House Hotel, London. In 1992, the award name was changed, for that year only, to 'Special Tribute', in recognition of the contribution and life of Queen's Freddie Mercury, who had died on 24 November 1991.

THE TOP 10 AMERICAN MUSIC AWARDS WINNERS

	Artist	Awards
1	Kenny Rogers	19
2=	Alabama	15
2=	Lionel Richie	15
4	Michael Jackson	14
5	Willie Nelson	12
6=	Whitney Houston	11
6=	Stevie Wonder	11
8	Randy Travis	10
9	Olivia Newton-John	9
10=	Hammer (aka MC Hammer)	8
10=	Janet Jackson	8

The only 'populist' music awards in the United States based on voting by the American public, the AMAs have been held annually since their 19 February 1974 inaugural ceremony which took place at the Aquarius Theater, Hollywood. Kenny Rogers' mighty total is largely due to his crossover appeal from Country to pop music in the early 1980s, during which he garnered the Favorite Male Artist award for four consecutive years (1979–82).

THE 10 ARTISTS WITH MOST BRIT AWARDS

	Artist	Awards
1	Phil Collins	6*
2	Michael Jackson	5
3=	George Michael	4**
3=	Prince	4†
3=	Annie Lennox	4
6=	Dire Straits	3
6=	Trevor Horn	3
6=	Paul McCartney	3#
6=	Seal	3§
6=	Paul Young	3

* Includes award for Best Film Soundtrack (1989, for Buster Original Soundtrack).

** Includes two awards with Wham! (1985 and 1986).

† Includes award for Best Film Soundtrack (1990, for Batman Original Soundtrack).

Includes one award with the Beatles (1983).

§ All three collected in one ceremony (1992).

The Brits, organized annually by the British Phonographic Industry, celebrated their 10th anniversary in 1992 when Seal won an unprecedented three trophies.

THE FIRST 10 INDUCTEES INTO THE COUNTRY MUSIC HALL OF FAME

	Artist	Born	Died	Year inducted
1	Jimmie Rodgers	8 Sep 1897	26 May 1933	1961
2	Fred Rose	24 Aug 1897	1 Dec 1954	1961
3	Hank Williams	17 Sep 1923	1 Jan 1953	1961
4	Roy Acuff	15 Sep 1903	23 Nov 1992	1962
5	Tex Ritter	12 Jan 1907	2 Jan 1974	1964
6	Ernest Tubb	9 Feb 1914	6 Sep 1984	1965
7	Eddy Arnold	15 May 1918	–	1966
8	James R. Denny	28 Feb 1911	27 Aug 1963	1966
9	George D. Hay	9 Nov 1895	8 May 1968	1966
10	Uncle Dave Macon	7 Oct 1870	22 Mar 1952	1966

Founded in 1961 by the Country Music Association in Nashville, the Country Music Hall of Fame recognizes outstanding contributions to the world of Country. Decided by a series of three ballots, the Hall of Fame inducted 54 members between 1961 and 1992.

THE TOP 10 COUNTRY MUSIC AWARDS WINNERS

	Artist	Awards
1=	Alabama	11
1=	Roy Clark	11
3	Chet Atkins	10
4	Loretta Lynn	8
5=	Judds	7
5=	Ronnie Milsap	7
5=	Willie Nelson	7
5=	Dolly Parton	7
5=	Hank Williams Jr	7
10=	Garth Brooks	6
10=	Johnny Cash	6
10=	Merle Haggard	6
10=	Ricky Skaggs	6

The Country Music Awards are the most prestigious Country awards, held as an annual ceremony since 1967. Veteran Country instrumentalist Roy Clark netted the Instrumentalist of the Year award for seven consecutive years between 1974 and 1980.

THE 10 ARTISTS WITH MOST GRAMMY AWARDS

	Artist	Awards
1	Sir George Solti	29
2	Quincy Jones	25
3	Vladimir Horowitz	24
4	Henry Mancini	20
5	Stevie Wonder	17
6=	Aretha Franklin	15
6=	John T. Williams	15
8=	Itzhak Perlman	14
8=	Leonard Bernstein	14
10=	Ella Fitzgerald	13
10=	Leontyne Price	13
10=	Robert Shaw	13

The Grammy Awards ceremony has been held annually in the United States since its inauguration on 4 May 1959, and the awards are considered to be the most prestigious in the music industry. The proliferation of classical artists in this Top 10 (not least, conductor Sir George Solti) is largely attributable to the large number of classical award categories at the Grammys, which have been latterly overshadowed by the rise of pop and rock. Grammy winners are selected annually by the 7,000-member Recording Academy of NARAS (the National Academy of Recording Arts & Sciences).

THE GRAMMY AWARDS

Among the dozens of music industry awards shows that annually populate American television each spring (including the American Music Awards, the Billboard Music Awards, the MTV Awards, the Country Music Awards, the Rock 'n' Roll Hall of Fame Awards, the BMI Awards and ASCAP Songwriters Awards), the oldest, largest and most prestigious has always been the Grammys.

Usually held in February in either New York or Los Angeles, the first Grammy ceremony was held on 4 May 1958 and was named after the gramophone: the trophy itself is a composite design of early gramophones. Initiated by the National Academy of Recording Arts & Sciences, based in Burbank, California, the membership of which was established as a body of creative contributors to the field of music recording, the inaugural Awards show presented 28 trophies including Song of the Year, which went to Domenico Modugno for *Volare (Nel Blu Dipinto Di Blu)*, and Album of the Year, awarded to Henry Mancini for *The Music From 'Peter Gunn'*. Today, with the Academy membership voting total now over 7,000, the number of standard categories, including rap, Country, R & B, pop, alternative, folk, jazz, New Age, instrumental, rock, gospel, latin, children, TV, film, and comedy, amounts to 80 awards. To these are added the Trustee Awards (special merit Grammys presented by the National Trustees to individuals who have made outstanding non-performing contributions to the recording industry), the Grammy Legend Award (introduced in 1989, designed to recognize ongoing contributions and influence in the recording field), the Lifetime Achievement Award (ebony and gold Grammy plaques awarded by the Academy to 'performers who have made creative contributions of outstanding artistic significance to the field of recordings') and the Hall of Fame Awards (established in 1973 to honour 'early recordings of lasting, qualitative or historical significance').

Heavily reliant in its early years on classical and jazz recording award categories, the Grammys ceremony, for all its prestige, has often been criticized for being behind the times. Elvis Presley did not win a Grammy until 1967, when, somewhat bizarrely, he received the Best Sacred Performance Award for his version of *How Great Thou Art*, while the Beatles were awarded only four Grammys throughout their career, and never won the much prized Song of the Year trophy. The most recent controversy erupted in 1989 when Jethro Tull won (over the more obvious candidate, Metallica) the Best Heavy Metal Performance Award for their entirely non-metal *Crest Of A Knave* album.

Regardless of these problems, the Grammys continue to be considered the Oscars of the recording world, while its ceremony is still the hottest ticket on the record industry calendar.

THE FIRST 10 RECIPIENTS OF THE GRAMMYS' LIFETIME ACHIEVEMENT AWARD

	Artist	Year
1	Bing Crosby, vocalist	1962
2	Frank Sinatra, vocalist	1965
3	Duke Ellington, jazz musician	1966
4	Ella Fitzgerald, jazz vocalist	1967
5	Irving Berlin, composer	1968
6	Elvis Presley, vocalist	1971
7=	Louis Armstrong*, jazz musician	1972
7=	Mahalia Jackson*, gospel vocalist	1972
9=	Chuck Berry, composer/performer	1984
9=	Charlie Parker*, jazz musician	1984

* *Presented posthumously.*

THE 10 ARTISTS WITH MOST GRAMMY AWARDS IN ONE YEAR

	Artist	Year	Awards
1	Michael Jackson	1983	8
2=	Quincy Jones	1990	6
2=	Eric Clapton	1992	6
4=	Bee Gees	1978	5
4=	Christopher Cross	1980	5
4=	Quincy Jones	1981	5
4=	Henry Mancini	1961	5
4=	Roger Miller	1964	5
4=	Roger Miller	1965	5
4=	Paul Simon	1970	5
4=	Stevie Wonder	1973	5
4=	Stevie Wonder	1974	5
4=	Stevie Wonder	1976	5

Michael Jackson won eight Grammys in one year for his global bestselling *Thriller* project. No one, however, can match Stevie Wonder's feat of 15 Grammys in four years.

THE 10 NON-CLASSICAL ARTISTS WITH MOST GRAMMY AWARDS

	Artist	Awards
1	Quincy Jones	25
2	Henry Mancini	20
3	Stevie Wonder	17
4=	Aretha Franklin	15
4=	John T. Williams	15
6	Ella Fitzgerald	13
7=	Michael Jackson	12
7=	Paul Simon	12
9=	Ray Charles	11
9=	Duke Ellington	11
9=	Roger Miller	11

Mancini and Williams have won a significant number of Grammys for film soundtrack scores, as has Quincy Jones – although the latter boosted his total considerably with a six-trophy win in 1991, all for his 1990 R & B album *Back On The Block*. The Beatles, perhaps surprisingly, only ever won four Grammys, two in 1964 and two in 1967.

THE FIRST 10 RECIPIENTS OF THE IVOR NOVELLO 'OUTSTANDING PERSONAL SERVICES TO POPULAR MUSIC' AWARD

	Artist	Year
1	Jack Payne	1955
2	Mantovani	1956
3	Ted Heath	1957
4	Billy Cotton	1958
5	Lionel Bart	1959
6	Eric Maschwitz	1960
7	Lawrence Wright	1962*
8	Beatles, Brian Epstein & George Martin	1963
9	Paddy Roberts	1964
10	BBC Television**	1965

* No award was presented at the 1961 ceremony.

** The BBC was presented with the trophy for the production of the series, A Song For Europe.

Source: BASC.

In 1963, the Ivor Novello Awards took a contemporary leap that was to alter the nature of the annual ceremony by being one of the first major awards to recognize the achievements of the Beatles, along with the band's manager and producer.

THE TOP 10 MTV VIDEO MUSIC AWARDS WINNERS, 1984–92

	Artist	Awards
1	Peter Gabriel	10
2	Madonna	9
3	a-ha	8
4	R.E.M.	7
5=	Don Henley	5
5=	INXS	5
5=	Janet Jackson	5
8=	Paula Abdul	4
8=	Guns N' Roses	4
8=	Herbie Hancock	4
8=	Michael Jackson*	4
8=	Prince	4
8=	U2	4
8=	Van Halen	4

* Includes the prestigious 1988 Video Vanguard Award which was subsequently renamed The Michael Jackson Video Vanguard Award.

Peter Gabriel's total is entirely due to the popularity of one video, the innovative clip he produced with Stephen Johnson in 1986 for the global chart-topper, *Sledgehammer*.

THE LAST 10 RECIPIENTS OF THE IVOR NOVELLO 'SONGWRITER OF THE YEAR' AWARD

	Songwriter	Year
1	Mick Hucknall	1991
2	Phil Collins	1990
3	Mike Stock, Matt Aitken & Pete Waterman	1989
4=	George Michael*	1988
4=	Stock Aitken Waterman*	1988
6	Stock Aitken Waterman	1987
7	Annie Lennox and Dave Stewart	1986
8	Roland Orzabel	1985
9	George Michael	1984
10	Annie Lennox and Dave Stewart	1983

* Michael and SAW shared this honour for the first time in Ivor Novello history.

Source: BASCA.

At an emotional ceremony in 1985, George Michael wept openly upon receiving his first 'Songwriter of the Year' award (for the 1984 year), presented to him by Elton John. At age 21, Michael was the youngest-ever recipient of this much-coveted trophy.

THE TOP 10 SONGWRITER RECIPIENTS OF THE IVOR NOVELLO AWARDS

	Songwriter	Awards
1	Paul McCartney	19*
2	John Lennon	15*
3	Andrew Lloyd Webber	13
4=	Barry Gibb	11**
4=	Robin Gibb	11**
6	Maurice Gibb	10**
7	Tim Rice	9
8	Mike Stock, Matt Aitken & Pete Waterman†	8
9=	Lionel Bart	7
9=	Leslie Bricusse	7
9=	Elton John	7
9=	Tony Macauley	7

* Both Lennon and McCartney received one award as members of the Beatles. All the others were garnered either as one-half of their songwriting team or individually.

** All of the brothers Gibb received two of their awards as members of the Bee Gees. The rest were as a result of different Gibb writing partnerships between the three of them.

† Stock Aitken Waterman are the only songwriting team listed together since all of their awards were made to them as a trio unit.

Widely regarded within the industry as the most prestigious UK music awards ceremony, the BASCA-organized Ivor Novello Awards have been held annually since 1955 and principally reward significant songwriting achievements by British writers and composers.

THE FIRST 10 RECIPIENTS OF THE NORDOFF-ROBBINS SILVER CLEF AWARDS

	Artist	Year
1	Who	1976
2	Genesis	1977
3	Cliff Richard & The Shadows	1978
4	Elton John	1979
5	Pink Floyd	1980
6	Status Quo	1981
7	Rolling Stones	1982
8	Eric Clapton	1983
9	Queen	1984
10	Dire Straits	1985

The Silver Clef has been awarded annually since 1976 at an awards lunch in London by the Nordoff-Robbins charity, the work of which is devoted to helping severely handicapped children through music therapy. This highly prized award recognizes a substantial contribution to the world of music by a British act.

Source: BASCA.

THE FIRST 10 INDUCTEES INTO THE ROCK 'N' ROLL HALL OF FAME

1	Chuck Berry
2	James Brown
3	Ray Charles
4	Sam Cooke
5	Fats Domino
6	Everly Brothers
7	Buddy Holly
8	Jerry Lee Lewis
9	Elvis Presley
10	Little Richard

These seminal artists were all inducted at the first ceremony which took place on 23 January 1986 at the Waldorf-Astoria Hotel, New York. While only 10 performing artists were inducted, two non-performing Rock 'n' Roll pioneers were also recipients: DJ Alan Freed and Sun record label owner Sam Phillips. Three official 'Early Influence' inductions were also confirmed at this inaugural dinner: Robert Johnson, Jimmie Rodgers and Jimmy Yantcey.

Chuck Berry, one of the first 10 inductees into the Rock 'n' Roll Hall of Fame, celebrates by doing his famous 'duck walk' across the stage.

THE 10 RECIPIENTS OF THE SONG-WRITERS' HALL OF FAME 'LIFETIME ACHIEVEMENT' AWARD, 1983–93

	Artist	Year
1	Willie Nelson	1983
2	Benny Goodman	1984
3	John Hammond	1985
4	Jerry Wexler	1987*
5	Dick Clark	1988
6	Quincy Jones	1989
7	B.B. King	1990
8	Gene Autry	1991
9	Nat 'King' Cole	1992
10	Ray Charles	1993

* No award was made in 1986.

THE TOP 10 LIVE CD ALBUMS OF ALL TIME, AS VOTED BY CD REVIEW MAGAZINE

	Title	Artist	Year
1	Live At The Apollo	James Brown	1963
2	Live At The Star Club	Jerry Lee Lewis	1964
3	Get Yer Ya Yas Out	Rolling Stones	1970
4	Live At The Opry	Patsy Cline	1959
5	Amazing Grace	Aretha Franklin	1972
6	Live At Winterland	Jimi Hendrix Experience	1991
7	Live At The Regal	B.B. King	1971
8	Live At Carnegie Hall	Buck Owens & The Buckaroos	1966
9	Live	Doug Sahm	1988
10	Live 1975–85	Bruce Springsteen & The E. Street Band	1986

Source: CD Review *magazine, October 1992.*

This subjective list, compiled by *CD Review*, America's bestselling compact disc magazine, is based on sound quality and performance quality, and serves as an excellent run-down of some of the more important live recordings now available on CD.

The Songwriters' Hall of Fame was initiated in June 1969 in New York by Johnny Mercer, Abe Olman and Howard Richmond, who were keen to formally establish a national academy to recognize the achievements of American songwriters. What started as a low-key ad hoc affair blossomed into a grand annual awards dinner whose most prestigious honour is the 'Lifetime Achievement' Award which is presented to a music veteran who is also a non-songwriter.

Nat 'King' Cole, in 1992 a posthumous recipient of a Songwriters' Hall of Fame 'Lifetime Achievement' Award.

ROLLING STONE MAGAZINE'S 10 'ALL TIME GREATEST ALBUMS OF THE EIGHTIES'

	Title	Artist
1	*London Calling*	Clash
2	*Purple Rain* (Original Soundtrack)	Prince & The Revolution
3	*The Joshua Tree*	U2
4	*Remain In Light*	Talking Heads
5	*Graceland*	Paul Simon
6	*Born In The USA*	Bruce Springsteen
7	*Thriller*	Michael Jackson
8	*Murmur*	R.E.M.
9	*Shoot Out The Lights*	Richard & Linda Thompson
10	*Tracy Chapman*	Tracy Chapman

Source: Rolling Stone.

This rather eclectic list, typical of the general mood of *Rolling Stone* magazine during the decade, was compiled from the assessments of the publication's editors.

THE 10 COUNTRIES WITH MOST WINS AT THE EUROVISION SONG CONTEST

	Country	Years	Wins
1=	France	1958, 1960, 1962, 1969*, 1977	5
1=	Luxembourg	1961, 1965, 1972, 1973, 1983	5
1=	Ireland	1970, 1980, 1987, 1992, 1993	5
4=	Netherlands	1957, 1959, 1969*, 1975	4
4=	UK	1967, 1969*, 1976, 1981	4
6	Sweden	1974, 1984, 1991	3
7=	Israel	1978, 1979	2
7=	Italy	1964, 1990	2
7=	Spain	1968, 1969*	2
7=	Switzerland	1956, 1988	2

* *All four countries tied as winners in 1969.*

The Eurovision Song Contest has been an annual event since its 25 May 1956 debut, which was won by Swiss singer Lys Assia. Johnny Logan completed a hat-trick of wins for Ireland (even though he is Australian by birth). Having won as a performer in 1980 and 1987, he wrote the Irish entry *Why Me* for the 1992 winner, Linda Martin.

THE 10 MOST SUCCESSFUL EUROVISION SONG CONTEST LOSERS IN THE UK*

	Title	Artist	Year	Contest position
1	*Congratulations*	Cliff Richard	1968	2
2	*Are You Sure*	Allisons	1961	2
3	*Knock Knock, Who's There?*	Mary Hopkin	1969	2
4	*Beg, Steal Or Borrow*	New Seekers	1972	2
5	*Jack In The Box*	Clodagh Rodgers	1971	4
6	*Power To All Our Friends*	Cliff Richard	1973	3
7	*One Step Further*	Bardo	1982	7
8	*Say Wonderful Things*	Ronnie Carroll	1963	4
9	*Go (Before You Break My Heart)*	Gigliola Cinquetti	1974	2
10	*I See A Star*	Mouth & McNeal	1974	3

* *Based on sales.*

Most of the non-victorious Eurovision songs that made the UK charts were, inevitably, the British competition entries, many of which have been major hits despite being pipped at the Eurovision post – Cliff Richard's *Congratulations* and the Allisons' *Are You Sure* both made No. 1 and Mary Hopkin and the New Seekers reached No. 2. A most unusual year, however, was 1974, when Abba won the competition (with *Waterloo*) and topped the UK chart, but then the Italian and Dutch entries (numbers nine and 10 in the list here) also made the UK Top 10, outselling that year's British entry, Olivia Newton-John's *Long Live Love*.

THE TOP 10 EUROVISION SONG CONTEST WINNERS IN THE UK

	Title	Artist	Country	Contest
1	Save Your Kisses For Me	Brotherhood Of Man	UK	Mar 76
2	Puppet On A String	Sandie Shaw	UK	Mar 67
3	Making Your Mind Up	Bucks Fizz	UK	Mar 81
4	All Kinds Of Everything	Dana	Eire	Apr 70
5	Waterloo	Abba	Sweden	Apr 84
6	Ein Bischen Frieden (A Little Peace)	Nicole	West Germany	May 82
7	What's Another Year	Johnny Logan	Eire	May 80
8	Après Toi (Come What May)	Vicky Leandros	Luxembourg	Apr 72
9	Boom Bang-A-Bang	Lulu	UK	Mar 69
10	Hold Me Now	Johnny Logan	Eire	May 87

Based on UK chart performance: the top five all hit the top of the charts, the remaining five peaking at No. 2.

Sandie Shaw's Puppet On A String *was the first British entry ever to win the Eurovision Song Contest, in 1967, and is the most successful Eurovision entry ever by a bare-footed performer.*

THE TOP 10 OF *YOUR HUNDRED BEST TUNES*

	'Tune'	Composer
1	In the Depths of the Temple (from The Pearl Fishers)	Georges Bizet
2	Chorus of the Hebrew Slaves (from Nabucco)	Giuseppi Verdi
3	Miserere	Gregorio Allegri
4	Violin Concerto No. 1 in G Minor (Adagio)	Max Bruch
5	Canon in D	Johann Pachelbel
6	Symphony No. 6 ('Pastoral') (last movement)	Ludwig van Beethoven
7	Piano Concerto No. 21 (Andante)	Wolfgang Amadeus Mozart
8	Lament: What is Life? (from Orfeo ed Euridice)	Christoph Willibald von Gluck
9	The Holy City	Stephen Adams
10	Nimrod (from Enigma Variations)	Sir Edward Elgar

BBC Radio 2's *Your Hundred Best Tunes* first went on the air as *The Hundred Best Tunes In The World* on 22 November 1959, and is still broadcast every Sunday night by its original presenter, Alan Keith. The Top 10 comes from the programme's listeners' poll of all-time favourites.

CAPITAL RADIO LISTENERS' 10 FAVOURITE SINGLES OF ALL TIME (1988)

	Title	Artist	1992 position
1	*Careless Whisper*	George Michael	2
2	*Stairway To Heaven*	Led Zeppelin	4
3	*Against All Odds*	Phil Collins	16
4	*I Owe You Nothing*	Bros	–
5	*Bohemian Rhapsody*	Queen	3
6	*Romeo And Juliet*	Dire Straits	27
7	*Sexual Healing*	Marvin Gaye	53
8	*Bad*	Michael Jackson	164
9	*Dock Of The Bay*	Otis Redding	123
10	*Crazy For You*	Madonna	19

Based on the 'Hall of Fame' compiled annually by the independent London radio station Capital Radio.

How the mighty are fallen: *I Owe You Nothing* does not appear anywhere in the 1992 Top 500, and nor does anything else from the entire oeuvre of 1988 flash-in-the pan group Bros.

CAPITAL RADIO LISTENERS' 10 FAVOURITE SINGLES OF ALL TIME (1992)

	Title	Artist
1	*(Everything I Do) I Do It For You*	Bryan Adams
2	*Careless Whisper*	George Michael
3	*Bohemian Rhapsody*	Queen
4	*Stairway To Heaven*	Led Zeppelin
5	*Sweet Child O' Mine*	Guns N' Roses
6	*Imagine*	John Lennon
7	*Hotel California*	Eagles
8	*Wonderful Tonight*	Eric Clapton
9	*I Will Always Love You*	Whitney Houston
10	*Stars*	Simply Red

Based on the 'Hall of Fame' compiled annually by the independent London radio station Capital Radio.

Led Zeppelin's seminal album track *Stairway To Heaven* frequently appears in many 'All-Time Favourite Singles' lists – despite never having actually been released as a single (it existed briefly on an EP in Australia, but the record was withdrawn on the group's instructions).

BBC RADIO 1 LISTENERS' 10 FAVOURITE SINGLES OF ALL TIME (1988)

	Title	Artist	1992 position
1	*I Owe You Nothing*	Bros	–
2	*Bohemian Rhapsody*	Queen	1
3	*Careless Whisper*	George Michael	7
4	*Stairway To Heaven*	Led Zeppelin	2
5	*Nothing's Gonna Change My Love For You*	Glenn Medeiros	–
6	*Drop The Boy*	Bros	–
7	*Angel Eyes*	Wet Wet Wet	–
8	*Bad*	Michael Jackson	63
9	*Tainted Love*	Soft Cell	34
10	*Thriller*	Michael Jackson	11

A poll of 20,000 BBC Radio 1 listeners completed in August 1988 established this list of 'all-time' Top 10 favourite singles. In the comparative 1992 poll, four of these 'all time' singles did not even make the Top 100, such is the transient nature of 'all-time' status and fan loyalty.

BBC RADIO 1 LISTENERS' 10 FAVOURITE SINGLES OF ALL TIME (1992)

	Title	Artist
1	*Bohemian Rhapsody*	Queen
2	*Stairway To Heaven*	Led Zeppelin
3	*(Everything I Do) I Do It For You*	Bryan Adams
4	*Imagine*	John Lennon
5	*Baker Street*	Gerry Rafferty
6	*Layla*	Derek & The Dominos
7	*Careless Whisper*	George Michael
8	*I'm Not In Love*	10cc
9	*Hey Jude*	Beatles
10	*Bat Out Of Hell*	Meat Loaf

Based on a survey conducted by BBC Radio 1FM in association with Pepsi, 31 August 1992.

KISS 100 FM LISTENERS' TOP 10 DANCE RECORDS OF ALL TIME (1990)

	Title	Artist
1	Hold On	En Vogue
2	Keep On Movin'	Soul II Soul
3	The Power	Snap!
4	Back To Life	Soul II Soul
5	You Can't Touch This	MC Hammer
6	Expansions	Lonnie Liston Smith
7	Tears	Frankie Knuckles (featuring Satoshi Tomie)
8	Rebel Without A Plause	Public Enemy
9	Poison	Bell Biv Devoe
10	The Masterplan	Diana Brown and Barrie K. Sharpe

This Top 10 is derived from a poll conducted at the time of its launch by London dance music radio station Kiss 100 FM. A former pirate radio station established in 1985, it attracted a wide following among young Londoners. It applied for a licence and went 'legit' on 1 September 1990, and has rapidly achieved substantial success as a commercial station.

KISS 100 FM LISTENERS' TOP 10 DANCE RECORDS OF ALL TIME (1992)

	Title	Artist
1	All This Love I'm Giving	Gwen McCrae
2	Optimistic	Sounds of Blackness
3	Sesame's Treet	Smart E's
4	Raving I'm Raving	Shut Up and Dance (featuring Peter Bouncer)
5	Ain't Nobody	Rufus & Chaka Khan
6	Strings Of Life	Rhythim Is Rhythim
7	The Power	Snap!
8	Sex Machine	James Brown
9	Expansions	Lonnie Liston Smith
10	Someone Else's Guy	Jocelyn Brown

Snap!'s The Power and Lonnie Liston Smith's Expansions are the only records that are common to both Kiss 100 FM's 1990 'all-time' chart and the 1992 version.

THE FIRST 10 WINNERS OF THE NME POLL WINNERS' BEST SINGLE OF THE YEAR AWARD

	Title	Artist	Year
1	Living Doll	Cliff Richard	1959
2	Apache	Shadows	1960
3	Johnny Remember Me	John Leyton	1961
4	I Remember You	Frank Ifield	1962
5	She Loves You	Beatles	1963
6	House Of The Rising Sun	Animals	1964
7	(I Can't Get No) Satisfaction	Rolling Stones	1965
8	Eleanor Rigby	Beatles	1966
9	A Whiter Shade Of Pale	Procul Harum	1967
10	Hey Jude	Beatles	1968

The New Musical Express began its annual Poll-Winners Poll, based on readers' votes, in 1952 when Dickie Valentine was named Best UK Male Singer, but only introduced the Best Single category in 1959. Until the early 1970s, voting for Best Single was restricted to British-recorded singles.

THE TOP 10 COUNTRY AMERICA COUNTRY SONGS OF ALL TIME*

	Title	Artist
1	He Stopped Loving Her Today	George Jones
2	When I Call Your Name	Vince Gill
3	The Dance	Garth Brooks
4	Crazy	Patsy Cline
5	I Fall To Pieces	Patsy Cline
6	El Paso	Marty Robbins
7	Your Cheatin' Heart	Hank Williams
8	I'm So Lonesome I Could Cry	Hank Williams
9	Sixteen Tons	Tennessee Ernie Ford
10	Lovesick Blues	Hank Williams

* As voted by readers of the magazine.

Source: Country America, October 1992.

The top three were all recorded in the 1980s, while the rest were all released before 1961. The godfather of Country music, Hank Williams, who merits three favourites on this list, died when he was only 29 on 1 January 1953.

THE 10 WORST RECORDS OF ALL TIME?

	Title	Artist
1	I Want My Baby Back	Jimmy Cross
2	Wunderbar	Zara Leander
3	Paralysed	Legendary Stardust Cowboy
4	The Deal	Pat Campbell
5	Transfusion	Nervous Norvus
6	This Pullover	Jess Conrad
7	Spinning Wheel	Mel & Dave
8	Laurie	Dickey Lee
9	A Lover's Concerto	Mrs Miller
10	I Get So Lonely	Tania Day

In 1978, London Capital Radio DJ Kenny Everett polled his listeners on their least favourites from the items which he regularly played in a 'ghastly records' spot. From 6,000 replies, these were the Top (or Bottom) 10, which went on to headline a special 'All-Time Worst' show. Mostly obscure before Everett dragged them up, several of these have since become bywords of bad taste on vinyl, particularly Jimmy Cross's 1965 tale of necrophilic love which proudly tops this grisly list.

NAME CHANGES QUIZ

Match the famous acts with their earlier names:

1	Graduate	A	Wham!
2	Pendletones	B	Stone Roses
3	New Yardbirds	C	Led Zeppelin
4	Swankers	D	Cult
5	English Rose	E	Beach Boys
6	Tom & Jerry	F	Tears For Fears
7	Executive	G	Simple Minds
8	Hawks	H	Simon and Garfunkel
9	Johnny & The Self Abusers	I	Sex Pistols
10	Southern Death Cult	J	Band

THE TOP 10 HYMNS REQUESTED ON SONGS OF PRAISE

1	Dear Lord And Father Of Mankind
2	The Day Thou Gavest, Lord, Has Ended
3	The Old Rugged Cross
4	How Great Thou Art
5	Abide With Me
6	Shine, Jesus, Shine
7	Make Me A Channel Of Your Peace
8	The Lord's My Shepherd
9	Love Divine
10	Great Is Thy Faithfulness

Compiled, much to the chagrin of Christian traditionalists, by BBC 1's Songs Of Praise programme in 1992, this list of the most-requested hymns was last collated in 1984 and reflects the growth in popularity of the more 'trendy' evangelical-style hymns, ousting such orthodox golden oldies as William Blake's Jerusalem.

BRITISH STUDENTS' 10 FAVOURITE ALBUMS OF ALL TIME (1988)

	Title	Artist
1	The Wall	Pink Floyd
2	The Joshua Tree	U2
3	Brothers In Arms	Dire Straits
4	Bat Out Of Hell	Meat Loaf
5	The Queen Is Dead	Smiths
6	Love Over Gold	Dire Straits
7	Graceland	Paul Simon
8	Steve McQueen	Prefab Sprout
9	Sgt Pepper's Lonely Hearts Club Band	The Beatles
10	Dream Of The Blue Turtles	Sting

BRITISH STUDENTS' 10 FAVOURITE ALBUM COVERS OF ALL TIME (1988)

	Title	Artist
1	Sgt Pepper's Lonely Hearts Club Band	Beatles
2	Dark Side Of The Moon	Pink Floyd
3	Tango In The Night	Fleetwood Mac
4	Script For A Jester's Tear	Marillion
5	A Kind Of Magic	Queen
6	Misplaced Childhood	Marillion
7	Love Over Gold	Dire Straits
8	Bat Out Of Hell	Meat Loaf
9	Somewhere In Time	Iron Maiden
10	The Beatles ('White Album')	Beatles

The various 'Students' Favourites' are based on an exhaustive poll conducted in 1988 by Nescafé and University Radio, York, in which questionnaires were sent to 24,000 students throughout the country via student radio stations. Regrettably, the survey has not been repeated, but it remains nonetheless fascinating as a time capsule of late-1980s taste, and a salutary indication of the sometimes ephemeral nature of 'all-time' listings.

BRITISH STUDENTS' 10 FAVOURITE SINGLES OF ALL TIME (1988)

	Title	Artist
1	Bohemian Rhapsody	Queen
2	Stairway To Heaven	Led Zeppelin
3	Vienna	Ultravox
4	Blue Monday	New Order
5	Baker Street	Gerry Rafferty
6	Don't You Forget About Me	Simple Minds
7	Romeo And Juliet	Dire Straits
8	Wuthering Heights	Kate Bush
9	How Soon Is Now?	Smiths
10	Will You?	Hazel O'Connor

BRITISH STUDENTS' 10 FAVOURITE FEMALE SINGERS OF ALL TIME (1988)

1	Kate Bush
2	Annie Lennox
3	Whitney Houston
4	Aretha Franklin
5	Suzanne Vega
6	Alison Moyet
7	Debbie Harry
8	Stevie Nicks
9	Tina Turner
10	Siouxsie Sioux

BRITISH STUDENTS' 10 FAVOURITE MALE SINGERS OF ALL TIME (1988)

1	Phil Collins
2	Peter Gabriel
3	David Bowie
4	Sting
5	Morrissey
6	Bruce Springsteen
7	Chris De Burgh
8	Elvis Costello
9	Michael Jackson
10	Elton John

The Top 50 contains four singles by Dire Straits, three by U2 and Peter Gabriel and two each by Eric Clapton, Phil Collins, the Police and the Beatles. Queen are in the unusual position of holding the number one spot, but not having any other single in the Top 50. Perhaps surprisingly, Bruce Springsteen has only one entry (*Born To Run* at number 33). Another oddity is the presence (at number 48) of the Canadian group, Martha & The Muffins, whose song *Echo Beach* was the only chart hit they ever had in the UK.

Annie Lennox scored highly on the 1988 poll of students' favourite singers while still in the Eurythmics.

BRITISH STUDENTS' 10 FAVOURITE MUSIC FILMS OF ALL TIME (1988)

	Film	Year
1	The Blues Brothers	1980
2	Pink Floyd The Wall	1982
3	Grease	1978
4	The Rocky Horror Picture Show	1975
5	Tommy – The Who	1975
6	Stop Making Sense – Talking Heads	1987
7	The Sound Of Music	1965
8	Little Shop Of Horrors	1986
9	Woodstock	1970
10	Highlander	1986

BRITISH STUDENTS' 10 FAVOURITE LIVE ACTS OF ALL TIME (1988)

1	Queen
2	U2
3	Genesis
4	Bruce Springsteen
5	Dire Straits
6	Peter Gabriel
7	Marillion
8	Rush
9	Pogues
10	Simple Minds

BRITISH STUDENTS' 10 FAVOURITE GROUPS OF ALL TIME (1988)

1	Genesis
2	Beatles
3	Queen
4	Smiths
5	Dire Straits
6	U2
7	Pink Floyd
8	Marillion
9	Police
10	Rolling Stones

MISCELLANY

10 MUSIC ARTISTS WHO WERE BORN ABROAD*

	Artist	Birthplace	Date of birth
1	Jackson Browne	Heidelberg, Germany	9 Oct 1948
2	David Byrne (of Talking Heads)	Dumbarton, Scotland	14 May 1952
3	Stewart Copeland (of Police)	Alexandria, Egypt	16 Jul 1952
4	Neneh Cherry	Stockholm, Sweden	10 Oct 1964
5	Thomas Dolby (Thomas Morgan Dolby Robertson)	Cairo, Egypt	14 Oct 1958
6	Holly (William) Johnson (of Frankie Goes To Hollywood)	Khartoum, Sudan	19 Feb 1960
7	Manfred Mann (Michael Lubowitz)	Johannesburg, South Africa	21 Oct 1940
8	Freddie Mercury (Frederick Bulsara)	Zanzibar	5 Sep 1946
9	Cliff Richard (Harry Rodger Webb)	Lucknow, India	14 Oct 1940
10	Gene Simmons (Chaim Witz, of Kiss)	Haifa, Israel	25 Aug 1950

* *i.e. not in the countries in which they became famous.*

10 'AUSTRALIAN' MUSIC ARTISTS WHO WERE NOT BORN IN AUSTRALIA

	Artist	Country of birth
1	Neil Finn (Split Enz/Crowded House)	New Zealand
2	Barry Gibb (Bee Gees)	England
3	Maurice Gibb (Bee Gees)	Isle of Man
4	Robin Gibb (Bee Gees)	Isle of Man
5	Colin Hay (Men At Work)	Scotland
6	Olivia Newton-John	England
7	Harry Vanda (Easybeats)	Holland
8	'Little' Stevie Wright (Easybeats)	England
9	Angus Young (AC/DC)	Scotland
10	Malcolm Young (AC/DC)	Scotland

10 MUSIC ARTISTS WHO WERE BORN IN BIRMINGHAM, UK

	Artist	Date of birth
1	Ali (Alastair) Campbell of (UB40)	15 Feb 1959
2	Tommy Iommi (of Black Sabbath)	19 Feb 1948
3	John Lodge (of the Moody Blues)	20 Jul 1945
4	Jeff Lynne	30 Dec 1947
5	Christine McVie (Christine Perfect)	12 Jul 1943
6	Nick Mason (of Pink Floyd)	27 Jan 1945
7	Ozzy (John) Osbourne	3 Dec 1948
8	Carl Palmer (of Emerson Lake & Palmer)	20 Mar 1951
9	John Taylor (Nigel John Taylor of Duran Duran)	20 Jun 1960
10	Roy Wood (of Wizzard)	8 Nov 1946

A lot of the personnel of groups which formed in Australia (AC/DC, Bee Gees, Easybeats and Men At Work) were actually born somewhere else, but since their musical roots were from Down Under, many people incorrectly assume (most often with the Bee Gees and Olivia Newton-John) that they were born there.

10 MUSIC ARTISTS WHO WERE BORN IN BROOKLYN, USA

	Artist	Date of birth
1	Pat Benatar (Patricia Andrzejewski)	10 Jan 1953
2	Neil Diamond (Noah Kaminsky)	24 Jan 1941
3	Arlo Guthrie	1 Jul 1947
4	Carole King	9 Feb 1941
5	Barry Manilow	17 Jun 1946
6	MCA (Adam Yauch of Beastie Boys)	15 Aug 1967
7	Eddie Money (Edward Mahoney)	2 Mar 1949
8	Harry Nilsson (Harry Nelson)	15 Jun 1941
9	Neil Sedaka	13 Mar 1939
10	Barbra Streisand	24 Apr 1942

10 MUSIC ARTISTS WHO WERE BORN IN CANADA

	Artist	Birthplace	Date of birth
1	Bryan (Guy) Adams	Kingston	5 Nov 1959
2	Paul Anka	Ottawa	30 Jul 1941
3	Randy Bachman (Bachman Turner Overdrive)	Winnipeg	27 Sep 1943
4	Leonard Cohen	Montreal	21 Sep 1934
5	Rick Danko (of the Band)	Simcoe	9 Dec 1943
6	Alex Lifeson (of Rush)	Fernie	27 Aug 1953
7	Gordon Lightfoot	Orillia	17 Nov 1938
8	Joni Mitchell (Roberta Joan Anderson)	Alberta	7 Nov 1943
9	Robbie Robertson	Toronto	5 Jul 1944
10	Neil Young	Toronto	12 Nov 1945

Canadian-born Bryan Adams had the top-selling single of 1991 with (Everything I Do) I Do It For You, *the love theme from the film* Robin Hood – Prince Of Thieves.

10 MUSIC ARTISTS WHO WERE BORN IN CHICAGO, USA

	Artist	Date of birth
1	Peter Cetera	13 Sep 1944
2	Sam Cooke	22 Jan 1935
3	Donny Hathaway	1 Oct 1945
4	Rickie Lee Jones	8 Nov 1954
5	Quincy Jones	14 Mar 1933
6	Roger McGuinn (James Joseph McGuinn of The Byrds)	13 Jul 1942
7	Ray Manzarek (of the Doors)	12 Feb 1935
8	Curtis Mayfield	3 Jun 1942
9	Grace Slick (Grace Wing)	30 Oct 1939
10	Patti Smith	30 Dec 1946

10 MUSIC ARTISTS WHO WERE BORN IN DETROIT, USA

	Artist	Date of birth
1	Anita Baker	20 Dec 1957
2	Sonny (Salvatore) Bono (of Sonny and Cher)	16 Feb 1935
3	Alice Cooper (Vincent Damon Furnier)	4 Feb 1948
4	Ted Nugent	13 Dec 1948
5	Freda Payne	19 Sep 1945
6	Suzi Quatro	3 Jun 1950
7	Martha Reeves	18 Jul 1941
8	Smokey (William Jr) Robinson	19 Feb 1940
9	Diana Ross	26 Mar 1944
10	Jackie Wilson	9 Jun 1932

It should also be noted that, in addition to former member Peter Cetera, six members of the band Chicago were also born there.

10 MUSIC ARTISTS WHO WERE BORN IN DALLAS/FORT WORTH, USA

	Artist	Birthplace	Date of birth
1	Ornette Coleman	Fort Worth	19 Mar 1930
2	Bobby Day (Robert James Byrd)	Fort Worth	1 Jul 1930
3	Dusty Hill (of ZZ Top)	Dallas	19 May 1949
4	Meat Loaf (Marvin Lee Aday)	Dallas	27 Sep 1947
5	Trini Lopez (Trinidad Lopez III)	Dallas	15 May 1937
6	Roger Miller	Fort Worth	2 Jan 1936
7	Steve Miller	Dallas	5 Oct 1943
8	Stephen Stills	Dallas	3 Jan 1945
9	Sly Stone (Sylvester Stewart)	Dallas	15 Mar 1944
10	Stevie Ray Vaughan	Dallas	3 Oct 1954

10 MUSIC ARTISTS WHO WERE BORN IN GLASGOW, UK

	Artist	Date of birth
1	Lonnie Donegan (Anthony James Donegan)	29 Apr 1931
2	Donovan (Donovan Phillips Leitch)	10 May 1946
3	Sheena Easton (Sheena Orr)	27 Apr 1959
4	Jim Kerr (Simple Minds)	9 Jul 1959
5	Mark Knopfler	12 Aug 1949
6	Lulu (Marie McDonald McLaughlin Lawrie)	3 Nov 1948
7	Lorraine McIntosh (of Deacon Blue)	13 May 1964
8	Jimmy Somerville	22 Jun 1961
9	Al Stewart	5 Sep 1945
10	Midge Ure (of Ultravox)	10 Oct 1953

10 MUSIC ARTISTS WHO WERE BORN IN HOUSTON, USA

	Artist	Date of birth
1	Billy Gibbons (of ZZ Top)	16 Dec 1949
2	Barbara Ann Mandrell	25 Dec 1948
3	Johnny Nash	19 Aug 1940
4	Mike Nesmith	3 Dec 1942
5	Billy (William Everett) Preston	9 Sep 1946
6	P.J. Proby (James Marcus Smith)	6 Nov 1938
7	Kenny Rogers	21 Aug 1938
8	Cleanhead (Eddie) Vinson	18 Dec 1917
9	Johnny 'Guitar' Watson	3 Feb 1935
10	Mason Williams	24 Aug 1938

10 MUSIC ARTISTS WHO WERE BORN IN NEW JERSEY, USA

	Artist	Date of birth
1	Jon Bon Jovi (John Bongiovi)	2 Mar 1962
2	Connie Francis (Concetta Rosa Maria Franconero)	12 Dec 1938
3	Whitney Houston	9 Aug 1963
4	Bette Midler	1 Dec 1945
5	Ricky Nelson (Eric Hilliard Nelson)	8 May 1940
6	Fred Schneider (of B52s)	1 Jul 1951
7	Paul Simon	5 Nov 1942
8	Frank Sinatra	12 Dec 1915
9	Bruce Springsteen	23 Sep 1949
10	Frankie Valli (Francis Castelluccio)	3 May 1937

10 MUSIC ARTISTS WHO WERE BORN IN IRELAND

	Artist	Birthplace	Date of birth
1	Bono (Paul Hewson)	Dublin	10 May 1960
2	Adam Clayton (of U2)	Dublin	13 Mar 1960
3	Brian Downey (of Thin Lizzy)	Dublin	27 Jan 1951
4	Enya (Eithne Ni Bhraonain)	Donegal	17 May 1961
5	Bob Geldof	Dublin	5 Oct 1954
6	Danny Hutton (of Three Dog Night)	Buncrana	10 Sep 1946
7	Phil Lynott	Dublin	20 Aug 1951
8	Larry Mullen Jr (of U2)	Dublin	31 Oct 1961
9	Sinead O'Connor	Glengeary	12 Dec 1966
10	Gilbert O'Sullivan (Raymond Edward O'Sullivan)	Waterford	1 Dec 1946

10 MUSIC ARTISTS WHO WERE BORN IN MANCHESTER, UK

	Artist	Date of birth
1	Stuart (William Stuart) Adamson (of Big Country)	11 Apr 1958
2	Wayne Fontana (Glyn Geoffrey Ellis)	28 Oct 1945
3	Martin Fry (of ABC)	9 Mar 1958
4	Kevin Godley (of 10cc)	7 Oct 1945
5	Roy Harper	12 Jul 1941
6	Mick Hucknall	8 Jun 1960
7	Davey Jones (of the Monkees)	30 Dec 1945
8	John Mayall	29 Nov 1943
9	Morrissey (Stephen Patrick Morrissey)	22 May 1959
10	Barney Sumner (Bernard Dicken of New Order)	4 Jan 1956

10 MUSIC ARTISTS WHO WERE BORN IN NEW ORLEANS, USA

	Artist	Date of birth
1	Louis Armstrong	4 Aug 1901*
2	Harry Connick Jr	11 Sep 1967
3	Dr John (Malcolm Rebenack)	21 Nov 1941
4	Fats Domino (Antoine Domino)	26 Feb 1928
5	Lee Dorsey	24 Dec 1924
6	Mahalia Jackson	26 Oct 1911
7	Art Neville	17 Dec 1937
8	Randy (Randolph) Newman	28 Nov 1944
9	Lloyd Price	9 Mar 1934
10	Allen Toussaint	14 Jan 1938

* For many years, Armstrong's accepted birthdate was the more romantic 4 July 1900.

10 MUSIC ARTISTS WHO WERE BORN IN PHILADELPHIA, USA – AND CHANGED THEIR NAMES

	Artist	Real name	Date of birth
1	Frankie Avalon	Francis Thomas Avallon	18 Sep 1940
2	Chubby Checker	Ernest Evans	3 Oct 1941
3	James Darren	James William Ercolani	8 Jun 1946
4	Fabian	Fabian Forte	6 Feb 1943
5	Buddy Greco	Armando Greco	14 Aug 1926
6	Joan Jett	Joan Larkin	22 Sep 1960
7	Patti LaBelle	Patricia Louise Holt-Edwards	4 Oct 1944
8	Mario Lanza	Alfredo Arnold Cocozza	31 Jan 1921
9	Al Martino	Alfred Cini	7 Nov 1927
10	Bobby Rydell	Robert Lewis Ridarelli	26 Apr 1942

10 MUSIC ARTISTS WHO WERE BORN IN WALES

	Artist	Birthplace	Date of birth
1	John Cale (of Velvet Underground)	Garnant	4 Dec 1940
2	Julian Cope	Bargoed	21 Oct 1957
3	The Edge (David Evans of U2)	Cardiff	8 Aug 1961
4	Dave Edmunds	Cardiff	15 Apr 1944
5	Green (Green Strohmeyer-Gartside of Scritti Politti)	Cardiff	22 Jun 1956
6	Mary Hopkin	Pontardawe	3 May 1950
7	Tom Jones (Thomas Jones Woodward)	Pontypridd	7 Jun 1940
8	Mike Peters (of the Alarm)	Prestatyn	25 Feb 1959
9	Shakin' Stevens (Michael Barratt)	Ely	4 Mar 1948
10	Karl Wallinger (of World Party)	Prestatyn	19 Oct 1957

'On the whole, I'd rather be in Philadelphia' was the comic actor W.C. Fields' probably apocryphal reply when asked what he would like inscribed on his tombstone. Fields, who came from Philadelphia, also changed his name, from Dukenfield. What is it about the city that makes people want to adopt new names?

REAL NAMES QUIZ

Match the famous artists with their birth names:

1	Marvin Lee Aday	A	Adam Ant
2	James Osterberg	B	Elvis Costello
3	Susan Ballion	C	Tina Turner
4	Stuart Goddard	D	Gary Glitter
5	Paul Gadd	E	Meat Loaf
6	Louis Firbank	F	Boy George
7	Declan McManus	G	Iggy Pop
8	Annie Mae Bullock	H	John Denver
9	George O'Dowd	I	Lou Reed
10	Henry John Deutschendorf	J	Siouxsie Sioux

10 MEMBERS OF THE FOUR SEASONS

1	Frankie Valli
2	Bob Gaudio
3	Nick Massi
4	Tommy DeVito
5	Dimitri Callas
6	Joe Long
7	Gerry Polci
8	Don Ciccone
9	Lee Shapiro
10	John Paiva

The first four names formed the original hit-making line-up from 1962 to 1965, but since the latter half of the 1960s, personnel changes have been regular. Only Frankie Valli has provided any continuity (although Bob Gaudio has usually been associated with the band in either a production or songwriting capacity since the beginning). Their major chart return between 1975 and 1977 saw the line-up of Valli and the last four names on the list stabilize until the end of that decade, turning out hits including *Who Loves You?* and *December '63.*

10 MEMBERS OF THE SUPREMES

1	Diana Ross
2	Mary Wilson
3	Florence Ballard
4	Cindy Birdsong
5	Scherrie Payne
6	Jean Terrell
7	Susaye Greene
8	Barbara Martin
9	Lynda Lawrence
10	Karen Jackson

The definitive Supremes line-up, which recorded such hits as *Baby Love, You Keep Me Hangin' On* and *Where Did Our Love Go,* consisted of the first three girls on the list. Jean Terrell replaced Diana Ross as lead singer in 1970 to score with *Nathan Jones* and *Stoned Love* among others, followed by a string of personnel changes thereafter which saw only founding member Mary Wilson maintain continuity in the line-up.

10 MUSIC ARTISTS WITH BETTER-KNOWN RELATIVES

	Artist	Relative	Relationship
1	Carlene Carter (Country)	Johnny Cash	Step-daughter
2	Nona Gaye (R & B)	Marvin Gaye	Daughter
3	Mickey Gilley (Country)	Jerry Lee Lewis	Cousin
4	Lalah Hathaway (R & B)	Donny Hathaway	Daughter
5	Cissy Houston (R & B)	Whitney Houston	Mother
6	Loretta Lynn (Country)	Crystal Gayle	Sister
7	Mike McGear (pop)	Paul McCartney	Brother
8	Sally Oldfield (pop)	Mike Oldfield	Sister
9	Kate Robbins (pop)	Paul McCartney	Cousin
10	Robin Sarstedt (pop)	Peter Sarstedt	Brother

Only the movie world (and, perhaps, that of royal families) can match pop music for the intricacies of its exponents' relationships with each other. Extending beyond those itemized here, Carlene Carter was also married to Nick Lowe, while Whitney Houston also has a famous cousin, Dionne Warwick. A third Sarstedt brother, Clive, was actually the most successful of the three charting relatives: under the pseudonym Eden Kane, Clive scored five Top 10 UK hits in the early 1960s. Both Nona Gaye and Lalah Hathaway have embarked on promising R & B careers in recent years, following the deaths of their respective fathers: Marvin Gaye was shot by his father, while soul legend Donny Hathaway committed suicide.

THE 10 HIGHEST-EARNING POP STARS IN THE WORLD

	Artist(s)	Income ($) 1991	1992	Total
1	New Kids On The Block	54,000,000	8,000,000	62,000,000
2	Michael Jackson	25,000,000	26,000,000	51,000,000
3=	Madonna	24,000,000	24,000,000	48,000,000
3=	Julio Iglesias	23,000,000	25,000,000	48,000,000
5	Guns N' Roses	21,000,000	26,000,000	47,000,000
6	Prince	10,000,000	35,000,000	45,000,000
7	Garth Brooks	20,000,000	24,000,000	44,000,000
8	U2	9,000,000	27,000,000	36,000,000
9	Grateful Dead	16,000,000	15,000,000	31,000,000
10	ZZ Top	11,000,000	18,000,000	29,000,000

Used by permission of Forbes *Magazine.*

Forbes Magazine's survey of top entertainers' income covers a two-year period in order to iron out fluctuations, especially those caused by successful tours. In 1991 both Aerosmith and Grateful Dead entered the Top 10 as a result of sell-out tours, but only the latter maintained their income over the subsequent year, while the Rolling Stones, having earned $44,000,000 in 1990 when they were touring, saw this fall to $11,000,000 in 1991 and $14,000,000 in 1992, thus evicting them from the Top 10. Conversely, after a relatively quiet 1991, the income from U2's massive global tour during 1992 reinstated them in the Top 10. In 1990 New Kids On The Block (previously at number three) sold almost $75,000,000 worth of concert tickets and over $1,000,000,000 worth of merchandise – hence their elevation in that year to number one, which they sustained in 1991, although they will clearly never be seen again in this list. In the 1990–91 period, Michael Jackson's income actually halved, but it remains so huge that he nevertheless remains a prominent member of this elite.

10 MEN HONOURED IN SONG

	Man	Title	Artist
1	Syd Barrett	*Shine On You Crazy Diamond*	Pink Floyd
2	Bob Dylan	*Diamonds And Rust*	Joan Baez
3	Brian Epstein	*Baby You're A Rich Man*	Beatles
4	Marvin Gaye	*Missing You*	Diana Ross
5	Jimi Hendrix	*Song For A Dreamer*	Procul Harum
6	Buddy Holly	*Old Friend*	Waylon Jennings
7	John Lennon	*Empty Garden (Hey Hey Johnny)*	Elton John
8	Don McLean	*Killing Me Softly With His Song*	Roberta Flack
9	Neil Sedaka	*Oh Neil*	Carole King
10	Vincent Van Gogh	*Vincent*	Don McLean

Shine On You Crazy Diamond, written about ex-Pink Floyd member, the highly reclusive Syd Barrett, appeared on their *Wish You Were Here* album. *Missing You* was written and produced (for Diana Ross) by Lionel Richie following the death of their friend and former Motown label-mate, Marvin Gaye. Elton John's eulogy to John Lennon appeared on the former's *Jump Up!* album, while *Killing Me Softly* was written by Lori Lieberman (although a hit for Roberta Flack), inspired after attending a Don McLean concert. *Oh Neil* was Carole King's 'answer' record to Neil Sedaka's hit, *Oh Carol* (see companion list overleaf).

Buddy Holly & The Crickets: Holly was the subject of Waylon Jennings' tribute Old Friend. *Jennings could have been in the same crash that killed Holly, but lost in a draw to see who got seats on the plane.*

10 WOMEN HONOURED IN SONG

	Woman	Title	Artist
1	Rosanna Arquette	*Rosanna*	Toto
2	Angie Bowie	*Angie*	Rolling Stones
3	Jenny Boyd	*Jennifer Juniper*	Donovan
4	Patti Boyd	*Layla*	Derek & The Dominos
5	Rita Coolidge	*Delta Lady*	Joe Cocker
6	Patti D'Arbanville	*Lady D'Arbanville*	Cat Stevens
7	Linda Eastman	*Linda*	Jan and Dean
8	Peggy Sue Gerrow	*Peggy Sue*	Buddy Holly
9	Carole King	*Oh Carol*	Neil Sedaka
10	Nancy Sinatra	*Nancy (With The Laughing Face)*	Frank Sinatra

Song-writer Jack Lawrence wrote *Linda* about the daughter of his attorney, Lee Eastman; Jan and Dean scored with the song in 1963, and she later became famous as Paul McCartney's wife. Jenny and Patti Boyd may be the only sisters in the world to have had hit songs written about each of them by different artists (Patti, who was originally married to George Harrison, was also the subject of *Wonderful Tonight*, a 1978 hit for Eric Clapton, whom she also married). Peggy Sue Gerrow married Buddy Holly's drummer (in the Crickets), Jerry Allison.

10 UK MUSIC ARTISTS WHO HAVE ALSO PURSUED ACTING CAREERS

	Artist	Acting projects include
1	David Bowie	*The Hunger, The Man Who Fell To Earth, The Elephant Man**
2	Phil Collins	*Buster, Miami Vice**, Hook*
3	Roger Daltrey	*Lisztomania, McVicar, Tommy*
4	David Essex	*That'll Be The Day, Stardust, The River***
5	Adam Faith	*Stardust, Budgie**, Beat Girl*
6	Marianne Faithfull	*Girl On A Motorcycle, Ned Kelly†, Three Sisters**
7	Mick Jagger	*Performance, Ned Kelly, Freejack*
8	Paul Jones (Manfred Mann)	*Privilege, Joseph & The Amazing Technicolor Dreamcoat*, Hamlet**
9	Olivia Newton-John	*Grease, Xanadu, Two Of A Kind*
10	Sting	*Dune, Quadrophenia, Brimstone & Treacle*

* Stage role.   ** Television role.

† *Marianne Faithfull was unable to complete filming for* Ned Kelly *(starring Mick Jagger) as a result of a drug overdose.*

Many of these artists continue to pursue acting careers despite consistently bad reviews from film, TV and stage critics, notably David Bowie, Mick Jagger and Sting. Phil Collins has, however, attracted more positive notices – he may benefit from an early acting start as a child, notably as the Artful Dodger in a London stage production of *Oliver!* and as an extra in the Beatles' *A Hard Day's Night* movie.

NATIONALITIES QUIZ

Match the act with its home territory:

1	Johnny Halliday	A	Switzerland
2	Golden Earring	B	Canada
3	Abba	C	Australia
4	Midnight Oil	D	France
5	Scorpions	E	Holland
6	Yello	F	Sweden
7	a-ha	G	Norway
8	Bee Gees	H	New Zealand
9	Rush	I	Germany
10	Split Enz	J	United Kingdom

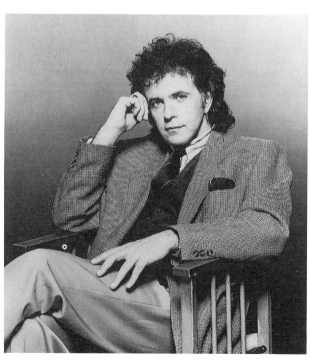

David Essex's acting career has encompassed the films That'll Be The Day, Stardust *and* Silver Dream Racer *and stage musicals* Evita *and* Mutiny.

10 NOTABLE ARTISTS WHO HAVE BEEN IMPRISONED

	Artist	Offence	Year	Sentence
1	Chuck Berry*	Transporting a minor across state lines for immoral purposes.	1962	3 years
2	James Brown**	Drug possession, unlawful possession of a gun and resisting arrest.	1988	6 years
3	David Crosby (Crosby, Stills, Nash & Young)	Possession of cocaine and carrying a gun into a bar.	1983	5 years
4	Hugh Cornwall (Stranglers)	Possession of cocaine, heroin and cannabis.	1980	3 months
5	Grateful Dead	Entire band detained for possession of cannabis.	1967	6 hours
6	Paul McCartney	Jailed in Tokyo for marijuana possession.	1980	9 days
7	Jim Morrison	Interfering with the flight of an aircraft (more specifically an air hostess) and public drunkenness.	1969	1 day
8	Keith Richards†	Allowing his house to be used for the illegal smoking of cannabis.	1967	1 day
9	Siouxsie Sioux	Obstruction following a Johnny Thunders gig.	1977	1 day/fined £20
10	Sid Vicious	Charged with murdering his girlfriend, Nancy Spungen.	1978	2 months (awaiting trial)

* *A prison regular throughout his career, Berry was also incarcerated at the age of 14 for three years for robbery and again in 1979, serving five months for tax evasion.*

** *Brown also has an illustrious crime record, including a four-year hard labour stretch for theft at the age of 16, a 1972 arrest for trying to incite a riot and several offences in 1988 including assaulting his wife with intent to murder and miscellaneous drug charges.*

† *Mick Jagger was also imprisoned for one night on the same day for unlawfully possessing four benzedrine tablets: Jagger spent the night in Brixton Prison, while fellow Stone Richards entertained inmates at Wormwood Scrubs.*

THE 10 MOST EXPENSIVE ITEMS OF POP MEMORABILIA EVER SOLD AT AUCTION*

	Item/sale	Price (£)**
1	John Lennon's 1965 Rolls-Royce Phantom V touring limousine, finished in psychedelic paintwork Sotheby's, New York, 29 June 1985 ($2,299,000)	1,768,462
2	John Lennon's 1970 Mercedes-Benz 600 Pullman four-door limousine Christie's, London, 27 April 1989	137,500
3	Elvis Presley's 1963 Rolls-Royce Phantom V touring limousine Sotheby's, London, 28 August 1986	110,000
4	John Lennon's handwritten lyrics for *A Day In The Life* Sotheby's, London, 27 August 1992	48,400
5	Elton John's 1977 Panther de Ville Coupé Sotheby's, London, 22 August 1991	46,200
6	Paul McCartney's handwritten lyrics for *She's Leaving Home* Sotheby's, London, 27 August 1992	45,100
7	Buddy Holly's spectacles, 1958 Sotheby's, New York, 23 June 1990 ($45,100)	26,027
8	An unreleased 8mm film of the Beatles in America, 1965 Christie's, London, 29 August 1986	24,000
9	Tape-recorded interview with John Lennon, 1968 Sotheby's, London, 5 August 1987	23,650
10=	Film by Mal Evans, the Beatles' road manager, of the group on holiday in India Sotheby's, London, 27 August 1992	23,100
10=	*Benny and the Jets*, a Surrealist collage by John Lennon, 1974 Sotheby's, London, 21 August 1990	23,100

* *Excluding clothing and guitars – see separate lists.*   ** *Including 10 per cent buyer's premium, where appropriate.*

THE 10 MOST EXPENSIVE SIGNED RECORDS EVER SOLD AT AUCTION BY CHRISTIE'S, LONDON

	Record/sale	Price (£)*
1	Single, *I Am The Walrus*, signed and annotated by John Lennon, 27 April 1989	2,200
2	Album, *Yesterday And Today*, signed by the Beatles, 25 August 1988	1,650
3=	Album, *Revolver*, signed by the Beatles, 24 August 1989	1,540
3=	Album, *Revolver*, signed by the Beatles, 25 April 1991	1,540
5	Album, *Sgt Pepper's Lonely Hearts Club Band*, signed by the Beatles, 28 August 1988	1,430
6=	Album, *Help!*, signed by the Beatles, 29 August 1986	1,320
6=	Album, *A Hard Day's Night*, signed by the Beatles, 27 April 1989	1,320
6=	Album, *Beatles For Sale*, signed by the Beatles, 27 April 1990	1,320
6=	Album, *Meet The Beatles*, signed by the Beatles, 29 August 1991	1,320
10	Single, *All My Loving*, signed by the Beatles, 7 May 1992	1,250

* *Including 10 per cent buyer's premium.*

All the most expensive signed records sold in Christie's auctions have been signed by members of the Beatles, whose domination of the pop memorabilia business has been maintained for many years.

THE 10 MOST EXPENSIVE ITEMS OF ROCK STARS' CLOTHING SOLD AT AUCTION IN THE UK

	Item/sale	Price (£)*
1	Elvis Presley's one-piece 'Shooting Star' stage outfit, *c*1972 Phillips, London, 24 August 1988	28,600
2	John Lennon's black leather jacket, *c*1960–62 Christie's, London, 7 May 1992	24,200
3	Michael Jackson's white rhinestone glove Christie's, London, 19 December 1991	16,500
4	Elvis Presley's blue stage costume, *c*1972 Phillips, London, 24 August 1988	15,400
5	Jimi Hendrix's black felt hat Sotheby's, London, 22 August 1991	14,300
6	Elvis Presley's one-piece stage costume, as worn on the cover of his *Burning Love* album Phillips, London, 25 August 1992	13,200
7	Elton John's giant Dr Marten boots from the film *Tommy* Sotheby's, London, 6 September 1988	12,100
8=	Michael Jackson's black sequinned jacket Sotheby's, London, 22 August 1991	11,000
8=	Prince's *Purple Rain* stage costume, 1984 Christie's, London, 19 December 1991	11,000
10	Hand-painted silk jacket worn in 1967 by Jimi Hendrix Experience drummer Mitch Mitchell Sotheby's, London, 27 August 1992	10,450

* *Including 10 per cent buyer's premium.*

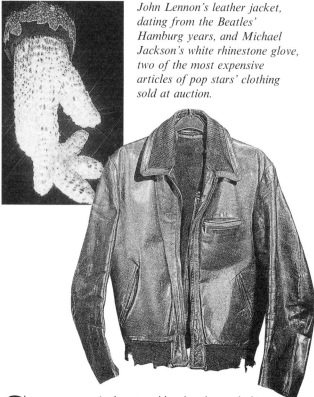

John Lennon's leather jacket, dating from the Beatles' Hamburg years, and Michael Jackson's white rhinestone glove, two of the most expensive articles of pop stars' clothing sold at auction.

Close runners-up in the second-hand rock star clothing market include two of Madonna's gold basques, designed by Jean Paul Gaultier, one of which made £9,900 at Sotheby's, London, on 27 August 1992, and another, which was auctioned twice – at Sotheby's, London, on 22 August 1991, when it fetched £8,800 and again on 27 August 1992, when it realized £9,000. Another of Prince's *Purple Rain* stage costumes was sold at Christie's, London, on 8 May 1992 for £9,020, and Michael Jackson's studded black leather jacket at Sotheby's, London, on 22 August 1991 for £7,480.

10 NOTABLE ROCK STARS' GUITARS SOLD AT AUCTION

	Guitar/sale	Price (£)*
1	Jimi Hendrix's Fender *Stratocaster* guitar Sotheby's, London, 25 April 1990	198,000
2	Buddy Holly's Gibson acoustic guitar, c1945, in a tooled leather case made by Holly Sotheby's, New York, 23 June 1990 ($242,000)	139,658
3	Elvis Presley's Martin D-18 guitar (formerly with a $5,000,000 asking price) Red Baron Antiques, Atlanta, Georgia, 3 October 1991 ($180,000)	106,825
4	Buddy Holly's Fender *Stratocaster* guitar, 1958 Sotheby's, New York, 23 June 1990 ($110,000)	63,481
5	Two pieces of a guitar personally smashed by Jimi Hendrix, June 1967 Sotheby's, London, 22 August 1991	29,700
6	John Lennon's Hofner acoustic guitar, c1960 Sotheby's, London, 30 August 1984	17,050
7	John Entwistle's Peter Cook customized Fender electric bass guitar (one of the few that survived a Who stage performance) Sotheby's, London, 7 April 1988	16,500
8	Bill Haley Aria electric guitar Christie's, London, 29 June 1986	15,500
9	Hofner *President* guitar, c1960, once owned by Stuart Sutcliffe, the 'Fifth Beatle' Sotheby's, London, 28 August 1986	10,450
10	John Entwistle's custom-built 'Streak of Lightning' guitar Sotheby's, London, 7 April 1988	9,350

Including 10 per cent buyer's premium, where appropriate.

Jimi Hendrix's Fender Stratocaster *guitar, sold in 1990 for a record £198,000.*

THE 10 MOST VALUABLE GUITAR MODELS IN THE WORLD

	Guitar	Estimated value ($)
1=	Martin D-45 (pre-war)	100,000
1=	Stromberg Master 400 Cutaway	100,000
3	Gibson Explorer	70,000
4	Gretsch White Penguin	60,000
5=	D'Angelico New Yorker Cutaway	50,000
5=	Martin OM-45	50,000
5=	Martin 1932 D-28 (12 fret)	50,000
5=	Gibson Flying V	50,000
9	Gibson Les Paul Sunburst	45,000
10	D'Angelico Excel Cutaway	35,000

Source: *Gruhn's Guitars, Nashville.*

The estimated sales value assumes that the guitar is a clean early example in good condition. These dollar estimates reflect market sales for these rare guitars during the past two years, when such prices have been achieved. If one of these guitars has a celebrity status, the value would increase beyond even these prices.

THE 10 MOST EXPENSIVE MUSICAL INSTRUMENTS EVER SOLD AT AUCTION

	Instrument	Sale	Price (£)*
1	'Mendelssohn' Stradivarius violin	Christie's, London, 21 November 1990	902,000
2	'Cholmondley' Stradivarius violoncello	Sotheby's, London, 22 June 1988	682,000
3	Jimi Hendrix's Fender *Stratocaster* guitar	Sotheby's, London, 25 April 1990	198,000
4	Steinway grand piano, designed by Lawrence Alma-Tadema and Edward Poynter for Henry Marquand, 1884–87	Sotheby Parke Bernet, New York, 26 March 1980 ($390,000)	163,500
5	Verne Powell platinum flute	Christie's, New York, 18 October 1986 ($187,000)	126,200
6	Flemish single-manual harpsichord made by Johan Daniel Dulken of Antwerp, 1755	Sotheby's, London, 27 March 1990	82,280
7	Kirkman double-manual harpsichord	Christie's, London, 26 June 1987	77,000
8	Columnar alto recorder made by Hans van Schratt, mid-16th century	Christie's, London, 16 March 1988	44,000
9	'Portable Grand Piano' made by John Isaac Hawkins, c1805 (a very early example of an upright piano, considerably pre-dating the modern type, and one of only three examples known)	Sotheby's, London, 4 July 1985	14,300
10	Miniature silver horn made by Johann Wilhelm Haas of Nuremberg, 1681	Sotheby's, Geneva, 5 May 1981 (SF46,200)	11,800

* Including 10 per cent buyer's premium, where appropriate.

This list represents the most expensive example of each type of musical instrument only. The two harpsichords and the two pianos are actually of different types, but as each belongs to the same family, it may by argued that numbers seven and nine should be disqualified from the ranking – in which case, the contenders for the new numbers nine and 10 would be a pair of German kettle drums, c1700, formerly the property of the Counts von Geich, sold at Sotheby's, London, on 21 November 1974 for £3,900 – the record price for a percussion instrument – and a Swiss sachbut made by J. Steimer of Zofinger in the early 18th century (Sotheby's, London, 6 May 1976, £3,080), which holds the record for a brass instrument (other than the current number 10, which is an unusual miniature model).

THE 10 MOST EXPENSIVE MUSIC MANUSCRIPTS EVER SOLD AT AUCTION

	Manuscript	Sale	Price (£)*
1	Nine symphonies by Wolfgang Amadeus Mozart	Sotheby's, London, 22 May 1987	2,350,000
2	Ludwig van Beethoven's *Piano Sonata in E Minor*, Opus 90	Sotheby's, London, 6 December 1991	1,000,000
3=	Robert Schumann's *Piano Concerto in A Minor*, Opus 54	Sotheby's, London, 22 November 1989	800,000
3=	Wolfgang Amadeus Mozart's *Fantasia in C Minor* and *Sonata in C Minor*	Sotheby's, London, 21 November 1990	800,000
5	Ludwig van Beethoven's first movement of the *Sonata for Violoncello and Piano in A Major*, Opus 69	Sotheby's, London, 17 May 1990	480,000
6	Johann Sebastian Bach's cantata *Auf Christi Himmelfahrt allein*	Sotheby's, London, 22 November 1989	390,000
7	Igor Stravinsky's *Rite of Spring*	Sotheby's, London, 11 November 1982	300,000
8	Franz Schubert's *Quartet in B flat Major* (No. 8) D.112, Opus 168	Christie's, London, 24 June 1992	270,000
9	Johann Sebastian Bach's cantata *O Ewigkeit, Du Donnerwort*	Sotheby's, London, 11 November 1982	190,000
10	Franz Schubert's overture to the opera *Fierabras*	Sotheby's, London, 28 May 1986	150,000

* Hammer prices', excluding premiums.

The collection of nine symphonies by Mozart not only holds the record for the highest price ever paid for a music manuscript, but also for any post-medieval manuscript.

THE 10 MOST VALUABLE JUKEBOXES IN THE UK

Jukebox	Value (£)*
1 Wurlitzer 950 (1942)	35,000

Made in 1942 when wartime restrictions were imposed on the supply of plastic and nickel (two crucial design elements), the result is a testament to the resourcefulness of Wurlitzer's chief designer, Paul Fuller. A combination of its aesthetic appeal and rarity – only 3,497 were made – makes it by far the most valuable jukebox.

2 Wurlitzer 850 (1941)	20,000

Known as the 'Peacock', this was the most spectacular jukebox designed by Paul Fuller. Its central feature was a silkscreened peacock illuminated from behind by polarized coloured filters that presented an ever-changing display of iridescent colour. Wurlitzer's last full production model before the Second World War, a total of 10,002 were made in 1941.

3 Elton John's Wurlitzer 750 (1941)	17,600

Sold at Sotheby's in London on 6 September 1988 with an estimate of £10,000, bidding reached a surprising £16,000 (£17,600 with the 10 per cent buyer's premium).

4 Rock-Ola Commando (1942–45)	14,000

In response to wartime restrictions on materials, Rock-Ola came up with a highly creative design which looked more like a sculpture than a conventional jukebox. Its uniqueness and rarity contribute to its high market value. It derived its extraordinarily apt name from its inventor, David Rockola, the founder of the Rock-Ola Manufacturing Company, who died on 26 January 1993.

5 Wurlitzer 81 (1940)	12,000

As well as full-sized jukeboxes, Wurlitzer also manufactured small 'tabletop' machines which played only one side of a dozen 78-rpm discs. Of all the tabletop models the 81 is regarded as the most desirable, partly because only 1,100 were made and also because its design incorporated marbled plastics not found in any other model. The countertops came with a stand almost as valuable as the machine itself — hence the high price of the two together.

Jukebox	Value (£)*
6 Wurlitzer 1015 (1946–47)	11,000

Arguably *the* archetypal jukebox, this post-war machine evokes the spirit of Rock and Roll. Wurlitzer manufactured 56,000 of this model and launched a massive advertising campaign to link the 1015 with every festival in American life, from Christmas to Thanksgiving. Mechanically reliable, numerous examples remained in use well into the 1950s. Its visual appeal, deriving from its rotating colour cylinders and streaming bubble tubes, and its associations with a nostalgic era account for the 1015's value, despite the relatively large numbers available.

7 Wurlitzer 1080 (1947)	10,000

Made in 1947 and known as the 'Colonial', this model was designed for elegant sites, although many regard its bizarre eighteenth-century styling as verging on the kitsch.

8 Wurlitzer 'Victory' Model (1943–45)	9,500

A wartime model in which glass replaced plastic, the Victory was essentially a cabinet that could be placed over any earlier Wurlitzer in order to keep the company name in the public consciousness.

9 Wurlitzer 800 (1940)	

A large jukebox made in 1940, the 800 was the first to use bubble tubes. Enormous illuminated pilasters on each side featured rotating colour cylinders that projected a moving zebra stripe pattern.

10 Wurlitzer 1100 (1948)	8,000

Paul Fuller's last jukebox before his retirement, it featured a state-of-the-art sound system for 78-rpm records, with a lightweight tone arm and pre-amp. Although the most colourful 1940s jukebox when lit up, it was not well received in its day, perhaps because stylistically it harked back to wartime design (its dome was even compared with that of a bomber!), but by the time it was manufactured in 1948, America was looking forward to the 1950s and so the 1100 marks the end of an era.

* *Based on average market price in the UK of a model in fine condition – with the exception of number three, the value of which was inflated by its connection with a celebrity owner.*

The jukeboxes made in the 1940s, which usually played one side of 20 or 24 78-rpm records, represent the most desirable, and hence valuable among collectors, although 1950s examples are also becoming more widely appreciated. Good original or sympathetically restored machines command the highest prices, but jukeboxes are generally bought for their visual appeal, nostalgic associations – and because they will also play one's favourite records. Additionally, in recent years, as prices have escalated, they have also become acknowledged as a sound investment. All but one of the 10 most valuable jukeboxes were made by the same company, Wurlitzer, all of these created by the same designer, Paul Fuller, during the 1930s and 1940s. Regarded as the doyen of jukebox cabinet designers, Fuller was responsible for 13 full-size jukeboxes and five tabletop models. His importance was such that some collectors bid only for his machines.

THE 10 MOST VALUABLE JUKEBOXES IN THE USA

1	Wurlitzer 950
2	Rock-Ola President
3	Rock-Ola Premier
4	Rock-Ola Spectrovox
5	Wurlitzer 850
6	Rock-Ola Commando
7	AMI 40 Selection Singing Towers
8	Wurlitzer 81
9	Wurlitzer Victory
10	Wurlitzer 1015

Source: Jukebox Collector Magazine (as of October 1992). The list assumes that the machines are in Grade One condition.

While the value of old jukeboxes fluctuates from year to year as different models drop in and out of favour, the number one item, the Wurlitzer 950, is currently worth approximately $35,000. The 10th most valuable jukebox listed would expect to achieve a $10,000 sale.

THE 10 MOST EXPENSIVE GRAMOPHONES AND PHONOGRAPHS SOLD AT AUCTION IN LONDON

	Gramophone or phonograph/sale	Price (£)*
1	Edison Opera phonograph Sotheby's, May 1990	17,500
2	Columbia Type K Graphophone (phonograph) Phillips, May 1992	13,005
3	HMV Model 203 cabinet gramophone Phillips, May 1991	9,350
4	Edison Stereoscopic Co tinfoil phonograph, c1880 Christie's, September 1980	8,000
5	Edison Class M phonograph Christie's, April 1987	7,700
6	HMV Model 203 re-entrant tone-chamber gramophone, 1930 Christie's, April 1990	6,050
7=	Edison *Perfected* phonograph, c1889 Christie's, September 1980	6,000
7=	Detective recording machine, 1892 Christie's, September 1980	6,000
9	HMV Model 202 teak cabinet gramophone Phillips, May 1992	5,940
10	Edison electric phonograph in floor standing case, c1892 Christie's, September 1980	5,800

* Including 10 per cent buyer's premium, where relevant.

Number five owes part of its value to its association with the explorer-journalist Sir Henry Morton Stanley (of 'Dr Livingstone I presume?' fame), to whom it was given by Edison's UK agent, Colonel Gouraud, as a wedding present when Stanley married the artist Dorothy Tennant on 12 July 1890.

THE 10 MOST VALUABLE ALBUMS OF THE 1950s IN THE USA

	Title	Artist	Special feature/label/cat. no.	Year	Estimated value ($)
1	*Billy Ward & His Dominoes*	Billy Ward & His Dominoes	10"/Federal 295-94	1954	7,500
2	*The Best Of The Five Keys*	Five Keys	Blue label/Aladdin 806	1956	5,000
3	*Their Greatest Jukebox Hits*	Midnighters	10"/Federal 295-90	1955	4,000
4=	*Mood Music*	Charles Brown	10" red vinyl/Aladdin 702	1952	3,000
4=	*Rockin' The Boogie*	Amos Milburn	10" red vinyl/Aladdin 704	1954	3,000
4=	*Party After Hours*	Amos Milburn, Wynonie Harris & 'Crown Prince' Waterford	10" red vinyl/Aladdin 703	1954	3,000
7=	*Johnny Burnette & The Rock 'n' Roll Trio*	Johnny Burnette & The Rock 'n' Roll Trio	Coral CRL 57080	1956	2,500
7=	*The Five Satins Sing*	Five Satins	Blue vinyl/Ember ELP 100	1957	2,500
9=	*Boyd Bennett*	Boyd Bennett	King 594	1956	2,000
9=	*Blue And Moody*	Lula Reed	King 604	1959	2,000

Source: Goldmine/Neal Umphred.

THE 10 MOST VALUABLE SINGLES OF THE 1950s IN THE UK

	Title	Artist	Label/cat. no.	Year	Estimated value (£)
1	*See You Later, Alligator*	Bobby Charles	London HLU 8247	1956	275
2	*Earth Angel*	Penguins	London HL 8114	1955	200
3	*Mama, Don't You Think I Know*	Jackie Lee Cochran	Brunswick 05669	1957	190
4	*You Ain't Treatin' Me Right*	Mac Curtis	Parlophone R 4279	1957	175
5	*Walking The Blues*	Willie Dixon	London HLU 8297	1956	165
6	*Latch On*	Ron Hargrave	MGM 956	1957	160
7	*Gee*	Crows	Columbia SCM 5119	1954	150
8=	*Would I Be Crying*	Flamingos	London HLN 8373	1957	145
8=	*Down Yonder We Go Ballin'*	Smiley Lewis	London HLU 8337	1956	145
10	*I Knew From The Start*	Moonglows	London HLN 8374	1957	140

These extremely rare artifacts are all 45-rpm 7″ singles issued in comparatively minuscule numbers during the era when most UK singles were 10″ 78s. Moreover, these are all lesser-known Rock 'n' Roll and R & B tracks which would have catered, at the time, for minority tastes. The prices quoted assume mint condition. Considering that there cannot be more than a handful of copies of each of these still in existence, the figures are probably conservative – in fact, an auctioned copy of *Earth Angel* fetched a four-figure sum in 1991.

THE 10 MOST VALUABLE BEATLES RECORDS IN THE UK

	Title	Special feature/label/cat. no.	Year	Estimated value (£)
1	*Please Please Me*	First UK stereo album with gold label/Parlophone PCS 3042	1963	1,000
2	*The Beatles At The Beeb*	BBC Transcription disc for broadcasters only/CN 3970	1982	400
3	*From Then To You*	Fan club album compiling Xmas flexis/Apple LYN 2153	1970	260
4	*Abbey Road*	Limited-edition picture disc LP/Parlophone PHO 7088	1978	250
5=	*First HMV Boxed Set*	First four albums on CD, in exclusive box/HMV BEACD 25	1987	200
5=	*Please Please Me*	Mono version of (1) above	1963	200
7	*Let It Be*	Original UK LP release with book and box/Apple PXS 1	1970	160
8	*The Beatles Mono Collection*	Mono versions of first 10 LPs in a box/ Parlophone BMC 10	1984	120
9	*The Beatles Collection*	Stereo versions of 13 LPs in a box/Parlophone BC 13	1986	110
10	*Sweet Georgia Brown*	7″ single made with Tony Sheridan/Polydor NH 52906	1964	80

These are all UK releases, and mint condition is assumed for the quoted prices. Items such as acetates and demonstration discs, which can fetch higher sums still, have not been included: all of those in the Top 10 had at least some degree of public availability.

THE 10 MOST VALUABLE BEATLES ALBUMS IN THE USA

	Title	Special feature/label/cat. no.	Year	Estimated value ($)
1=	Introducing The Beatles	'Ad back' cover/Vee Jay SR 1062 (mono)	1963	9,000
1=	Hear The Beatles Tell All	White label promotional LP/Vee Jay PRO 202	1964	9,000
3=	The Beatles And Frank Ifield On Stage	Full-colour painted Beatles portrait cover/ Vee Jay LPS 1085 (stereo)	1964	7,500
3=	Yesterday And Today	Initial state 'butcher' cover/Capitol ST 2553 (stereo)	1966	7,500
5=	Introducing The Beatles	'Ad back' cover/Vee Jay LP 1062 (stereo)	1963	3,000
5=	Introducing The Beatles	Blank back cover/Vee Jay SR 1062 (stereo)	1963	3,000
5=	Yesterday And Today	Initial state 'butcher' cover/Capitol T 2553 (mono)	1966	3,000
8=	The Beatles And Frank Ifield	Portrait cover/Vee Jay LP 1085 (mono)	1964	2,500
8=	The Beatles Vs The Four Seasons	Double-LP/Vee Jay DXS 30*	1964	2,500
10	A Hard Day's Night	White label promotional LP/United Artists UAL 3366	1964	2,000

* This double set combined the contents of Introducing The Beatles with The Golden Hits Of The Four Seasons, and, if found with a fold-open poster, is worth an additional $300.

Source: *Goldmine/Neal Umphred.*

THE 10 MOST VALUABLE BEATLES SINGLES IN THE USA

	Title	Special feature/label/cat. no.	Year	Estimated value ($)
1	My Bonnie/The Saints	Black label/Decca 31382	1962	10,000
2=	Ask Me Why/Anna	Sample from the label's 4-track EP/ Vee Jay Special DJ #8	1964	8,500
2=	Souvenir Of Their Visit To America	Picture sleeve EP/Vee Jay 903	1964	8,500
4	I Want To Hold Your Hand	WMCA radio station staff picture sleeve/Capitol 5112	1964	2,500
5=	Please Please Me/Ask Me Why	Promotional picture sleeve/Vee Jay 581	1964	2,000
5=	A Hard Day's Night	Promotional interview/United Artists – no cat. no.	1964	2,000
5=	The Beatles Introduce New Songs	Promotional EP/Capitol PRO 2720/21	1964	2,000
5=	A Surprise Gift From The Beatles, The Beach Boys & The Kingston Trio	Flexi-disc EP with mailing envelope/ Evatone 8464	1964	2,000
9=	Open-End Interview With The Beatles	Promotional picture sleeve EP/Capitol PRO 2548/49	1964	1,950
9=	The Beatles' Second Open-End Interview	Promotional picture sleeve EP/Capitol PRO 2598/99	1964	1,950

Source: *Goldmine/Neal Umphred.*

Beatles recordings remain the most valuable overall body of work in pop history. Number one was the first Beatles release in the USA, credited to The Beats backing Tony Sheridan. Only four known copies exist of number two, which was technically a two-track sample from the label's four-track EP. Number seven features Lennon and McCartney introducing new recordings of their compositions by Peter & Gordon and Cilla Black.

THE 10 MOST VALUABLE NON-BEATLES ALBUMS OF THE 1960s IN THE USA

	Title	Artist	Special feature/label/cat. no.	Year	Estimated value ($)
1	The Freewheelin' Bob Dylan	Bob Dylan	Original pressing including Talkin' John Birch Blues/ Columbia CS 8786 (stereo)	1963	16,000
2	The Freewheelin' Bob Dylan	Bob Dylan	Original pressing including Talkin' John Birch Blues/ Columbia CL 1986 (mono)	1963	10,000
3	River Deep–Mountain High	Ike & Tina Turner	Without cover/Philles PHLP 4011	1966	5,000
4=	Mule Skinners Blues	Fendermen	Translucent black vinyl/Soma MG 1240	1960	2,500
4=	The Jefferson Airplane Takes Off!	Jefferson Airplane	Original release with Runnin' Round The World/ RCA LPM 3584	1966	2,500
6=	Hey! Boss Man	Frank Frost	Philips Intl. 1975	1961	2,000
6=	The Return Of The Blues Boss	Amos Milburn	Motown 608	1963	2,000
8=	Rhythm Blues Party	Frank Ballard	Philips Intl. 1985	1962	1,500
8=	The Freewheelin' Bob Dylan	Bob Dylan	White label promo/Columbia CL 1986	1963	1,500
10	The International Hotel Presents Elvis 1969	Elvis Presley	Boxed set/RCA – no cat. no.	1969	1,400

Source: *Goldmine/Neal Umphred.*

The distinction between numbers one and two is that the first version was in stereo, the latter released in mono, the kind of apparently minor detail which can make all the difference in the serious business of record collecting.

THE 10 MOST VALUABLE ALBUMS OF THE 1970s AND 1980s IN THE USA

	Title	Artist	Special feature/label/cat. no.	Year	Value ($)
1	The Black Album	Prince	Two 45 rpm promotional discs/ Warner Bros. 25677	1987	6,000
2	Diamond Dogs	David Bowie	With 'genitals' cover/RCA APL1-0576	1974	5,000
3=	Blood On The Tracks	Bob Dylan	Test pressing with alternative tracks/ Columbia PC 33235	1976	4,000
3=	The Black Album	Prince	Warner Bros. 25677	1987	4,000
5	Ram	Paul McCartney	Mono promotional disc/Apple MAS 3375	1971	3,000
6	Aloha From Hawaii Via Satellite	Elvis Presley	With 'Chicken Of The Sea Tuna' sticker/RCA VPSX 6089	1973	1,500
7=	International Hotel Presents Elvis, 1970	Elvis Presley	Boxed set/RCA – no cat. no.	1970	1,400
7=	Moody Blue	Elvis Presley	'Splash' coloured vinyl/RCA AFL1-2428	1977	1,400
9	Songs Of The Rolling Stones	Rolling Stones	'Rock 'n' Roll Circus' cover/Abkco MPD 1	1975	1,250
10	Hey Jude/The Beatles Again	Beatles	Alternative prototype cover/Apple SO 385*	1970	1,100

* A number of alternatives for the cover of this compilation reached the prototype stage. If offered at an open auction by a reputable source, this item may fetch a much higher sum.

Source: *Goldmine/Neal Umphred.*

The estimated values given are sums which have either been achieved in 1992 or reasonable estimates of what a title might expect to fetch at an open auction. Prince's *Black Album* is the much cassette-copied album which was scheduled for release by Warner Bros, but pulled from release schedules at the last minute and never officially issued. While cassette copies are 10-a-penny, the original vinyl release, particularly in the two-disc 45-rpm format, are worth a royal ransom.

THE 10 MOST VALUABLE DAVID BOWIE RECORDS IN THE USA

	Title	Special feature/label/cat. no.	Year	Estimated value ($)
1	Diamond Dogs	LP with 'genitals' cover/RCA APL1 0576	1974	5,000
2	Time/The Prettiest Star	Picture sleeve 45/RCA APBO 0001	1973	500
3	Can't Help Thinking About Me	Retail 45/Warner Bros 5818	1966	400
4	Fashion/It's No Game/Teenage Wildlife	45/RCA JE 12087	1980	300
5	Can't Help Thinking About Me	White label promotional 45/Warner Bros 5818	1966	200
6=	David Bowie	LP/Deram DBS 18003	1969	150
6=	Man Of Words, Man Of Music	LP/Mercury SR 61325	1969	150
6=	Changesonebowie	LP featuring alternative version of John, I'm Only Dancing/ RCA APL1 1732	1976	150
9=	Memory Of A Free Festival, Parts 1 & 2	Retail copy 45/Mercury 73075	1970	100
9=	All The Madmen	One-sided promotional 45/Mercury DJ 311	1971	100

Source: Goldmine/Neal Umphred.

A few early copies of Diamond Dogs featured plainly visible 'Bowiedog' genitals in the fold-open cover drawing. These were subsequently air-brushed into shadow, making the original 'uncensored' release highly collectable.

THE 10 MOST VALUABLE BOB DYLAN RECORDS IN THE USA

	Title	Special feature/label/cat. no.	Year	Estimated value ($)
1	The Freewheelin' Bob Dylan	Original pressing containing John Birch Paranoid Blues, Ramblin' Gamblin' Willie, Rocks And Gravel and Let Me Die In My Footsteps (Stereo LP)/Columbia CS 8786	1963	16,000
2	The Freewheelin' Bob Dylan	Original pressing containing John Birch Paranoid Blues, Ramblin' Gamblin' Willie, Rocks And Gravel and Let Me Die In My Footsteps (Mono LP)/Columbia CL 8786	1963	10,000
3	Blood On The Tracks	Original test pressing LP containing alternative versions of five songs/ Columbia PC 33235	1975	4,000
4=	The Hit Pack	Promotional set of three singles on coloured vinyl, one each by Dylan, Barbra Streisand and Andy Williams/Columbia – no cat. no.	1965	1,500
4=	The Freewheelin' Bob Dylan	White label promotional pressing listing the four deleted tracks on the label (although the record contains the new cuts)/Columbia CL 1986	1963	1,500
6=	Mixed Up Confusion/ Corrina, Corrina	Single/Columbia 42656	1963	750
6=	Subterranean Homesick Blues	Black and white picture sleeve promotional single featuring a photo of the Beatles/Columbia 43242	1965	750
6=	Blowin' In The Wind	Black and white picture sleeve promotional single featuring 'Rebel without a cause' slogan/Columbia 42856	1965	750
9	Blonde On Blonde	White label promotional double LP/Columbia C2L 41	1966	600
10	The Freewheelin' Bob Dylan	White label promotional pressing listing the four deleted tracks on a special front cover strip together with track times (although the record contains the new cuts)/Columbia CL 1986	1963	500

Source: Neal Umphred/Goldmine.

Perhaps more than any of the collectable lists, this Dylan ranking shows the extraordinary difference a seemingly trivial feature can make to the value of records which are essentially similar, with no fewer than five positions taken up by subtly different versions of The Freewheelin' Bob Dylan album.

THE 10 MOST VALUABLE ELVIS PRESLEY RECORDS IN THE UK

	Title	Special feature/label/cat. no.	Year	Estimated value (£)
1	*Legend*	Limited-edition box of three gold CDs/RCA PD 89000	1985	180
2	*Elvis (Rock 'n' Roll No. 2)*	First UK pressing of second LP/HMV CLP 1105	1957	160
3	*Rock 'n' Roll*	First UK pressing of first LP/HMV CLP 1093	1956	150
4	*The Best Of Elvis*	10" UK-only compilation LP/HMV DLP 1159	1957	120
5=	*A Mess Of Blues/The Girl Of My Best Friend*	78-rpm single; very limited availability in 1960/RCA 1194	1960	100
5=	*Legend*	Silver-CD boxed version of (1) above/RCA PD 89000	1985	100
5=	*I Forgot To Remember To Forget/Mystery Train*	UK-pressed single for export. No UK equivalent/HMV 7ML 42	1957	100
8=	*Rip It Up/Baby Let's Play House*	Original 45-rpm pressing with gold label script/HMV POP 305	1957	80
8=	*Blue Suede Shoes/ Tutti Frutti*	Original 45-rpm pressing with gold label script/HMV 7M 405	1956	80
8=	*Mystery Train/Love Me*	Original 45-rpm pressing with gold label script/HMV 295	1957	80

This list includes only records that were commercially available and originated in the UK. Items like demonstration copies of UK early singles on the HMV label would theoretically carry higher prices if they ever came on to the market, as would a host of imported rare Presley records from around the world.

THE 10 MOST VALUABLE ELVIS PRESLEY ALBUMS IN THE USA

	Title	Special feature/label/cat. no.	Year	Estimated value ($)
1	*Aloha From Hawaii Via Satellite*	With 'Chicken Of The Sea Tuna' sticker/RCA VPSX 6089	1973	1,500
2=	*International Hotel Presents Elvis, 1969*	Boxed set/RCA – no cat. no.	1969	1,400
2=	*International Hotel Presents Elvis, 1970*	Boxed set/RCA – no cat. no.	1970	1,400
2=	*Moody Blue*	'Splash' coloured vinyl/RCA AFL1 2428	1977	1,400
5=	*Elvis*	Featuring an alternative version of *Old Shep*/RCA LPM 1382	1956	1,000
5=	*Special Christmas Programming*	Promotional radio show LP/RCA UNMR 5697	1967	1,000
5=	*Moody Blue*	Coloured vinyl/RCA AFL1 2428	1977	1,000
8=	*Elvis' Gold Records, Volume 4*	Mono LP/RCA LPM 3921	1968	900
8=	*Speedway*	Mono LP/RCA LPM 3989	1968	900
10	*Special Palm Sunday Programming*	Promotional radio show LP/RCA SP 33 461	1967	750

Source: *Goldmine/Neal Umphred.*

THE 10 MOST VALUABLE ELVIS PRESLEY SINGLES IN THE USA

	Title	Special feature/label/cat. no.	Year	Estimated value ($)
1	*Elvis Presley*	Triple EP/RCA SPD 23; available only by mail order to purchasers of an RCA gramophone	1956	4,000
2	*Elvis Presley/Jaye P. Morgan*	Double EP/RCA EPA 992	1956	2,500
3	*Can't Help Falling In Love*	Compact 33-rpm with picture sleeve/RCA 37-7968	1961	2,400
4	*Good Luck Charm*	Compact 33-rpm with picture sleeve/RCA 37 7992	1961	2,350
5	*The Most Talked About New Personality In The Last Ten Years Of Recorded Music*	Promotional EP with picture sleeve/RCA EPB 1254	1956	2,300
6	*Don't/Wear My Ring Around Your Neck*	Double A-side promotional 45 withpicture sleeve/SP 45-76	1960	2,150
7	*Surrender/Lonely Man*	Compact 33-rpm, stereo/RCA 68 7850	1961	1,750
8	*TV Guide Presents Elvis Presley*	White label promotional 45/RCA 8705	1956	1,350
9=	*Old Shep*	One-sided promotional 45/RCA CR 15	1956	1,250
9=	*Moody Blue/She Still Thinks I Care*	Two-coloured vinyl/RCA PB 10857	1976	1,250
9=	*Blue Christmas/Blue Christmas*	White label promotional 45/RCA 0808	1957	1,250
9=	*This Is His Life*	Biographical cartoon picture sleeve/ RCA – no cat. no.	1956	1,250

Source: *Goldmine/Neal Umphred.*

THE TOP 10 SOUVENIR ITEMS AT GRACELAND

1 'Jungle Room' postcard

2 Key chain: 'I ELVIS' licence-plate

3 Label pin: 'TCB'*

4 Float liquid pin (depicting Elvis's pink Cadillac floating past Graceland)

5 Elvis signature coffee mug

6 Elvis spoon

7 Graceland thimble

8 Necklace (gold-plated): 'TCB'*

9 'I've Been To Graceland' T-shirt

10 *Elvis: The King Of Rock 'n' Roll – The Complete 50s Masters* CD/tape boxed set of 1950s recordings

* *'TCB' stands for 'Taking Care Of Business', a catch-phrase Elvis made his own.*

The 'Jungle Room' postcard (35 cents) is the most popular of the dozens of Elvis postcards available at the Graceland souvenir shops which are located across the street from his Memphis home. Elvis bought the house on 19 March 1957 for $100,000 from Dr and Mrs T. D. Moore, who had originally named the mansion after Mrs Moore's aunt, Grace Toof.

THE 10 MOST VALUABLE ROLLING STONES RECORDS IN THE USA

	Title	Special feature/label/cat. no.	Year	Estimated value ($)
1=	Street Fighting Man	Picture sleeve 45/London 909	1968	4,000
1=	12 x 5	Blue vinyl LP/London LL 3402	1969	4,000
3	I Wanna Be Your Man/Stoned	45/London 9641	1964	2,250
4=	The Rolling Stones	White label promotional LP/London LL 3375	1969	1,500
4=	Songs Of The Rolling Stones	LP with 'Rock 'n' Roll Circus' cover shot/Abkco MPD 1	1975	1,500
6	The Promotional Album	LP/London RSD 1	1969	1,000
7=	I Wanna Be Your Man/Stoned	White label promotional 45/London 9461	1964	500
7=	Beast Of Burden	Picture sleeve 45/Rolling Stones 19309	1978	500
9=	Heart Of Stone	Picture sleeve 45/London 9725	1964	400
9=	Songs Of The Rolling Stones	LP with 'Between The Buttons' cover shot/Abkco MPD 1	1975	400

Source: Goldmine/Neal Umphred.

*S*treet Fighting Man's scheduled picture sleeve, depicting police in full riot gear battling demonstrators, was deemed unsuitable by record label executives prior to release, though enough copies surfaced to make this the most collectable of Rolling Stones 45s.

THE 10 MOST VALUABLE BRIAN WILSON RECORDS IN THE USA

	Title	Artist	Special feature/label/cat. no.	Year	Estimated value ($)
1	Girls On The Beach	Beach Boys	Promotional EP/Capitol – no cat. no.	1964	*
2	The Surfer Moon	Bob & Sherri	Blue label 45/Safari 101	1962	1,500
3=	Surfin' Safari	Beach Boys	Complete recording sessions EP/Capitol 2185/6	1962	750
3=	The Surfer Moon	Bob & Sherri	White label promotion 45/ Safari 101	1962	750
3=	Barbie	Kenny & The Cadets	Red and gold vinyl 45/Randy 422	1962	750
6=	Shoot The Curl	Honeys	Picture sleeve 45/Capitol 4952	1963	600
6=	Selections From 'Beach Boys Concert'	Beach Boys	EP/Capitol 2754/5	1964	600
6=	Spirit Of America	Beach Boys	Promotion paper sleeve 45/Capitol – no cat. no.	1963	600
9=	Excerpts From 'Beach Boys Party'	Beach Boys	EP/Capitol 2993/4	1965	500
9=	Heroes And Villains	Beach Boys	Discarded Capitol picture sleeve, never officially released 45/Capitol 5826	1967	500

* No value can be reasonably estimated for this priceless item. There are no known copies in the hands of collectors, although the EP was pressed as a promotional item for the Beach Boys film of the same name.

Source: Goldmine/Neal Umphred.

Most records in which Brian Wilson had a hand, either as a writer, performer or producer, are regarded as collectable. The Bob & Sherri record features longtime friend Bob Norberg and an unknown female vocalist duetting on an early Wilson composition. Kenny & The Cadets features Wilson and his brother Carl performing as a separate unit from the Beach Boys, while the Honeys, a female surf trio, performed Wilson songs and were produced by him.

THE 10 MOST VALUABLE JAZZ ALBUMS IN THE USA

	Title	Artist	Special feature/label/cat. no.	Year	Estimated value ($)
1	*The Bird Blows The Blues*	Charlie Parker	Dial LP 1	1949	*
2	*Poetry For The Beat Generation*	Jack Kerouac	Dot DLP 3154	1959	**
3=	*Charlie Parker Quintet*	Charlie Parker	10″ LP/Dot LP 201	1949	600
3=	*Charlie Parker Quintet 2*	Charlie Parker	10″ LP/Dot LP 202	1949	600
3=	*Charlie Parker Quintet 3*	Charlie Parker	10″ LP/Dot LP 203	1949	600
3=	*Charlie Parker Sextet*	Charlie Parker	10″ LP/Dot LP 207	1950	600
3=	*Battle Of The Blues Volume 3*	Jimmy Weatherspoon & Eddie Vinson	King 395-634	1959	600
8=	*The Jackie McLean Quintet*	Jackie McLean	Adlib ADL 6601	1955	500
8=	*Piano Red In Concert*	Piano Red	Groove LG 1002	1956	500
8=	*George Wallingford Quintet At The Bohemia*	George Wallingford	Progressive PLP 1001	1955	500

* Yet to appear in the collectors arena, this debut Dial disc was a compilation of 78s issued as a 12″ album in 1949. It was available originally only as a $5 mail-order item, but, should it ever surface, would expect to achieve a sizeable four-figure sum today.

** Again, there is no documented transaction of this title to date. It had a minimal press run in 1959 and would easily fetch four figures if offered for sale.

Source: *Goldmine/Neal Umphred.*

THE TOP 10 POP MUSIC MAGAZINES IN THE UK, 1992

	Magazine	Circulation*
1	*Smash Hits*	368,258
2	*Q*	161,104
3	*Fast Forward*	129,714
4	*Sky*	129,055
5	*New Musical Express*	116,415
6	*Vox*	114,213
7	*Select*	75,617
8	*Melody Maker*	68,596
9	*Kerrang!*	45,504
10	*Raw*	24,044

* Average sale per issue, 1992.

Source: *Audit Bureau of Circulations.*

Fast Forward became the BBC's only pop weekly following the demise of its *No. 1* magazine in 1991, a year which also saw the end of the road for longtime music rags, *Sounds* and *Record Mirror*. The fall-out effect from the Maxwell empire collapse also closed *Rage* in the same year, during one of the most difficult periods ever experienced by the traditionally buoyant music magazine market.

THE TOP 10 POPULAR MUSIC MAGAZINES IN THE USA, 1992

	Magazine	Circulation
1	*Rolling Stone*	1,202,082
2	*Country America*	804,970
3	*Entertainment Weekly*	803,101
4	*Country Music*	637,455
5	*Spin*	305,016
6	*Guitar World*	180,381
7	*Guitar For The Practical Musician*	180,229
8	*Guitar Player*	134,565
9	*Circus*	131,322
10	*Guitar School*	120,702

Source: *Magazine Publishers Association.*

Circulation figures are for average weekly, fortnightly or monthly sales. The 11th most popular is the highly respected *Musician* publication with 110,702 sales while the bestselling music trade magazine is *Billboard* (62,354).

THE TOP 10 RECORD-BUYING COUNTRIES

	Country	% of global market	Retail sales ($)*
1	USA	31	7,834,000,000
2	Japan	13	3,435,600,000
3	Germany	10	2,574,100,000
4	UK	9	2,311,700,000
5	France	7	1,632,400,000
6	USSR**	2	696,600,000
7	Italy	2	695,500,000
8	Spain	2	680,200,000
9	Canada	2	650,600,000
10	Netherlands	2	600,200,000

*1991, except ** (1990).

Source: *IFPI*.

In 1991 worldwide record sales accounted for a retail value of over $25 billion. Cassettes were the leading sales choice with global sales of 1,279,000,000 units versus 1,092,000,000 compact discs. CD shipments rose by some 330,000,000 units from 1990 and were reckoned to have become the world's leading format by the end of 1992.

THE TOP 10 RECORD COMPANIES IN THE UK

	Label	Market share %*
1	Polygram	23
2	EMI	14
3=	Warner Music/WEA	12
3=	Sony Music	12
5	Virgin	7
6	BMG	6
7=	MCA	4
7=	Telstar	4
9	Chrysalis	3
10	PWL	2

* Based on 1991 market share performance of chart records for both the UK singles and albums surveys.

Source: *MRIB*.

Multi-national Polygram (owned by Dutch electronics giant, Philips) benefits from its ownership of a number of successful labels, including Mercury, Vertigo, London, ffrr, Polydor and their two most recent acquisitions, the formerly independently owned A&M and Island record companies.

THE TOP 10 RECORD RELEASE FORMATS IN THE UK, 1992

1	Compact disc albums
2	Cassette albums
3	5″ compact disc singles
4	7″ singles
5	12″ vinyl singles
6	Cassette singles
7	Vinyl LP albums
8	10″ vinyl singles
9	Digital compact cassette albums
10	3″ compact disc singles

Source: *MRIB*.

The sale of compact disc albums overtook those of vinyl LPs in 1989, and became the most-bought format by record buyers (over cassette albums) in 1991. Vinyl LP sales have fallen to only 7 per cent of overall UK album business, while compact discs now account for approximately 55 per cent of all albums sold, though a challenge to its popularity was initiated by Philips in the autumn of 1992 with the launch of their new Digital Compact Cassette album. Sony's 3″ mini-disc (not to be confused with the existing 3″ compact disc single which became popular in 1988) was also brought into an increasingly crowded market at the same time. In June 1992 5″ CD singles became the most popular format for singles release and currently account for 30 per cent of that declining market.

THE TOP 10 PIRATE RECORD COUNTRIES

	Country	Estimated value ($)*
1	Paraguay	200,000,000
2	United Arab Emirates	108,000,000
3	Thailand	85,000,000
4	Mexico	75,000,000
5	Taiwan	50,000,000
6=	India	33,000,000
6=	Saudi Arabia	33,000,000
8=	Italy	30,000,000
8=	Korea	30,000,000
10	Greece	21,000,000

* IFPI figures for the last accountable year, 1990.

Piracy consists of counterfeit recordings of original albums and bootlegs (illegal recordings of a performance broadcast or live concert). Worldwide, it is estimated that the record piracy industry is responsible for a $2 billion loss to the legitimate music business community.

THE TOP 10 MUSIC RETAIL CHAINS IN THE USA

	Store	Total locations*
1	Musicland Group (Musicland, Sam Goody, Discount Records On Cue, Music Play)	884
2	Target Stores, Inc. (Target)	508
3	Trans World Music Group (Coconuts, Record Town, Tape World, Great American Music, Good Vibrations, The Music Company)	502
4	Camelot Enterprises, Inc. (Camelot Music, Spectrum)	328
5	Wherehouse Entertainment, Inc. (The Wherehouse, Leopold, Odyssey)	315
6	Super Club Music Corporation (Turtles, Tracks)	286
7	Blockbuster Music (Sound Warehouse, Music Plus)	237
8	Wee Three Records Shops (Wee Three, Wall To Wall, Mothers Record World, Square Circle, The Wall)	169
9	Strawberries, Inc. (Strawberries, Waxie Maxie's)	138
10	Hastings Books, Music & Video (Hastings)	128

* To January 1993.

There are over 7,000 retail chains and independent stores in the United States. The recent buyout of Sound Warehouse by the largest video chain, Blockbuster, and the arrival on the US scene of British record retailer Virgin (which opened its first American store on Sunset Boulevard, Los Angeles, and entered into a retail co-venture with Blockbuster in December 1992) will undoubtedly change the picture.

DILLONS' TOP 10 MUSIC BOOKS, 1992

	Author	Title
1	Paul Gambaccini, Jonathan Rice & Tim Rice	British Hit Singles
2	Jerry Hopkins & Danny Sugarman	No One Here Gets Out Alive
3	Ivan March, Edward Greenfield & Robert Layton	The Penguin Guide to Compact Discs
4	Mark Lewisohn	Complete Beatles Chronicles
5	Ralph Denyar	New Guitar Handbook
6	Jackie Gunn & Jim Jenkins	Queen: As It Began
7	Johnny Rogan	Morrissey and Marr: The Severed Alliance
8	Ivan March, Edward Greenfield & Robert Layton	The Penguin Guide to Bargain Compact Discs
9	Tony Bacon	Ultimate Guitar Book
10	Marcus Gray	REM Companion: It Crawled From The South

W. H. SMITH'S TOP 10 MUSIC BIOGRAPHIES, 1992

	Author	Title	Subject
1	Rick Sky	The Show Must Go On	Freddie Mercury
2	Michael Jackson	Dancing The Dream	Michael Jackson
3	Stephen Rider	These Are The Days of Our Lives	Queen
4	Adua Pavarotti	Pavarotti: Life with Luciano	Luciano Pavarotti
5	Ken Dean	Queen: The New Visual Documentary	Queen
6	Jackie Gunn & Jim Jenkins	Queen: As It Began	Queen
7	Ross Clarke	A Kind of Magic	Freddie Mercury
8	Jerry Hopkins & Danny Sugarman	No One Here Gets Out Alive	Jim Morrison
9	Mike Clifford	The Beatles	The Beatles
10	Michael McCartney	Remember – The Recollections and Photographs of Michael McCartney	The Beatles

W. H. SMITH'S TOP 10 MUSIC REFERENCE BOOKS, 1992

	Author	Title
1	–	*Proms '92*
2	Paul Gambaccini, Jonathan Rice & Tim Rice	*British Hit Singles*
3	Paul Gambaccini, Jonathan Rice & Tim Rice	*British Hit Albums*
4	Ivan March, Edward Greenfield & Robert Layton	*The Penguin Guide to Compact Discs*
5	*Gramophone*	*Good CD Guide*
6	Nick Hamlyn	*Price Guide for Record Collectors*
7	W. H. Smith/*New Musical Express*	*Rock 'n' Roll Years*
8	Paul Gambaccini, Jonathan Rice & Tim Rice	*Top 40 Charts*
9	Ivan March, Edward Greenfield & Robert Layton	*The Penguin Guide to Bargain Compact Discs*
10	Music Master	*CD Catalogue*

FULL METAL T-SHIRT: VIRGIN RETAIL'S TOP 10 HEAVY METAL T-SHIRTS, 1992

	Group	T-shirt
1	Guns N' Roses	Use Your Illusion II
2	Queen	Blue Crest
3	Metallica	Gargoyle
4	Ugly Kid Joe	America's Least Wanted
5	Guns N' Roses	Use Your Illusion I
6	Faith No More	Angel Dust
7	Guns N' Roses	Civil War
8	Levellers	Black logo
9	Queen	Black logo
10	Ugly Kid Joe	Ugly As You Wanna Be

WATERSTONE'S TOP 10 MUSIC BOOKS, 1992

	Author	Title
1	Norman Lebrecht	*The Maestro Myth: Great Conductors in Pursuit of Power*
2	Humphrey Carpenter	*Benjamin Britten: A Biography*
3	Johnny Rogan	*Morrissey and Marr: The Severed Alliance*
4	Anthony Storr	*Music and The Mind*
5	Mark Lewisohn	*Beatles Chronicle*
6	Jon Savage	*England's Dreaming*
7	Richard Cook & Brian Morton	*The Penguin Guide to Jazz*
8	Miles Davis & Quincey Troupe	*Miles: The Autobiography*
9	Stan Cullimore & Jules Sharpe	*Fighting For Fame: How to be a Popstar*
10	Christopher Headington	*Peter Pears: A Biography*

If Madonna's *Sex* were classified as a 'music' book, rather than what it is (a book of photographs of and text by a woman who happens to sing), it would actually head this and the Dillon's list opposite.

VIRGIN RETAIL'S TOP 10 BOOKS BY AND ABOUT ROCK STARS, 1992

	Author	Title	Subject
1	Madonna	*Sex*	Madonna
2	Jerry Hopkins & Danny Sugarman	*No One Here Gets Out Alive*	Jim Morrison
3	Johnny Rogan	*Morrissey and Marr: The Severed Alliance*	Smiths
4	Ken Dean	*Queen: The New Visual Documentary*	Queen
5	Marcus Gray	*REM Companion: It Crawled From The South*	REM
6	Stephen Rider	*These Are The Days of Our Lives*	Queen
7	Rick Sky	*The Show Must Go On*	Freddie Mercury
8	Jackie Gunn & Jim Jenkins	*Queen: As It Began*	Queen
9	Michael Jackson	*Dancing The Dream*	Michael Jackson
10	John W. Duffy	*Illustrated Biography*	Prince

10 MUSIC ARTISTS WHO DIED AS A RESULT OF ACCIDENTS

1 Johnny Ace

American R & B star, accidentally shot himself while playing Russian roulette backstage at Houston Civic Auditorium, 24 December 1954.

2 Graham Bond

Founder of the British group Graham Bond Organization, died mysteriously under a tube train at Finsbury Park station, London, 8 May 1974.

3 Johnny Burnette

Singer (*You're Sixteen*, etc), drowned in a boating accident in Clear Lake, California, 1 August 1964.

4 Sandy Denny

Lead singer of Fairport Convention, died of a cerebral haemorrhage after falling down stairs, London, 21 April 1978.

5 'Mama' Cass Elliot

Substantial Mamas and Papas vocalist, died in Harry Nilsson's London flat after choking on a sandwich, 29 July 1974.

6 Brian Jones

Ex-Rolling Stones guitarist (he had quit the group the previous month), drowned in his swimming pool at Hartfield, Sussex, as a result of 'misadventure', 3 July 1969.

7 Terry Kath

Member of rock band Chicago, shot himself, 23 January 1978, playing Russian roulette. His last words were: 'Don't worry, it's not loaded.'

8 Keith Moon

Who drummer, died as a result of taking an accidental overdose of Hemineverin, a drug prescribed to assist him in overcoming alcoholism, 7 September 1978 (in the same London apartment in which Mama Cass had died).

9 Keith Relf

Lead singer of the Yardbirds, electrocuted while tuning his guitar at his London home, 14 May 1976.

10 John Rostill

Ex-member of the Shadows, electrocuted by his guitar at his home recording studio, 26 November 1973. (Electrocution is an occupational hazard among rock musicians: another notable victim, Les Harvey, singer in the British rock band Stone the Crows, died after receiving a shock on stage during a gig at Swansea University, 3 May 1972.)

10 MUSIC ARTISTS WHO WERE KILLED IN ROAD ACCIDENTS

1 Duane Allman

American guitarist Allman (of Allman Brothers), who played with Eric Clapton on *Layla*, was killed in a motorcycle accident in Macon, Georgia, 29 October 1971. Berry Oakley from the same group was also killed in a motorcycle accident just three blocks away, 11 November 1972.

2 Jesse Belvin

R & B singer (Jesse & Marvin) and co-composer of *Earth Angel*, killed in an automobile crash in Los Angeles, 6 February 1960.

3 Marc Bolan

British singer (T. Rex) died when a Mini driven by his American girlfriend, Gloria Jones, crashed into a tree on Barnes Common, 16 September 1977. The tree is now a shrine for T. Rex fans.

4 Harry Chapin

American singer-songwriter, was killed in Jericho, New York, 16 July 1981, when a tractor-trailer rammed his car which then exploded.

5 Eddie Cochran

American rock star, died of head injuries following a taxi crash in Chippenham, Wiltshire, 17 April 1960. Gene Vincent was injured in the same crash, and the first policeman to arrive on the scene was 16-year-old cadet, Dave Dee, who later fronted Dave Dee, Dozy, Beaky, Mick & Tich. Cochran's first posthumous single would be *Three Steps To Heaven*.

6 Richard Fariña

Folk singer, died in a motorcycle accident after the party to launch his book, *Been Down So Long It Looks Like Up To Me*, Carmel, California, 30 April 1966.

7 Johnny Horton

Country singer who had US No. 1 (UK No. 16) hit with *The Battle Of New Orleans*, died in a car accident, Austin, Texas, 5 November 1960.

8 Johnny Kidd

Lead singer of British group Johnny Kidd & The Pirates, killed in a car crash, 7 October 1966.

9 Bessie Smith

American Blues singer, died after the car in which she was a passenger crashed into the rear of a truck near Clarksdale, Mississippi, 26 September 1937.

10 Clarence White

Guitarist with the Byrds, died after being run over by a truck, Palmdale, California, 14 July 1973.

10 MUSIC ARTISTS WHO WERE MURDERED

1 Sam Cooke

Cooke was shot dead at the Hacienda motel, Los Angeles, 11 December 1964, by the manager, Bertha Franklin, who claimed she was saving 22-year-old Elisa Boyer from being raped (verdict: 'justifiable homicide').

2 King Curtis

Curtis (Curtis Ousley), sax player on Coasters hits, including *Yakety Yak*, was stabbed to death in a brawl in New York, 13 August 1971.

3 Marvin Gaye

Shot dead by his father, an apostolic church minister, in Los Angeles the day before his 45th birthday, 1 April 1984.

4 Samuel George Jr

Lead singer of the Capitols, stabbed to death during a family row, 17 March 1982.

5 Al Jackson

Drummer with jazz combo Booker T. & The MGs, shot dead by an intruder, 1 October 1975.

6 Little Walter Jacobs

Blues harmonica player with Muddy Waters, stabbed to death in a street fight in Chicago, 15 February 1968.

7 John Lennon

Shot dead outside the Dakota Building, New York, by Mark David Chapman, 8 December 1980.

8 Sal Mineo

Actor-singer, stabbed to death in Hollywood, apparently during a robbery, 12 February 1976.

9 James 'Shep' Sheppard

Member of American groups Heartbeats and Limeliters, his body was found in his car on the Long Island Expressway, assumed murdered by robbers, 24 January 1970.

10 Peter Tosh

Jamaican reggae star, shot dead by raiders at his home, 11 September 1987.

10 MUSIC ARTISTS WHO DIED IN PLANE CRASHES

1 Patsy Cline

American Country singer, killed (with Cowboy Copas and Hawkshaw Hawkins) when her single-engined aircraft crashed after takeoff from Dyersburg, Tennessee, 5 March 1963.

2 Jim Croce

American singer, died in a plane crash at Natchitoches, Louisiana, 20 September 1973. His song *Time In A Bottle* became a posthumous US No. 1 hit later that year.

3 Buddy Holly

Holly, The Big Bopper (aka J.P. Richardson) and Ritchie Valens, three Rock 'n' Roll legends, died in the same accident aboard a Beechcraft Bonanza on 2 February 1959, on a flight from Clear Lake, Ohio to Moorhead, Minnesota.

4 Glenn Miller

American big band leader, was lost on a wartime flight from England to France on 16 December 1944. His body was never discovered.

5 Ricky Nelson

With his fiancée and other band members, Nelson died in a plane crash near DeKalb, Texas, on 31 December 1985.

6 Otis Redding

Died with the Bar-Kays group when his plane crashed into a lake near Madison, Wisconsin, 10 October 1967.

7 Jim Reeves

American Country singer, killed in a plane crash near Nashville, Tennessee, 31 July 1964.

8 Kyu Sakamoto

Japanese singer Sakamoto, who had a 1963 No. 6 UK hit with *Sukiyaki*, was killed in the crash in Japan of a Japan Air Lines Boeing 747 on 12 August 1985. A total of 520 died in this, the worst single-plane aviation disaster of all time.

9 Ronnie Van Zant

Lynyrd Skynyrd band members Van Zant and Steve Gaines, his sister Cassie and their manager, were killed on 20 October 1977 when their rented single-engined Convair 240 ran out of fuel and crashed into a swamp in Gillsburg, Missouri.

10 Stevie Ray Vaughan

Guitar great Vaughan died in a helicopter in foggy weather on 27 August 1990, travelling to Chicago following a concert in East Troy, Wisconsin. Four others died in the accident including Eric Clapton's agent, Bobby Brooks.

10 MUSIC ARTISTS WHO COMMITTED SUICIDE

1 Ian Curtis

Lead singer of Joy Division, hanged himself in his Manchester garage while listening to Iggy Pop's *The Idiot* album, 18 May 1980.

2 Nick Drake

British folk singer-songwriter, died of a deliberate drug overdose, 25 October 1974.

3 Bobby Fuller

Leader of Texas band, Bobby Fuller Four, found dead in his car, Los Angeles, 18 July 1966, presumed to have committed suicide.

4 Pete Ham

Ham, of Badfinger (signed by Paul McCartney to Apple Records in 1968 and joint composer of Nilsson's global No. 1 hit *Without You*), hanged himself in his garage, 23 April 1975. Tim Evans, also of Badfinger, hanged himself under identical circumstances, 23 November 1983.

5 Donny Hathaway

American R & B singer, plunged 15 floors to his death, Essex House Hotel, New York, 13 January 1979, his death being officially registered as suicide.

6 Joe Meek

Notable British producer, shot himself in London, 3 February 1967, after killing his landlady.

7 Phil Ochs

American folk singer, hanged himself, Queens, New York, 9 April 1976.

8 Del Shannon

American singer, shot himself, Santa Clarita, California, 8 February 1990.

9 Paul Williams

Founder member of Temptations, shot himself, 17 August 1973.

10 Al Wilson

Canned Heat singer-guitarist, died of barbiturate poisoning, 3 September 1970.

10 UNUSUAL POST-MORTEM INCIDENTS INVOLVING MUSICIANS

1 Ludwig van Beethoven

German composer, died 26 March 1827. His grave was opened in 1863 and again (with that of Schubert) in 1888 and his bones examined before reburial in the Zentralfriedhof (Central Cemetery), Vienna.

2 Enrico Caruso

Italian tenor, died 2 August 1921 after bungled medical treatment. His body was displayed until 1927 – with an annual change of clothes – but was finally buried in Del Planto Cemetery near Naples, Italy.

3 Franz Joseph Haydn

Austrian composer, died 31 May 1809. His head was stolen soon afterwards by grave robbers on the instructions of amateur phrenologist Johann Peter and, after extensive changes of ownership, was eventually reunited with Haydn's body in 1984.

4 Jim Morrison

Lead singer of the Doors, died in Paris 3 July 1971. His wife Pam, who died in 1974, and the doctor who signed the death certificate were reportedly the only two people to have seen the body, and there have been persistent rumours ever since that he is still alive – one suggesting that his Alsatian dog is buried in his grave at Père-Lachaise, Paris.

5 Gram Parsons

Guitarist with American group the Byrds, died of unspecified causes, Joshua Tree, California, 19 September 1973. His body was stolen by his manager Phil Kaufmann and burned.

6 Wolfgang Amadeus Mozart

Austrian composer, died in Vienna, 5 December 1791. His suspected poisoning by his rival Antonio Salieri (a theme explored in the film *Amadeus*) can never be proved, since his grave was unmarked and his remains have never been found.

7 Elvis Presley

Died of heart failure after years of massive drug abuse, 16 August 1977, at his home, Graceland. He was originally buried with his mother at Memphis Forest Hill cemetery, but the remains of both were later reinterred at Graceland after threats of body-snatching.

8 Franz Schubert

Austrian composer, died 19 November 1828. He was buried at Wahring cemetery, Vienna, but reburied at the Zentralfriedhof, Vienna, after his bones (with those of Beethoven) were examined in 1888.

9 Thomas 'Fats' Waller

American jazz musician, died on board a train, 15 December 1943. His ashes were scattered from a plane over his birthplace, Harlem, New York.

10 Dennis Wilson

Member of American group the Beach Boys, drowned at Marina del Rey, California, 28 December 1983. He was buried at sea after the personal intervention of Ronald Reagan (sea burial is usually reserved for naval personnel).

INDEX

ACKNOWLEDGEMENTS

AGB (Penny MacKie)
Amusement & Music Operators Association
Amusement Business (Marie Ratliffe)
ASCAP (Jeff Sapan)
Audit Bureau of Circulation
Australian Record Industry Association
BARB (Bob Hulks)
BASCA (Eileen Stow)
BBC Radio 1
BBC Radio 2
BBC Radio 3
BBC Radio 4
BBC Written Archives
Bellows Karaoke/Peter Frailish
Billboard
Billboard Entertainment & Marketing (Liz Nevins)
Don Black
BLMS
BMI (Pat Baird, Betsy Schutt)
BPI
Capital Radio
David Chesterman
Chicago Sound Co
Christie's
Dick Clark Productions (Patricia Carroll)
Classic FM
Coca-Cola Company (Phil Mooney)
Don Cornelius Productions
Country Music Association
Dillons (Anthony Keates)
Christopher Forbes
Forbes Magazine
Goldmine
Graceland
Gruhn's Guitars, Nashville

IFPI (and associate members)
IMP (Donna Bird)
Impact Agency
Alan Jones
Jukebox Collector (Rick Botts)
Jukebox Journal (Ian Brown)
Kiss FM
MIRO
MRIB
MTV (Maggie Sherman)
MTV Europe (Judith Daniel)
Joseph Murrells
Music Exchange, New York
Music Sales (Peter Evans)
NARAS
NATAS
Nielsen Media Resarch (Maria Zimmann)
NME (Fiona Foulgar)
Nordoff-Robbins Music Therapy
Pepsi-Co
Phillips West Two
PRS (Terri Anderson)
RADAD
Radio & Records (Ken Barnes)
Realsongs (Doreen Dorion)
RIAA
RIAJ
Rock and Roll Hall of Fame (Bonnie Oviatt)
Rolling Stone
Royal Opera House
RPM
Shefrin Company
W.H. Smith (Jacqui Palmer-Jones)
Songwriters Hall of Fame (Chris Malone)
Sotheby's
Theatre Record

Neal Umphred (*Collectible Record Albums/Goldmine's Price Guide*)
Virgin Retail (Maria Arthur)
Waterstone's (Claire Hungate)

Various record company press offices

Special thanks to Peter Compton, Lorraine Jerram, Dave McAleer Dafydd Rees, Linda Silverman, Kim Whitburn, Steve Wright, and of course to Caroline, Alexander and Nicholas Ash, Elaine Crampton and Marilyn, Stephanie and Joanne Lazell.

Picture Credits

Clive Barda: 206
BBC: 188, 194
Christie's Colour Library: 232
Ronald Grant Archive: 94, 130, 202
The Kobal Collection: 201
Courtesy of MRIB: 13 (left), 17, 31 (middle), 43, 47, 72, 76, 97, 101, 106, 109, 116, 125, 136, 138, 147, 216, 222, 230
Popperfoto: 57, 67
Redferns: 9, 11, 15, 18, 20, 21, 22, 24, 27, 33 (bottom), 52, 53, 55, 61, 66, 69, 73, 77, 81, 84, 132, 134, 149, 156, 176, 179, 184, 186, 218, 224, 229
Retna Pictures: 13 (right), 31 (top), 33 (top), 36, 82, 119, 129, 137, 139, 148, 150, 160, 190, 210, 215
Sotheby's: 233

QUIZ ANSWERS

Beatles (p. 24) **1** *Yellow Submarine.* **2** *Hey Jude,* written by Paul McCartney about Julian Lennon. **3** Pete Best. **4** Brian Epstein. **5** *Something,* written by George Harrison. **6** Billy Preston. **7** Phil Spector. **8** The Cavern. **9** *Magical Mystery Tour.* **10** 1964 – on 7 February, Pan Am flight 101 brought the Beatles to New York's JFK airport.

Labels (p. 45) **1** Motown. **2** Memphis, Tennessee. **3** Apple. **4** Specials. **5** Ahmet Ertegun. **6** Jake Riviera. **7** Sugarhill. **8** Frank Sinatra. **9** Anxious. **10** Warner Brothers.

Duos (p. 57) **1** Kim Weston. **2** Donny and Marie Osmond. **3** David & Jonathan. **4** *Summer Nights.* **5** Laurel & Hardy. **6** Sheena Easton. **7** Everly Brothers. **8** Dave Stewart and Annie Lennox. **9** Righteous Brothers. **10** Carpenters (Karen died on 4 February 1983).

Numbers (p. 71) **1** City Boy. **2** Byrds. **3** 50. **4** Pete Wingfield. **5** Meat Loaf. **6** 68. **7** Queen. **8** Wilson Pickett. **9** Iron Maiden. **10** Prince (*I Would Die 4 U, Nothing Compares 2 U*).

One-Hit Wonders (p. 90) **1**–E. **2**–H. **3**–D. **4**–G. **5**–C. **6**–B. **7**–A. **8**–F. **9**–J. **10**–I.

Initials (p. 93) **1**–F. **2**–E. **3**–H. **4**–G. **5**–D. **6**–B. **7**–I. **8**–C. **9**–J. **10**–A.

Comedy (p. 113) **1** Vic Reeves. **2** Derek & Clive. **3** Ken Dodd. **4** Peter Sellers. **5** Benny Hill. **6** *The Streak.* **7** Harry Enfield. **8** Lindsey Buckingham (of Fleetwood Mac). **9** Monty Python; *The Life of Brian.* **10** *Brush Strokes.*

Rolling Stones (p. 145) **1** Mick Taylor. **2** *It's All Over Now.* **3** Peter Tosh. **4** Lennon & McCartney. **5** Bill Wyman. **6** Faces. **7** Marianne Faithfull. **8** Glimmer Twins. **9** Bill Wyman. **10** Keith Richards.

Songwriters (p. 156) **1** Neil Diamond. **2** David Bowie. **3** Jimmy Webb. **4** Joni Mitchell. **5** Lionel Bart. **6** Bob Dylan. **7** Dolly Parton. **8** Bruce Springsteen. **9** John Stewart. **10** John Lennon.

Lyrics (p. 163) **1** *Bette Davis Eyes* (Kim Carnes). **2** *Crazy* (Seal). **3** *Billie Jean* (Michael Jackson). **4** *Wuthering Heights* (Kate Bush). **5** *Tears Of A Clown* (Smokey Robinson & The Miracles). **6** *Bohemian Rhapsody* (Queen). **7** *Uptown Girl* (Billy Joel). **8** *Goody Two Shoes* (Adam Ant). **9** *Let's Dance* (David Bowie). **10** *Don't You Want Me* (Human League).

DJs & Radio (p. 190) **1** Richard Skinner. **2** Dave Lee Travis. **3** Wolfman Jack. **4** Capital Radio. **5** Janice Long (sister). **6** Steve Wright. **7** Sir James (Jimmy) Savile. **8** Paul Gambaccini. **9** The Simon Bates Show (Radio 1). **10** Paul Burnett and Dave Lee Travis.

Rock & the Movies (p. 204) **1** David Essex. **2** *A Hard Day's Night* (1964). **3** Sting. **4** *The Man Who Sold The World.* **5** Bee Gees. **6** Keith Carradine. **7** Gary Busey. **8** *Give My Regards To Broad Street.* **9** Neil Diamond. **10** *Mad Max: Beyond Thunderdome.*

Name Changes (p. 221) **1**–F. **2**–E. **3**–C. **4**–I. **5**–B. **6**–H. **7**–A. **8**–J. **9**–G. **10**–D.

Real Names (p. 227) **1**–E. **2**–G. **3**–J. **4**–A. **5**–D. **6**–I. **7**–B. **8**–C. **9**–F. **10**–H.

Nationalities (p. 230) **1**–D. **2**–E. **3**–F. **4**–C. **5**–I. **6**–A. **7**–G. **8**–J. **9**–B. **10**–H.